TE KOOTI'S LAST FORAY

TE KOOTI'S LAST FORAY

The extraordinary story of Te Kooti's 1870 abduction of two Whakatōhea communities into the Waioeka Gorge and how Whanganui's pursuit won the day but never the credit

RON CROSBY

Oratia

Front and back cover image Early morning scene of the upper Kahunui River that flows into the Waioeka River. Stu Spicer

Back cover images, from top Te Kooti Arikirangi Te Turuki. Laishley, Richard, 1816–1897. [Ryan, Thomas Aldworth] 1864–1927. Ref: A-114- 004-2, Alexander Turnbull Library, Wellington; Huhana Tamati. Binney, Judith Te Tomairangi o te Aroha (Dame), 1940–2011. Ref: PAColl-9928-46, Alexander Turnbull Library, Wellington; Topia Pehi Turoa. New Zealand Tourism Department. Ref: PAColl-5671-42, Alexander Turnbull Library, Wellington; Samuel Austin. Harding, William James, 1826–99. Ref: 1/4-004715-G, Alexander Turnbull Library, Wellington; Te Kēpa Te Rangihiwinui. Ref: PA2-2562, Alexander Turnbull Library, Wellington

Half-title page Artist's impression of Ōmarumutu pā with Makeo maunga in the background. Stu Spicer

Title page Aerial view looking down the Raetakahia valley (at right). Raupō ridge is at centre, and mist lies in the Waioeka valley, at left. Stu Spicer

Published by Oratia Books, Oratia Media Ltd, 783 West Coast Road, Oratia, Auckland 0604, New Zealand (www.oratia.co.nz).

Copyright © 2023 Ron Crosby
Copyright © 2023 Oratia Books (published work)

The copyright holders assert their moral rights in the work.

This book is copyright. Except for the purposes of fair reviewing, no part of this publication may be reproduced or transmitted in any form or by any means, whether electronic, digital or mechanical, including photocopying, recording, any digital or computerised format, or any information storage and retrieval system, including by any means via the Internet, without permission in writing from the publisher. Infringers of copyright render themselves liable to prosecution.

The publisher acknowledges the generous support of Creative New Zealand for this publication.

ISBN 978-1-99-004234-8

First published 2023
Reprinted 2024

Editors: Susan Brierley, Peter Dowling
Designer: Sarah Elworthy

Printed in China

CONTENTS

Foreword *by Justice Sir (Tā) Joe Williams*	6
Preface	8
Chronology	13

PART 1 BACKGROUND TO AN ABDUCTION
1 Difficult years for Whakatōhea	22
2 Te Kooti's relationship with Whakatōhea	36

PART 2 THE ŌPAPE RAID AND THE PURSUIT OF TE KOOTI
3 Te Kooti's arrival at Maraetahi and the raid on Ōpape	49
4 Whanganui's resolute determination	69
5 Ngāti Porou traverse Te Urewera	99
6 Whanganui capture Waipuna pā	120
7 Ngāti Porou assault Maraetahi pā	135

PART 3 THE CONTINUING AFTERMATH
8 The end of the campaign and the development of a myth	160
9 The impacts of war	182
10 The fruits of war — and the last word to Te Kooti	201

Epilogue The effect of the Porter 'myth' on the historical record	211
Appendix 1 Food and other resources	218
Appendix 2 Te Kooti's Te Urewera routes in February and March 1870	221
Appendix 3 Following in their footsteps	231
Appendix 4 Porter's questionable reliability	251
Glossary	252
Select bibliography	253
Acknowledgements	256
Endnotes	258
Index	262
About the author	272

FOREWORD

Nau mai ka haere tāua, ki roto o Tūranga
Kia whakangungua koe ki te mīni
Ki te hoari, ki te pū hurihuri
Nga rākau kōhuru a te Pākeha e takoto nei

Come we will go to Turanga [modern Gisborne]
That you may be tested by the Minnie rifle
By the sword and the revolver
Those Pakeha instruments of murder lying everywhere

Thus reads a small excerpt from Te Kooti's adaptation of the famous Ngāti Kahungunu oriori 'Pinepine te Kura'. In this book Ron Crosby returns to the bitter chapter of the New Zealand Wars so graphically described in that oriori: the pursuit of Te Kooti and the whakarau (the name given to the Chatham Islands captives) by predominantly Māori kāwanatanga forces. Ron first wrote on the subject nearly twenty years ago in *Gilbert Mair: Te Kooti's Nemesis* and returned to it a decade later in *Kūpapa: The Bitter Legacy of Māori Alliances with the Crown*. This time, as the title suggests, his focus is on the end game (at least militarily) of that chapter.

Ron brings two indispensable qualities to his writing of our colonial military history. First, the forensic exactitude of a fine litigation lawyer (I know, I had the misfortune to appear against him a couple of times); and second, an intimate knowledge of the whenua upon which the drama played out. (I witnessed the latter first-hand when my whānau and I spent five days in the summer of 2019 trekking through the Urewera with him and his wife Mākere. This consisted primarily of struggling to keep up with them.) In *Te Kooti's Last Foray*, he again demonstrates command of both the documentary and physical landscapes of his subject to a degree only too rarely attained by modern historians.

This is a military history. It does not purport to be a political history of the period, still less a biography of a man who, though defeated, would eventually become one of New Zealand's most important spiritual leaders. That work has been done by others. Rather Ron follows (literally), over forested ridges and down riverine gorges, the narratives written by or about those trying, in vain, to catch Te Kooti. Ron has found key locations in the narrative of pursuit by walking the whenua and comparing what he saw with descriptions of battle sites, geographical features and landforms recorded by kāwanatanga forces at the time. The physical challenge of the traverse ought not to be underestimated. It was the subject of repeated comment by kāwanatanga officers at the time. Had Ron not committed himself to his task, the places and their kōrero might, in time, have faded from memory altogether. New Zealand history owes him a debt of gratitude.

The author also provides important new insights about the contribution of Major Kēpa Te Rangihiwinui and his Whanganui force. And, relatedly, it challenges some of the orthodoxies written into the historical record by Lt (later Lt Col) Porter who fought under the command of Major Rapata Wahawaha as part of the latter's Ngāti Porou force. The evidence in support of the conclusions drawn is compelling.

This book is well worth the read.

Justice Sir (Tā) Joe Williams
February 2023

PREFACE

Just two mass abductions occurred during the era of the New Zealand wars. The first, carried out by Te Kooti in November 1868, after his raid on Matawhero at Tūranganui (Gisborne), is well known and documented. The second, however, has almost disappeared in the mists of time.

This book concerns the second of these events, which also involved Te Kooti, and had lasting significance for him, his victims, and all those who became involved in his pursuit. On 7 March 1870, Te Kooti abducted two communities of Whakatōhea — the occupants of the pā at Ōpape and at nearby Ōmarumutu, east of Ōpōtiki. Te Kooti's men compelled some 218 people — 57 men, 83 women and 78 children — to travel on foot for around three days into the difficult, heavily bushed area of the upper Waioeka River, about 45 kilometres from the coast. At the end of this arduous journey they then had to build whare for shelter, forage for food, and begin to prepare gardens to see them through the looming winter.

No other forced movement of people on that scale, involving such a degree of hard physical effort, occurred in the 12 years of the New Zealand Wars, which lasted from 1860 to 1872. Even after Te Kooti's earlier raid on Matawhero, when he had compelled, or 'persuaded', a possibly similar number of people to move up the Wharekopae River to Ngātapa, the trek to Ngātapa from Tūranganui was nowhere near as difficult.*

In the weeks following the abduction, the pursuit of Te Kooti began in earnest through the remote fastnesses of the mid Waioeka River valley. It was led principally by contingents of Whanganui and Ngāti Porou, who faced similar

---

* Unlike the situation in the Waioeka, where careful counts were later made of those taken captive, no similar record exists to establish the numbers taken captive from Tūranganui.

physical challenges to Te Kooti's captives — extraordinarily harsh country, shortages of food and shelter — in addition to a lesser knowledge of the terrain than Te Kooti.

But the story of the abduction of the Whakatōhea from Ōpape and Ōmarumutu, and the subsequent pursuit, is not a straightforward one of physical and mental hardship. It involves mixed and changing loyalties within and between iwi and hapū, and between iwi and the settler government, often as a result of past conflicts and harsh land confiscations. This was also a time of transition for many Māori, as the settler government increasingly saw Māori forces as a significant part of a new policy of 'self-reliance' for the country, and acknowledged their skills and leadership in the field.

In addition to all these elements, the story of these events provides a stark illustration of the effect on history of the editing of memory. Not only have details been 'misremembered', but the whole episode has almost disappeared from history, as discussed in the Epilogue to this book. To take one example, James Belich's otherwise very perceptive *The New Zealand Wars and the Victorian Interpretation of Racial Conflict*, published in 1986, simply refers in passing to these Waioeka events as one of two 'minor forays to the coast' undertaken by Te Kooti in March and July 1870. The memory of these events has largely become lost outside of the Whakatōhea rohe surrounding Ōpōtiki, and even within that rohe few details are known. But these were much more than 'minor forays', and the consequences were far-reaching.

One major outcome of the events in the Waioeka was that the defeat of Te Kooti and the dispersion of his forces led Hira Te Popo, the leading rangatira of Ngāti Ira hapū of Whakatōhea, to change his allegiance. Repudiating Te Kooti at that stage, within months he had led his people out of the rugged Urewera bush country to a more benign, cultivatable area just north of the mouth of the Waioeka Gorge. Other wavering Tūhoe rangatira also withdrew their support for Te Kooti after these events.

Although Te Kooti himself was not captured, his power was completely undermined by these events. Ever since his brutal attacks on Matawhero and Mohaka in late 1868 and early 1869, Te Kooti's potential to launch raids on both Māori and Pākehā communities surrounding his Te Urewera refuges had been a constant threat. After the events of March 1870, however, Te Kooti was never again able to assemble the large numbers of people who he had gathered together in the Waioeka through a mixture of compulsion and loyalty.

The question of whether the people at Ōpape and Ōmarumutu were compelled to go with Te Kooti or chose to do so is one of the many intriguing aspects of these events. The possibility that some of those 'compelled' to migrate inland may in fact have been sympathetic to Te Kooti and his cause raises the interesting, and probably unanswerable, question as to who were really the 'abductors' — Te Kooti, or those who later 'released' the Whakatōhea from him? Modern adherents of the Ringatū religion probably favour the latter view, but the Whakatōhea rangatira at Ōpape at the time expressed a strong view against Te Kooti and enthusiastically joined Whanganui in his pursuit, with the aim of releasing their people.

This raises another intriguing consequence arising out of these events that has an ongoing impact. Today, a significant proportion of the Whakatōhea hapū in Ōpape and Ōpōtiki actively practise the Ringatū religion. And the prophet who established that religion was, of course, Te Kooti. There is more than a touch of irony in the fact that many of those hapū who follow the Ringatū faith today have direct whakapapa links to those who were forced from Ōpape and Ōmarumutu by Te Kooti in March 1870.

At the heart of this story, however, is the fact that the northeast Waioeka catchment and the southwest Waiau/Te Hoe catchments contain some of the steepest ridges, and hence the longest gorges, in the block of continuous bush country known as Te Urewera. It is rugged, heavily bushed, extremely difficult country. It almost defies belief that a whole community, comprising 218 people from two pā, could have been compelled to make such a trek through such challenging country. As discussed in later chapters, there would have been limited numbers of military-aged men among the captives, and the 57 men, 83 women and 78 children would have included elderly kuia and kaumatua, younger and possibly hapū (pregnant) women, and very young children and babies.

The impacts on these people included loss of freedom; the uncertainty of confinement and its length; the dangers of conflict; and very real physical hardship. These Whakatōhea people, and the people involved both in their abduction and in their release, deserve to have these events and their impacts recorded in the national memory. It is a tale that demands retelling to ensure its memory and significance are not lost.

AUTHOR'S NOTE

On a personal note, my interest in these events has stemmed from a well-nigh lifelong interest in Te Urewera, and over later decades in the history of the pursuit of Te Kooti in those widespread ranges. In the early 1970s I made a number of deerstalking trips into the headwater streams of the upper Waioeka, initially climbing over the range from the Moanui area in the upper Koranga valley. In 1987 I spent two weeks walking from the Wairata area up into the head of the Makakoere Stream, one of the feeder headwaters of the Waioeka River itself, and a third week with friends descending the length of the river from the Makakoere back to Wairata. At that time, sadly, I did not have the knowledge of the history I was literally walking through.*

In later years, as my knowledge developed, the significance of the events surrounding the mass abduction at Ōpape and Ōmarumutu became clear. In order to check on the ground what had occurred, and where, it was necessary to make a number of trips into the area, usually in the company of friends who shared my interest, albeit I dare say less obsessively. The knowledge gained during these trips inform the main text, with the details described in Appendix 3.

Another very significant source of information, particularly with respect to the role of the Whanganui Contingent, was the diaries of Samuel Austin. In 2013, when I was carrying out research for the book *Kūpapa: The Bitter Legacy of Māori Alliances with the Crown*, I became aware of the recently published book by Barbara Mabbett, *For Gallant Service Rendered: The Life & Times of Samuel Austin*. It was here that I first became aware that this experienced Pākehā NCO had served with Te Kēpa's contingent of Whanganui kūpapa in 1870 in the Bay of Plenty. When I finally came clear of other obligations late in 2019 I approached Barbara for access to her copies of the Austin diaries, and received her willing assistance, for which I am very grateful.

As described in more detail later in this book, what recognition of the Ōpape and Waioeka events that does exist has until now concentrated on Ropata Wahawaha and Ngāti Porou at Maraetahi. Contemporary newspaper reports and later histories became predominantly based on accounts provided by Thomas Porter, a Pākehā officer who accompanied the Ngāti Porou contingent. His accounts gave most credit to Wahawaha and his Ngāti Porou, with Te Kēpa and his Whanganui often receiving only passing acknowledgement as providing a supporting role. It is clear from Austin's diaries, however, that this was a completely inaccurate picture of events. Austin's diaries, and the immediate post-operational reports of the Whanganui rangatira Te Kēpa and Topia Turoa, make very clear the significant role that Te Kēpa's men played, particularly at Waipuna pā.

---

* Nor, intriguingly, in 1987 was I aware that Barry Crump had based part of his very popular book *Wild Pork and Watercress* in the upper catchments of the Waioeka. Although the book was published in 1986, I only became aware of it after I emerged from the Waioeka in late 1987. Some 30-odd years later that book was itself to form the basis of Taika Waititi's equally popular film *Hunt for the Wilderpeople*.

Samuel Austin.
Harding, William James, 1826–99. Ref: 1/4-004715-G, Alexander Turnbull Library, Wellington, NZ

There are two matters of typographical style that need to be recorded. One of these is the vexed issue of tohutō or macrons for the long vowels in te reo Māori. I have endeavoured to use these for iwi/hapū names, as some level of certainty can usually be obtained about these usages. With the names of individuals and places, however, that certainty is not so easy to establish, and I have endeavoured to use tohutō only when I have been confident of their accuracy.

The other issue relates to the misspellings in diaries and other contemporary documents. Samuel Austin could certainly have benefited as a child from more time on spelling lessons. I have not attempted to correct his or other misspellings, nor have I attempted to reproduce Austin's random use of capitalisation.

CHRONOLOGY

A: GENERAL CHRONOLOGY, APRIL 1864 TO FEBRUARY 1870

1864

April — A Tai Rāwhiti taua, seeking to join the Kingitanga in Waikato, is defeated at the battle of Kaokaoroa Beach, east of Maketū. Whakatōhea under Hira Te Popo suffer many casualties at the hands of Te Arawa, and Hira Te Popo narrowly escapes.

Paimārire religion, established by Te Ua Haumēne in south Taranaki, leads to the first attack on British troops in Aotearoa.

1865

February — Kereopa and Patara arrive at Ōpōtiki as emissaries of Paimārire.

March — Murder of the Rev. Carl Volkner at Ōpōtiki.

September — A government invasion force arrives in Ōpōtiki and occupies the coastal area.

October — Ngāti Ira, Hira Te Popo's hapū, suffer heavy losses at Te Tarata pā and withdraw up the Waioeka River to live predominantly at Maraetahi pā.

November — The Waerenga a Hika siege occurs inland of Tūranga (Gisborne); a combination of Ngāti Porou and other allied iwi and government Armed Constabulary defeat Paimārire; Te Kooti serves with the government forces.

1866

January — Proclamation of confiscation of Whakatōhea and Ngāti Awa lands in and around Ōpōtiki and Whakatāne respectively. Whakatōhea, other than Ngāti Ira, are later compelled to live at the Ōpape reserve east of Ōpōtiki; Ūpokorehe at the small Hiwarau reserve at Ōhiwa; and Ngāti Ira predominantly remain at Maraetahi and other locations further up the Waioeka.

March — Te Kooti arrested at Tūranga and accused of assisting Paimārire at the Waerenga a Hika siege.

June — Te Kooti exiled with other whakarau (captives) to Wharekauri (Chatham Islands) or Rēkohu without trial or finite sentences.

1866–67

Te Arawa establish a redoubt at the eastern entry to Ōhiwa harbour as part of a government occupation force.

1868

July	Te Kooti and his 300 whakarau followers escape from Wharekauri by seizing the *Rifleman*, and land at Whareongaonga Bay, south of Tūranga.
July–August	Te Kooti's force repels repeated attacks by government forces in the ranges between Whareongaonga Bay and the Ruakituri River.
November	Te Kooti attacks Matawhero, at Tūranganui, and kills some 70 Māori and Pākehā.
November–December	Joint Ngāti Kahungunu and Ngāti Porou forces heavily defeat Te Kooti at Makaretu pā, and besiege him at Ngātapa.

1869

January	Ngāti Ira invite Te Kooti to come to Maraetahi pā.
4 January	Ngātapa pā falls to attacks by Ngāti Porou under Ropata Wahawaha and Te Arawa under Lt George Preece, as well as Armed Constabulary. Te Kooti escapes, but an estimated 120 of his followers are tracked down, captured and killed.
Mid January	Te Kooti and some of the whakarau arrive at Maraetahi pā, and gather more recruits over the next month.
February	Te Kooti and Ngāi Tūhoe enter into a covenant at Tawhana pā in the upper Waimana/Tauranga valley whereby Te Kooti gains refuge in Te Urewera in return for his leadership against the government.
March	Te Kooti's forces attack the Ngāti Pukeko pā of Ngāti Awa, called Raupōroa, just south of Whakatāne, and the associated millhouse called Te Poronu. Te Kooti is pursued up the Rangitaiki River to Tauaroa pā, and escapes into Te Urewera up the Horomanga River.
April	Te Kooti attacks the Ngāti Pahauwera pā at Mohaka and settler farms nearby, killing about 70 more Māori and Pākehā.
May	Conventional government forces under Col George Whitmore invade Te Urewera in pursuit of Te Kooti, penetrating as far as Ruatāhuna from the north and west, but fail to capture him.
June–October	Te Kooti emerges from Te Urewera, attacks Ōpepe redoubt, and heads around Lake Taupō for the kingitanga (King Country), where King Tāwhiao refuses to meet him. He suffers heavy losses in battles at Te Pōnanga and Te Pōrere at the hands of Te Arawa, Ngāti Kahungunu, Whanganui under Te Kēpa, some Ngāti Tūwharetoa hapū, and small numbers of Pākehā.
November	The Whanganui Contingent under Te Kēpa returns to Whanganui.
19–20 November	Hui are held by various Whanganui rangatira at Te Ao Marama wharenui at Ōhinemutu on the Whanganui River to debate their

	varying attitudes to Te Kooti. Topia Turoa announces that he agrees to serve with Te Kēpa's Whanganui Contingent.
29 November	Premier William Fox meets with Topia Turoa, Te Kēpa and other Whanganui rangatira at Rānana and agrees to provide weapons for Topia's men.
December	The Whanganui Contingent regather under Te Kēpa and Topia Turoa and head up the flooded Whanganui River, taking most of the month to reach Taumarunui. They then traverse west of Lake Taupō to meet up with Lt Col McDonnell's Armed Constabulary forces at the Waikato River, just north of Tapuaeharuru (modern Taupō).
	Te Kooti is pursued by Whanganui, Te Arawa and Pākehā forces to and around Tirau, at the Tapapa pā of Hakaraia, his prominent Waitaha rangatira supporter.

1870

January	Intermittent clashes continue in the Mamaku ranges west of Rotorua and in the Kaimai ranges south of Tauranga.
February	Most of the Whanganui Contingent under Te Kēpa and Topia Turoa arrive in Tauranga and are shipped to the beach area east of the Ōhiwa harbour entrance.
7 February	Te Kooti attacked successfully south of Rotorua by a Te Arawa force led by Lt Gilbert Mair, losing about 20 killed in a day-long engagement south to Tumunui.
8 February	Te Kooti's forces escape across the Kaingaroa Plains and enter Te Urewera, arriving at Ruatāhuna.
	From there he and his followers take two different routes to Tauaki pā north of Maungapōhatu, then continue north and east across the Urewera ranges from the Waimana/Tauranga River valley to arrive at Maraetahi pā.
18 February	The Minister of Defence and Native Affairs, Donald McLean, issues orders that only Māori forces are now to be involved in the pursuit of Te Kooti.
21 February	Te Kēpa and Topia Turoa are visited by Ropata at Ōhiwa, and they plan to invade Te Urewera from the north and southeast respectively, to meet at Maungapōhatu.
	Ropata continues on by sea to the East Coast to raise his force.
24 February	The balance of the Whanganui Contingent arrives at Ōhiwa from Tapapa.
28 February	Te Kooti attacks Kōkōhinau flour mill in the Rangitaiki valley, west of Whakatāne and just north of Te Teko.

B: DETAILED CHRONOLOGY OF EVENTS IN THE WAIOEKA, 1870–83

1870

4 March	Ngāti Porou under Ropata Wahawaha (accompanied by Lt Thomas Porter) leave Tūranga (Gisborne), heading west for Te Urewera.
	The Whanganui Contingent under Te Kēpa and initially Topia Turoa, with Ngāi Tai under Wiremu Kingi Tutahuarangi and some 40 young Whakatōhea as allies, heads up the Waimana River. They are joined at Waimana by 60 Ngāti Awa under Hori Kawakura.
5 March	Topia Turoa returns to Ōhiwa.
	The Whanganui Contingent under Te Kēpa has an initial engagement with Tūhoe under Tamaikōwha at Ōtara, midway up the Waimana/Tauranga River.
6–7 March	Te Kēpa's force continues up the Waimana/Tauranga but is forced to camp because of floods in the river.
6–12 March	Ngāti Porou traverse the Hangaroa and Ruakituri valleys in the eastern Urewera ranges, taking some 11 Ngāti Kōwhatu people captive.
7 March	Te Kooti raids Ōmarumutu and Ōpape pā and seizes Whakatōhea communities in both. Some Whakatōhea rangatira escape by sea with weapons to Tōrere.
	On receipt of this news Topia Turoa heads for the Ōpape area to protect Ngāi Tai at Tōrere.
8–11 March	Te Kooti takes his Whakatōhea captives up the Tutaetoko valley, into Raetakahia Stream, along the Raupō ridgeline and over into the Ōmaukora valley, then down to Wairata in the mid Waioeka River.
11–12 March	Te Kooti's force splits at Wairata, with Whakatōhea captives and some of the whakarau heading upriver and establishing Waipuna/Raepawa pā at Te Pato junction.
	Te Kooti and the balance of the whakarau travel downriver to Maraetahi pā.
12–13 March	The Whanganui Contingent reaches Tawhana pā, well up the Waimana/Tauranga River, and Te Kēpa and Tamaikōwha enter a rongopai (peace agreement).
13 March	Ngāti Porou attack and capture two Maungapōhatu pā, called Horoeka and Toreatai, losing only one man and taking 40 prisoners.
	News of the rongopai reaches Maungapōhatu.
	Tamaikōwha heads from the Waimana valley toward Ruatāhuna to take news of the rongopai to other Tūhoe rangatira.
16 March	Ngāti Porou head north from Maungapōhatu toward Waimana and stay overnight at Tauaki pā.
17 March	The Whanganui Contingent under Te Kēpa arrives back at Ōhiwa.

CHRONOLOGY

18–20 March	The Whanganui Contingent makes preparations in Ōpōtiki to link up with Topia Turoa and locate traces of Te Kooti's route with his Whakatōhea captives.
	The Whanganui Contingent makes plans with Ngāi Tai under Wiremu Kingi Tutahuarangi and Whakatōhea under Te Ranapia and Tiwai to head off in pursuit of Te Kooti and the captives.
20 March	Ngāti Porou reach Ōhiwa.
	Ropata and Te Kēpa meet at Ōhiwa, then Te Kēpa returns to Ōpōtiki from where the Whanganui Contingent departs at 10 p.m. for the Tutaetoko valley.
21 March	The Whanganui Contingent stops for the night well up the Tutaetoko River.
	Ngāti Porou arrive at Ōpōtiki, and resupply and overnight there.
22 March	The Whanganui Contingent ascends the Raetakahia Stream and continues up onto the Raupō ridgeline.
	Ngāti Porou leave Ōpōtiki at 5 p.m., heading up the Waioeka River.
23 March	The Whanganui Contingent drops down into the Ōmaukora Stream, descends and reaches Wairata at 4 p.m.
	The Whanganui Contingent commences attacks on a pā at 6.30 p.m., and later attack six puni (temporary camps). These attacks take all night, culminating in the contingent surrounding Waipuna/Raepawa pā at dawn on 24 March.
	Ngāti Porou continue travelling up the Waioeka all day, camping for the night near the old Matahanea pā location.
24 March	Whanganui attack Waipuna pā at dawn, releasing all the Whakatōhea captives without loss, capturing 87 of Te Kooti's people and over the night and dawn attacks killing about 22, including Hakaraia.
	Ngāti Porou reach Kairakau pā at about midday and continue until camping somewhere probably just north of the gorge of Te Karoro a Tamatea (Hell's Gate).
25 March	Ngāti Porou are fired on by a picquet consisting initially of two sentries at Te Karoro Gorge, where they are delayed for two hours by the need to descend the river to cross and fire at the picquet that had by then been reinforced; they wound two members of the picquet.
	Ngāti Porou then advance for 2 km to take Maraetahi pā two hours after first being fired upon at the gorge; by the time they arrive all the occupants have gone.
	The Whanganui Contingent set up an ambuscade at Wairata, 6 km upriver, where they capture 18 and kill four more.
	Meanwhile Whanganui pursuit patrols from Waipuna pā capture 11 and kill one more.

26 March	Ngāti Porou send out a pursuit patrol of 120 men over ranges to the west, which reaches Te Ponga on the Waimana/Tauranga River at its junction with the Waiiti Stream.
	At 8 a.m. the Whanganui Contingent burns all the whare at Waipuna pā and heads downriver with 321 captives, killing four more men encountered on the way.
	The contingent arrives at 2 p.m. at Maraetahi pā to link up with Ngāti Porou.
27 March	The Ngāti Porou pursuit patrol returns from the Waimana, having taken three prisoners and killed one man.
	The Whanganui contingent sends out a pursuit patrol from Maraetahi, which kills one more man.
28 March	Two pursuit patrols of 150 men each are sent out by Whanganui and Ngāti Porou from Maraetahi; they return the following day without making contact with any of Te Kooti's people.
	Samuel Austin, of the Whanganui Contingent, oversees the burning of all whare at Maraetahi pā in an effort to draw Te Kooti out of the bush.
30 March	The Whanganui Contingent, Ngāti Porou and all the captives head down the Waioeka River.
	Porter, Austin, and small groups of their men arrive at Ōpōtiki.
	Lt Col St John sends a hurried report to his superior officer by boat.
31 March	The main bodies of Whanganui, Ngāti Porou and all the captives arrive at Ōpōtiki.
	Ropata recovers a gunpowder cache after gathering intelligence from Whakatōhea captives.
	Porter hands Lt Col St John his original unpublished report in diarised form, which St John sends on to his superiors.
	Te Kēpa, Topia Turoa and Ropata Wahawaha all write reports to Donald McLean.
1 April	Wiremu Kingi Tutahuarangi of Ngāi Tai writes a report to McLean.
8 April	McLean and Henry Clarke meet at Ōpōtiki with the Whanganui Contingent and Ngāti Porou, and then Ngāi Tai and Whakatōhea.
12 April	Ngāti Porou leave for Te Tai Rāwhiti by sea, accompanied by McLean and Clarke.
	The Whanganui Contingent heads home by sea together with the captives committed for trial in the Wellington Supreme Court.
13 April	McLean signs a memorandum with Ngāti Porou rangatira agreeing not to continue with confiscations in Te Tai Rāwhiti.

15 April	The captives are landed at Wellington and held as prisoners pending trial.
16 April	Premier William Fox writes to Te Kēpa and Topia Turoa promising no further confiscations of their lands.
20 April	The Whanganui Contingent reaches Whanganui.
23 April	Lt Col St John attacks Tamaikōwha at Whakarae pā near Ōhiwa and kills his uncle, Tipene.
4 May	Ngāti Porou under Ropata head into Te Urewera once more for two weeks, emerging at Wairoa on 17 May; they do not reach the Waioeka.
7 May	Donald McLean writes a letter dismissing Lt Col St John from his command at Ōpōtiki (the letter not arriving until after 12 May).
12 –24 May	Lt Col St John and Wiremu Kingi Tutahuarangi of Ngāi Tai conduct a long raid into Waipuna and Maraetahi pā without contact with any enemy.
17 June	Hira Te Popo and his remaining Ngāti Ira people emerge from the bush and surrender.
20 June	Swords of honour are presented by the governor to Te Kēpa and Ropata Wahawaha, and another Ngāti Porou rangatira, Mōkena Kōhere.
27 June	The trial of the captives opens in the Wellington Supreme Court and lasts a week, with all except two sentenced to death.
26 July	Ropata meets with Hira Te Popo and Paora Te Uaaterangi and reports on them favourably to McLean, as well as recommending mercy for Whakatōhea captives.
26–27 July	Te Kooti attempts a raid at Uawa (Tolaga Bay) and is rebuffed, with one of his wives, Huhana Tamati, being captured.
4 August	McLean writes back to Ropata and confirms that the prisoners will not be executed.

1871

14 January	Ropata and Porter lead Ngāti Porou into the eastern Urewera once more.
February	A Ngāti Porou expedition visits Maraetahi, which is unoccupied.
	Ngāti Porou traverse into the Waimana valley, where Ropata at last meets Tamaikōwha, but they find no sign of Te Kooti at or near Maraetahi.
6 June	Ngāti Porou enter Te Urewera once more for an extended expedition, which lasts until September.
18 August	The Arawa Flying Columns attack Te Kooti's puni at the Waipaoa, in the Ruakituri catchment, but he escapes.
September	Porter's Ngāti Porou ope attacks Te Kooti's puni at Te Hapua, on the northern flanks of Maungapōhatu, but again he escapes.
October	Porter's resupply ope heading from Ōpōtiki to the Waimana passes through the Maraetahi site, which is still unoccupied.

18 November	Kereopa is captured in the Whakatāne River valley by Ngāti Porou, with assistance from a Tūhoe guide, Te Whiu Maraki; he is taken out by Porter to be prosecuted at Napier.
1872	
5 January	Kereopa is executed by hanging at Napier.
11 January	Governor Bowen reports to the British government that all prisoners' sentences have been commuted and none are now imprisoned.
31 January	The Arawa Flying Column under Preece fires the last shots at Te Kooti south of Lake Waikaremoana, in the Waiau catchment.
May	Te Kooti escapes from Te Urewera and reaches refuge in the Kingitanga.
1883	Te Kooti is pardoned and afterwards embarks on an extended reconciliation process in areas where he has previously been engaged in war, garnering widespread support for Te Hāhi Ringatū.
	The government vests a block of land in Te Kooti at Ōhiwa.
1889	Te Kooti's followers are held near Ōpōtiki; Te Kooti is arrested by Ropata and the newly promoted Major Porter at Waiotahi, and prosecuted for disturbing the peace after he attempts to visit the Tūranganui area.
1892	Te Kooti dies, but leaves a flourishing Ringatū religion.

PART 1
BACKGROUND TO AN ABDUCTION

1

DIFFICULT YEARS FOR WHAKATŌHEA

The events described in this book originated indirectly in the invasions and confiscations that occurred in the years after 1863, as the New Zealand Government followed up its earlier aggressive military actions against Māori. These confiscation actions were in their own way as devastating as the physical invasions, because they involved the passing of the legislation that enabled widespread land confiscation from Māori.

Māori who experienced the initial invasions and confiscations in Taranaki, Waikato and Tauranga from 1860 to 1864, and those anxiously looking on, like Whakatōhea in the Ōpōtiki area, realised there was no protective government authority to which they could turn, or that they could rely on, to uphold their entitlements under the Treaty of Waitangi.

In Article 2 of the Treaty, the Crown had solemnly covenanted with Māori that it would protect their rights of tino rangatiratanga over their lands. Yet just 20 years later, here was the Crown itself embarking on a series of aggressive military campaigns, beginning in 1860, which were followed by land confiscations on a massive scale against Māori who were branded as rebels for defending their lands against Crown aggression. When these confiscations occurred the loss of land was in perpetuity, depriving the Māori customary owners of the vital resources on which their very lives depended. They were stripped of their homes and cultural links, and their hereditary resources. Whakatōhea in the Ōpōtiki area were one of the iwi who were most seriously affected by such confiscations.

As a nation we are still grappling with the consequences of the callous conduct that involved cynical, flagrant breaches of the Treaty by governors, and later settler governments, bent on massive land acquisition for Pākehā settlement. The underlying arrogance that led to this type of Crown conduct is typified in a speech relating to the South Island as late as 1907, given by Dr T.M. Hocken, whose name in the Hocken Library at Dunedin is associated with the protection of our historical memories as a nation:

> It may be of interest to you to know that from time to time large blocks of land have been purchased from the Natives of this Island for ourselves, until now we possess the whole. The total area is roundly about 38,000,000 acres, which have cost us in round numbers, and very roughly speaking, about £50,000. Of course, reserves have been made for the benefit of the interesting people who were the original owners of the soil. It is right, perhaps, and in accordance with the principles of evolution and of the advancement of the human race, that those should possess the land who use it to best advantage, even though this should involve dispossession of the original inhabitants.[1]

It is hard to imagine an attitude more in conflict with the principles underlying the Treaty than that last sentence, yet Hocken was one of the leading Pākehā thinkers of his era in the country.

RELIGION AS A REACTION TO CROWN AGGRESSION IN THE MID 1860S

Understandably, for many Māori the direct consequence of the Crown's aggressive acquisition processes, which included resorting to war, was a mixture of deep anger and hurt on the part of those directly affected; and frustration, anxiety, disbelief and despair for many of those watching on, such as Whakatōhea. When they could no longer perceive any lawful authority from which to obtain protection or fair and just treatment, it is hardly surprising that they turned to other sources of comfort or belief. In some cases this took the form of following religious prophets, or a mixture of religious guidance and direct resistance.

In 1864, Governor George Grey lost the ability to utilise British Imperial troops aggressively. The British Government, increasingly perturbed at what it perceived as his improper use of Imperial forces to dispossess Māori of land, directed the withdrawal of its forces from active operations, and confined their use to garrison roles only. Notwithstanding this loss, Grey felt that by the end of the first half of 1864 Māori opposition to his invasions had been crushed. However, even as he was reaching that conclusion, the Paimārire religious movement erupted, with the first attacks linked to the movement occurring in the Taranaki and Whanganui areas, where serious further fighting had commenced in early 1864.

The Paimārire movement derived from the teachings of Te Ua Haumēne, a self-proclaimed prophet from the Taranaki iwi. In common with other later prophets he utilised predominantly Old Testament texts and drew parallels between the burdens inflicted by biblical authorities against the Israelites and those now being inflicted by the Crown on Māori. As Bronwyn Elsmore writes:

> They saw themselves as captive in their own land — subject to the Pakeha as the Israelites had been to a number of other peoples throughout their history. As the earlier overlords had plundered Israel, so had the substance of Aotearoa been taken over by a foreign race. The Maori saw similarities in many of the passages of the Old Testament scripture, and so his religious response was built upon that foundation.[2]

Typical Paimārire scene — this one being at Tataroa in the Waikato.

Meade, Herbert George Phillip, 1842–68. Ref: B-139-014. Alexander Turnbull Library, Wellington, NZ

This phenomenon of indigenous people turning to Old Testament scripture in response to the fate they faced when government authorities acted in breach of solemn treaty obligations to protect them and their lands was not restricted to Māori. In many other countries around the world where indigenous peoples were undergoing similar pressures of settler expansion involving repeated treaty breaches (as in the United States), or colonialism (as in India, China, Melanesia or Africa), religious movements seeking a salvation based loosely on a mix of Old Testament texts and indigenous beliefs were relatively common.[3]

However, what had begun as a peaceful religious belief — the very word 'Paimārire' embodies a sense of peace — quite rapidly developed into a mixed concept of religion and armed resistance to the settler government. In time this aggressive style of Paimārire worship became more commonly referred to by Pākehā as the Hauhau movement. Its most readily recognised signature became its extended prayer ceremonies, often chanted by adherents circling around very tall symbolic niu poles, and including the rhythmic chanting of the phrase 'Hau, hau'.

In early 1865 Te Ua Haumēne sent out Patara Raukatauri and Kereopa Te Rau as emissaries to the Bay of Plenty and Te Tai Rāwhiti (East Coast) areas. The arrival of the Paimārire message occurred against a setting of frustration and despair for many eastern Bay of Plenty Māori such as Whakatōhea.

Te Ua Haumene.
Cowan, James, 1870–1943. Ref: 1/2-005495-F, Alexander Turnbull Library, Wellington, NZ

WHAKATŌHEA IN THE FIRST 20 YEARS AFTER THE TREATY

As with all iwi groups during the period up to and including the New Zealand Wars, Whakatōhea communities functioned principally at a hapū level. At that time, Whakatōhea comprised six main hapū with common whakapapa threads interweaving among them. Generally from east to west nearer the coast those hapū comprised Ngāti Rua (takenga), Ngāti Ngāhere, Ngāti Patu(moana) and Te Ūpokorehe, with Ngāi Tamahaua and Ngāti Ira predominantly more to the south in the various feeder contributors to the Waiaua, Ōtara, Waioeka and Takaputahi valley catchments.*

The Whakatōhea response to the outbreak of war between the Kingitanga (the Māori King movement) and the Kāwanatanga (being initially the governor, and later the settler government) in 1863 had echoed that on the East Coast and the Māori nation generally: many Whakatōhea hapū sympathised strongly with the Kingitanga in the face of overwhelming Crown assault. Others, while unsettled by the government's actions, nonetheless clung to the hope that there could still be trading and other benefits from the Treaty, such as an ordered, peaceful society supported by Crown authority.

In the Ōpōtiki area there were significant physical manifestations of those Treaty benefits. During the period from the Treaty signing until 1864 many Whakatōhea rangatira led the way in growing commercial quantities of produce, and acquiring the farm equipment and horses necessary to carry on a lucrative trade with rapidly growing Pākehā settler centres. The other perceived Treaty benefits included the belief that adherence to the Treaty accorded with the messages of peace and good order they had heard and accepted through the Anglican and Roman Catholic churches.

Moreover, some argued that the Treaty guarantees provided protection from any repetition of the ravages they had endured as an iwi at the hands of other iwi during the Musket Wars. It is often overlooked that the Whakatōhea people had suffered particularly badly at the hands of recurrent taua by Ngāpuhi and Ngāti Maru over the period from 1820 to 1830. At various times from the late 1820s until about 1836 they had also been engaged in fighting against hapū of their near neighbours to east and west, Ngāi Tai and Ngāti Awa, as well as against Te Aitanga a Māhaki in Gisborne and Ngāti Porou, who they fought alongside Whānau a Apanui at Te Kaha.

The consequence, then, of all these travails was that all hapū of Whakatōhea had suffered severe disruptions and losses in the Musket Wars era. It must therefore have been with a major sense of relief that from 1840 Whakatōhea entered a period of extended peace, free from the threat of musket raids with the development of the more equal balance of musket power between iwi. They enjoyed about 25 years of relative calm, during which they re-established themselves on their coastal plains, with all their rich land, riverine and marine food resources. They also enjoyed the growth of a new economy based on the

---

* Even in modern times, and as at the date of writing in 2022, Whakatōhea and their hapū are still locked in struggles over their identities and interrelationships. One of the more major of those issues in recent times has been the stance of Ūpokorehe in particular in asserting an independent iwi status.

agricultural produce able to be grown on the high-quality soils on their Waiaua, Ōtara and Waioeka river flats, and acquired horses, drays, ploughs and all the other accoutrements needed for a growing agricultural industry. In turn, that led to the construction from local timbers of a number of sea-going vessels to carry their produce to the new population centres in Tauranga and even Auckland. The vessels returned with a wide range of trade goods and other personal items.

This period brought an increased uptake of the Christian religion, with its messages of peace conveyed by both Anglican and Roman Catholic missionaries. One of those missionaries was the Reverend Carl Sylvius Volkner, an Anglican who arrived in Ōpōtiki with his wife in August 1861, and in a few years had arranged the building of the impressive wooden church initially called Hīona (or Zion, and now called St Stephens) in the centre of the settlement.

Yet by 1863–64 the whole way of life of the Whakatōhea people appeared to be at increasing risk as the Crown guarantee in the Treaty of Māori lands and tino rangatiratanga came under threat. Many Whakatōhea observed with considerable disquiet as the Crown rode roughshod over Māori customary communal rights to land, and invaded first Taranaki, then the Waikato basin.

The Reverend Carl Volkner.
Kinder, John, 1819–1903. Ref: 1/2-059698-F, Alexander Turnbull Library, Wellington, NZ

INCREASING TENSIONS IN THE BAY OF PLENTY AND EAST COAST AREAS

When the Crown invaded the Waikato in July 1863 the Kingitanga sought the support of various Te Tai Rāwhiti and eastern Bay of Plenty iwi. Many eastern hapū, including some of Whakatōhea, were sympathetic to the Kingitanga's requests for support.

In February 1864, a large taua of about 800 men assembled in the eastern Bay of Plenty intending to head for the Kingitanga. The following month, however, Te Arawa refused to let the Tai Rāwhiti taua move through their rohe to support the Tainui Kingitanga, largely as a result of longstanding enmities following conflicts between Tainui and Te Arawa during the later Musket War era, from 1836 to after 1840. Heavy fighting ensued between the taua and Te Arawa at Lake Rotoiti and east of Maketū, culminating in a drawn-out battle on 28 April 1864 along the long, sandy beach and dune area east from Ōtamarakau known as Kaokaoroa. Casualties inflicted by Te Arawa there exceeded the combined losses suffered on both sides the following day at the battle of Gate Pa, back in Tauranga.

One of the leading Whakatōhea rangatira on the taua was Hira Te Popo of the Ngāti Ira hapū. He narrowly escaped with his life as he and his ope, or detachment of men, made their escape inland up a gully near the final stand of the taua at the Pikowai Stream, just west of Matatā. Many other Whakatōhea were not so fortunate, and scores were killed or wounded.

WHAKATŌHEA CONCERNS AT VOLKNER'S PRESENCE AT ŌPŌTIKI

During these rapidly intersecting events in 1864 officials of the settler government and the governor were determined to prevent the arrival of any support for the Kingitanga, and were constantly seeking intelligence as to possible sources of such support.

In the Bay of Plenty to the east of Tauranga, and right around the northern East Coast, the presence of Europeans was almost entirely limited to one or two traders at locations like Whakatāne and Ōpōtiki. However, there were also a handful of European missionaries who were either scattered in remote permanent residences or more commonly were travellers through these remote areas. The government began to look to those individual missionaries and traders for information, as well as to the passengers and skippers of the various trading vessels that were still plying to and fro with trade goods, particularly from Tauranga. In Ōpōtiki, Volkner soon became a source about the Whakatōhea. It is now known that in February 1864 Volkner wrote a number of letters to Governor Grey providing valuable military

Hira Te Popo(ki).
Author copy of the original at Ōpeke marae taken with permission of Te Rua Rakuraku

intelligence, although this was not known to Whakatōhea at the time.

One of Volkner's problems as an Anglican minister was that when the Waikato invasion occurred tales of biased Church actions, such as the Anglican Bishop Selwyn appearing to side with the Crown against Māori by ministering to the British Army forces, spread rapidly around the country. The bishop's actions did not help the situation for isolated missionaries such as Volkner. As tensions grew, and messengers from the Kingitanga passed back and forth, Whakatōhea became increasingly suspicious of Pākehā in their midst, such as Volkner, particularly as in 1864 he made a number of visits to Auckland. In about March 1864 he had taken his wife Emma to Auckland to live, perhaps indicating his awareness of the vulnerability of his position. It is plain that by early 1865 Whakatōhea held strong suspicions about Volkner.

PAIMĀRIRE ARRIVAL AT ŌPŌTIKI AND VOLKNER'S DEATH

Volkner was on an extended visit to his wife in Auckland when the Paimārire messengers Kereopa and Patara arrived in Ōpōtiki from Whakatāne, on Saturday 25 February 1865. They were accompanied by some 190 supporters.

Te Ua Haumēne's written instructions to Patara and Kereopa had been to carry his teachings in a peaceful manner. While Patara may have endeavoured to abide by this instruction, it is plain from the ensuing events that Kereopa did not feel any restraint in this respect. Tragically for Volkner, Patara did not stay long in Ōpōtiki before heading further along the eastern Bay of Plenty, leaving Whakatōhea to take their initial instruction from Kereopa alone. Kereopa was strident in his denunciation of Volkner as an agent of the Crown, and it is clear from subsequent events that his words fell on receptive ears.

What would have added fuel to the fire was the fact that in January that year the first declarations confiscating large

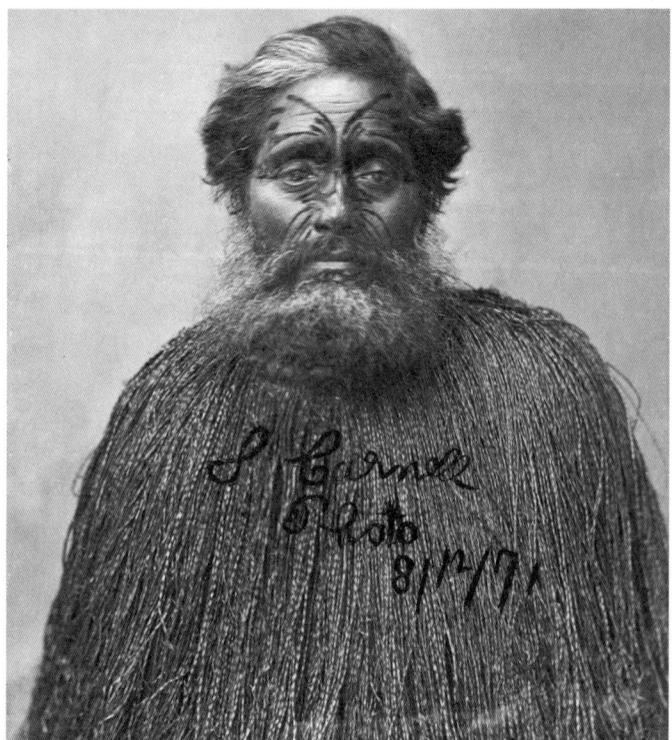

Kereopa Te Rau.
Carnell, Samuel 1832–1920. Ref: 1/4-022207-G, Alexander Turnbull Library, Wellington, NZ

areas of land in Taranaki and Waikato had been gazetted under the authority of the New Zealand Settlements Act of 1863. Many Whakatōhea feared that at some time in the near future the involvement of some of their people in the Tai Rāwhiti taua was highly likely to be cast by the settler government as rebellious activity, and used as justification to confiscate Whakatōhea lands. If this occurred, they knew from what had happened in other areas that there would be no regard for the niceties of whether or not the occupiers of the confiscated lands had been members of the 'rebellious' taua.

By the end of February, when the Paimārire prophets arrived with their message of a means of religious salvation from Pākehā, Whakatōhea must have been in a state of considerable anxiety about the potential confiscation of their lands. Their anxiety would also have been exacerbated by the heavy losses they had suffered the previous year from illness and war. At the end of 1864 Volkner had estimated that Whakatōhea had suffered 22 deaths on the Tai Rāwhiti taua, and about another 80 in two months from a severe 'fever'. These were significant losses out of a population he gave as being about 500 strong. Kereopa's urgings of a future path for Māori through the Paimārire religion and the rejection of Pākehā Christian beliefs were thus well received by many Whakatōhea. He arranged for a niu pole to be erected at Ōpōtiki, which could perhaps be seen as a physical symbol of the sudden swing in sentiment by many Whakatōhea away from Pākehā authority and religion.

It was into this cauldron of induced excitement and distrust of Pākehā ways that Carl Volkner returned. On his arrival at Ōpōtiki on 1 March, he was seized at the quayside by a large crowd made up of Whakatōhea and members of Kereopa's group. Within a day, Kereopa's urgings for him to be killed as a government spy had resulted in Volkner's being hanged. Whakatōhea had no previous culture of hanging, and those involved in Volkner's killing achieved it in a particularly gruesome manner. He died slowly as he was hoisted from the ground by a rope around his neck, the rope being threaded through a block and tackle from the *Eclipse*, the vessel on which he had travelled to Ōpōtiki. The block and tackle was tied to a branch of a willow tree near the Hīona church.

The callous manner of Volkner's killing was matched by the way in which his body was then treated. At Kereopa's direction his head was cut off and taken to his church, where the chalice was filled with his blood. Kereopa then harangued the crowd using Volkner's head for emphasis, concluding by plucking out Volkner's eyes and eating them. As a result of this action, something he did again two months later at the siege of the Ngāti Manawa pā at Te Tāpiri, southeast of modern Murupara, he became known as Kereopa Kaiwhatu or Kaikaru, the 'eye-eater'.

The Martyr's Tree, Ōpōtiki.
ATL Nat Lib
1/2-C-012123

The news of Volkner's killing, the manner in which it occurred, and Kereopa's subsequent actions caused widespread revulsion outside Ōpōtiki. Despite the fact that Ngāti Ira and Ngāti Ngahere people had not supported the killing, and Ngāti Rua had been specifically forbidden by their rangatira Hoera Pōaka to drink Volkner's blood, in the eyes of the settler government the die was now cast for Whakatōhea as a whole.

GOVERNMENT REACTION TO VOLKNER'S KILLING

The government soon became aware that it was Kereopa who was the main motivator behind the events that resulted in the killing of Carl Volkner, and that he and Patara and their Taranaki group had left Ōpōtiki, heading for Tūranganui, or the East Coast.

An attempt was made to locate Kereopa and Patara further along the Bay of Plenty coast using the naval vessel HMS *Eclipse*, with brief landings at Ōpōtiki and Hicks Bay in March, but without success. Among those on board HMS *Eclipse* was James Te Mautaranui Fulloon, a Crown agent and interpreter who had Ngāti Awa rangatira whakapapa. After HMS *Eclipse* returned to Tauranga Fulloon set out to covertly investigate the religious and political settings at Whakatāne and Ōpōtiki by taking a trip on the trading vessel *Kate*. The trip ended disastrously on 22 July, with Fulloon and two Pākehā crew being killed on board the *Kate* off the mouth of the Whakatāne River.

The killings of Volkner and Fulloon became the pretext for the settler government to send major invasion forces to attack Ngāti Awa and Whakatōhea communities later in 1865. The government's lack of interest in ensuring it was actually apprehending the individuals involved in the two murders — instead, ruthlessly attacking whole iwi — was summed up concisely by the Waitangi Tribunal when it commented on the attack at Ōpōtiki in its *Ngāti Awa Raupatu Report*: '[t]he force was aggressive from the outset, bombarding the village and shooting at Maori indiscriminately, with no attempt made to ascertain who was involved in the missionary's murder and who was not.'[4]

At Ōpōtiki the heaviest casualties in the invasion that began in September 1865 happened to be inflicted on Ngāti Ira hapū, whose pā were strongly defended near the entrance to the Waioeka Gorge, and particularly at Te Tarata pā in early October. At Te Tarata alone some 35 were killed and 40 wounded. Their prominent fighting rangatira was Hira Te Popo. He drew many of his hapū back with him well up the

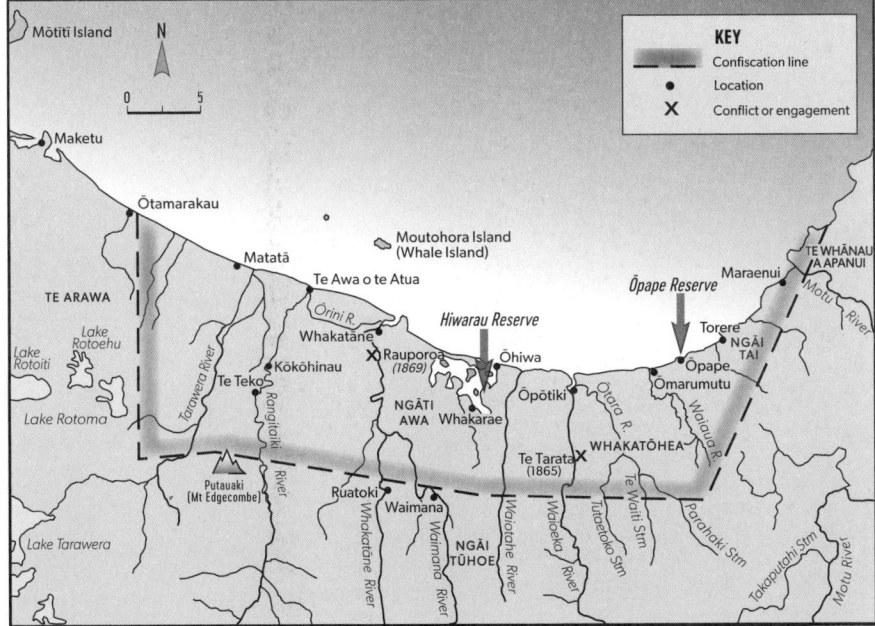

Map showing extent of area confiscated by the Crown and locations of Ōpape and Hiwarau reserves.

Waioeka Gorge to a pā called Maraetahi, at Ōponae, near the modern Wairata area.

During the invasion, Whakatōhea not only suffered heavily from the number of casualties, but their whole economic world was also shattered. The invasion forces, who totalled about 500 soldiers, stripped away everything of value from the abandoned farming operations, well-developed orchards and neat kāinga that Whakatōhea had developed over the previous 25 years. In response to the understandable resistance to the invading forces in Whakatāne and Ōpōtiki, on 17 January 1866 the settler government declared both Ngāti Awa and Whakatōhea lands to be confiscated to a considerable distance inland from the coastline. It was no accident that the confiscation line was drawn at a sufficient distance inland to ensure it encompassed most of the high-value, fertile plains that surrounded both Whakatāne and Ōpōtiki.

ŌPAPE NATIVE RESERVE

The only slight hint of reasonableness on the part of the government came in mid 1866 when it recognised that some lands must be returned to Whakatōhea to enable them to provide food for themselves. Its initial answer was to move most of Whakatōhea to a reservation area of 20,789 acres (8413 ha) called the Ōpape Native Reserve. The easternmost hapū of Whakatōhea were all compelled to live on these much more limited land holdings, where they struggled to survive. The Ōpape reserve was based around 2–3 kilometres of coastline near Ōpape pā and Ōmarumutu pā, to which most surviving Whakatōhea on the coastal plains had to move. Ūpokorehe were confined to the western end of the rohe on the much smaller Hiwarau reserve, comprising 1073 acres (434 ha), at Ōhiwa.

The only exceptions were a relatively limited number, mainly of the Ngāti Ira hapū, who followed Hira Te Popo to Maraetahi pā, and some other small groups who moved inland into more elevated and steeper bush-covered valleys, such as the Takaputahi and Whitikau areas of the upper Motu catchment. In all of these heavily bushed inland valleys it was a struggle to survive in the harsher elevated winter conditions.

CONTINUED MILITARY OCCUPATION 1865–70

In addition to the confiscation of their land, Whakatōhea also had to cope with the loss of mana and hapū and iwi pride in their own rangatiratanga that flowed from having an occupation force living at Ōhiwa and Ōpōtiki. The reason for the continued military occupation was that the government was keenly aware that the process of placing settlers on disputed confiscated lands throughout the country exposed them to attack from dispossessed Māori living in the adjacent hinterlands.

In the lower Waioeka, settler soldiers and farmers faced ongoing risks both from the Tūhoe rangatira Eruiti Tamaikōwha, operating from the adjacent lower Waimana and Waiotahe river valleys, and from Hira Te Popo and his people in the mid Waioeka. From 1866 there were intermittent raids on stock and produce in the lower Waioeka and Ōhiwa harbour areas, and these continued until 1868. From late 1867, the military force based at Ōpōtiki comprised a volunteer Pākehā militia, the Ōpōtiki Volunteer Rangers, which was further supplemented in mid 1868 by the establishment of a contingent of about sixty Te Arawa located at a redoubt site at Ōhiwa, near the coast.

Eruiti Tamaikōwha.
Ref: 1/2-073839-F, Alexander Turnbull Library, Wellington, NZ

The late 1860s, therefore, were troubled years for Whakatōhea in a range of ways, although there was some lessening of tension in 1869–70. Some of those living at Ōpape and Ōmarumutu were able to develop limited trade with the soldiers and storekeepers at nearby Ōpōtiki. For many, however, there probably remained a deep sense of resentment. It is almost certain that some among the communities at Ōpape and Ōmarumutu, at least among the younger men, would have been maintaining contacts with the Whakatōhea people who had remained in the hinterland since the 1865 invasion. Overall, loyalties among the Whakatōhea people would have been mixed, with some muted loyalty to the Treaty and the Crown, combined with varying degrees of sympathy for the views of those in the hinterland bush areas, such as Hira Te Popo.

It was into this atmosphere of continued anxiety over what effectively amounted to an ongoing military occupation that news arrived of the escape of Te Kooti Arikirangi Te Turuki from Wharekauri (the Chatham Islands) in July 1868. The news probably reached Whakatōhea some time in early August. There would also have been the news that Te Kooti had brought with him from Wharekauri about 340 whakarau, or followers, of his new variant of the Paimārire religion (later to become known as Ringatū). Sooner than they could have expected, Whakatōhea were to be at its very centre.

2

TE KOOTI'S RELATIONSHIP WITH WHAKATŌHEA

The background to any events surrounding Te Kooti Arikirangi te Turuki has to commence with his wrongful exile in 1866 to Wharekauri (the Chatham Islands, the Moriori name for which is Rēkohu).

Toward the end of that year Te Kooti had been present at the extended siege of Waerenga a Hika, inland of Tūranga (Gisborne), where he had served alongside the besieging government forces. Following the surrender on 22 November of those who had been besieged, about 340 of a dissident grouping of Māori from a range of iwi and hapū were taken prisoner.

The extremely time-consuming and costly tasks of transporting the prisoners to a suitable place and conducting trials were effectively avoided by the simple, but illegal, expedient of exiling them to Wharekauri en masse, without charging them with any specific offences. Te Kooti was accused of being a supporter of the Waerenga a Hika dissidents and, despite his protestations of innocence, was forced to join the other prisoners who were taken to Wharekauri.

This action, effectively a mass abduction, was not only illegal but also constituted a clear and egregious breach of the rights of those exiled in terms of the Treaty of Waitangi. Article 3 of the Treaty, signed just 25 years earlier, stated that

Te Kooti Arikirangi Te Turuki.
Laishley, Richard, 1816–1897. [Ryan, Thomas Aldworth] 1864–1927. Ref: A-114-004-2, Alexander Turnbull Library, Wellington, NZ

the Crown would extend Royal protection over Māori, and provide them with all of the rights and privileges that British subjects of the Crown enjoyed. The basic rights enjoyed by British subjects in 1840, which applied continuously to 1865 and persist today, included the right to face charges, and to have a fair trial of any such charges, before any form of loss of liberty could be imposed.

EXILE ON WHAREKAURI

On their arrival at Wharekauri the prisoners found there was no permanent accommodation available for them, and that they would be compelled to build their own. In addition, they would have to grow most of their own food. There was also no prospect of an end to their harsh imprisonment on the island, which was only terminated by their escape under Te Kooti's leadership on 4 July 1868.

Te Kooti's leadership role on Wharekauri had arisen over time as he developed his own style of religious belief. As he accomplished this, his following grew steadily, most likely fanned by the hopelessness his fellow prisoners felt at their imprisonment with no end in sight. Te Kooti's teachings were based on a mixture of Old Testament and traditional Māori beliefs and predictions that would have closely accorded with the similar Paimārire teachings, to which most of the prisoners had earlier responded. This new, increasingly mystical, leader had a receptive, and literally captive, audience.

ESCAPE FROM WHAREKAURI

By July 1868, Te Kooti had devised a plan to seize the *Rifleman*, which intermittently brought supplies to the island. The plan succeeded and the vessel made landfall at Whareongaonga Bay, just south of Tūranga, close to the home areas of Te Kooti's whakarau, as his followers came to be called. They landed with only a limited number of weapons and supplies that they had brought with them from Wharekauri. Aiming to reach their homes, or the Kingitanga, they headed inland, first ascending a steep and rugged landform.

As they moved inland, they were intercepted by a group of militia from Tūranganui who were under orders to compel them to surrender. Unsurprisingly, in view of their past treatment by the government, Te Kooti and his whakarau were unwilling to give up their newfound freedom. Thus began a series of engagements against government forces that continued for the next two months. In the Ruakituri they successfully defeated a force under Lt Col George Whitmore on 8 August, although Te Kooti himself was wounded in the foot during that engagement. After Whitmore's force had withdrawn, Te Kooti continued to occupy the Puketapu pā site, situated on the modern Pāpuni station in the middle reaches of the Ruakituri River.

From Puketapu Te Kooti sent messengers to surrounding iwi inviting them to join him, a gathering of forces from diverse sources that became a common practice he used to supplement his force right through until 1871.

THE MATAWHERO RAID

It was from Puketapu, on 10 November 1868, that Te Kooti led a brutal assault on the Māori and settler communities at Matawhero and other localities surrounding Tūranga. The raid seems to have been carried out for a mixture of reasons, including a measure of utu for Te Kooti's own treatment as well as to obtain further supplies of weaponry, gunpowder and ammunition, and in part possibly to gain more supporters — either by persuasion or by compulsion. In the course of the night raid on Matawhero, and over following days in surrounding areas, Te Kooti and the whakarau killed some 70 people, as well as wounding numerous others.

Members of both the Māori and settler communities in and around Tūranga, and further afield, were shocked at the number of killings and their senseless brutality. Many of the victims were old men or women and, even worse, they included a number of children. Thirty-seven of those killed were Māori, and 33 were Pākehā.

Whatever may be the legal and moral arguments among historians more than a century and a half later with regard to any justification for these killings, it is an incontrovertible fact that for many Māori at the time Te Kooti's actions were unforgivable. In addition to those who had lost relatives in the course of the killings, there were others for whom such acts of brutality were an offence against their Christian beliefs, and rangatira who regarded Te Kooti's actions as a dangerous threat to their own rangatiratanga. These included Mōkena Kōhere and Ropata Wahawaha of Ngāti Porou, and Ihaka Whaanga and Renata Kawepo of Ngāti Kahungunu, all of whom immediately offered to pursue Te Kooti alongside government forces.

Te Kooti was now perceived by many Māori as a very real threat to any isolated Māori or settler community on which he might choose to descend. And as he moved about the interior of the North Island in 1869–70, his wanton killings of other Māori increased the number of rangatira and hapū who were set on his capture or destruction.

The strength of the revulsion felt among both Māori and settler communities at the killings at and after Matawhero, and a similar raid on Mohaka some months later, meant that Te Kooti would be relentlessly pursued by the government, who could now rely on the support of many rangatira from a range of powerful iwi. That support spread even more widely across the country as Te Kooti's raids involved the killing of more Māori in other locations.

MAKARETU AND NGĀTAPA, AND INITIAL CONTACTS WITH WHAKATŌHEA

After the Matawhero raid, Te Kooti and his whakarau, together with possibly a few hundred others from the Tūranganui area who were compelled, persuaded or volunteered to accompany them, pulled back up the Wharekopae River into the Makaretu and Ngātapa pā. Soon after they arrived there Te Kooti sent out messengers to gather assistance from other iwi whom he was aware were disaffected with the actions of the settler government — primarily hapū of Ngāi Tūhoe of Te Urewera, and Whakatōhea under Hira Te Popo at Maraetahi pā in the Waioeka. By that time, Te Kooti was doubtless aware of the bitter dissatisfaction felt by both of those iwi over the confiscations of their customary interests in the Ōhiwa harbour and Ōpōtiki areas.

Ngātapa pā from the north.
Stuart Spicer

Wiremu Kingi Te Paia was one of those of Rongowhakaata whakapapa who later asserted he was compelled under threat of death to accompany Te Kooti as he left Tūranganui and pulled back into the Wharekopae. Te Paia, who also had Te Aowera whakapapa to Ngāti Porou, described the warm response Te Kooti's message received from Hira Te Popo and the Whakatōhea at Maraetahi pā:

> The very night that Te Kooti escaped from Ngatapa, the Whakatohea arrived from Waioweka to fetch him. Timoti was one of them (since killed at Rotorua).* The Whakatohea and the Urewera were the chief support of Te Kooti — the first supplying him with ammunition and caps, and the second with men.[5]

Te Kooti embarked on the refortification of the defensive hill pā site at Ngātapa, where he was besieged at the end of 1868 and again in the first week of 1869, with Ropata Wahawaha of Ngāti Porou playing a major part in these actions. Other iwi who supplied forces to the government included Ngāti Kahungunu and Te Arawa.

The second of these sieges lasted some days before Ngātapa fell after it was abandoned when the defenders were cut off from their water supply. Most of them initially escaped after Te Kooti led a dramatic night-time descent in heavy weather

---

* Timoti Te Kaka was wounded on 7 February 1870 by Lt Gilbert Mair and killed the next day by one of his Te Arawa men.

conditions, down vine ropes lowered over the precipitous northern cliffs below the tihi or summit portion of the pā. The pursuit that followed, however, as the defenders dispersed in all directions, involved some particularly ruthless conduct on the part of their pursuers. It seems clear that about 120 of Te Kooti's followers were either shot where they were captured or were taken back up to the top of Ngātapa and shot there by Ngāti Porou, their bodies falling over the northern cliffs. Te Kooti and some of his followers made the difficult descent of the gorge country along the Waioeka River, linking up some days later with Hira Te Popo and his Ngāti Ira at Maraetahi pā.

REFUGE WITH WHAKATŌHEA AT MARAETAHI

Wiremu Kingi Te Paia was one of those who survived after fleeing from Ngātapa. When he was finally captured in the Waioeka the following year he made the statement in which he described some events relevant to Whakatōhea:

> We went on to Waioweka, and there I met Te Kooti again … I remember at this time a sum of money (£100) being sent down to Opotiki to buy clothing and rum; it was collected in small sums from many men; it was brought down to Opotiki by a man named Hera, and about £30 was expended. The balance was returned, the reasons assigned being that the people were afraid lest the Pakeha should wonder where so much money came from, and conclude there were Hauhaus at Waioweka.[6]

Although 'Hera' is the spelling used in Te Paia's statement, it is almost certain he was referring to Hira Te Popo, whose name was often misspelt in contemporary documents as Hera. If it was indeed Hira Te Popo himself who went to Ōpōtiki in January 1869, it would have been a risky personal action.

Te Kooti did not actually stay for many weeks at Maraetahi after the fall of Ngātapa. His resilience, energy, drive and magnetism were such that, even after such a disastrous defeat as Ngātapa, he was quickly able to attract a reasonable number of new recruits from a wide range of sources. Importantly for his later plans, some were from Ngāti Tūwharetoa from the Tauranga-Taupō area. Other Tūhoe soon joined him in Te Urewera, where he moved in early 1869.

ACCORD WITH NGĀI TŪHOE

In February 1869 Te Kooti had moved west to attend a major hui at Tawhana pā, on the lower Waimana River, with most of the major Tūhoe rangatira. Somewhat surprisingly, Eruiti Tamaikōwha did not attend the hui, even though his own rohe was centred on the pā at Tawhana and Tauwharemanuka. He always maintained an independence from Te Kooti, although at this stage he made no effort to refuse him access to the lower Waimana.

At the Tawhana hui Te Kooti obtained an agreement from Tūhoe for sanctuary in Te Urewera in return for his leadership in a campaign against government confiscation policies. Confiscation had already impacted badly on Tūhoe by cutting them off from access to their customary coastal resources in the Ōhiwa harbour area, which they shared with Te Upokorehe of Whakatōhea. Because of his accord with Tūhoe, not only did Te Kooti derive a huge, very effective bush-covered sanctuary, but many Tūhoe rangatira and their younger fighting men now directly allied themselves with his forces.

WHAKATĀNE AND MOHAKA RAIDS, MARCH–APRIL 1869

Less than two months after the events at Ngātapa, then, Te Kooti had managed to gather about him a completely fresh force, with which he launched two major raids — one in March on the Whakatāne area, and the other in April at Mohaka.

While these raids were a success from Te Kooti's viewpoint — providing much-needed ammunition, men and horses — once again the nature and extent of the ruthless killings that occurred led to further enmity from other iwi and hapū to the north and east of Te Urewera. It is hardly surprising, then, that Te Kooti found that while he had gained refuge in Te Urewera, a growing list of hapū were now willing to join in his pursuit. These included most hapū of Ngāti Kahungunu, many from Ngāti Pukeko, Ngāti Awa and also Ngāti Rangitihi, and most Te Arawa hapū, as well as Ngāti Porou.

THE IMPACT OF THE ACCORD WITH TE KOOTI ON NGĀI TŪHOE

In May 1869 Te Kooti returned from Mohaka into Te Urewera, arriving at Ruatāhuna just in time to assist Tūhoe in repelling major government invasion forces, two columns of which had penetrated as far as Ruatāhuna that month. While the invaders failed to inflict many casualties among Te Kooti's forces, they did cause serious deprivations for Ngāti Whare at Ahikereru (Te Whaiti) and Tūhoe at Ruatāhuna.

Te Arawa government forces had taken a whole community of women and children from Ahikereru to Matatā, on the coast to the west of Whakatāne, so as to persuade their menfolk to follow. At Ruatāhuna and other small kāinga on their routes, the invasion forces had destroyed gardens and whare, leaving devastation and food shortages behind for people facing the onset of winter.

For Ngāi Tūhoe, succour provided to Te Kooti in Te Urewera was to have an increasingly bitter taste.

TE KOOTI'S CONDUCT LEADS TO MOUNTING ENMITY

By the end of May 1869, Te Kooti still retained a powerful fighting force, and in early June he led his followers southwest out of Te Urewera, heading initially for Lake Taupō, and from there to the King Country.

As he passed through the Taupō area he killed some Ngāti Tūwharetoa who were related by whakapapa to the upper Whanganui people. News of these killings incensed one of the leading rangatira of the upper Whanganui, Topia Turoa, who was a kinsman of some of those killed. After hearing the news his alignment changed from one of armed reaction against the government — years earlier he had fought for the Paimārire movement against government forces — to enthusiastic support for Te Kēpa Te Rangihiwinui's Whanganui Contingent in their pursuit of Te Kooti.

Te Kooti then moved further west into the Kingitanga in his attempt to garner support from both Ngāti Tūwharetoa and the Waikato/Ngāti Maniapoto peoples for his declared intention of expelling the Europeans. But his efforts fell on stony ground, probably in large part because of the assertive, often threatening stance he adopted towards those who would not support him. The Māori King, Tāwhiao, made it plain Te Kooti was not welcome in the Kingitanga, declining even to meet him, so he had little choice but to leave.

In mid August 1869 he moved off a little to the east, and over the next few months based himself in or near Moerangi in the upper Whanganui area of the Volcanic Plateau. The government hurriedly moved to gather support from iwi who had cause to support it in attacking Te Kooti, concentrating these forces at a camp established by Lt Col Thomas McDonnell at Poutū, at the southeastern end of Lake Rotoaira.

Three major engagements occurred over the next two months, at Tauranga-Taupo, Tokaanu

Tawhiao Tukaroto Matutaera Potatau Te Wherowhero.
Preston, G.M. Ref: PA1-0-423-01-1, Alexander Turnbull Library, Wellington, NZ

and Te Porere. In the first two of these clashes Te Kooti was rebuffed from assaults he launched, suffering some casualties. At Te Porere, however, on 4 October, he was heavily defeated, losing 37 killed while defending an incomplete defensive pā. Te Kooti himself and many others were wounded, but he managed to escape.

In strategic terms the worst effect for Te Kooti's cause was a loss of mana with Rewi Maniapoto, the prominent Ngāti Maniapoto fighting rangatira who was one of King Tāwhiao's main military advisers. Rewi was unimpressed by Te Kooti's military skills. After a period of recovery from his wounds, Te Kooti found the Māori King even less supportive than before of any alliance with him. Consequently, in December 1869 he headed away to the northeast across the Waikato River towards Tapapa pā in the Mamaku ranges, near modern Tirau. Tapapa was the home pā for Hakaraia, an enthusiastic supporter who had recently joined Te Kooti.

Te Kooti was pursued to Tapapa by a mixed force of Armed Constabulary, Whanganui and Te Arawa, and a number of skirmishes occurred. Only limited casualties were inflicted on Te Kooti's forces, however, despite the very large numbers of Crown forces, which included the Whanganui Contingent under Te Kēpa and Turoa. Nevertheless, their pressure on Te Kooti led him to decide to return to Te Urewera by way of Rotorua in the first week of February 1870.

TUMUNUI – TE ARAWA INFLICT A HEAVY BLOW

On 7 February 1870 a small force of about forty young Te Arawa fighting men led by the Pākehā officer Lt Gilbert Mair engaged Te Kooti's force in a day-long running battle from Ōhinemutu to Tumunui, south of Rotorua. Despite the Te Arawa men being outnumbered by Te Kooti's force, which included about 200 fighting men, they inflicted substantial casualties. Te Arawa suffered the loss of only one killed and probably six wounded, while Te Kooti's men lost about twenty killed, and an unknown number wounded.

Gilbert Mair was promoted to the rank of captain on 18 February, with the formal promotion backdated to the date of this action. Many years later, in April 1886, Mair was awarded the New Zealand Cross for his efforts and leadership that day.

Some more recent histories have asserted that Te Kooti's advance north to Ōhinemutu, which required a considerable detour from the direct route to Te Urewera, was peaceful and intended merely to obtain consent to pass through Te Arawa lands. However, Hoani Te Paiaka, who was present as one of Te Kooti's leading fighters, viewed Te Kooti's intentions very differently:

I was in the fight at Tapapa. We lost five men there, and one afterwards died of his

Gilbert Mair (far left) and his Arawa men at their Kaiteriria base at Lake Rotokakahi on 8 February, 1870 the day after their day-long running battle with Te Kooti's forces.
Mundy, Daniel Louis, 1826–81. Ref: PA7-17-30, Alexander Turnbull Library, Wellington, NZ

wounds. I was nearly taken prisoner at Ohinemutu. Te Kooti intended to attack Ohinemutu, but we, the Urewera, would not consent. All the men killed at Rotorua were Chatham Islanders, except Timoti Te Kaka.[7]

Paiaka's contemporary statement of events as to Te Kooti's intentions is supported by the objective fact that Te Arawa were among Te Kooti's most vehement enemies. They had been involved in some of his most significant defeats, at Ngātapa, Te Ponanga and Te Pōrere.

Following this action Te Kooti made a rapid withdrawal across the Kaingaroa Plains to Tauaroa, at the Horomanga River mouth, in the western Urewera ranges. From there he headed into Te Urewera, arriving at Ruatāhuna some days later. Then, within a matter of about ten days, he and his followers had traversed Te Urewera and returned to Maraetahi pā in the Waioeka.

For Whakatōhea, Te Kooti's arrival at Maraetahi meant that the impacts of war were about to be unleashed upon them once more.

THE DECISION TO USE ONLY MĀORI FORCES IN THE PURSUIT OF TE KOOTI

A significant tactical decision by Donald McLean, the Minister of Defence and Native Affairs, also followed the action on 7 February. Henceforth, only Māori forces were to be engaged in the pursuit of Te Kooti, with the exception of a very few Pākehā officers and NCOs (such as Thomas Porter and Samuel Austin).

McLean's thinking was that during this action small, fit, lightly equipped and mobile irregular Māori forces had proved capable of achieving better results, at far less cost, than the unwieldy conventional forces of the Armed Constabulary. The latter were expensive and difficult to supply logistically in rugged bush country where there were no supply roads.

On 11 February, McLean wrote to Lt Col McDonnell, the commander of the Armed Constabulary forces in the Bay of Plenty pursuit of Te Kooti. He informed McDonnell that Ropata Wahawaha was to be directed into the Urewera from the east with his Ngāti Porou; another column was to come in from the southeast under Ngāti Kahungunu rangatira from the Hawke's Bay and Wairoa districts; and a third entry into the Urewera was to be from the Bay of Plenty by Whanganui. At that stage McDonnell was to retain overall command.

Just a week later, however, on 18 February, McLean followed up with further orders that contained a personal bombshell for McDonnell, as they deprived him of his fighting command: '... the Government, after full consideration, have decided that no European force should be engaged on this expedition, as it is contemplated to give the chiefs of each tribe the command of their own followers.'[8]

This was immediately followed by a series of letters issued by McLean, containing orders to Ropata to command the East Coast invasion force, and to Te Kēpa Te Rangihiwinui and Topia Turoa to command the Whanganui — all with the rank of Major. However, McLean also now deviated from the normal daily rates of pay, with an arrangement that he communicated on 19 February to Ropata and other rangatira:

> You alone are to have the management and to give orders to your tribe; there will be no European over you. If you should succeed in catching that bad man five thousand pounds (£5,000) will be given to you and your tribe; if you do not, there will be no payment. It will be for you to explain these words to your soldiers.[9]

On 3 March, McLean clarified to Te Kēpa and Topia Turoa the ambiguity around the circumstances in which the £5000 was payable:

> The arrangement for this work is a lump sum of money. If Te Kooti is caught or killed, five thousand pounds (£5,000) will be given. It matters not if another tribe should

catch him; this money will still be paid, for all who will have taken part in the work. All that the Government are considering about is food for the road.¹⁰

RUTHLESSNESS OF MCLEAN'S INSTRUCTIONS

McLean's instructions to Ropata Wahawaha continued by addressing the treatment of Te Kooti and any prisoners in the following terms: 'Should fighting actually take place, remember to save the women and children. ... There is no other word to you, because you know the objects of the fighting: that evil is to be exterminated, so that peace may be in our places.'¹¹

While McLean's instruction was explicit in stating that women and children were to be spared, it left an ambiguity as to Te Kooti's men. On one interpretation it can be seen as opening the door to execution of the male prisoners. In his statement that 'evil is to be exterminated', McLean does not make clear whether the term 'evil' related solely to Te Kooti or if it encompassed his men. In a communication on 18 February to Mohi Turei, a Ngāti Porou church leader whom he asked to assist Ropata in his recruitment of soldiers, McLean was more specific, writing: '... these murderers ought to be exterminated as soon as possible, so that the quietness, prosperity, and peace of the former days may return.'¹²

The die was thus cast for a ruthless campaign as Whanganui were shipped from Tauranga to Ōpōtiki to enter Te Urewera from the north, and Ropata travelled to the East Coast to raise his Ngāti Porou force to enter Te Urewera from the southeast. The later brutal killings by the Whanganui forces in the Waioeka must therefore be considered against the background of these ruthless instructions from the nation's Minister of Defence, Donald McLean.

PART 2
THE ŌPAPE RAID AND THE PURSUIT OF TE KOOTI

3

TE KOOTI'S ARRIVAL AT MARAETAHI AND THE RAID ON ŌPAPE

It is believed that Te Kooti had entered the western Te Urewera with a force of about 100 to 120 fighting men, and a similar number of supporting older men, women and children. He and his people had endured harsh conditions and travelled through remote, difficult country between June 1869 and February 1870, and they had displayed extraordinary resilience. But their numbers had waxed and waned during that time, as a result of the attacks that his forces had launched or suffered, the casualties sustained, the repeated dispersions of his forces, and the pursuits they had endured.

Many of those who were with him when he entered the Horomanga River area on the edge of Te Urewera were of Tūhoe or related Te Urewera iwi and hapū, such as the western hapū of Ngāti Whare, Ngāti Haka and Patuheuheu. It appears that even some people from the catchments draining the eastern Urewera areas were still with him, such as Ngāti Kōhatu of the upper Mangaaruhe and Waikaretaheke catchments, and Ngāti Ruapani around Lake Waikaremoana. However, events such as the government's invasions of the central Urewera in May 1869, the Māori King's rejection of Te Kooti later that year, and his heavy defeats at Te Porere and at Ōhinemutu in October 1869 and

February 1870 all meant that his mana had taken heavy blows in the eyes of Tūhoe rangatira.

Most likely, then, in mid February 1870 Te Kooti felt only reserved enthusiasm from some Tūhoe rangatira in the centre of Te Urewera. He quickly resolved to move east to the Waioeka. He was still confident he could securely base himself at Hira Te Popo's fastness at Maraetahi pā in the Waioeka Gorge area. By then, his active support had dropped away further as some of his supporters returned to their homes in and around Te Urewera. By the time he completed this further hard walk to arrive at Maraetahi pā he probably had with him only about 100 fighting men and a lesser number of supporters.

THE LONG TRAVERSE ACROSS THE KAINGAROA AND TE UREWERA

Dating exactly when Te Kooti arrived at Maraetahi pā is impossible, but an estimate can be made by tracing the events that followed the running battle with Gilbert Mair and his Te Arawa fighters on 7 February. In the early hours of 8 February Mair and his men also attacked Te Kooti's overnight puni (temporary camp) at Lake Ōkaro, just northeast of Maunga Kākaramea (Rainbow Mountain). Te Kooti's people fled under fire, and started to cross the Kaingaroa Plains in the dark. From the edge of the plains they had to descend the steep pumice faces to the broad Rangitaiki valley, then cross the valley to arrive at Tauaroa pā at the junction with the Horomanga River. The total distance from Lake Ōkaro to the edge of Te Urewera at the Horomanga is about 40 kilometres.

In a statement made a month or so later, Wiremu Kingi Te Paia (who was captured on the fall of Waipuna pā in March 1870) said: 'We broke, continuing our running night and day for two nights and days, merely resting by the way side, and reached Te Rangitaiki.'[13] Given the ambiguity of whether Te Paia was talking of them having 'broken', or fled, on 7 February or 8 February, their arrival at the Rangitaiki would have occurred by nightfall on 9 February or early on the 10th. That would have meant that on 10 or 11 February they started up the Horomanga River heading for Ruatāhuna.

Te Paia described the route they had taken after crossing the Rangitaiki, and the run-down condition of Te Kooti's people by that stage:

> We crossed it at the Horomanga ford, and followed up that gorge until we got to Omaruteangi. We were about one hundred strong, but had very few guns, many having been thrown away. If it had been Ngatiporou following us we must all have been killed, as we moved along very slowly, from hunger and fatigue.[14]

The likely location of Omaruteangi on the Whakatāne River north of Ruatāhuna, and a more detailed description of this traverse of Te Urewera, can be found in Appendix 2 and on the colour map on page A2.

TE KOOTI'S ARRIVAL AT RUATĀHUNA AND THE JOURNEY TO MARAETAHI PĀ

Te Paia's account continued by describing the extraordinary lengths Tūhoe went to at Ruatāhuna in order to provide manaakitanga (hospitality) for Te Kooti and his supporters:

> From Omaruteangi a letter was sent up to Ruatahuna telling them we were come, and had escaped leaving many of our men in the hands of the Kawanatanga and unburied, and we went up after the letter. The Urewera killed for us one hundred sheep and three cows. The sheep came from the Waikare Hauhaus, who had taken them from the Pakeha at Wairoa.

If one allows for two to three days' travel from the Rangitaiki valley to Ruatāhuna, that means they would not have arrived until 12 or 13 February. It then probably took some days for Te Kooti and his people to recover from their recent ordeals and the pressure of pursuit, while enjoying the generous amounts of food provided by Ngāi Tūhoe. Over those days Te Kooti would have had opportunities to engage with Tūhoe rangatira at Ruatāhuna about their respective intentions, and he did not waste any time before launching a raid to try to replenish his supplies of munitions.

Te Paia described how the very morning after their arrival at Ruatāhuna Te Kooti sent out an ope of about a hundred men to attack the stockade of Runanga on the southeastern side of the Rangitaiki Plains:*

> At daylight next morning Te Kooti told two chiefs, Te Rangikaitupuaki and Hapurona, to take one hundred men and fetch the guns and ammunition from the barracks near Runanga. They were to take possession of the store of powder and to cut the wire. Information respecting that place came from the Maoris living at Runanga; I think also from one of the Ngatiawa living inland at Whakatāne.

---

* Runanga is identified in Nigel Prickett's book *Fortifications of the New Zealand Wars* (Dept of Conservation, 2016) at p. 90 as being 'Rangitaiki; 1.6 km southwest of the Napier–Taupo Road and Waiarua Stream on a broad ridge, c. 1000 m a.s.l.' (The Waiarua Stream has its junction with the Waipunga River at the Waipunga Falls.) Established in 1869, the Runanga redoubt was abandoned in 1876. It was one of a series of stockades or redoubts on the Taupō–Napier road. From Taupō the distances were: to Ōpepe 12 miles (19 km); Runanga 36 miles (58 km); Tarawera 48 miles (77 km); and Te Haroto 54 miles (87 km); with Titiokura stockade being the last, on the high point of that name.

As it turned out, the raiding party did not get very far, for reasons Te Paia went on to describe:

> Word came to us that the Kawanatanga were at Motumako [the Ngāti Manawa pā on the edge of the Rangitaiki Plains not far southwest of modern Murupara] and Horomanga. The hundred men had left, but returned on the news of the approach of the Kawanatanga. On this news we ran in the direction of Whakatāne to Omaruteangi, leaving Te Kooti in Ruatahuna. We ascended Te Wharau, and went on through the swamps till we got to Neketuri.[15]

Neketuri is located on the upper Waikare River about an hour downstream of the old Tauaki pā site to the north of Maungapōhatu. From Tauaki an old Tūhoe trail ran over a long, high ridgeline to the Tawhana Stream headwaters in the Waimana catchment. Te Kooti's supporters would have joined that route at Neketuri. From there they faced a long, steep climb to link over to the Tawhana Stream within the rohe of Tamaikōwha. His pā was at Tawhana, a beautiful location at the junction of the Tawhana Stream and the Tauranga River.*

Tawhana pā location — Rēti Hēmi and Margy Crosby in 2002. Author collection

---

* The Tauranga River, as it is called on Topomaps, is very commonly called the Waimana. At most places in this book it is called the Waimana/Tauranga, or the Waimana, particularly to avoid confusion with the Tauranga Stream that flows into the Waioeka River.

Te Paia's description was simply, 'From Neketuri we went down to Tawhana.' The simplicity of this statement belies what is a significant distance on ridge and riverbed, involving much physical effort to move from one catchment to the other. With the same classic understatement of the effort involved, Te Paia then concluded his account by stating that having reached the Tawhana, 'we descended the river, and after two nights on the road reached Waioweka'.[16]

The 'road' Te Paia was describing in such straightforward terms could hardly have been rougher or harder. For a start there was no road as such, merely the typical Urewera mixture of riverbed walking and steep bush-covered ridges. However, they did have Whakatōhea guides with them, as Te Paia recorded: 'I forgot to mention that while in Ruatāhuna Te Kooti wrote to Waioweka, telling the Whakatohea to be prepared for his coming, and to send some people to Opotiki as scouts. Aporo took the letter. Some of the Whakatohea then came to visit us ...'[17]

Te Paia's lack of any emphasis on the hardships involved on those long routes is an indication of the toughness of the people of those times, but even taking this and their powers of endurance into account, the trip would have taken them at least five or six days. If they left Ruatāhuna on or about 16 or 17 February that would have had them, and possibly Te Kooti, arriving at Maraetahi somewhere between 22 and 24 or 25 February.

According to Te Paia's statement, Te Kooti had been left at Ruatāhuna when his supporters fled down the Whakatāne River after hearing news of another possible government force coming into Te Urewera from the Rangitaiki, to the west. Most likely, though, while in central Te Urewera, Te Kooti would have wanted to meet with those Ngāi Tūhoe rangatira at Maungapōhatu who had not heard of his arrival at Ruatāhuna in time to meet him there. Given that likelihood, he could have then taken the route through Maungapōhatu, which offered another more direct way to reach the Tauaki pā route over to the Waimana. That would have enabled him to make up a day or so on his supporters, even allowing time for discussions at Maungapōhatu on the way. Wiremu Kingi Te Paia does not state where Te Kooti linked back up with the whakarau, but he would likely have done so at or about Tawhana pā.

Despite their earlier generous support, after the return to Ruatāhuna from the abortive raid on the Runanga stockade Tūhoe did not seem to accept any of Te Kooti's proposals. Hoani Te Paiaka, the Te Atihaunui rangatira who was with Te Kooti in February 1870, said in a later statement he provided to Gilbert Mair, 'The Urewera would not go with Te Kooti to Waioeka. I went with ten; two were killed, and the rest came back with me to Ruatahuna on the 27th April.'[18]

SUPPORT FROM NGĀTI IRA AT MARAETAHI

Before leaving Maraetahi the previous year, Te Kooti had urged that a whare karakia (a church or meeting house for prayers) should be built for him; he must have been delighted when he and his whakarau returned to find this large and impressive whare nearly complete. Lt Thomas Porter, who accompanied the Ngāti Porou contingent, later described it as being:

> ... a fine house 80 ft long, 30 ft broad, and 9 ft high at the eaves. The floor was covered with two flax mats or takapau, the whole length of the building. A great deal of time and labour must have been expended in the manufacture of the Maori carpets; they were worked in various patterns and devices in wools of different colours.[19]

In June 1870, Wiremu Kingi Te Paia gave evidence in the Supreme (now High) Court at Auckland in which he stated that after they had fled from Ngātapa the previous year Te Kooti and many others from Ngātapa had made their home at Maraetahi pā. He said it was then that the Whakatōhea at the pā were captured by the fervour of Te Kooti's religious message: 'We fled from Ngatapa to Waioeka, and from there Kooti took me and the prisoners to all the places. Kooti made some of his prisoners fight for him, others he did not. ... The Whakatoheas joined Kooti's worship at Waioeka.'[20]

Te Paia asserted that it was not only the Ngāti Ira hapū of Whakatōhea at Maraetahi who lent their support to Te Kooti at this stage, stating:

> We were told by Pera that the Whakatohea outside (i.e. the friendly Whakatohea) were prepared, waiting for Te Kooti.
>
> Here, in the evening, Arapera and an old man, a relation of mine, told me that he had seen twenty casks of powder which had been taken by the Whakatohea up the Waihau, and left in a secret spot for Te Kooti. ... There is not one of the Whakatohea, chiefs or otherwise, who has not been all for Te Kooti.

This issue of the differing loyalties of other Whakatōhea hapū 'outside' the Waioeka Gorge was to be a constant right through until after the capture of Waipuna and Maraetahi pā; the subject is traversed in Chapter 9.

In addition to the whare karakia, Te Kooti found on his return to Maraetahi that the extensive gardens he had requested had also been planted. Crops of taro, corn and potatoes would now have been ripening in the extensive garden areas on terraces around the pā site. Porter was later to state: 'We found very large quantities of food planted here, some five acres of "taro", and many acres of maize, &c. It is the largest Native plantation I ever remember to have seen.'[21]

The efforts that had been put into the construction of the whare karakia, including the woven mats, as well as the extensive gardens that had been established, and the warm welcome he received from Ngāti Ira are all marks of Te Kooti's success in garnering spiritual and physical support from Ngāti Ira the previous year. However, the actions he took immediately after his arrival at Maraetahi pā show that he was plainly not seeking just a refuge.

ATTACK ON KŌKŌHINAU FLOUR MILL – A DIVERSIONARY TACTIC?

Just as he had done at Ruatāhuna, Te Kooti showed his inexhaustible energy by immediately planning his next attacks. He began with two operations straight away, both outside the Waioeka. His intention was to increase his forces, and in some manner to supplement his low resources in gunpowder, percussion caps, bullets and other munitions.

He must have headed away from Maraetahi pā on his first expedition within a few days of his arrival there. This first expedition consisted of an attack on the Kōkōhinau flour mill site in the lower Rangitaiki valley, which occurred as early as 28 February. Yet even to get there required hard travel as it entailed taking a northerly route into the lower Waimana valley area near Nukuhou, before heading west into the Whakatāne valley. From there it is about 10 kilometres further across to the Rangitaiki valley.

In the lower plains area of the Rangitaiki River, a few kilometres north of Te Teko, lies the historic Kōkōhinau pā of the Te Pahipoto hapū of Ngāti Awa. In 1870 it was the location of a flour mill, processing wheat grown on the surrounding plains. Te Kooti was aware that while some Ngāti Awa sympathised with him and actively adopted his beliefs, others were strongly opposed, and had joined forces sent against him. He was also aware of the enmity that had resulted from his raid into the lower Whakatāne areas in March 1869 and the killings his forces had carried out there. To his mind, then, parts of the area such as Kōkōhinau were enemy territory and therefore open to a raid.

Very little is known about the attack itself, or the direction taken across the Waimana/Whakatāne areas to and from Kōkōhinau, although in all probability he would have taken the Pōkirikiri route from Maraetahi (discussed in detail in Chapter 7 and Appendix 2). This would have enabled him to gain direct access to the Waimana/Tauranga river valley and avoid getting too close to the government forces at Ōpōtiki and Ōhiwa. Whatever route he took, it would have required considerable travel over some days to reach the site and then return to Maraetahi. In addition, the goal of seizing men, gunpowder, or other weapons or munitions from Kōkōhinau did not seem a realistic one. Instead, it appeared initially that the flour mill was burnt down solely as retribution for the fact that the rangatira at Kōkōhinau, Te Rangitukehu, had sided with the government in the past and allowed Te Arawa to use the pā as a redoubt in earlier fighting.

Some days later, however, after Te Kooti had attacked Ōpape, Major William Mair suggested to H.T. Clarke, the civil commissioner at Tauranga, in his report on the Ōpape raid: 'The burning of the Rangitaiki Mill by a party of Hauhaus on the 28th ultimo, was in all probability intended as a draw to attract attention in that direction while the Opotiki move was made.'[22]

Given the lack of other apparent reasons for the attack, Mair looks to have been correct in his supposition. If so, then the Kōkōhinau raid demonstrated yet again Te Kooti's broad thinking in planning his raids, travelling to and from a location some three valleys away from the Waioeka to lull government officials into thinking his aims lay in the west. Having attacked Kōkōhinau on 28 February, he turned around almost immediately, and headed back inland to the east. Not that the government knew that.

WHANGANUI CONTINGENT RAID UP THE WAIMANA/TAURANGA RIVER

While Te Kooti was slowly returning toward Te Urewera in February 1870, the Whanganui Contingent had made their own gruelling journey. They had traversed the whole width of the central North Island during December 1869 and January 1870, at first by waka and then on foot, before finally enjoying the luxury of a short journey by sea from Tauranga to Ōhiwa in early February 1870.

A clear indication of government officials' lack of knowledge of Te Kooti's whereabouts or intentions can be seen in the instruction to the Whanganui Contingent under Te Kēpa Te Rangihiwinui to head into the Waimana valley on 4 March. Their aim was to attack and suppress the Tūhoe rangatira Tamaikōwha, whose rohe in the lower Waimana they would be passing through, then to move on up to Maungapōhatu to link with Ropata Wahawaha's Ngāti Porou. By effecting a pincer movement with Ngāti Porou it was intended that Ngāi Tūhoe support for Te Kooti at Maungapōhatu, and in the Waimana valley, would be destroyed. As it transpired, Te Kēpa led part of the contingent up the Waimana while Topia remained at Ōhiwa for reasons that are unclear.

The irony was that as the major government force in the Whakatāne/Ōpōtiki area was heading south, it was moving away from Te Kooti, not towards him. By 4 March he was either back at Maraetahi pā or on his way to attack Ōpape. Te Kēpa's Whanganui moved on up the Waimana/Tauranga valley without being aware that in the dark they had crossed over Te Kooti's tracks as he was heading back from the Kōkōhinau raid.

On 13 March, after making peace with Tamaikōwha at Tauwharemanuka, well up the Tauranga River, Te Kēpa reported to the Minister of Defence, Donald McLean. In his report, he lamented the fact that no one had reported the evidence of Te Kooti's passage to him, which he had not seen because he had passed by at night:

> The following day we returned to the Waimana, and we saw the place where Te Kooti had encamped. I said, 'Why did not the Arawa and Topia and party, when they saw this encampment, send men up to me, because we came along here at night.' We then slept there. The next day we arrived at Ohiwa, at 9 o'clock at night. A letter from Captain Walker reached me to come here to Opotiki. I wrote to him telling him that I would leave at 4 o'clock in the morning.
>
> The next news I heard about Te Kooti was that Te Whakatohea had been captured, and that Topia had gone and was aiding Ngaitai.[23]

In his diary for 9 March, Samuel Austin, the Pākehā NCO who was serving with Te Kēpa's men, supported Te Kēpa's account of why Te Kooti's tracks were not seen when Te Kēpa advanced up the Waimana:

> And when Kepa went on the 4th inst. he marched at night so as to get into the bush before daylight, and through this he crossed over the track that was taken by the Hau Haus. If it had been daylight it would have been seen by him or his men and it would have been followed up and things would have been different.
>
> Topia and his men, it appears, had seen it when they were returning but took no notice of it but came on to Ohewe. The track crossed the Waimana and then on to Opotiki. It was a good beaten track and through this the Hau Haus were left to do just as they wished in this part.

From the little information that is available on Te Kooti's movements, it appears he did return to Maraetahi pā before launching his raid out to Ōpape and Ōmarumutu. In his later evidence to the Supreme Court, Wiremu Kingi Te Paia implied that he had not personally accompanied Te Kooti on the Kōkōhinau raid, but that Te Kooti had reported seeing the Whanganui Contingent crossing the Ōhiwa harbour: 'We remained some time at Waioweka when we heard that Te Kooti was on the way, and had seen at Ōhiwa the army crossing over.'

Given that Te Kēpa travelled up the Waimana at night, the movement Te Kooti reported to his people that he had seen at Ōhiwa must have been an earlier movement of Te Kēpa's force, which had gone to Whakatāne on 23 February in response to rumours Austin recorded of a large 'Hau hau' force approaching there. Austin noted that Te Kēpa had returned from Whakatāne to Ōhiwa on 27 February. This would fit perfectly with Te Kooti's seeing 'an army' crossing the Ōhiwa harbour while he was going in the other direction to attack Kōkōhinau on 28 February.

THE RAID ON ŌPAPE AND ŌMARUMUTU

On 7 March, Te Kooti made his raid first on Ōmarumutu, then Ōpape. The only contemporary account of his approach to the pā and the numbers of men involved is that Wiremu Kingi Te Paia made the following month. Even that needs to be regarded with caution at times: Te Paia was intent on casting himself in a good light, as being personally opposed to, but very fearful of, Te Kooti. At the same time he was keen to cast suspicion on Whakatōhea.

From Te Paia's statement it would appear that Te Kooti did return to Maraetahi after the Kōkōhinau raid, and that Te Paia was among the men who accompanied him on the Ōpape raid:

> He then moved in the direction of Waioweka, and keeping through the country about the lower part, reached Waihaua [the Waiaua river, adjacent to the Omarumutu pā]. The Whakatohea were expecting him there; therefore, when he told them to go up the country they went. They started by themselves, and Te Kooti remained with his men and killed two Arawa. His force was about 100 men, but badly armed.[24]

What is known from other reports is that Te Kooti's force suddenly appeared on the Waiaua River flats south of Ōmarumutu, and that those at Ōpape (about 1.5 kilometres from Ōmarumutu pā) received a warning that Te Kooti's men were on their way, presumably as a result of shots being fired by his people. In response, the Whakatōhea rangatira in control at Ōpape — Te Ranapia, Te Teira and Piahana Tiwai — immediately gathered together the few remaining men of fighting age left in the pā, and all the government weapons that had been issued to them.*

By now able to see Te Kooti's force approaching, and believing that they did not have enough men of fighting age to oppose him, the Whakatōhea rangatira ordered their younger men to load all the weapons into their waka or rowing boats on the shore in front of the pā. Then, before Te Kooti's force could reach them, they launched the waka and boats and headed off by sea around Tarakeha Point and on to the security of the Ngāi Tai pā at Tōrere, to the east. Te Ranapia

---

* The fact that 34 of the younger Whakatōhea fighting men had joined Te Kēpa for his move up the Waimana is addressed in Chapter 4.

and Tiwai knew that Ngāi Tai had a government force at Tōrere protecting them while their rangatira Wiremu Kingi Tutuhuarangi and many of their younger fighting men were away serving with the Whanganui Contingent.

Time would later show that for Whakatōhea, and Te Ranapia personally, the move to Tōrere with their weapons was a very wise decision. But in the immediate future the Whakatōhea rangatira and their men were devastated when they learnt that Te Kooti had headed back into the inland ranges, taking with him all the women, children and older people from both Ōpape and Ōmarumutu pā. Their sense of deep despair and anger was apparent in a letter Te Ranapia and Tiwai jointly wrote on 17 March to H.T. Clarke, the civil commissioner at Tauranga, seeking his assistance:

> This is to inform you that we have been surprised by Te Kooti, and our women and children taken captives by him; the total number taken by him, including men, women, and children, amounts to 170 persons. This has made us very sorry ...
>
> Te Kooti is at present at Waioeka. He has stated that the settlements he is anxious to attack are Opotiki, Torere, and Ohiwa.
>
> ... we, the persons who escaped when Te Kooti made his attack, are anxious to be enrolled or attached to the expedition against Te Kooti, to assist in the work now going on, lest we make the same mistake as we made before.
>
> We have made this proposal to Major Kemp, and he expressed himself willing that we should do so.[25]

The precise details of what had occurred at the pā are sparse. The first official reports were written by Captain G.P. Walker, the officer in command of the small group of volunteer militia based at Ōpōtiki who worked in with mounted Te Arawa patrols from Ōhiwa. These reports were necessarily very rushed. On the day of the attack at Ōpape, just before heading out with a mounted patrol in response to news of the raid, Walker wrote two brief and nearly identical reports to his superior officers at Tauranga, Major William Mair and Lt Col Fraser. In his report to Mair, Walker stated:

> A party of the Urewera are at Opape. They have come down to tamper with the Whakatohea, and have taken some of them prisoners whom they met with. Ranapia and the others have abandoned the settlement. He has gone by sea to Torere, and others to the Kaha [Te Kaha, well up the coast], so that if the Hauhaus go there they will be warmly received. Their numbers are not known, but I should say they are not in force.
>
> The Whakatohea seem to have bolted at the first appearance of the Hauhaus, most of their young men being with Kemp.

Captain G.P. Walker, c.1900.
William Francis Gordon. Purchased 1916. Te Papa (O.013580)

> I have sent to Ōhiwa for 100 of the Whanganui Natives, to try and intercept them if possible.[26]

Walker's report to Lt Col Fraser provides a little more detail about the situation of the Whakatōhea as he knew it at that time:

> I have just received information to the effect that a party of the Urewera have made their appearance at Opepe. They fell in with some of the Whakatohea, whom they asked to join them, and on their refusing were made prisoners.
>
> The Whakatohea have abandoned their settlements, some taking to the bush, and the remainder have gone by sea to Torere and Te Kaha. The object of the Hauhaus is evidently to try and get the friendlies to join them.
>
> I have sent to Ohiwa for 100 of the Whanganui Natives in order to intercept the party on their return, and in the meantime I proceed with a small mounted party to ascertain the track they have taken.[27]

Before leaving with his mounted patrol, Walker also sent out a message to all the settlements in the district:

> This Address is to OHIWA, as far as Whakatane, and to all the other Settlements northward.
>
> Friends,—
>
> This is to inform you that the Hauhaus have made a descent on Opape. It was on Monday that they made the attack, and the people of that place have in consequence been obliged to fly. Some have gone to the eastward, while others are wandering in the bush, and it is not yet known whether they will find their way here, or whether they will remain in the open bush country.
>
> This is the end of my address to you.
>
> To Topia, Ohiwa.   Captain Walker.[28]

William Gilbert Mair.
Hartley Webster (–1906). Ref: PA2-1870, Alexander Turnbull Library, Wellington, NZ

William Mair had obviously received a little more news by the time he reported to H.T. Clarke, the civil commissioner, four days later, and he expanded on Walker's initial report with details of some casualties:

On the 7th instant a party of Hauhaus came down the Waiaua Valley, near Opotiki, and surprised the inhabitants (Whakatohea); most of them escaped by the sea to the eastward, but a number of women and children are supposed to have fallen into the hands of the enemy. Captain Walker made a demonstration, and two of his party, Arawa from Ohiwa, were killed. Later information received by the officer commanding here makes it appear that the Whakatohea Pa, Omarumutu, is occupied by the Hauhaus. I attach a copy of letter from Captain Walker; the news furnished is very meagre.[29]

The news received by those of the Whanganui Contingent who were at Ohiwa at the time (which did not include Te Kēpa's men, who were still returning from the Waimana/Tauranga expedition) appears in Samuel Austin's diary on 7 and 8 March:

> 7th Fine again ... News arrived this afternoon, shortly after Topia's arrival from Opotiki that the Hau Haus had made an attack on Opotiki. Topia fell in all the men in camp except 58 of all ranks. He, Topia, marched for Opotiki. We all kept under arms all night as we expected to be attacked by the Hau Haus.
>
> 8th Fine again. All on the lookout for Kepa, also news from Opotiki. There was a number of fires on the hills last night. No news from Opotiki as yet. An orderly arrived hear at 1.30 p.m. from Opotiki on his way to Tauranga with dispatches. He informed us that the Hau Haus had killed two (2) men of the Arawas and took a number of the Ahakatohu [Austin's misspelling of Whakatōhea] tribe prisoners and also took a quantitie of ammunition and arms out of the pa. About 3 p.m. Aperaniko of the Wanganui Natives arrived with the same statement, also that Capt. Walker of the Opotiki troop of Volunteers and his men had bolted, and left the friendly natives to fight it themselves and there was only a few natives. And those Cavalry of troopers, as they were called, were going to clear Te Kooti and his gang out of the district. Instead of that they bolted back to Opotiki with the news of their own defate without ever firing a shot. It was disgraceful for white men.

Captain Walker's much more detailed report, furnished on 8 March, provided a very different picture:

> Acting on the information which I received (as stated in my report of yesterday's date), I proceeded to the Waihoua, where I was informed the Hauhaus were at 2 a.m. this morning, with 25 of the Arawa from Ohiwa (who arrived here last evening), and one sergeant and 17 men of the Militia on pay. The Whanganui Natives whom I had sent for, not having arrived till late at night, were unable to

march through fatigue. My object in proceeding with so small a party was simply to ascertain the position of the enemy, or, if they had retired, to find out the direction they had taken, as I was apprehensive of the safety of William King's kainga at Torere, most of whose men were absent, doing duty in the field with Major Kemp, and whose pa is greatly weakened in consequence. After proceeding some distance up the Waihoua Valley, I found that the Arawa had returned and left me unsupported. We here found a Maori boy who had been hiding in the scrub, and by him I was told that both his parents had been killed by Te Kooti the night before, and that the Hauhaus were at a cultivation about two miles from where we then were, and that they were going back that morning. He also stated that Omarumutu Pa was occupied by the Hauhaus. At this time I heard some firing from the direction of the pa, and thinking that the Arawa were engaged, I returned to support them. On arriving at the beach I saw six or seven of the Arawa posted behind a sandhill about 300 yards in front of the pa, firing into it, without, however, their fire being returned, or seeing any sign of its being occupied. The rest of the Arawa were some distance from them, stationed on a point terminating the sandhills on to the beach. As the six Natives kept up their firing for a considerable time without its being returned, and no sign of life being visible in the pa, I ordered the Europeans to return to Opotiki, and stayed with the Arawa on the sandhill for nearly an hour. As there still continued to be no movement in the pa, I told the Arawa to return, some of them now having already followed the Europeans. They told me that two of their men had gone to the pa, and that they would return when they came back. I then left them, and, shortly after arriving in Opotiki, a Maori came in and reported that Hetaraka Mahi and Te Awaawa had been shot. The Arawa shortly after arrived with the bodies of the unfortunate men. It appears that they must have left the main body when proceeding up the Waihoua, and gone towards the pa, at the foot of which they were killed. The Arawa, on hearing the shots, must have returned; but at the time of my leaving them they had no idea that such a melancholy event had happened.

    All accounts seem to agree that Te Kooti himself is with this body of Hauhaus, which is not numerous, and that his main force is at Waioeka. The Whanganuis decline doing anything unless re-inforced, except sending out scouting parties, which I have prevailed upon Topia to do.

    My information says that 40 or 50 of the Whakatohea women and children are prisoners, which is not at all improbable, as there are few of them here, the majority, I am told, having taken to the bush on Te Kooti's first appearance, and the men, as I stated in my report of yesterday, having taken to their boats. No arms or ammunition have fallen into the enemy's hands, Ranapia having taken the precaution of putting them into the boats. The cultivations of the Whakatohea are likewise comparatively untouched. The enemy's retreat is towards Waioeka.[30]

One difficulty that arises from this report is in trying to reconcile the location where the two Arawa men were killed with a statement later provided by one of Te Kooti's wives, Huhana Tamati. Huhana was taken prisoner and interviewed by Thomas Porter after Te Kooti unsuccessfully attacked Uawa on the East Coast in late July 1870. She gave two statements three days apart, on 5 and 8 August, which are closely similar in her general recall but provide some variation in details.[31] In her statement of 5 August, Huhana described arriving at the Waioeka with Te Kooti after what she described as 'the retreat from Rotorua', before going on to recount some of the events at Ōpape:

> We came on to Waioeka; I then went with the kokiri [raiding party] to Opape to fetch the Whakatohea.
>
> While we were in the pa at Opape in the morning we were asleep and the government people came; I, Te Kooti, Otiwa/Oriwa [the handwriting of this name is indecipherable] and some soldiers were in one whare when the sentries reported the government people coming along the beach, we then went outside. When we were going out, six of the government people had already come to the pa; we then fired and two of the Arawa were killed. One of the Hauhaus Pinere was wounded in the shoulder. He escaped in the direction of Waihaua.

Huhana's account of the shooting of the Arawa men at Ōpape pā accords with her statement that they saw the 'government people' coming along the beach to the pā, Ōpape being much closer to the sea than Ōmarumutu. Walker's account, however, appears to place the firing he observed as occurring at Ōmarumutu, or near the Waiaua River mouth, which is some distance away from that pā — about the 300 yards (275 metres) that Walker mentioned. However, there is little doubt that Te Kooti took both pā, and it probably matters little in the end precisely where the killing of the two Te Arawa men occurred. The important thing is that it occurred after the two pā were taken.

A newspaper report in the *Daily Southern Cross* on 1 April 1870 provided some more second-hand details from a Whakatōhea man who came into Ōpōtiki on 9 March:

> They, by some circuitous route, managed to get back on the top of a large hill at the back of Omarumutu, and saw the enemy in force in the bed of the Waiaua river and cultivations below. They were very busy hurrying about catching horses, and securing prisoners. He calculated they were about 100 strong, and that

Te Kooti is amongst them. They left and went up the valley about three o'clock this afternoon, forming an open square, with their prisoners in the centre, consisting of men, women, and children of all ages.[32]

The hill on which this Whakatōhea man stood was most probably the impressive flat-topped peak of Makeo, directly south of Ōmarumutu pā. This is the only elevation near the back of the pā that is likely to have enabled views across and up the Waiaua riverbed.

On 16 March, Wiremu Kingi Tutahuarangi of Ngāi Tai wrote to William Mair expressing his thanks to the government for the reinforcement of Tōrere by 50 men, an action that he believed prevented the pā being attacked by Te Kooti when he was absent at Tawhana:

> While on our march from Waimana to Opotiki, the enemy made an attack on Waiaua. Some of the Arawa fell at Omarumutu. The Whakatohea retreated quietly and in good order.
>
> Te Ranapia and Te Teira with their people were the only ones who fled to the settlement of Torere. As it was, it was through their relatives among the Hauhaus that they escaped and were saved. Rawiri, the Ngatirua, and the Ngatingahere were taken. Te Awanui and thirty of his people joined us, having heard of our movements by letter.
>
> Had they been at Waiaua at the time the attack was, they also would have been taken; but even now they also are disposed to fly.
>
> The reason why Te Kooti did not make an attack upon Torere was because the Whakatohea told him that there was a strong party defending that settlement.
>
> Te Kooti inquired of them how many men there were, and he was told that there were fifty men; and it was in consequence of this information that it was not taken. …
>
> I am much pleased with the arrangement made by Mr. Clarke and yourself for stationing fifty men at my settlement, by which means my people were saved from an attack.[33]

Makeo maunga from Ōmarumutu pā in March 2022.
Stuart Spicer collection

Deep emotions at a tangihanga

The two young Te Arawa men killed at Ōpape were Hātaraka Maihi (spelt in contemporary documents as Heteraka) and Te Awaawa. The father of Hātaraka Maihi was the redoubtable Wiremu Maihi Te Rangikāheke (often referred to as Wi or William Marsh by Pākehā). A prominent Ngāti Rangiwewehi rangatira with kinship ties to Ngāti Rangitihi, he had become particularly well known both for his long years working closely on the recording of te ao Māori and te reo Māori me ona tikanga for Governor George Grey, and for his own prolific writings on the same subjects as well as Māori mythology and genealogy. Wiremu Te Rangikāheke and his wife Mere Pinepire were devastated to lose their eldest son, and the tangihanga for such a prominent Te Arawa man was naturally a major event.

Samuel Austin observed the tangihanga and recorded that it commenced on 9 March and continued until the 11th. His diary entries show both the intensity of tangihanga for the rangatira class, and his lack of appreciation of the cultural significance of that tikanga:

> 9th ... At 3.30 p.m. the remains of the two (2) men who was killed on the 7th inst were brought into the camp at Ohewe and such a tanga I never heard before since I came to New Zealand. They were crying the greatest part of yesterday and all last night. Men and all joined in today. Young Marsh's mother had his vest on and his trowsers tied around her waist. His sister had two pairs of his trowsers tied around her and the bridle of his horse over her shoulders. His wife was covered all over with all sorts of feathers etc. etc. same as if she was going to a wedding. And she carried a long pole in her hand, and as she stood upon his coffin, first tapping one end and then the other with the pole. She had a number of his mats tied around her, she had his saddle and his shawls on her back. All his things was laid out around his coffin from time to time.

> As soon as those men of the tribe who were in the fight where he was killed came in she pitched into two of them with the long pole and called them cowards etc. etc. ...

> I enquired the reason that Marsh's wife had the long pole. I was informed that a number of the men came away and left her husband and she wanted to strick those men when they came in to where her husband lay so as to brand them as cowards for leaving her husband behind them. The Hau Haus stripped all his clothes off and left him naked.

TE KOOTI RETURNS TO WAIOEKA AND ESTABLISHES WAIPUNA PĀ

It is difficult to be sure exactly when Te Kooti's force left Ōpape and Ōmarumutu, and what route they followed. Ordinarily the path back to the Waioeka would have been readily observable after being trodden by approximately 300 people, but the very dry conditions at the time may have made it harder to follow.

The only markers available in the contemporary documentation are the comments of Huhana and the diary of Samuel Austin, coupled with the physical actions of the Whanganui Contingent in following up Te Kooti's trail over two weeks later on 21 March.

Huhana stated that after Ōpape:

> We went to Waioeka to a place named the Tahora. We seperated and the main body of the people; the old men, women, and children, and some of the chiefs went to Raipawa further back.*
>
> Te Kooti with all his soldiers, every one of them, went to Maraetai. I do not know the exact number but there were a great many at that time.
>
> Te Kooti when going to Maraetai warned the main body to be cautious, as our friends the government people would likely be after us.
>
> When we reached Maraetai, picquets were sent out to the Karoro.** We had only been there two nights when the government people attacked us.[34]

For the two groups to have split at the Tahora Stream (modern Ōpato) would have required them to have followed up the Tutaetoko River and over the long, high Raupō ridge route to descend into the Ōmaukora Stream. That stream descends in a southerly direction to meet the Waioeka River immediately downriver from the junction of the Tahora Stream and the Waioeka.

The separation into two groups occurred when they reached the Tahora, at the modern location known as Wairata.***

Austin, in his diary entry on 21 March, notes:

> At 4.30 p.m. we came to where the Hau Haus had halted and cooked their food. Marched on and at 6.30 p.m. we came to where the Hau Haus had camped for the night. This place is pretty clear. We came about 15 miles today. It is a frightful

---

* Raipawa or Raepawa are names for Waipuna pā in Huhana's statement.

** A reference to Te Karoro a Tamatea or the Hell's Gate gorge downriver from Maraetahi pā.

*** Even the use of the name of Wairata for that location is a little confusing, and possibly relates as much as anything else to the school of that name, which was at that location for decades. The actual Wairata Stream is a major sidestream located about 3.5 km further up the Waioeka on its western side, at the end of Redpath Road.

road, we are about 25 miles from Opotiki. Now the name of the river that we are going up is the Tutae Toka.

From this it can be deduced that the route followed by Te Kooti went up the Tutaetoko Stream from its junction with the Ōtara River.

There is one more interesting comment, made by Te Kēpa in his report to Premier William Fox on 30 March:

> On the 20th, the force under Topia and myself started, 490 in number, at 10 o'clock at night, being anxious not to be discovered by Te Kooti's scouts. In the morning we saw the party of Hauhaus that had gone out to catch the Whakatohea. After going for about half a mile they disappeared; they were going in single file. Well, we went on through streams and over mountains. On the 23rd we came out at the Waioeka Gorge ...[35]

Whatever the exact route, the people from the Ōpape and Ōmarumutu pā had to undertake an extraordinarily difficult journey. This is particularly striking when one considers the make-up of the group: the total number, established as 218 people, comprised 57 older men, 83 women, both kuia and younger women, and 78 children.*

Wiremu Kingi Te Paia's statement of 2 April showed that he remained with the group that went upriver to Waipuna pā. His account continued:

> The Whakatohea were expecting him there; therefore, when he told them to go up the country they went. They started by themselves, and Te Kooti remained with his men and killed two Arawa. His force was about 100 men, but badly armed. He then came up the river, opened his church and had prayers. (This church was destroyed at Maraetahi.)** He also sent thirty men with food to the Whakatohea.
>
> He then came up himself to see us, stayed two nights with us, and told the Whakatohea to come down to his pa to get food and to be organized in one body. He then went back, and afterwards the Kawanatanga came and took us.[36]

Assuming the accuracy of Te Paia's statement as to the events after Ōpape and Ōmarumutu were taken, the Whakatōhea captives, doubtless with some guards, headed off straight away on 7 March. They probably took about three days to make the hard trip of some 50 kilometres to get from Ōpape to the Tahora Stream

---

* The precise number of Whakatōhea is difficult to ascertain from the records. However, Samuel Austin later recorded in his diary, just before the descent down the Waioeka, that 218 Whakatōhea were being released. It was his contingent that carried out the attack that led to their release and stayed with them for a day before meeting up with Ngāti Porou. During that time Austin counted up their numbers and he would accordingly seem to be the most reliable source. Te Kēpa's report also gave the figure of 218.

** This note in brackets was obviously added by Porter, who translated Te Paia's statement.

junction where the two groups split.* Te Kooti and his fighting men would have caught up with the group and their guards before the two groups split. From there another three hours would have seen the Whakatōhea captives arrive at the Te Pato Stream junction, opposite which they would have started clearing land for Waipuna pā. Gathering resources for the construction of whare for about 260 people would have taken many days, particularly as one large whare was erected capable of holding over 100 people, as described in Chapter 6.

The reference by Te Paia to 30 men bringing up food from Maraetahi makes it reasonably plain that Waipuna pā was indeed a new pā site specifically established to contain the Whakatōhea captives, but still without a major food source of its own. Maraetahi pā, with its extensive gardens, was plainly considered by Te Kooti to be the food basket for the groups at each pā.

In later evidence before the Supreme Court in July 1870 at the treason trial of some others of Te Kooti's men, Te Paia added detail that confirmed the location of Waipuna pā in relation to Maraetahi, although the distances he gave are too short: 'When the Wanganuis and Ngatiporou came up all five prisoners were with me at Tahore, when they were caught. Tahore is about one mile from Martahi, and Ripawa is further off. ... I remained with Te Kooti until captured at Ripawa.'[37]

When the misspellings are corrected in that evidence, they accurately place Maraetahi as the downriver location, with the Tahore Stream (or modern Ōpato) upriver from Maraetahi pā, and the Waipuna or Raepawa pā further upriver again. This juxtaposition of the various locations was also confirmed in the evidence of Piahana Tiwai, the Whakatōhea rangatira who was allied with the Whanganui Contingent, at the same trial:

> I know all the prisoners. Tamati was caught a little way from Ripawa, and the others were caught in the 'stream', except Hare, who was caught by the Ngatiporo in retreating from Maraetahi. I did not see any of them with arms, and I saw Hare captured. Te Kooti and his men were at Maraetahi. We went down to Maraetahi with the prisoners taken at Tahore and Ripawa.[38]

The work of clearing a garden area on the upriver side of the pā would have been a major priority at Waipuna, as winter was nearly upon them. Proper weatherproof shelter and food were essential to get them through those cold months up the Waioeka valley. The forthcoming winter must have been a particularly concerning prospect for the Whakatōhea captives, but they were not to know what was looming in just a few weeks.

---

* See Appendix 3 as to distance calculations, assumed routes and the most likely site of Waipuna pā.

4

WHANGANUI'S RESOLUTE DETERMINATION

The confidence of the government, and in particular of Minister of Native Affairs and Defence Donald McLean, in Māori fighting qualities and leadership had been hard earned. The ground had been laid in the conflicts on the Volcanic Plateau in September and October 1869, in which the various Whanganui, Ngāti Kahungunu and Te Arawa contingents had performed well under their own rangatira. After the battle at Te Porere no direct clashes occurred until near the end of January 1870, as Te Kooti recovered from his wounds and regathered his forces in the Tuhua area within the Kingitanga. However, much hard patrolling by government forces occurred, covering long distances, often in very cold weather in the alpine climate of the Volcanic Plateau.

By the end of October 1869 Lt Col McDonnell, the commander of the Armed Constabulary, was able to report in glowing terms to the General Government Agent at Napier, J.D. Ormond, with regard to Major Te Kēpa (Major Kemp):

> Before closing this despatch, I beg leave to bring especially before the notice of the Government the very excellent conduct of Major Kemp; he has been my right-hand all through, and every order has been well carried out by him, and a great

proportion of the late success has been owing to his conduct, and the bravery of my old friends the Wanganuis.[39]

McDonnell's recognition of Whanganui and Te Kēpa was not unique, as many other senior government officials, including Ormond and McLean themselves, made similar observations in their reports as to Te Kēpa's qualities. However, events in February and March 1870 would demonstrate that the hard service in the field that Whanganui gave to the pursuit of Te Kooti could also be easily overlooked or undervalued, often by the very same officials or officers who had so recently praised Te Kēpa.

Also often overlooked was the fact that in early April 1869 most of Te Kēpa's men had only just been paid off after nearly eight months of hard campaigning in south Taranaki against Titokowaru. That campaign had involved many months of continuous travel over long distances in rugged bush country, as well as assaults on a series of pā across the whole width of south Taranaki. After that difficult campaign, the men serving as the Whanganui Contingent under Te Kēpa had a little less than five months to recuperate at their homes before they were again in the field on active operations in pursuit of Te Kooti.

EARLY INVOLVEMENT OF THE WHANGANUI AGAINST TE KOOTI

The initial involvement of the Whanganui Contingent in the pursuit of Te Kooti lasted from early September until the end of November 1869, up on the Volcanic Plateau. Just to reach the active field of operations meant a gruelling trip the full length of the Whanganui River. The field of operations in which the Whanganui Contingent had to operate was always hard and uncompromising in terms of geography and climate. In addition, government provision of food and other logistical supplies, such as tentage, groundsheets or boots, was most noticeable by its frequent absence.

After leaving Whanganui on 11 September, the Whanganui Contingent, which included the Pākehā NCO Samuel Austin, faced an arduous paddle upstream by canoe right into the headwaters of the Whanganui River. From there they climbed up through difficult bush conditions to emerge on the windswept Volcanic Plateau. The mountains in the Tongariro, Ngāuruhoe and Ruapehu cluster were heavily snow covered, and the nights were extremely cold for men equipped only with blankets. As they traversed east they encountered bitterly cold rains and finally snow, which on one day fell to a depth of some six inches (15 centimetres). Finally, on 1 October, they arrived at the base camp at Poutū, at the southeastern end of Lake Rotoaira, which Lt Col McDonnell had recently established. They were just in time to link up with McDonnell's forces before the attack on Te Pōrere, and just three days later, on 4 October, Te Kēpa's men played a leading role in the fighting during that assault.

In fact, not all was as rosy in McDonnell's relationship with the Whanganui Contingent as his report at the end of October suggested. The lack of satisfactory, or often any, provision of food and other equipment was an issue that would plague them throughout the campaigns of late 1869 and early 1870. Much to the men's chagrin, while being told no supplies were available for them, they would at times observe McDonnell ensuring that the Pākehā Armed Constabulary received supplies of food. Even worse, on one occasion McDonnell supplied Pākehā gold prospectors on the same day that he told Austin there was no food available for Whanganui.

One of Sergeant Samuel Austin's principal roles with the Whanganui Contingent was that of quartermaster, charged with the acquisition and provision of whatever shelter, food and ammunition supplies he could access. Not surprisingly, in view of what he saw as inequitable and harsh treatment of the Whanganui men he had to provision, many of his diary entries indicate the low regard in which he held McDonnell.

Over nearly three weeks in late October and early November 1869 their potato sources in locations near the camp were used up. After desperate foraging for potatoes, Austin made furious diary entries over two days in November as they tried to gather provisions, or find the means for provisions, before heading south on their long journey home:

> 20th Fine morning went to Col McDonnell for our account for rations so as we can leave for Wanganui before that we are starved to death as we have not got anything to eat.
>
> 21st Fine morning fell in and marched at 4 a.m. for Wanganui bidding good by to Poutu hoping never to serve under such a selfish commander and commissariat as we were leaving behind.

It is an old saying but true, that an army marches on its stomach. And there is no doubt from Austin's diary entries that the lack of food influenced his opinion of McDonnell, who in his eyes was the one to blame.

To be fair to McDonnell, it is clear from correspondence in late 1869 between McLean, Premier William Fox and their senior officials that budgetary pressures, lack of roads and flooded rivers were impinging on the ability of government officials to provide adequate food supplies and other resources to their forces in the field. Moreover, the dispersed nature of the pursuit of Te Kooti, and the fact that the various columns were in untracked country, made it very difficult for pack-trains of horses to maintain a regular logistical supply.

The Whanganui Contingent, driven by hunger, achieved the extraordinary feat of making the return trip from Poutū to Whanganui in just five days, arriving on 25 November. Austin recorded on that day that he and some of the force had reached Whanganui, with others following days later: 'So ends this short expedition and hoping never to be under the same command again … it was the beginning of December before the force all arrived in Wanganui.'

NEGOTIATIONS OF PREMIER WILLIAM FOX WITH TOPIA TUROA AND TE KĒPA

While there was no firm news of Te Kooti's exact location or the size of the threat he posed, in late November and early December 1869 the government knew that he was likely gathering forces somewhere near the head of the Whanganui River in the Kingitanga. The government's main source of intelligence arose out of the close relationships between Ngāti Tūwharetoa men and Tainui or Ngāti Maniapoto in the Kingitanga. The only obvious force the government could gather near the Kingitanga in December was the Whanganui Contingent, which had so recently returned home.

In the meantime the premier, William Fox, had become aware that as a result of the killing of some of Topia Turoa's relatives by Te Kooti, Topia was close to committing his support for a renewed campaign. Fox then heard that Topia Turoa and other Te Atihaunui and Ngā Rauru rangatira had met on 19 and 20 November, at the opening of the Te Ao Marama wharenui at Ōhinemutu on the Whanganui River. It was reported to Fox that during this hui the upper- and lower-river Whanganui rangatira had discussed the depth of the differences between the Kingites and those supporting the Crown within their iwi. Although Te Kēpa himself was not present, as he was still with the contingent on the Volcanic Plateau, Fox was informed that Topia Turoa had spoken strongly against Te Kooti, and expressed a willingness to serve against him, if the government provided him and his people with arms and ammunition.

These meetings were followed by a hui at Rānana a week later that lasted for some days, at which both Topia Turoa and Te Kēpa were present. Fox made sure there was a supply of weapons and ammunition for Topia. In its 1999 report on the Whanganui River Inquiry, the Waitangi Tribunal succinctly summarised the outcome of these delicate negotiations, and the important commitments given on both sides:

The opening of the house turned into a dramatic meeting, the Kingites favouring Te Kooti, others supporting the Government, and two days of plain speaking proving inconclusive. Some tension was eased when a message from King Tawhiao renounced Te Kooti; thereafter, the Kingite, Turoa Topia, declared that he would pursue Te Kooti if he were given guns to do so. That raised two more questions: whether neutral hapu would allow a taua against Te Kooti to use their part of the river and whether those supporting the Government, and the Government itself, could trust the Kingite warriors with guns and ammunition.

Discussion continued at Rānana nine days later, with Te Keepa present, followed by a meeting with the Premier, William Fox, who was conciliatory. He assured all that they would not be punished with land confiscations if they now rejected Te Kooti, whatever their history in the recent war. Advised by Te Keepa and Mete Kingi, Fox agreed to trust Turoa Topia to fight Te Kooti, and let him have a stand of arms. In return, Topia promised to work with the Native Minister, Donald McLean, in the cause of peace.[40]

Topia Pehi Turoa.
New Zealand. Tourism Department.
Ref: PAColl-5671-42, Alexander Turnbull Library, Wellington, NZ

THE WHANGANUI CONTINGENT REASSEMBLES

In early December 1869 news of a possible move by Te Kooti from the Kingitanga towards the Tapuaeharuru (Taupō) area galvanised senior officials into action. Ormond issued orders for McDonnell and his remaining Armed Constabulary to head for Tapuaeharuru. At the same time Fox instructed Major Te Kēpa to reassemble the Whanganui Contingent, and to travel to Tapuaeharuru.

Te Kēpa Te Rangihiwinui.
Ref: PA2-2562, Alexander Turnbull Library, Wellington, NZ

Sudden impetus for the Whanganui Contingent's assembly plans followed a rash action on the part of Te Kooti, which was recorded in a telegram Fox sent to Ormond from Whanganui on 7 December:

> News just brought down river that Te Kooti has plundered Mamaku's cattle and crops, and is going to attack him. All Wanganui furious. Kemp wants to go 500 strong; they will feed themselves. The news is from Pehi [the senior upriver rangatira Te Pēhi Turoa]. No white man will be allowed by me to accompany them except Mr. Booth as far as Pipiriki. [The vessel] 'Sturt' will be sent to you.[41]

Austin's diary also records in the first week of December that William Fox and Donald McLean had asked Te Kēpa to send messages to the members of the contingent to regather, because of news the government had received that Te Kooti was now in the upper Whanganui catchment. The principal difference now was that Topia Turoa was so committed in his opposition to Te Kooti that he and his men intended to join up with the contingent when it reached his pā at Ōhinemutu.

Te Kēpa wasted no time. By 8 December most of the contingent had gathered and were heading upstream by waka, with other members joining at many of the small kāinga they passed as they travelled up the river. By 10 December they had reached Rānana. Suddenly the challenges facing the Whanganui Contingent had an added edge, with Austin's diary entry recording some disquieting news they received there: '… pulled on to Rannana where we were informed that Topini Mamaku had joined Te Kooti and that the force in all numbered 500 men but Topia still stuck to it that up the river we would go.'

Topine Te Mamaku was a leading Te Atihaunui rangatira from the upper reaches of the Whanganui River, whose rohe included the large feeder tributary catchment of the Ōhura. He had previously fought against the Crown alongside Topia Turoa. The news that he was intending to join Te Kooti, if it proved correct, would mean that even when combined Te Kēpa's and Topia Turoa's forces would be facing potentially overwhelming numbers of opponents. Among that opposing force was Topine and his men, now very close at hand, and possibly to be encountered within a day of leaving Ōhinemutu, which was Topia Turoa's own principal pā. The combined force under Te Kēpa and Topia reached Ōhinemutu the next day, 11 December, and by the 13th they had arrived at Tieke, north of the Maunganuioteao junction, but without encountering Topine Te Mamaku or his men.

At this point the journey became even more challenging as it started raining heavily that night, and over the next weeks the men had to struggle repeatedly with the river rising by up to one to two metres or more after periods of heavy rain. The extra effort required to paddle and pole against the swiftly flowing river had an effect, with Austin recording on 22 December that a number of the older men had turned back for Whanganui that morning. The same day they received intelligence of a potential threat: '... we received information that a canoe was seen belonging to Te Kooti we now moved on in silence and 3 canoes with the best men went to the front.' No actual threat materialised that day, or on any of the following days on the river, although Austin's diary includes repeated comments about rumours that Te Kooti was not far away.

A CONFRONTATION WITH TOPINE TE MAMAKU

The main concern remained Topine Te Mamaku's attitude and that of the Māori King as the contingent drew nearer to the Kingitanga. At a location well upriver, which Austin recorded as 'Tewha Ra Hora', but which was most likely Whakahoro pā at the Retaruke junction, he recorded interactions with both Te Mamaku and the Māori King as they developed over the day:*

> Topine was there when we arrived and a number of his men. At 5 p.m. a number of canoes came down the river filled with men. A good number of those men were

Topine Te Mamaku.
Burton Brothers (Dunedin, NZ). Ref: PA7-05-07, Alexander Turnbull Library, Wellington, NZ

---

* Whakahoro, at the junction of the Retaruke and Whanganui rivers, was a major pā belonging to Topine Te Mamaku. A few days later Austin's diary records their arrival at Tawata, and then Maraekowhai, both of which are upriver from Whakahoro.

from Waikato. An orderly or rather messenger from the King was one of them. This was a great Hau Hau settlement and at 7 p.m. our men fell in and marched under the Hau Hau flagstaff and had prayers. This was putting down Hauism as it was here that they had Capt Lloyds head and Hewetts at one time.*

The Whanganui Contingent's inflammatory action in conducting their own prayers under the flagstaff was followed up the next morning by an even more provocative act, as Austin described: 'Our men hoisted three Ensigns on the Hau Hau flagstaff this morning at 8 a.m. so where the Hau Hau Flag was yesterday the Flag of our Queen flew today.'

The racheting up of tensions continued both in the evening of the 24th and on into 25 December as whaikōrero occurred between the various factions — Te Pehi Tūroa, Topia Tūroa and Te Kēpa adopting a hostile approach to Te Kooti; Topine Te Mamaku, at least initially, expressing an opposing view; and Aporo, the king's messenger, yet another, asserting that the king had the Te Kooti situation under his control and urging the Whanganui force to return home.

Topia and Te Kēpa stressed their determination to carry on, and Topia announced he would not let Topine Te Mamaku or Aporo leave, posting guards to ensure they remained. Faced with this determined, somewhat heavy-handed approach, Topine finally declared on the following day that he would assist in the pursuit of Te Kooti. It is clear from Austin's diary that not much weight was placed on that assurance: 'Topini and his men left today for his place after giving a promise to assist in getting Te Kooti which promise he never intends to fulfil.'

The heightened sense of tension was marked by a guard of 30 men being set at each corner of the camp that night. However, there was no action during the night, and as they progressed further up the river over the next ten days they still did not encounter Te Kooti.

THE WHANGANUI CONTINGENT REACHES TAUMARUNUI AND TURNS INLAND

The first day of the new year, 1870, at last saw a slow drop in the river as the regular bouts of rain finally ceased for a while, enabling the Whanganui to recommence their journey upriver. However, over the following days the river rose and fell, with repeated rainfall once more making progress very slow. It was 9 January before Austin recorded their arrival at the Ōngarue junction, at the

---

* The references are to the severed heads of Captain Lloyd and a settler, Captain Hewett, who were killed in 1865 and whose heads the Paimārire prophet Te Ua Haumēne had sent inland.

'village called Tamanurni'. It had taken them a month of hard work to travel that far upriver. Once more news was received at Taumarunui of Te Kooti's forces being tantalisingly close. On 14 January Te Kēpa sent a messenger overland from Taumarunui with a report to McDonnell, who was at Tokaanu, as part of the process of linking up with his forces:

> I have arrived here, and Te Kooti has run away. Aporo, of Waikato, gave him information; that is the reason of his retreat. I hear he has gone to Waotu, then I hear he has gone to Taupo.* Topia and I are following him up. You can know about that side (S.E.) of the lake. If you come to Ti Ti Raupeka, it will be good to see us.** Bring food for us with you. I intend to follow him to Tauranga, &c., if he goes there. This is all.⁴²

> **Volcanic Plateau changes**
>
> At this time the whole western side of Lake Taupō was in poor grasslands, with only pockets of bush surviving after the colossal effects of the Taupō eruption about 1800 years earlier. The Volcanic Plateau had been engulfed in massive deposits of pumice sands and other volcanic ejecta deficient in cobalt. Since World War II, treatments with cobalt-based fertilisers have transformed the land coverage.

Te Kēpa was not the only one to decide at Taumarunui that he would follow Te Kooti wherever he might be heading. Topia Turoa wrote in similar terms from Taumarunui to Premier William Fox:

> We have come to this place; on the 9th instant we arrived here. On our arrival, we found Te Kooti had made his escape. We are therefore going on in pursuit of him, and we intend to go on until we find him, wherever he may be, excepting in the case of his going to Te Kuiti. We will not follow him to that place; the thought about him at that place will be with the King.⁴³

McDonnell forwarded Te Kēpa's message on to Ormond by telegram on the evening of 14 January, with advice that he intended to link with Te Kēpa's force.⁴⁴ Meanwhile, the Whanganui Contingent spent three days at Taumarunui finalising their arrangements to leave the river and travel overland to the Volcanic Plateau. Austin's two final entries on the river were made on 11 and 12 January:

> 11th Fine again. All the men fell in on parade at 6 a.m. The whole forse wanted to follow up Te Kooti or els all return back again to Wanganui, but

---

* Waotu is a location well down the Waikato River, south of modern Cambridge.

** Titiraupenga is the well-known pā site in the northern Pureora Forest area northwest of modern Taupō.

> **Hakaraia Māhika**
>
> Hakaraia Māhika was a prominent rangatira who was one of Te Kooti's well-known supporters. He had risen to prominence for a number of reasons.
>
> His original name was Māhika, and his principal iwi affiliation was Waitaha in the Tauranga area, though he also had links to Te Arawa. In the Musket Wars era he had been captured as a child by a Ngāpuhi taua and taken back to Pēwhairangi (the Bay of Islands) as a slave. He had attended a missionary school while there and learnt to read. While in captivity, he had converted to Christianity and adopted the baptismal name of Hakaraia. Because of his obvious intelligence and religious commitment, the missionaries had persuaded Ngāpuhi to let Hakaraia return south to his homelands with the missionary Thomas Chapman and his wife, who were setting up a new mission at Rotorua. For the next ten years or so he led a life of piety, helping Chapman and his wife establish their mission station. By 1845 he had achieved a reconciliation that allowed his Waitaha people to return to the Tauranga area, and he established a flourishing Christian kāinga called Kenana on the Kaituna River near Maketū. By this time his mana had increased greatly.
>
> When the Crown launched its invasions of the Waikato and Tauranga, Hakaraia actively supported the Māori King and was one of the prominent rangatira involved in the defeat of the British Imperial Army's assault on Pukehinahina (Gate Pa) in April 1864. After the defeat a few months later at Te Ranga, just southeast of Tauranga, when British forces inflicted heavy casualties on the Kingitanga supporters, Hakaraia withdrew into the Kaimai ranges. Later, after the confiscations of Waitaha lands at Tauranga, he headed inland, spending time both in the Kingitanga and also in Ngāti Raukawa's rohe at Tapapa pā. He was by then disenchanted with the conservative Pākehā churches, and in 1869 became a keen adherent of Te Kooti's Ringatū religion and an active supporter of his campaign.

this was overruled by Kepa, Topia and the other chiefs. Two (2) men was selected to each canoe to take them back from hear to Wanganui. ...

12th Fine again. Fell in at 7 a.m. Had a war dance before parting. ... All hands fell in at 12 o'clock, 371 men to follow up Te Kooti, 130 men to return back to Wanganui. We fell in and marched away at 6.30 p.m. after seeing the canoes and men away to Wanganui. We halted for the night at Wata Wata Orangi.*

---

* Presumably this location lay under the high peak known on modern topographical maps as Whatawhata, 3–4 km east of Taumarunui near the modern Wharauroa marae.

Austin's diary entry for 12 January provided some idea of the number of waka used to transport the Whanganui Contingent from the lower river areas up to Taumarunui. With two men allotted to each waka for the return journey, the fleet must have comprised about 65 waka to transport the 500 men under Te Kēpa and Topia who had headed upriver, together with all their weapons, gear and food supplies.

Now without waka, for the next few days the contingent was to find that the river flows were still strong, making crossings on foot concerning. They continued on for two more days, on the 15th crossing the Waipari River, which flows into the Whanganui on the true right or east bank (the Whanganui at that point is still flowing north).* They seem to have followed the Waipari River northeast, as they soon crossed the Waione Stream, which flows into the Waipari. After recording that they had crossed the Waione they then climbed what Austin called 'a great hill, verry steep indeed'.

On 16 January, after a 5 a.m. start, Austin recorded that they finally broke out of the bush a few hours later and halted at 'Teruamata', or Ruamata, to cook breakfast.** It must have come as a major relief finally to reach open country after five weeks of hard slog by waka and on foot. The elevated open country on the Volcanic Plateau enabled faster travel, and by 18 January they were north of the Waihaha River crossing, at a location called Hurakia.*** Austin described this area as being easy to travel through — 'splendid country about hear, all level land with plenty of grass'.

WHANGANUI REJOIN MCDONNELL AND APPROACH TE KOOTI

From Hurakia it took the contingent one more day, and a night at a location called Hora Aruhe about 15 miles (24 km) from Hurakia, before they reached the Waikato River bank early on 20 January.**** Here Lt Col McDonnell and his force of Pākehā and Te Arawa were waiting for them. (Austin's hope for

---

* Austin, at page 71 of his diary, refers to the 'Waipore', a misspelling of the Waipari.

** This location is not marked on modern topographical maps but on a cadastral map referred to as 'MapColl-832.17gbbd/[n.d.]/Acc.39820: [Creator unknown]: Whangaipeke Block, [Piopiotea and Maungaku survey districts] [ms map]. [n.d.]', which was accessed on the web, an area is described as Ruamata just northeast of the head of the Waione Stream, which flows from northeast to southwest into the Waipari. (Just to add to the confusion, another larger Waione Stream flows direct into the Whanganui on the true left just upriver. It flows south to north into the Whanganui.)

*** Hurakia no longer exists as a kāinga but the name continues in Hurakia Station, located by the Tihoi Trading Post on SH32.

**** No longer shown on modern topographical maps, Hora Aruhe was located near the head of the Maraemanuka Stream.

Whanganui never to serve under McDonnell again had taken less than two months to be shattered.) As the Whanganui Contingent had been travelling on a fairly direct route through the open country west of Lake Taupō it can be reasonably assumed it reached the Waikato somewhere west of Atiamuri, having taken just over three days to reach the Waikato River after emerging from the bush at the head of the Whanganui onto the open areas of the Volcanic Plateau.

It took an hour and half for the whole contingent, now numbering 371 men, to cross the wide and deep Waikato River using only one waka, described by Austin as being 'hardly fit to float cats in, both old and rotten and leaking'. Once they had crossed, the now combined force marched west for a short distance before heading north, spending that night at a location called Waimahana.*

From Waimahana the force headed inland towards Hakaraia's Tapapa pā, government officials having received reliable reports from Hitiri Paerata, a Ngāti Raukawa and Ngāti Te Kōhera rangatira, that Te Kooti was now there.**

McDonnell would have seen Hitiri Paerata's correspondence when he was at Taupō on 17 January, before he continued on foot down the Waikato to meet up with the Whanganui Contingent on the 20th. In one letter, Paerata provided news of Te Kooti's numbers and location:

> I have met with Te Kooti at Pouakani on the 10th January, he has above 100 men, and including women and children, 200. On the 14th of January they reached Tapapa. The news from there is, that the whole of the tribes and hapus of Ngatiraukawa, on the other side of Waikato and extending to Tauranga, have joined Te Kooti.[45]

For two more days the combined government force travelled north from Waimahana on a route that took them inland, but basically parallel to the Waikato River. Until the deviation inland towards Tapapa, they followed approximately the course of modern SH1. McDonnell reported from Waimahana on 21 January:

> ... am now on my way to Patetere with Europeans and Arawas. Majors Kemp and Topia joined us yesterday morning, and move on with us to-day. ... I move on with as little delay as possible, and trust to meet with the enemy the day after

---

* Waimahana was a well-known kāinga site on both sides of the river, which has since been swamped by the waters behind the dam at Whakamaru. It lay about midway between the Waipapa River in the east and the Maraemanuka Stream in the west, probably near the Okama Stream junction.

** Hitiri Paerata's mana was particularly established by his leadership at the battle of Orākau in 1864. In 1888 he was chosen to speak at Parliament to provide a Māori defender's account of that battle, with Gilbert Mair acting as interpreter.

tomorrow; the strength of the force is:—Europeans, 98; Maoris, 150;* Wanganuis with Topia, 370.⁴⁶

FIRST CONTACT WITH TE KOOTI'S FORCES

The following day Austin recorded that the combined forces had reached the Tokoroa Stream, at the site of modern Tokoroa, then moved on to stop for the night at the Pokaiwhenua River, which flows west down from the Patetere range.** Now, once again Austin began to note reports of Te Kooti's close proximity: '22nd … orders was given that no fires was to be lit untill after dark as according to the reports we are only a few miles from where Te Kooti is supposed to be stopping.'

The first encounter with Te Kooti's forces finally came after a long night-time approach, as Austin recorded:

> 23rd … here we halted until 10 p.m. Fell in and marched all the remainder of the night, crossed several small rivers or creeks.
>
> 24th A fine morning after all of last night. We came in sight of Te Kooti and his men at break of day. We rushed the village and the party I was in charge of they killed (2) men, took 4 men prisoners, 8 women and 12 children, making in all (2) killed & 24 prisoners.
>
> The remainder got away into the bush. This was Tapapa, a verry hard place. We cooked a few potatoes and moved into the hills after Te Kooti and his men.

By this stage the men of the contingent had not slept for over 36 hours, and they were to have only a short sleep before more action on 25 January:

> 25th Fine. Up and cooked breakfast at 4 a.m. and ready to march as soon as McDonnell's forse joines us. No sign of him, that is McDonnell. Kepa fell in his men about 6 a.m. As we were falling in we heard firing in the direction of Tapapa. When the firing had been continued for some time Kepa gave the order to advance on Te Kooti's stronghold at Panetaonga, this being his chief place hear, as it was called his headquarters.***
>
> We advanced and we were received with a heavy fire from the Hau Haus. After about half an hours fighting we rushed the place and took it. We shot about 45 horses that were tied up — they were tied up like the Cavalry tie up theirs. Those

---

* This was a Te Arawa force with whom George Preece was serving.

** In his diary entry for 22 January, Austin spells Pokaiwhenua as 'Pakaiwenura'.

*** The location of Panetaonga has not been established.

were the troop horses. The men got saddles and bridels and spurs and plenty of blankets and brandy. We caught about 100 fine horses and we shot a good number that we could not catch. ...

We returned to camp at Tapapa without the loss of a man.

On their return to Tapapa they realised that the two sides had each launched an attack on the other's base. The firing they had heard was Te Kooti attacking McDonnell's camp, which was near Tapapa, while unbeknownst to Te Kooti, Te Kēpa and most of his men were in the bush waiting to attack his base at Panetaonga. Te Kēpa launched his attack only after the firing of Te Kooti's attack at Tapapa was heard.

Austin's diary for the period from 26 January to 3 February records much tough patrolling in difficult bush country, resulting in few contacts with Te Kooti's men and the capture of several prisoners. What stands out most in Austin's diary is the fact that by the end of January relations had again deteriorated between the Whanganui Contingent and their overall commander, Lt Col McDonnell, once more over issues of food:

31st... We are kept moving about and all the provisions we get is what potatoes we can find, as the officer in command will not issue us rations, so we must do on what we can pick up from time to time. It was a bad morning when we joined the European forse at the Waikato River, we would have either beaten Te Kooti or he us, that is how it stands at present. None of our natives like McDonnell from Kepa down, they are all against him and no wonder for the way we are treated by him.

Despite Austin's comment on the lack of rations, however, two days later the majority of the contingent were given provisions for four days, and sent in the direction of Paengaroa, near Te Puke, where Te Kooti's forces had ambushed Lt Col Fraser's column, killing three of Fraser's men. After they had met up with Lt Col Fraser, the day after his contact with Te Kooti, Te Kēpa's men effectively passed out of McDonnell's control for some days. On 8 February, this major part of the Whanganui Contingent marched into Tauranga, keen to reunite with the 159 men who had remained at the Tapapa camp.

INITIAL STEPS AT ŌHIWA

On 10 February, however, the men at Tauranga were shipped to Ohope, and the next morning to Ōhiwa harbour, where they disembarked in steady rain. Not being supplied with tents, they were fortunate to find some unoccupied huts on the beach east of the harbour entrance. But Austin's diary entry for the 10th struck a familiar note of optimism in one respect: 'We all thought that we had seen the last of Lt Col. McDonnell and his orders & counter-orders.'

There is no doubt that by the time the Whanganui Contingent reached Ōhiwa harbour the continuing food shortages had lowered their capability, if not enthusiasm, for campaigning. In late February and through most of March, while they were at Ōhiwa, there was a growing focus by the Whanganui men on food-gathering, from whatever sources they could find. This contributed to a delay in operations, which by mid March had generated a negative effect on their reputation, not just in McDonnell's and H.T. Clarke's eyes, but particularly among Whakatōhea.

Moreover, for Te Kēpa and Topia Tūroa, it was now necessary to undertake a period of familiarisation and negotiation to assess the attitudes of iwi in the wider area toward Te Kooti. This involved discussion with rangatira of Ngāti Awa and Ngāti Pukeko to the west; Te Arawa at Ōhiwa stockade above them; Whakatōhea at Ōpape and Ōmarumutu; Ngāi Tai at Tōrere, and even with Whānau a Apanui from the area around the Motu River mouth and Te Kaha further east. The process of reconnaissance, familiarisation and fraternisation with locals was particularly important for a force of Whanganui and Ngā Rauru who were from the other side of the North Island. If the local iwi or even some hapū were opposed to Te Kooti, the Whanganui rangatira also needed to know just how reliable they might be as guides, or how willing they were to contribute to any force heading into Te Urewera to confront Tūhoe, and/or Hira Te Popo's Ngāti Ira.

It was a process that paid great dividends, with Te Kēpa and Topia able to persuade most of these rangatira to provide either guides or limited small forces to support their forays into Te Urewera, up the Waimana/Tauranga River in early March, and later that month into the Waioeka Gorge area. Local knowledge of these difficult areas, with their tangle of steep, heavily bushed ranges, would prove vital to the success of any expedition.

The formal orders that Te Kēpa received from Donald McLean, dated 19 February, were completely open-ended:

This is a word of mine to you: The management of the fighting against Te Kooti is given by me into the hands of you the Maori chiefs, for you know his tactics; so I have said that only you, the Maoris, are to pursue him. I have instructed Colonel McDonnell that he and the Europeans are not to go.

If that murderer, Te Kooti, is caught by you, the Government will make some arrangement with you, the chiefs; and the European people will praise you, and make you great.

I have selected the chiefs who are to have the conduct of the fighting, viz., you and Topia Turoa for your own party, and Ropata Wahawaha to be the leader of his own tribe, the Ngatiporou; they will come by way of Waikare-Moana. The chiefs of Ngatikahungunu will lead their own men.

Well, my desire is that you, the chiefs of these tribes, should work together in unity. Do not be jealous of one another, but do the work well, so that that bad man may soon disappear from our sight.[47]

ROPATA WAHAWAHA MEETS TE KĒPA AND TOPIA AT ŌHIWA

Ropata had been at Tauranga in the first week of February, and he had been involved in the negotiations with McLean that led to the minister's decision to use only Māori forces. McLean informed McDonnell of his decision in his letter of 18 February, as described in Chapter 2.[48]

On 21 February Ropata arrived at Ōhiwa on the *Sturt*, en route back to Te Tai Rāwhiti to gather his own force. He brought with him McLean's instructions of 19 February to Te Kēpa and Topi Turoa, as well as rations and stores for the Whanganui Contingent, in addition to provisions for his own force of Ngāti Porou.

The new arrangements left much to Te Kēpa's discretion with regard to the

Sir Donald McLean.
Ref: PA2-2603, Alexander Turnbull Library, Wellington, NZ

detailed planning and route selection, but Ropata's visit at Ōhiwa provided an opportunity for the three rangatira to liaise in person. It appears from later reports that Ropata, Te Kēpa and Topia agreed they would each lead their forces into Te Urewera heading towards Maungapōhatu, and that they intended to meet there. It was a challenging arrangement in such a major set of bush-clad ranges: none of the contingents would know where the others were, or even when they were likely to be near Maungapōhatu.

TE KĒPA'S WHANGANUI HEAD UP THE WAIMANA VALLEY

Te Kēpa's plan was to head into the Waimana valley, but he was determined not to do so without all his men, including the 159 still on their way from the camp at Tapapa pā. He knew that Tamaikōwha, the prominent Tūhoe rangatira, was likely to oppose his passage up the Waimana to Maungapōhatu, and understandably wanted to have a superior force. In addition, at that point he was awaiting the outcome of his agreements with surrounding rangatira whose contributions of small forces would augment his numbers even further.

They did not let him down. Wiremu Kingi Tutahuarangi of Ngāi Tai arrived at Ōhiwa with 60 of his men on 22 February; Ngāti Awa confirmed they would head up the Whakatāne into the Waimana and meet Te Kēpa in the lower Waimana valley with about 30–40 men; and on 24 February Austin noted that 34 young Whakatōhea fighting men had arrived at Ōhiwa to join the force.

On 23 February Austin wrote that Te Kēpa had taken a force of 300 men to Whakatāne in response to rumours of a 'Hau Hau' force being in that vicinity. The Tapapa men would probably have rejoined Te Kēpa by the time he returned to Ōhiwa on 27 February, possibly linking up at Whakatāne, as Austin makes no specific mention of their arrival at Ōhiwa.

The diary records that on 1 March ammunition was issued for the invasion force to head into Te Urewera, but heavy rain that day delayed the departure. That proved fortuitous, as the next day a pack train of 12 horses arrived with supplies of biscuits and sugar; Austin recorded that eight days of rations were to be issued the following day. That duly occurred on 3 March, but through lack of a local guide the start was once again delayed.

A guide finally arrived from Whakatāne on 4 March, enabling Te Kēpa to report formally to McLean:

> We have received the letter addressed by you to Topia and myself, urging us to go in pursuit of Te Kooti, — good. Having now completed the arrangements which detained me here, waiting also for my party left behind at Tapapa, and making

arrangements with the people of this East Coast, that is to say, the tribes of the Ngatipukeko, Ngatiawa, Whakatohea, Ngaitai, Te Whanau-apanui, and other tribes, and Ngatikereru.*

On this day the march has commenced by the road to Waimana and thence to Maungapowhatu. ... The party which accompanies me consists of 428. Then Ngatipukeko, Ngatiawa — they will move by the other road.[49]

Austin's diary records the commencement of these, the first operations in the Bay of Plenty solely under Māori command, and also explains why Topia Turoa did not accompany this first group:

4th ... The expedition marched today at 2 p.m. composed as follows:

Wanganui natives 300 strong – Ngati Kereru 32 strong – Whanauapuni – 32 strong –Ngaite [Ngāi Tai] 42 strong – Whakatohi 34 strong – making in all 440 of all ranks under the command of Major Kepa of the Wanganui Native Contingent. Those who were left behind were very dissatisfied. Topia remained in camp as he could not march, having his leg hurt a few days ago but most of his men went.

Unfortunately, Austin himself was among those who were left behind, so no diary account exists for this Waimana expedition.

On 5 March, Te Kēpa met up with a force of 60 Ngāti Awa under Hori Kawakura at Te Waimana before pushing on up the Tauranga River into Tamaikōwha's rohe. Austin records that Topia went out to the south with some of his men on 5 March to join the rest of the force at Waimana, but having met them there, for some unexplained reason he returned late that night, with two of his companies also returning the next day, 6 March.

NEWS OF TE KOOTI'S RAID ON ŌPAPE AND ŌMARUMUTU

A period of nervous waiting now ensued as McLean and Clarke, the civil commissioner, both distant from the action, awaited news of Te Kēpa's and Ropata's expeditions. In political terms a lot hung on the outcome of these expeditions, both for McLean and for his Premier William Fox. Their critics were vociferous in decrying the decision only to use Māori forces in the hunt for Te Kooti.

Even as late as 11 March, four days after Te Kooti's attack on the Ōpape and Ōmarumutu pā, Major William Mair could report about Te Kēpa only in the following way:

---

* Ngāti Kereru were a hapū of Ngāti Rangiwewehi of Te Arawa. Some of their men were among the Arawa men based at Ōhiwa.

About the 4th instant, the Ngatihau, under Kemp, left Ohiwa for Maungapowhatu, with about 150 Rawhiti Natives, including 40 Whakatohea. Hori Kawakura with 60 Ngatiawa marched up the Whakatāne to join Kemp at Te Waimana. Ngatipukeko, influenced, it is said, by Ngatipikiao, decline to go. No news from this expedition has come in.

Mair's report then continued, however, with the startling news of Te Kooti's raid on the Ōpape and Ōmarumutu pā on 7 March:

On the 7th instant a party of Hauhaus came down the Waiaua Valley, near Opotiki, and surprised the inhabitants (Whakatohea); most of them escaped by the sea to the eastward, but a number of women and children are supposed to have fallen into the hands of the enemy. Captain Walker made a demonstration, and two of his party, Arawa from Ohiwa, were killed. Later information received by the officer commanding here makes it appear that the Whakatohea Pa, Omarumutu, is occupied by the Hauhaus. I attach a copy of letter from Captain Walker; the news furnished is very meagre.[50]

Topia's return from the Waimana to Ōhiwa with his men meant that when on 8 March news reached there of Te Kooti's raid on Ōpape and Ōmarumutu pā the previous day, and the killing of the two Arawa men, he was able to head away immediately to Ōpōtiki with his two companies. His immediate aim was to save Tōrere from attack and if possible to engage Te Kooti. At this point, Austin and the ten men of the Whanganui Contingent who remained on the beach at Ōhiwa moved up into the Ōhiwa redoubt for greater security.

MCLEAN RECEIVES A BOMBSHELL

On 13 March Te Kēpa reported to McLean on the Waimana expedition after returning to Ōhiwa, which Austin's diary confirms occurred in the dark on the 12th. Te Kēpa conveyed news that was startling to McLean, who had been expecting to read of the contingent's engagements with Tamaikōwha or Te Kooti. He had certainly not envisaged, nor authorised, a peacemaking role for Te Kēpa, or even contemplated such a thing.

Te Kēpa's report began along the lines that McLean might have expected:

On the 5th instant we reached Te Waimana at 4 o'clock in the morning, but did not see any Hauhaus. In the forenoon, or later in the morning, Topia and his tribe and the Arawa also came back to Opotiki; we proceeded and reached Otara, where the Hauhaus asked 'Who are you?' The question was not answered, and they fired down their guns at us from the top of the precipice, and we fired up. They retreated: we then went on and slept at Motuohau, in consequence of the heaviness of the rain on that day. The next day we proceeded, and slept at Ngatuoha;* the river Waimana was flooded. Three days elapsed and the flood in the river subsided.

At this point, Te Kēpa's report took a completely unexpected turn. By 10 March the river had subsided enough that they were able to cross it and continue their advance upriver to Tauwharemanuka pā, which Tamaikōwha was occupying. Te Kēpa continued:

On the following day we reached Tauwharemanuka, and all the chiefs of my war party — Te Hata, Te Kani, Wiremu Kingi, Kerei Kawakura, and others — held a consultation as to sending a messenger to Tamaikowha. I assented to their word, and he was sent to those people, i.e., Tamaikowha and his people. On his arrival he found they had scattered about on the same day that they fired down on us. Afterwards those people came, and I said to them, 'Where is Te Kooti?' He, Tamaikowha, said, 'I have not seen him, but I heard he had gone to Waioeka, and do you go back quickly; soon he will arrive to capture the Whakatohea, Ngaitai, and Whanau a-Apanui, and kill them and the Europeans of Opotiki.' I said, 'Where are the Urewera?' He replied, 'They have been taken thither by (gone with) Te Kooti, as they think they will be put to death by Government. The chiefs only remained. Rakuraku has separated from Te Kooti.' I said, 'Have you no thought (desire) to make peace?' He said, 'I am willing; that is the reason why I questioned down to you on the day that you were fired down at by us, for I heard that that was Topia Turoa's war party, because we belong to the King party.' However, I am unable to write to you all that was said. The following day we returned to the Waimana …

The next news I heard about Te Kooti was that Te Whakatohea had been captured, and that Topia had gone and was aiding Ngaitai. This morning I sent Te Hata, Te Kani, and Wiremu Kingi and their tribe. Should the messenger from them arrive to-day, we shall march into the forest.[51]

Both the content of Te Kēpa's report and the reasons for the peace accord were supported by a report from Wiremu Kingi Tutahuarangi of Ngāi Tai, who was on the expedition with Te Kēpa. In his report to Major William Mair on 16 March, he stated:

---

* The location of Ngutuoha pā is still shown on topographical maps — it is well elevated on the ridge immediately to the south of the Ngutuoha Stream, just south of Te Urewera Education Lodge (commonly referred to as the 'Lion's Hut' complex).

I wish to tell you that I have been to Tamaikowha's place. We have actually seen him and his companions. Peace was made with him by Major Kemp. Peace is now made with his tribe; there are fifty of his own tribe. It was through this that our force did not go to Maungapowhatu. It would take one night to get from Tauwharemanuka to Maungapowhatu. We came back from Tauwharemanuku.[52]

The news of the peace accord, or rongopai, that had been made with Tamaikōwha, and the fact that Te Kēpa's powerful force had withdrawn without compelling Tamaikōwha and his people to surrender, was a bombshell to McLean and Clarke. It was even more so to Ropata, who had just arrived at Maungapōhatu when news of the rongopai arrived by urgent messenger. The ramifications of the rongopai, in terms of both Ropata's expedition and its broader effects among Tūhoe, are addressed in Chapter 5. Yet in the immediate future, of greater significance was the equally surprising news that greeted Te Kēpa on his return — that of Te Kooti's raid on the Ōpape and Ōmarumutu pā. The priority instantly turned to the pursuit of Te Kooti, and the release of his Whakatōhea captives.

DELAYS AT ŌPŌTIKI

The first few days after Te Kēpa's return to Ōhiwa were occupied with trying to establish the route that Te Kooti's forces, and several hundred captives, had taken after the raid on the two pā. Austin's diary entry on 13 March recorded that the whole contingent moved into Ōpōtiki that day, and that: 'Several partys has been trying to find the direction he has taken, but they cannot find out any signs of him or his men.' On 14 March, similarly: 'we cannot find anything as to the whereabouts of Te Kooti as yet.' It was not until 15 March that Austin was able to record, 'They have found the track that was taken by Te Kooti.'

Austin also recorded on the 15th that some men had gone from Ōpōtiki to Ōpape to dig potatoes, in preparation for the pursuit of Te Kooti once Topia returned. On 16 March, as Te Kēpa's men were waiting at Ōpōtiki, the sound of firing was heard from the direction of Ōpape. Te Kēpa marched his whole force in that direction, only to find that it was some of Topia's men shooting. However, at least the two Whanganui forces had finally met up again. Te Kēpa returned to Ōpōtiki, but sent a message to Topia asking him to follow.

On 17 March Austin recorded that rations, including 5 lb of flour per man, were issued for the forthcoming expedition, observing, 'it is a treat to see the natives cooking it'. On the morning of 18 March he recorded, 'We are waiting for Topia to come in with No. 5 & 6 companys', later adding, 'Topia and his men arrived all well this afternoon.'

The various delays that occurred sparked negative comment from the government's critics that was widely reported in the media. It must have been difficult for the government to answer this criticism when the Whanganui Contingent did not appear to be advancing into Te Urewera in pursuit of Te Kooti. The abduction of a whole community of over 200 people, with no apparent response, was bound to raise questions.

A typical example appeared in the editorial of the *Evening Post* of 19 March:

… the recent news from Opotiki justifies the opinion we have repeatedly expressed that the recent operations directed against the arch rebel have utterly failed to render him powerless for mischief. So far from being compelled to seek safety in the mountains from the bands who have undertaken to catch him by contract, he is able to make raids on the coast settlements at his pleasure, killing and capturing whom he chooses, and laughing at the spasmodic efforts made to destroy him. We read — 'He has returned again into the ranges. Kemp and Topia are in pursuit. The Arawas are furious at Marsh's loss.' How often have we heard of Kemp and Topia 'being in pursuit'? But we have never heard of them, overtaking the object they pursued, and never will until different measures are adopted.

… It is worse than absurd — it is insane — to commit the defence of the country to separate bands of Maoris, acting entirely according to their own ideas, unrestrained by any European control.[53]

The practical response from officialdom came from Henry Clarke, the civil commissioner in Tauranga.

COLONEL MCDONNELL'S INVOLVEMENT

Clarke had become very concerned about the actions, or apparent inactions, of the Whanganui Contingent, considering that an attack on the Māori settlements at Ōpape and Ōmarumutu pā had taken place when supposedly large government forces were in that very area. In addition, there was no sign of any immediate pursuit. The decision Clarke took on how to address these concerns, however, was extraordinary. Of all people, he chose to instruct Lt Col McDonnell to go urgently to Ōpōtiki, inspect and report.

McDonnell happened to be still in Tauranga after arriving from Tapapa, so he would almost certainly have received Clarke's letter of instructions delivered by courier on the day it was written, 15 March. The decision was unfortunate because McDonnell was the very man who had been ignominiously dumped by McLean from command of the Bay of Plenty forces less than a month earlier, and replaced by a number of Māori officers of lesser rank, as majors. Now, he had handed to him on a plate a golden opportunity to express his deprecation of those mere majors.

Clarke's letter of instruction was very broad in the parameters it set for McDonnell's report:

> From reports received from Opotiki, it appears that a portion of Te Kooti's followers made a raid upon Opape, one of the Whakatohea settlements in that neighbourhood, and carried off some men, women, and children; but from the very meagre nature of those reports, it is impossible to arrive at a correct estimate of the exact position of matters in that district, or of the operations (if any) being carried on against the enemy.
>
> I have therefore the honor to request, (unless the instructions you have received to proceed to Taupo are imperative), that you would be good enough to visit Opotiki, and from personal inspection and investigation furnish the Government with a full report, so as to enable it to take such measures as will be necessary to prevent further disasters to our allies on the shores of the Bay of Plenty.[54]

Henry Tacey Clarke.
In *Te Arawa*, Don Stafford, 1967.
Source unknown.

McDonnell clearly wasted no time in travelling to Ōpōtiki, Samuel Austin recording his arrival there on 17 March. Austin also recorded that McDonnell left again the very next day. Austin was naturally curious as to what lay behind McDonnell's visit, but he misread his purpose: '18th … Col McDonnell left again for Tauranga, it turns out that his coming hear was to see and get Kemp to let him go into the bush with us, but Kemp would not agree to it.'

McDonnell arrived back at Maketū by ship in the early hours of the morning of the 19th, and completed his report that day. The level of his bitterness and his determination to denigrate his Māori replacements were displayed fully in his report. He gave no opportunity for Te Kēpa or Topia to rebut his criticisms, as he gave no hint of any responses they might have made, and they would certainly have rejected as inaccurate many of his assertions of 'fact'.

A few examples suffice to portray the tone of underlying malice and some of the inaccuracies in McDonnell's report:

> Hori Kawakura of Ngatiawa, Tiwai and Te Ranapia of the Whakatohea, especially the latter, who are mad at the loss of their women, children, and relations, are most thoroughly disgusted with the apathy displayed by Major Kemp. He is, they say, 'Major of eating and fishing, hakas and pukanas.' That this Ope has no chance of falling in with or capturing Te Kooti. Hoani Ngamu, of the Arawa, and others say the same. So do Wi Kingi's Natives; and Kawana Paipai told me they were all at loggerheads. All concur in saying that they are disgusted with Native officers and majors, and that if the information which has been given from time to time to Ngatihau (particularly since the last raid of Te Kooti's) had been furnished to European officers, majors or colonels, they would have acted like men, and Te Kooti might have been caught like a rat, for he was gorged with his late capture of the Whakatohea. …
>
> Topia and Kemp are not pulling together, and the Whanganui apart from Topia's force are much disunited. Kemp has now, he appears to think, full powers and a separate command; just what he has been trying for ever since he served with Colonel Whitmore — I won't say under that officer. He is now eaten up with vanity, and appears to have lost his head, and gives orders to the small tribes, round him, causing much offence. I do not think things are at all improved by the counsels of Sergeant Austin, who is attached to his staff.

In a vain effort to appear unbiased and balanced, McDonnell ended his report with the extraordinary assertion that he had stuck to the facts and had not made comments of his own:

> In your letter, as you merely requested me to obtain, from personal inspection, a report for the Government, I have done so to the best of my ability; but have

refrained from comments of my own, or suggesting any plan of action suitable to the state affairs seem to be in.[55]

A cynic might be forgiven for thinking that McDonnell could hardly have done more to make 'comments'.

Together with his report, McDonnell enclosed a report from Ensign Rushton of the Opotiki Volunteer Rifles, who was equally derogatory towards the Māori commanders. Again, one example suffices to show the similar tone of malice:

> I think it my duty also to state that nothing has been done with the exception of marching up the Waimana, and making peace with Tamaikowha, who has murdered three Natives and three Europeans in this district during the last three years. The force is now at Opotiki, living on Government rations and eating up the cultivations of the Whakatohea, although Te Kooti's track is well known both by Kemp and Topia.[56]

Whakatōhea rangatira also expressed anxiety and complaints that would have caused Clarke concern. They delivered a formal letter of complaint to McDonnell, who forwarded it as another enclosure with his report. After expressing their anxiety and sorrow about Te Kooti taking away their people, the Whakatōhea rangatira turned to their frustrations with the Whanganui Contingent:

> ... and our sorrow has been increased by the fact that, in addition to the loss of our women and children, our plantations and food have been taken by Kemp and Topia Turoa. We should not be surprised if Te Kooti had done this, as he is an enemy, and not one of us. As it is, we have been sufferers at the hands of two parties, viz., Te Kooti, and Whanganui — I mean Major Kemp. On account of these things we are much cast down.
>
> This is another subject we are going to speak upon :— The movements of this war-party seem to me to be conducted in a very foolish manner. We have several times accompanied European expeditions but we never saw anything like this. This is the first time we have seen this war-party; and if it is left to them to follow up Te Kooti, they will never be able to come up with him. As things are, we are very much cast down. We grieve much for our children. ... As it is, we are much cast down, on account of the proceedings of this war-party. By whom shall these our grievances be removed? Should any person hasten to our relief, there may be hope to see the day dawn upon us. It rests with you to put down or remove these evils; and when, that is done, then peace and prosperity will follow.
>
> Friend, Mr. Clarke, this matter is now in your hands. It is for you to remove the evil.[57]

That the Whanganui Contingent had taken potatoes from Ōpape is quite correct, as Samuel Austin had recorded this in his diary. That should not have happened without Whakatōhea approval being sought, but one imagines that Te Kēpa and Topia at that point considered that no Whakatōhea were living at Ōpape, or seemed likely to be returning soon. It is interesting to note that McDonnell did not recommend that steps be taken to ensure that large government forces did not need to scavenge for supplies in this way. It was a repetition of a basic failing of logistical supply for Māori forces (about which Austin had been complaining for over six months) and a failing that McDonnell himself had ignored the previous year with Whanganui up on the Volcanic Plateau.

THE INFLUENCE OF THE RONGOPAI ON CLARKE

By the time Clarke received McDonnell's report he had had further reason to lose confidence in Te Kēpa, having by then Te Kēpa's own reports on the unauthorised rongopai that he had entered into with Tamaikōwha up the Waimana/Tauranga River. On 20 March Clarke sent McDonnell's report on to the Under Secretary of the Native Department in a fairly neutral manner, but he did manage to express his upset at Te Kēpa's peace dealings with Tamaikōwha:

> I have the honor to transmit, for the information of the Hon. the Native and Defence Minister, the enclosed original report from Lieut.-Colonel McDonnell, on the recent successes of Te Kooti in the neighbourhood of Opotiki.
>
> I would draw your attention to the copy of a letter from the Whakatohea chiefs Ranapia and Piahama Tiwai, which is one of the enclosures of Colonel McDonnell's report. And I cannot forbear drawing a marked contrast between the conduct complained of, and the treatment by Major Kemp, of Wanganui of the notorious Urewera murderer and cannibal Tamaikowha.[58]

It remains possible that the firm attitudes Clarke adopted against Whanganui at this time, so heavily influenced by McDonnell's report and its enclosures, were reflected in the way he reported in April on the whole of the later Waioeka events, where he elevated Ropata's and Ngāti Porou's efforts and gave limited credit to Whanganui.

THE WHANGANUI CONTINGENT RECEIVES SUPPORT IN THE PRESS

A more balanced account of why the delays had occurred appeared in a despatch by a *Southern Cross* newspaper reporter from Ōpōtiki dated 19 March, perhaps providing some relief for government officials. The account was published in the *Otago Witness* on 9 April, at about the time news of the later events in the Waioeka reached the mainstream media. It began:

> I am enabled to send you some particulars of the movements of the force under Kemp and Topia, from the time of its leaving Ohiwa Bay until its arrival here on the morning of the 13th. Apart from the value of the details, the account shows that all that has been said about Kemp's indisposition to follow Te Kooti, and to do the utmost to capture him, has been falsely said.*

The reporter then detailed Te Kēpa's march up the Waimana/Tauranga River, his engagements there, and the entry into the rongopai with Tamaikōwha. The account emphasised the fact that all that activity had involved Te Kēpa's force in marching, and some fighting, for days on end in steep bush country as they negotiated a way up a rough riverbed before the rongopai was achieved.

The distance from the old Whakarae pā by Ōhiwa harbour to Tauwharemanuka is about 42 kilometres. The expedition had taken from 4 March to 12 March, with food supplies becoming very short over the last few days. The newspaper article stated that by 13 March Te Kēpa had learnt what detail was available about Te Kooti's raid on Ōpape so he had started for Ōpōtiki at daylight, 'but on reaching Opotiki nothing could be learned of Te Kooti. Topia had arrived a day or two before; and when Kemp reached here Topia was out searching in the neighbourhood.'

The article continued by describing the tracking undertaken over the next two days, 14 and 15 March, and Te Kēpa's frustration at the lack of willing cooperation from local Whakatōhea:

> The Whakatoheas told Kemp that they did not know the country well enough to guide the force up the Waioeka gorge to Te Kooti's cultivations. Kemp replied, strongly, that they ought to know their own country — that he knew his own district thoroughly. This ignorance, real or otherwise, of the Whakatoheas was not likely to lessen Kemp's doubts as to these men; and hearing of a man who was in the neighbourhood of Whakatāne, and who was said to be able to act as guide, Kemp sent for him.

Topia arrived back at Ōpotiki from Ōpape on 16 March, according to the report, 'but he brought no news.' On 18 March the guide who Te Kēpa had been waiting

---

* *Otago Witness*, 9 April 1870, p. 7. At that time the *Southern Cross* was a weekly newspaper published only on a Saturday. The article may have appeared in the *Southern Cross* on Saturday 25 March but that copy is not held by Papers Past. It did not appear in the *Southern Cross* on 1 April or 8 April.

for finally arrived from Whakatāne, and the article concluded by saying that on 19 March:

> There were not sufficient rations in Opotiki to enable the force to go into the bush; but fortunately this morning the Sturt came in with a supply of biscuit, &c. I can only add that, it is not at all improbable Kemp will to-morrow morning go into the bush, and that he and his force are certainly in good spirits, and seem most anxious to kill or capture Te Kooti.

On 19 March Austin had entered in his diary: 'Under orders to march tomorrow morning after Te Kooti.'

It had taken 12 days after Te Kooti's raid for the Whanganui Contingent to join up together, to ensure it was properly provisioned, and to become adequately informed about where it was to head. In political terms, that was too great a delay for Henry Clarke, the civil commissioner at Tauranga.

TE KĒPA MEETS WITH ROPATA WAHAWAHA AT ŌHIWA

Despite the Whanganui Contingent being ready to head away at first light on 20 March, yet another urgent complication now arose.

Austin's diary entry for that day commenced:

> 20th Fine again. An orderly came in to camp this morning with a report that there was a great number of natives at Ohawe, which he took for Te Kooti and his men. Kemp fell in 200 men and marched at once to see who they were as he thought it might be the chief Ropata and his men that had come through the bush. We have all packed ready to march since daylight. At 5 p.m. Kemp and Topia returned to camp from Ohawe as those natives seen, turned out to be Ropata and his men which had arrived.

Thomas Porter's contemporary account in the diarised report that he sent to McLean before heading up the Waioeka recorded:

> 20th March, Sunday.— Reached the crossing at Ohiwa this morning ... We found Major Kemp there, with some of his men. After having eaten a welcome meal of kumaras, maize, &c, we had some talk with Kemp, who was then leaving for Opotiki, he promised to meet us next morning. Te Kooti is supposed to be at Waioeka. We intend to be on his track at once.[59]

Nearly 45 years later Porter wrote a similar account of these events that was published in the *Auckland Star* of 6 June 1914:

At Ohiwa, Bay of Plenty, we overtook Major Keepa's force, which had remained inactive some days, but which was spurred to activity now on hearing from Major Ropata that we knew the whereabouts of Te Kooti, and were marching at once to attack him. Moving on to Opotiki Kemp's force marched by the Otara route ...[60]

However, strangely, an account that Porter wrote in 1897 for the *Poverty Bay Herald* provided a much more 'racy' account of what happened at Ōhiwa. This account was republished in book form in 1923, in Porter's book on Ropata Wahawaha's life. Porter's slurs in this account not only reflected on the reputation of Te Kēpa, but also besmirched the reputations of Te Arawa and Ngāti Tūwharetoa. His 1897 account read:

At this pa of the Arawa they found Major Keepa with part of his force comfortably quartered in camp, well rationed, and wasting valuable time. Ropata, still feeling indignant at the miscarriage of the expedition so far by reason of Keepa's treaty with the Urewera, used very strong and taunting language to the chiefs of the West Coast division, accusing them of being half-hearted, calling them Kupapas (waverers), and stating that though his men were footsore, hungry, and tired, he would next day march to attack Te Kooti unaided. Major Keepa, who had proved his courage and loyalty during the West Coast fighting, took the taunts to heart, not caring to cast blame upon the chiefs of the Arawa and Taupo tribes allied with him, whose laggard movements had trammelled his actions. ... Spurred to action by Ropata's plain speaking, Keepa struck camp, and marched at 3 a.m. to rejoin the remainder of his force at Opotiki, intending to get ahead of Ropata and retrieve his laurels. It was a matter of severe reproach that at the time Keepa's force was inactive Te Kooti descended upon Opape.[61]

There was no basis in fact to most of Porter's assertions, which were made in this account for the first time 27 years after the event. It was the beginning of Porter's consistent distortion of history.

Te Kēpa's and Topia's force had specifically travelled out the 10 km to Ōhiwa to protect the small Arawa force that was based there from a perceived threat. It was not 'comfortably quartered in camp' there; it had been provisioned and prepared that very morning to head out into the upper Waioeka from Ōpōtiki. Nor had Arawa or Ngāti Tūwharetoa 'trammelled' Te Kēpa's actions at all. And nor had Te Kēpa been 'inactive' on 7 March when Te Kooti attacked Ōpape. In fact, on that day he was two days' travel away from Ōhiwa, about 42 kilometres up the Tauranga River valley intending still to engage Tamaikōwha at Tauwharemanuka.

Finally on this issue, Henry Clarke's report of 18 April was written after speaking with both Whanganui and Ngāti Porou soon after their return to Ōpōtiki after the Waioeka engagements. As discussed in the Epilogue, Clarke wrote that report with an obvious mindset against Te Kēpa because of the rongopai he had entered into with Tamaikōwha. However, even against that background, Clarke provided an account that again did not suggest any abusive 'lecture' by Ropata in the terms Porter later asserted. Rather, his report was relatively mild:

> At Ohiwa Ropata met Major Kemp, whose protracted inaction can hardly be explained away. Ropata exclaimed, 'Why, I left you here when I went to the East Coast to raise my men, and here you are still.' Ropata arranged to be at Opotiki on the following day.
>
> Kemp returned to his people at Opotiki the same afternoon, and seemed to be infused with a new life, and effectually roused from his late inactivity, it may be presumed, by the vigour displayed by his fellow in arms. He ordered his men to march forthwith in pursuit of Te Kooti.
>
> On arriving the next morning, Major Ropata was astonished to find that the Wanganuis had already left.[62]

Clarke's account, however, did perpetuate Porter's erroneous assertion that Te Kēpa was inactive and had not planned any advance on Te Kooti, when in fact he had planned for just such an advance to occur on the very morning of 20 March. The only reason he had not advanced that day was because he was diverted to the defence of the Ōhiwa redoubt of Te Arawa in response to the report of a large body of unknown Māori fighting men heading toward it.

Where all accounts do agree is that after meeting with Ropata, Te Kēpa returned with his force to Ōpōtiki, arriving there according to Austin's diary at 5 p.m. on 20 March. His men were to have only five hours of rest, as Austin's diary entry for that day concluded: 'The Whanganui natives under command of Major Kemp fell in at 10 p.m. and marched all night so as to get into the bush before daylight.'

5

NGĀTI POROU TRAVERSE TE UREWERA

The success of Gilbert Mair's Te Arawa force against Te Kooti on 7 February, south of Rotorua, had led to Donald McLean's initial discussions with Ropata and some Te Arawa rangatira at Tauranga. That had in turn resulted in the decision to use only Māori forces in the pursuit of Te Kooti in Te Urewera.

The manner in which the government officially recorded that policy was somewhat unusual. It was the first document published on 1 July 1870 in the *Appendices to the Journal of the House of Representatives (AJHR)*, which covered the period from 1 February. The item appeared under the heading 'Further Papers Relative to Military Operations Against the Rebel Natives'. Strangely, it took the form of a memorandum issued by Major Ropata Wahawaha:

No.1

Memorandum by Major Ropata Wahawaha.

The chiefs of Te Arawa and myself have had a consultation with Mr. McLean in reference to all orders connected with the movements of the Native forces at Waikare. It is arranged that the Maori chiefs shall assume the entire command, are to have the management of the military operations, and that they are to make their reports to the Government of the names of the killed and wounded in the engagements in these districts; whether at Waikare-Moana, Ruatahuna, or elsewhere, the same action is to be taken. No Europeans are to take part in any of these movements, lest confusion should arise from there being two different commands; and moreover the Maoris are very impatient, and incapable of obeying and carrying out the instructions or commands of European officers while engaged in field operations.

Tauranga, 11th February, 1870. Na Meiha Ropata Wahawaha

Wahawaha's memorandum had been followed by McLean's formal orders to Major Ropata on 19 February, the same day on which he had written similarly to Major Te Kēpa. McLean's orders left Ropata a very large area of discretion as to the force he gathered, from where he was to source his men, and the route they were to follow:

> This is my word to you: You are to go by the 'Sturt', to make arrangements with your tribe, the Ngatiporou, about going to hunt for Te Kooti and Kereopa, at Waikare-Moana.

Ropata (Rapata) Wahawaha.

Carnell, Samuel 1832–1920: Maori portrait negatives. Ref: 1/4-022027-G, Alexander Turnbull Library, Wellington, NZ

You alone are to have the management and to give orders to your tribe; there will be no European over you. If you should succeed in catching that bad man five thousand pounds (£5,000) will be given to you and your tribe; if you do not, there will be no payment. It will be for you to explain these words to your soldiers.[63]

As noted earlier (see Chapter 2), McLean's orders as to the treatment of prisoners, and his statement that 'evil is to be exterminated', were somewhat ambiguous.

GATHERING OF THE NGĀTI POROU CONTINGENT

Ropata left Ōhiwa on the *Sturt* on 21 February, faced with a series of major challenges that would require all his mana and determination to overcome.

Initial assistance came from McLean and J.D. Ormond, the Government General Agent at Napier, who wrote to a number of rangatira and other government officials or officers to ensure recruitment, shipping and provisioning steps were in place to support Ropata as he gathered his forces. By 19 February the Resident Magistrate at Napier, Mr S. Locke, was able to report on steps he had taken to ensure Ropata had forces waiting for him on his arrival at Te Tai Rāwhiti:

> I have the honor to inform you of my arrival at Poverty Bay on the evening of the 18th. No information whatever has yet been received from Major Ropata; it is believed here that he is in Auckland; therefore I have sent messengers up the coast with letters to Te Mokena, Captain Hotene, and Major Ropata, requesting them to push on with Ngatiporou as quickly as possible.
>
> I have also desired Mr. Campbell, R.M., who goes with his family to Waiapu by the 'Coomerang', to see Ropata and the Ngatiporou chiefs.[64]

Just over a week later, on 27 February, Major Westrup was able to report from Tūranga: 'Major Ropata Wahawaha, with the Natives under his command, started for their destination yesterday afternoon, all the men in high spirits ... The force numbers about 400 men.'[65] (In fact, Lt Porter recorded that the number of men who had assembled at the mouth of the Waipaoa River just southwest of modern Gisborne was 370.[66])

Notwithstanding the official support, this outcome was a demonstration of the phenomenal drive that had always marked Ropata Wahawaha. On 21 February he had been at Ōhiwa in the Bay of Plenty having just completed his discussions with Te Kēpa and Topia, with no accompanying forces. Now here he was, six days later, heading up the Waipaoa River at the head of 370 men collected from Te Tai Rāwhiti.

Lieutenant Thomas Porter (second from left, front) and Tuta Nihoniho (centre back) with other Ngāti Porou.
Photographer unknown, Kohere Collection, from Kohere, R.T., *The Autobiography of a Maori*, Reed Publishing Ltd, 1951

Neither McLean and his officials, nor Te Kēpa and Topia, were to hear anything from Ropata and his men for the next three weeks. They were on their own, heading into Te Urewera on a route that had not previously been penetrated so far by government forces, and they were heading for Maungapōhatu — a Tūhoe stronghold of almost mystical reputation, which no government force had ever reached.

The only readily available accounts of this expedition into Te Urewera are found in the diary of Lt Thomas Porter and the private account of Tuta Nihoniho, a Ngāti Porou rangatira. The latter was written many years later as part of a record of all of Ropata's expeditions; it says little of the approach march, and does not refer to the hard trek through Te Urewera up to Maungapōhatu and down to Ōhiwa.

THE ROUTE FOLLOWED INLAND FROM TŪRANGANUI

Porter's description of the route the expedition followed as it headed inland is difficult to trace because some of the old names have fallen into disuse on modern topographic maps. The first day's travel, however, was a rarity in that it did not involve much distance at all. The first night was spent just after a trying crossing of Te Arei River a few kilometres up the Waipaoa:

Reaching the Arai Stream, we found the tide high, and were compelled to cross the swags upon mokihi*, and the men by swimming. By the time the last of the stragglers had crossed, it was dark. We therefore deemed it prudent to encamp for the night.[67]

Porter included an intriguing comment on the uninspiring quality of provisions supplied to fighting men in those days, and the very heavy weights they were expected to carry, describing in his diary entry for 28 February 'most of the men carrying from 90 lb to 100 lb of biscuits'.

Maungapōhatu

Maungapōhatu is one of the higher areas of the central Te Urewera massif. Heavily bushed, it comprises a large, craggy mountain feature that rises in the form of a horseshoe to over 1360 metres above sea level. The huge Ruakituri catchment cascades off its southeastern side, from which the Ngāti Porou approached it in 1870. Off its northern flanks it gives rise to the large Whakatāne catchment to the west, and the Waimana catchment to the north and northeast.

For centuries hapū of Ngāi Tūhoe have occupied pā on large clearings on the northeastern flanks of Maungapōhatu. It was so distant from coastal enemies, and its rivers and ridges so broken and difficult to traverse, that it was an inviolate refuge for Tūhoe, whose traditional enemies had been unable to attack it.

Its craggy peaks are often encircled by mist, adding to its air of mystery — the true home of Ngāi Tūhoe, the People of the Mists. In the early twentieth century the prophet Rua Kēnana set up his community here, adding to its mystical allure.

The rocky peaks of Maungapōhatu.
Gillian Warren collection, 2019

---

* Mōkihi were rafts made usually of dry flax or harakeke flower stalks. They were able to be constructed relatively quickly by collecting large numbers of dry stalks, bundling them up and tying them in layers with improvised ropes made of flax leaves.

It is plain that Ropata used that first night to set the scene for the approach he wanted to adopt for their mission:

> When all were assembled, after supper, Major Ropata arose, and addressed the taua after the old Maori custom, by relating the deeds of their ancestors, and their own doings in former expeditions and fights. The men always pay great attention to his discourse, and seem to place great reliance upon him. He has great command over his men. In the course of his speech, he told them to consider well before they started on this expedition, as any man falling sick by the way must not expect assistance. He therefore advised those who did not consider themselves able to travel to return at once. Three men only availed themselves of this offer, and left in the morning.

The next few days followed an old route that Ropata had used twice just over a year earlier, in the direction of Ngātapa pā.* On 3 March the expedition arrived at the mid reaches of the Wharekopae River. Porter's diary entry for the following day provides some insights into the practices followed during the march:

> 4th March — Started at our usual hour (5 o'clock) this morning. It never requires a bugle and a number of non-commissioned officers to arouse the men. Their food is always prepared before daylight. With Natives, a man lagging behind is a subject of ridicule to the others. After having marched about five miles a halt was called that the men might rest, during which time Ropata got up and sang three waiatas to the taua, inciting them to bravery.

That night the force moved above the site of the Te Karetu battle of December 1868 (by the Rere Falls) as they travelled toward the headwaters of the Hangaroa River and its tributaries draining part of the northeastern Urewera ranges. Porter concluded his 4 March diary entry, 'To-morrow we commence to ascend the hills and break into the Urewera country, following Te Kooti's track.'

EVENTS IN EASTERN TE UREWERA

The climb into the ranges marked the start of a series of repetitive ascents and descents over the next few days as they headed into and across the headwaters of the Hangaroa River system, into the upper Ruakituri valley. Porter's diary entry for 5 March described a fairly typical day's march:

---

* The Ngātapa pā battle site is different from the modern location of Ngātapa, on the Waikakariki Stream just west of Patutahi, although it is highly likely they may have passed through there.

5th March.— To-day's march has been a most fatiguing one, all up hill; the sun very hot, and no water to be obtained. We were nearly three hours climbing up one hill, from the top of which we looked down upon Ngatapa. Turanganui could be plainly seen with a glass. Hikurangi appeared quite close to us. Looking in a westerly direction, Maungapowhatu was visible, rising considerably above all the surrounding hills, or, more correctly speaking, mountains. Its appearance from a distance is that of an immense white cliff.

Then suddenly, on the morning of 8 March, a partial success was recorded:

8th March. — The men were out last night following the tracks of footprints, and returned this morning, bringing in as captives one woman and four children. The husband had escaped. As on the men getting to the whare of the woman and children they found the husband absent, they laid wait for his return, and warned the woman to remain quiet. They had been concealed for some time, when they saw the man returning with a pig on his back. The woman called out to him 'Haeremai', upon which he stopped and dropped the pig, no doubt thinking it a most unusual thing to be welcomed by his wife in that manner. Some of the men moving, the eldest boy was alarmed, and called out, 'Don't kill Papa.' This was a final warning to the man, who darted off like a deer, and, though fired at, escaped.[68]

The woman's clever use of a formal greeting had plainly saved her husband, at least for the time being, and his escape raised some concern among Ngāti Porou that he could head for Maungapōhatu to warn Te Kooti of their presence. Porter later noted Ropata's pragmatic reasons for dismissing that concern: 'We are afraid the woman's husband may have gone on to that place and given them warning. Ropata thinks not, saying he will follow on our track, seeking the body or blood of his wife and children.'[69]

At the same time, the capture of the woman enabled the Ngāti Porou force to gain some initial appreciation of Te Kooti's likely whereabouts and the numbers of his supporters:

The woman reports herself as one of a bush tribe named Ngatikohatu, having been living out for over eighteen months without any settled abode, and depending solely upon animal food for subsistence. She said that her husband had visited Maungapowhatu some three months previously, to fetch Torori.* He then reported Te Kooti at Ruatahuna, and that 100 of the Urewera were with him.

---

* Described in the Māori online dictionary 'Te Aka' as 'home-grown tobacco, native-grown tobacco' and confirmed orally by Ngāi Tūhoe rangatira Tā Pou Temara as being a reference to locally grown tobacco.

That news supported the general objective of an attack on Maungapōhatu, previously agreed upon between Te Kēpa and Ropata:

> Consequent upon the information gained from this woman, it is our intention to endeavour to surprise Maungapowhatu, and take them all prisoners, so that none can escape to warn other kaingas. ... We hope to get positive information of his whereabouts at Maungapowhatu — if he is not there himself.[70]

The immediate direction now taken was towards Maungapōhatu, but they seem to have taken an approach across country from the lower Hangaroa area by heading overland into the Ruakituri catchment. On 10 March, Porter's diary records, 'We passed Puketapu to-day, where Te Kooti stayed after being followed by Colonel Whitmore. We are camped to-night at the Pa Puni, the site of an old pa.'*

On the evening of 9 March, Porter noted that scouts had returned to camp with five more prisoners — one man, two women and two children. On the morning of 10 March the husband of the woman caught earlier was also captured. By now the increasing number of prisoners must have added to the pressure on food supplies. After 12 days' marching this was becoming a concern, as Porter noted at the end of his entry for 10 March: 'We are still three days' march from Maungapowhatu, and our food is getting short. If we meet with much resistance there, I am afraid that we shall be badly off for food.'

There was an advantage to having the prisoners, however, since they were acting as guides and leading the way through the tangle of ridges and watercourses that lay between them and Maungapōhatu.

THE ASCENT TO MAUNGAPŌHATU

In fact, the guide who led them to Maungapōhatu was the husband and father of the woman and children captured on 8 March. His reasons for agreeing to guide them are intriguing, and were described by Porter in the account he wrote in 1897:

> The husband, a fine-looking fellow, escaped, but was afterwards captured by means of a ruse of Ropata's. At each camp Ropata caused some little article belonging to the family to be left behind, so that the husband and father, who, he said, was sure to follow, expecting to find the remains of his wife and children, might be caught. With this end in view, Ropata left a garment of one of the children behind and planted a small party in ambuscade near. True to paternal instincts, the father came,

---

* Papuni is today the name of a station at the end of the Ruakituri valley road, the homestead of which is close by the old Puketapu pā site, high above the Ruakituri.

and whilst mourning over the garment of the child, he was surprised by the party and captured after offering considerable resistance. Finding his family spared and himself well treated, this man became a most useful guide.[71]

The route the guide took would probably have avoided the potential for difficult river crossings by staying well up the heavily bushed northern ranges of the wide Ruakituri catchment. This assumption is provided with some support by Porter's contemporary diary, in which he noted:

> 11th March. — To-day's march has been a very fatiguing one, climbing some very steep ranges from the top of one of which a splendid view was obtained of the surrounding country. I do not ever remember seeing scenery so beautifully grand. Our track has been up tremendously steep ridges, very thickly timbered. It is from occasional breaks in the forest that a clear view can be obtained of the country around. In a torrent called the Arini, which takes its rise at Maungapowhatu, we saw a beautiful waterfall, with a fall of about 200 feet, and in width about 100, pouring over a smooth papa rock.[72]

It appears likely Porter confused the location of that huge waterfall, which would be understandable if they were climbing and descending up and out of, and back into, sidestreams of considerable size. What Porter called the 'torrent' of the 'Arini' would have been the Anini River, which flows into the Ruakituri not too many hours' walk above the magnificent Waitangi Falls.* These are the only falls in the huge Ruakituri catchment that would have the volume to meet Porter's description of being 200 feet high and 100 feet wide. The falls are indeed as beautiful and impressive as Porter describes, and still can only be reached on foot.

They must have been moving at quite an elevation above the main river (which

---

* The modern Topo map for these falls shows them as being 72 metres high (236 feet).

Maungapōhatu pā locations

Porter noted that the area known as Maungapōhatu comprised three separate small pā, which in those days were referred to in combination as Maungapōhatu. One of those he named in his diary was Toreatai (although he spelt it Toriatai), which was the pā attacked by Ropata. Some distance away from Toreatai to the east was a pā called Horoeka, so named because of the profusion of horoeka or lancewood that grew in the locality. This was the pā Porter's group attacked. The other one that he included as being part of a cluster of three pā at Maungapōhatu, without naming it, was probably Te Kākari to the west. Ngāti Porou seized that pā the following year, in February 1871. To the north, but probably too far distant to be regarded as part of Maungapōhatu, was Tauaki pā (which Porter variously spelt in two different entries as Tawika and Taueka).

would have made it difficult for Porter to work out exactly where the Anini and Ruakituri met) because when they stopped for the night of 11 March Porter recorded: 'We are camped to-night in the ranges; our supply of water is obtained from decayed logs, by squeezing the rotten wood with our hands, and catching the moisture in our pannikins.'

They must have camped close enough to Maungapōhatu that night to have had glimpses of the bluffs on the peak in the distance through breaks in the bush, as Porter closed his diary entry with a note of anticipation: 'To-morrow we sleep close to Maungapowhatu, the reputed impregnable pa. Next day we shall attack. I have heard much of bad country and have seen a great deal, but never worse than that we passed over to-day. It is raining ...'

FINAL APPROACH TO MAUNGAPŌHATU

If the weather had been uncomfortable on 11 March, it deteriorated badly as the force made the last long ascent up the ranges towards Maungapōhatu itself on 12 March. Notwithstanding, they were driven on by a combination of the hope of satisfying their hunger at Maungapōhatu and the anticipation of forthcoming action:

> 12th March.—During the whole of to-day's march it has been raining, consequently we are all miserably wet. Our track still lies through a dense bush and along the beds of mountain torrents, and it has been almost as dark as night. ... Our food is now getting short. We are in hopes of getting plenty from the enemy to-morrow.[73]

The Ngāti Porou were probably following an old Māori route that later became the modern, roughly marked Rua's Track. When travelling as they were from the east, the route curls in a westerly direction around the northern side of Maungapōhatu mountain. That would have taken them to a location just to the southeast above the various pā known as Maungapōhatu.

Anyone who has spent any time in the more elevated reaches of Te Urewera can attest to the misty effects of high-altitude cloud, rain or drizzle swirling among stunted, heavily moss-laden trees at the altitude of Maungapōhatu. Its height, at over 1360 metres, and its sheer bulk, ensure that it captures high-level rain clouds as they traverse Te Urewera. Ngāti Porou were now entering a type of bush country that was quite alien to their own home areas closer to the coast. Because fires could not be lit for fear of warning Tūhoe, they would have endured a miserable night on 12 March.

SEIZURE OF MAUNGAPŌHATU PĀ

On the morning of 13 March the force was divided in preparation for the assaults on the various Maungapōhatu pā, with Ropata leading one ope to attack Toreatai, and Porter Horoeka. Porter's approach to Horoeka pā went unnoticed by its occupants, and he later noted: 'I then deemed it advisable to surprise at once. We then charged from all sides, and took them completely by surprise, without firing a single shot; number of prisoners taken, forty.'

Some firing was then heard coming from Toreatai, but it took some time for Porter's men to reach Toreatai to provide support:

> Firing was then heard in the direction Ropata had taken to Toriatai. I then felt anxious to rejoin the main body, as I found the support of thirty men that should have followed us had not done so. It was arranged between myself and Ropata that no shots were to be fired, unless in the event of any of the prisoners trying to escape. Just after starting, we saw, at a pa called Tawika, a flag flying, which we supposed to be Major Kemp's.* Before reaching the position of Ropata at Toriatai, firing had ceased. On getting to that place, I found the main body cooking food in umus. Ropata then informed me that on approaching the pa they found it evacuated, but some of the men afterwards going out for food, were fired into by the enemy, killing one of our men, named Pene Kerikeri, the ball having passed through his brain. The men were at once in pursuit, but could not succeed in getting any of the Hauhaus.

Porter's diary account the following day seems to have been made after an ascent to the summit of this mountain, which was sacred to Ngāi Tūhoe:

> 14th March.— We are now encamped at the celebrated Maungapowhatu — the first war-party that has ever penetrated so far. The Ngapuhi could not succeed in getting here in days when they ravaged the Island. The mist and clouds have now cleared away, and we can obtain a splendid view of the surrounding country. Maungapowhatu is not what it has hitherto been represented to be, nor yet what it appears from a distance — a mountain rising from amidst a number of lesser ones. It is the termination of the highest range in the centre of the Urewera country. Maungapowhatu is a perpendicular rock, of about 500 feet in height, on the summit of which is the original pa, which has for many years been abandoned.
>
> There are now three small pas lying upon terraces, separated by deep gullies, yet all forming part of Maungapowhatu itself.

---

* The reference to 'Tawika' must be to Tauaki pā, which lay at the northern extremity of the Maungapōhatu group and hence was closest to the direction from which Te Kēpa's forces might be expected to arrive.

NEWS OF THE RONGOPAI REACHES ROPATA'S MEN

On the night of 13 March, after Ngāti Porou had captured two of the three pā at Maungapōhatu, Porter recorded that they had heard a weapon being fired in the dark:

> At night a gun was fired from the top of a range in front of our position, and a man called out that he was bringing a rongo pai (news) from Major Kemp, and telling us that it was to Major Ropata, and that he came from Major Kemp, who was at Tawhana. We called to the man to come in, but he was evidently afraid. Some men went in search but could not find him.

It is likely that the reference by their unknown visitor to his bringing a 'rongo pai' from Major Kemp would have been regarded as a Tūhoe ruse. However, events the following day indicate the deep upset the more definite news of the rongopai between Te Kēpa and Tamaikōwha caused to Ropata:

> Among the prisoners taken yesterday is a Urewera, proper name Iharaia Motu, whom Ropata had sent out to the tribe, telling them to give themselves up to us. He had not been gone long before he returned, having met a kokiri of Ureweras coming to attack us.* The chief of the party, Ihaka Whareraupo, getting Ropata's letter, returned an answer telling us they had received a flag of truce from Major Kemp, who had gone back from Tawhana, and that they would adhere to the terms if we returned to our wives and families at once. We have been greatly perplexed by this rongopai. Ropata is greatly annoyed at the steps Kemp has taken, but is determined to keep what prisoners we have already taken. We are now determined to march towards Tawhana to get correct information of Kemp's doings.

The Ngāti Porou force remained at Maungapōhatu the following day awaiting replies to messages Ropata had sent out to Tūhoe. As they waited, the men remained alert: 'We expect an attack to be made upon us, not knowing if Te Kooti is in the neighbourhood or not. Raining all day and frightfully cold.' On 16 March, with no replies having been received, Ropata decided to continue north to cross over the ranges and descend the Waimana River to Ōhiwa to meet up with Te Kēpa.

DEPARTURE FROM MAUNGAPŌHATU FOR ŌHIWA

Once again Porter's diary records Ropata's intense frustration at having to adhere to a rongopai as he passed through Tūhoe's rohe, when Ngāti Porou had

---

* Kōkiri, as used here, can mean a small war party.

made such a major effort to traverse the eastern Urewera and gain possession of Maungapōhatu. Porter recorded only a few shots being fired as they left:

> 16th March.— Left Toriatai going in the direction of Taueka, where we saw the white flag flying.* Expect to get information there. ... A short time after our leaving, a few shots were fired in our rear — no doubt by some of the enemy, who watched our departure. When we got to Taueka Pa, we found it deserted, and a letter left for Ropata from Kemp, ... Kemp tells us that he has left with the Urewera a rongo pai, and wishes us to respect it, and to follow on and join him as soon as possible. ... Ropata sent more letters to the Urewera, warning them not to protect Te Kooti if he returned to them. He also told them that he would respect the rongo pai this time, but not to let him come again.

It would seem that the march that day was very short and ceased at Tauaki pā, which lies only about 5 km away from Maungapōhatu itself, on the northern side of the Waikare River. This was probably to enable Ropata to confer with his senior leaders as to the force's next movements, and to write the threatening letters to Tūhoe that he issued from there. Once the decision had been made to head over to the Waimana and Ōhiwa, time was also needed to prepare for the long walk out to the Bay of Plenty.

On 17 March the usual early morning start was followed by yet another long ascent, this time followed by a long downhill gradient all the way down the Waimana. The initial observation in Porter's diary entry assumes some significance given his later, more dramatic accounts of what happened on the trip down the Waimana/Tauranga river:

> 17th March.— After leaving camp this morning, we ascended a range which took us exactly seven hours in reaching its top. We captured a prisoner here, who told us he was one of Tamaikowha's men, and intended going to join his chief, who had proceeded to Ruatahuna, with rongo pai to Urewera. On the evening we reached Tawhana, the pa of Tamaikowha ... Our march for to-morrow will be along the bed of the river leading into the Waimana. We make a forced march to-morrow. We had some pork to-night, which was the first piece of animal food we had tasted for a fortnight.[74]

The high ridgeline route the Ngāti Porou men followed is still a marked track. Once they had made the long descent down the northern ridgeline they would have descended the gentle Tawhana Stream to its junction with the Waimana/Tauranga River at Tawhana pā.

---

* Taueka refers to Tauaki pā, to the north of Maungapōhatu.

Tamaikōwha's
pā — probably at
Tauwharemanuka
but possibly Tawhana.
Scott, A.E.
Ref: PAColl-1894-3,
Alexander Turnbull
Library, Wellington, NZ

As Porter had predicted, on the following day the Ngāti Porou force left extremely early for a long forced march that lasted until late afternoon. Once again this contemporary diary entry is notable for the lack of any drama, and very different from the version of events that appears in the account he wrote 27 years later, as described in Chapter 4. In his diary, Porter wrote:

> 18th March.— Left Tawhana at 2 o'clock this morning, marching through the bed of the river nearly all the way, many parts of which are very deep, and the boulder rocks very trying to the feet. Our march to-day has been fifteen hours; some of the men were quite knocked up. We are also now very short of food. Two men were obliged to be carried. Our camping place to-night is at Te Punga.*

To reach the hill location Te Punga (or Te Ponga) from Tawhana involved a walk of close to 20 kilometres through rough bush country, with many river crossings. (Today, an easy, well-formed track follows a high-level terrace past many of the trickier crossings.) Significantly, about a quarter of the way along the route they would have passed Tauwharemanuka, Tamaikōwha's pā — where Tamaikōwha had met with Te Kēpa and his Whanganui Contingent about ten days earlier, and agreed upon the rongopai.

---

* This location was spelt Te Ponga in some accounts and Te Punga in others. It is not marked on modern topographical maps, but in his book *Te Waimana: The Spring of Mana*, at p. 130, Jeffrey Sissons locates it on the peninsula-like spur between the Waiiti Stream and the Tauranga River, immediately south of their junction. It was the site of an indecisive engagement between Tamaikōwha and Lt Col St John just over two years earlier, on 11 March 1868. It was also known as Panewhero.

DID ROPATA MEET TAMAIKŌWHA AT TAUWHAREMANUKA?

Porter's contemporary diary account of this day, 18 March 1870, made no mention of Ropata encountering Tamaikōwha at Tauwharemanuka. The passage quoted above is the complete entry for that day, which he forwarded some weeks later to McLean under cover of a letter dated 28 April.[75] The original diary entries for 16 to 20 March were forwarded as part of Porter's report to McLean on 21 March, before heading up the Waioeka. In these, he stated:

> 16th March.— The Urewera was here released by Ropata at Taueka. We have since heard it was he who murdered Bennett White, and took him to Maungapowhatu to eat him.
>
> 17th March.— Captured two of Tamaikowha's men, but were afterwards compelled to release them. Tawhana, Tamaikowha's Pa, was abandoned when we approached it.
>
> 20th March.— Reached Ohiwa. Ropata saw Kemp at the pa.

However, in the series of articles Porter wrote for the *Poverty Bay Herald* in 1897, a series he wrote for the *Auckland Star* in 1914, and in his book on Ropata Wahawaha's life published in 1923, he made much of a supposedly heated encounter between Ropata and Tamaikōwha at Tauwharemanuka on 18 March. That dramatic account has been repeated by a number of historians ever since (as discussed below).

In each of the three later accounts Porter also described a long-running assault by Tūhoe on Ngāti Porou on 16 March as they headed for Tauaki pā and up and over into the Waimana catchment. Yet there was no mention of such a pursuit in either of Porter's contemporary diary accounts of 16 or 17 March. The only other reference to any firing came several days later on 19 March, as they reached Waimana itself before crossing the Ōhiwa harbour to the Arawa redoubt. Of that event, he noted in the account published in 1870: 'Just before getting to the Waimana this morning, a shot was fired in our rear, doubtless by one of Tamaikowha's people, who had watched our march.'[76]

The *Poverty Bay Herald* account published in 1897 was the first of the more colourful versions, in which Porter now asserted for the first time:

> On the force advancing from Toreatai, the Urewera attacked front and rear in their characteristic mode of warfare before referred to. Ropata commanded the rear guard, which was the most harassed, and the narrator the advance. Having to fight their way a good distance, the party succeeded in traversing the country, and reached the headwaters of the Waimana, where straggler's of Tama-i-Koha's

people confirmed the news of the treaty made by Major Keepa's column. Meeting the chief Tama soon after, a long and angry talk was indulged in between Ropata and he, ending ultimately in peace and promise.[77]

A similar but even more dramatic account was published in the *Auckland Star* in 1914, and these assertions were repeated in Porter's 1923 book on the life of Ropata Wahawaha.[78]

However, the critical point is that in writing the series of newspaper articles 27 years and 44 years after the events Porter must have overlooked, or forgotten, an aspect of the contemporary diary entry he made on 17 March 1870 about their ascent from Tauaki pā. In his original diary he recorded: 'We captured a prisoner here, who told us he was one of Tamaikowha's men, and intended going to join his chief, who had proceeded to Ruatāhuna, with rongo pai to Urewera.'[79] It is clearly a matter of fact that when the Ngāti Porou passed through Tauwharemanuka, on the very next day, 18 March, Tamaikōwha was no longer there. It is entirely understandable that Tamaikōwha would have wished to carry the vital news of his rongopai with Whanganui to the Ruatāhuna rangatira. And his absence from Tauwharemanuka would explain the lack of any mention in Porter's contemporary diary of a meeting between Ropata and Tamaikōwha.

Many years after these events Ropata himself wrote a lengthy account running to over seventy pages in te reo Māori about his involvement in the East Coast campaigns. It culminated in a detailed account of his pursuit of Te Kooti in Te Urewera, but there was no mention of any meeting with Tamaikōwha at Tauwharemanuka. Ropata recorded that on reaching Tauaki pā they had taken captive a Hauhau man who told him Tūhoe had dispersed among the ngāhere (bush); Ropata had released the man, telling him to go back to his kāinga. His account then continued:

> Ka tae ki Tawhana, ka mau ano tetahi Hauhau, pera ano te tikanga me to te tuatahi; tae noa ki Tauwharemanuka pera ano te tikanga me o te tuatahi.
>
> I tetahi ra ka puta ki Ohiwa; i reira a Te Keepa ratou ko tona ope e tatari ana mai, a no te ahiahi ka hoki atu a Te Keepa ma ki Opotiki ...[80]

This can be translated as:

> We then arrived at Tawhana where we captured another Hauhau who had the same approach as the captive encountered at Tauaki. At Tauwharemanuka the approach seemed to be the same.
>
> The next day we arrived at Ohiwa where Te Kēpa and a group of his men were waiting, but in the afternoon Te Keepa and his men left for Opotiki ...

From Ropata's account, it appears that since Tūhoe had dispersed from their kāinga and pā, Tauwharemanuka had no occupants in March 1870. It is possible that when Porter wrote of this 1870 'meeting' decades later, he may have conflated these events in his own mind with others a year later, when Ropata did meet with Tamaikōwha at Tauwharemanuka. In light of these discrepancies, Porter's later account of events at Maungapōhatu and after the Ngāti Porou had left it is fanciful.

Nonetheless, this account was taken up and repeated by the respected historian Judith Binney in her books *Redemption Songs: A Life of Te Kooti Arikirangi Te Turuki* (1995) and *Encircled Lands: Te Urewera 1820–1921* (2009). In both books Binney noted the lack of a contemporary reference by Porter to the 'meeting' at Tawhana, but appears to have overlooked the fact that this was because, as Porter's earlier diary entry recorded, on 17 March Tamaikōwha was actually at Ruatāhuna, not Tawhana or Tauwharemanuka.

In *Encircled Lands*, Binney wrote in definitive terms about this so-called 'meeting':

> On 17 March, Ropata found Tamaikoha at Tawhana. There are no contemporary accounts to indicate what happened, but Porter's retrospective history is clear: there was an angry passage of words between Ropata and Tama-i-koha almost leading to an open fight. But, in the end, Ropata continued to respect the peace.[81]

Unfortunately, Porter's seriously questionable accounts have come to capture the historical record, notwithstanding their demonstrable flaws.

HOW MANY PRISONERS WERE TAKEN?

There are other clear inaccuracies in Porter's later accounts, such as just how many prisoners were taken by the Ngāti Porou force. In his contemporary diary he records that as they started the final ascent towards Maungapōhatu they had with them as prisoners two men, three women and six children — a total of eleven prisoners. In his diary entry of 13 March, when they took Horoeka pā, Porter recorded: 'We then charged from all sides, and took them completely by surprise, without firing a single shot; number of prisoners taken, forty.' After meeting up again with Ropata at Toreatai, he notes, 'Ropata then informed me that on approaching the pa they found it evacuated …'

Based on Porter's figures, as at 14 March the total number of prisoners was at most 53. Over the next few days several more prisoners were taken, but a few others were released with messages for Tūhoe. This figure coincides closely with the number of prisoners held by Ngāti Porou that Henry Clarke reported on 18 April, after the Waioeka engagements, when he recorded:

> [Ropata] at once gave orders for his people to march by the Waimana river to Ohiwa. This he did in forced marches, arriving at Ohiwa in two days and a half. The march from Turanga was accomplished in twenty days, which is a clear proof that not much time was lost, considering that the force was encumbered with above fifty prisoners, men, women, and children.[82]

And later in Clarke's report, 'Ropata carried with him the fifty prisoners he had taken in his expedition, with the intention of looking after them until the country was more settled.'[83]

Yet 27 years after these events, Porter wrote in his *Poverty Bay Herald* article: 'By a flank movement, the right division at daylight next morning completely surrounded the pa Horoeka, and by a kokiri (charge) rushed through the gates, capturing all within without a shot being fired. The total number of prisoners taken was 93 ...' The figure of 93 prisoners was not explained, but Porter repeated it in his *Auckland Star* article in 1914, and in his book on Ropata's life, published in 1923.

The most conclusive contemporary account was contained at the end of a short report Ropata himself sent to McLean from Ōpōtiki on 21 March, which was the day they headed up the Waioeka. Ropata concluded that report by saying:

> I have also to inform you that the captives are suffering from the effects of cold. There are twenty-four adults, male and female; and twenty-five children, male and female. They require blankets, shirts, trousers, gowns, and calico; also some spades with which to cultivate ground for food.

Ropata's prisoners at this stage, then, totalled 49. It is plain from the contemporary records — Porter's own diary entries, Clarke's report, and most conclusively Ropata's report to McLean — that the figure of 93 prisoners that Porter later used was completely wrong, and in fact was nearly double the actual figure. Nonetheless, once again Porter's figure was taken up and repeated by James Cowan in 1923 in his book *The New Zealand Wars*: 'There were ninety-three prisoners, about half of whom were women and children.'[84] Even more clearly than the supposed meeting between Ropata and Tamaikōwha, the almost doubling of the number of prisoners taken shows Porter seeding the historical record with demonstrably inaccurate material.

NGĀTI POROU ARRIVE AT ŌHIWA AND ROPATA MEETS WITH TE KĒPA

The final evening the Ngāti Porou spent in the mid Waimana/Tauranga River area was 18 March, at Te Ponga, or Te Punga, at the junction of the Waiiti Stream and the Tauranga River. From Te Punga, another long, hard riverbed walk took place on 19 March, the intention being to reach Ōhiwa that day. However, the physical state of the men was by now so depleted that they camped just short of the crossing over the harbour to the Ōhiwa redoubt of the Arawa. Notwithstanding their fatigue, they still had the energy to perform a celebratory haka on emerging at last from the bush-clad Te Urewera after three weeks of hard walking. Porter's diary recorded:

> 19th March.— Our march to-day has been another very fatiguing one; men all very foot-sore and hungry. My food to-day was some biscuit-dust and kauka tree roasted.* Our track has been through the bed of the river all day. When reaching the plain leading from the Waimana to Ohiwa, the men were so delighted at the sight of a little open country that, after plunging into the river to refresh themselves, they all joined in a war dance. I myself felt quite refreshed at the sight of a little level country. We expected to have reached Ohiwa to-night, but many of the men were quite unable to walk from fatigue and hunger.[85]

Finally, on 20 March, the weary Ngāti Porou force arrived at Ōhiwa, where they met Te Kēpa. Once again, Porter's later accounts are at variance with his diary entries, so it is worth repeating the entirety of his handwritten diary entry for that day, which he had sent on to McLean on 21 March before heading up the Waioeka: '20th March.— Reached Ōhiwa. Ropata saw Kemp at the pa.'[86]

The diary that Porter forwarded to McLean under cover of a letter dated 28 April 1870, and which was also later published in the *Appendices to Journals of the House of Representatives*, understandably records his relief at finally obtaining a decent meal, but otherwise is best described as bland:

Wiremu Maihi Te Rangikaheke, also known as William Marsh.
Thatcher, Frederick (Rev.), 1814–90.
Ref: PA1-q-232-10-2, Alexander Turnbull Library, Wellington, NZ

---

* 'Kauka' was tī kōuka or cabbage tree.

20th March, Sunday.— Reached the crossing at Ohiwa this morning, but were compelled to wait until afternoon for low water, to allow of our crossing. When we approached Marsh's pa, they mistook us for Hauhaus of Te Kooti.* I fortunately went on in advance, thinking it strange that no one should be about to meet us. When I got close to the pa two men came out to meet me, and asked me who we were? I replied Ngatiporou; upon which the people came out of the pa to welcome us. We found Major Kemp there, with some of his men. After having eaten a welcome meal of kumaras, maize, &c, we had some talk with Kemp, who was then leaving for Opotiki, he promised to meet us next morning. Te Kooti is supposed to be at Waioeka. We intend to be on his track at once.[87]

In 1897, however, Porter described the meeting between Ropata and Te Kēpa at Ōhiwa in far more dramatic terms for his article in the *Poverty Bay Herald*. Once again, this version of events was repeated word for word in his 1923 book on Ropata Wahawaha's life:

Ropata, still feeling indignant at the miscarriage of the expedition so far by reason of Keepa's treaty with the Urewera, used very strong and taunting language to the chiefs of the West Coast division, accusing them of being half-hearted, calling them Kupapas (waverers), and stating that though his men were footsore, hungry, and tired, he would next day march to attack Te Kooti unaided.[88]

If Ropata had used such strong words, one would expect at least one of Porter's two contemporary diary accounts to record that fact, as it would have been a very tense and extraordinary event between the two commanders who were about to head off up the Waioeka in alliance with each other. One might also have expected Samuel Austin to have recorded the exchange, just as he had when Topia spoke harshly to Topine Te Mamaku in the Whanganui River. No such entries were made at the time by either diarist.

Once again, however, Porter's later account has become the historical record, as demonstrated by the description in Thomas Lambert's detailed *Story of Old Wairoa and the East Coast* published in 1925, two years after Porter's book on Ropata. Lambert states, 'When Ropata reached the Bay of Plenty and met Kemp there were angry words between them ...'[89] It is a description that simply does not accord with any of the contemporary accounts.

---

* As noted earlier, Marsh was the name commonly used by Pākehā for Wiremu Maihi Te Rangikāheke of Te Arawa

NGĀTI POROU ARRIVE AT ŌPŌTIKI

On the afternoon of 20 March, after the meeting between Ropata and Te Kēpa at Ōhiwa, the latter took the 200 men of the Whanganui Contingent back to Ōpōtiki, Austin recording their arrival there at 5 p.m. The following day, Porter's handwritten diary recorded Te Kēpa's movements in neutral terms: '21st March.— Reached Opotiki, and found Major Kemp and force had started last night. We march to-morrow for the Waioeka, where Ropata fully expects to fall upon Te Kooti. During our march we could not obtain any information as to his whereabouts.'

Unsurprisingly, Porter's later published diary expanded on how Ngāti Porou felt at finding that Te Kēpa had already left:

> 21st March.— Left Ohiwa at 4 a.m., expecting to get to Opotiki in time for the tide, but getting to the crossing we found the tide well in, and were therefore compelled to cross in canoes. Kemp started away last night, immediately on his return from Ohiwa. He has gone by a track that will bring him on the flank of the pa where Te Kooti is supposed to be. We start to-morrow by the direct track up the Waioeka. Ropata was annoyed at Kemp leaving without arranging some plan of attack. I find that we cannot get a supply of rations until to-morrow, they having been all consumed by the Wanganuis.

Both Ropata and Porter used some of their time on 21 March to send in reports to McLean on their experiences in traversing Te Urewera and capturing the two pā at Maungapōhatu. Ropata stressed the severity of the trip and their privations because of the lack of food. He also requested permission to take the 49 prisoners back with him to his home at Mataahu on the East Coast.* Porter's report essentially took the form of short diarised notes, some of which are quoted above.

Finally, on 22 March, Porter was able to record that Ngāti Porou were on their way to engage Te Kooti directly. They were weary and knocked about, having endured much gruelling travel for over three weeks. They knew they had a demanding river trip ahead of them, but for once they also knew they were heading for Te Kooti himself:

> 22nd March,— Despatches sent to Tauranga reporting our return. I have been busy all day in getting rations for the march. Succeeded only in getting five days' rations, and that partly in potatoes. Obtained two guides for the expedition. At 5 p.m. started, leaving our sick, some forty in number, behind us.[90]

---

* Ropata's home pā of Akuaku was at that time a well-populated location lying just to the south of the high point Mataahu, at the northern end of Waipiro Bay on the flats of Te Maire Stream as it reaches the sea. The location of Akuaku is now devoid of permanent population and is no longer even named on modern topographical maps.

6

WHANGANUI CAPTURE WAIPUNA PĀ

Despite agreeing to wait for Ropata Wahawaha at Ōpōtiki before heading inland, Te Kēpa wasted no time once he, Topia Tūroa and their group of 200 men arrived back there in the late afternoon of 20 March. Their force again included Ngāi Tai under Wiremu Kingi Tutahuarangi, and the young fighting men of Whakatōhea who had all been with Te Kēpa at Waimana when Te Kooti's raid occurred — on this expedition, led by their own rangatira, Piahana Tiwai and Te Ranapia.

Te Kēpa's decision to leave so quickly was a bold one. Some 200 of the approximately 450 men in the column had accompanied Te Kēpa and Topia Turoa on the journey from Ōpōtiki to Ōhiwa and back, a distance of about 20 km. Having arrived back at Ōpōtiki at 5 p.m., they had only a five-hour break before being ordered to head off into the darkness. They were not to stop until 6.30 p.m. the following night.

In addition to the state of fatigue of many of the men, darkness would obviously accentuate the inevitable problems of control and cohesion to be found in such a large force. There was, of course, no ability in those days to communicate along the length of the column. Moreover, the level of discipline was limited, although the force was divided into six companies, which would have enabled a closer level of management by NCOs.

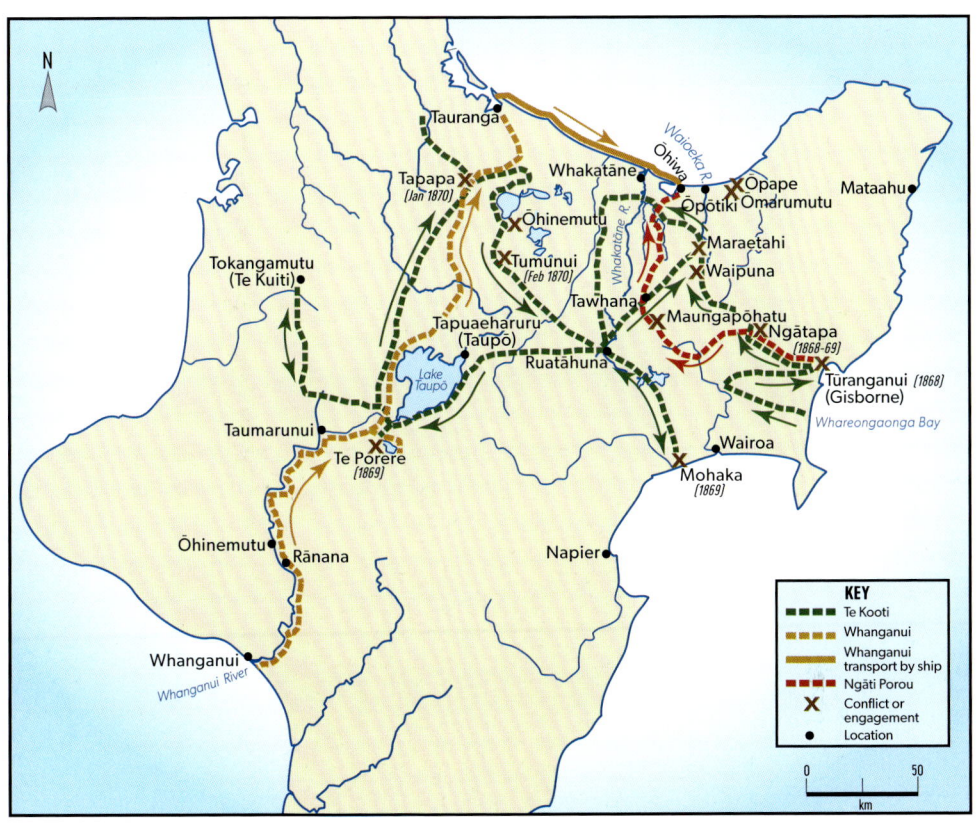

Map showing movements of Te Kooti and his Whanganui and Ngāti Porou pursuers prior to the raid on Ōpape and Ōmarumutu by Te Kooti.

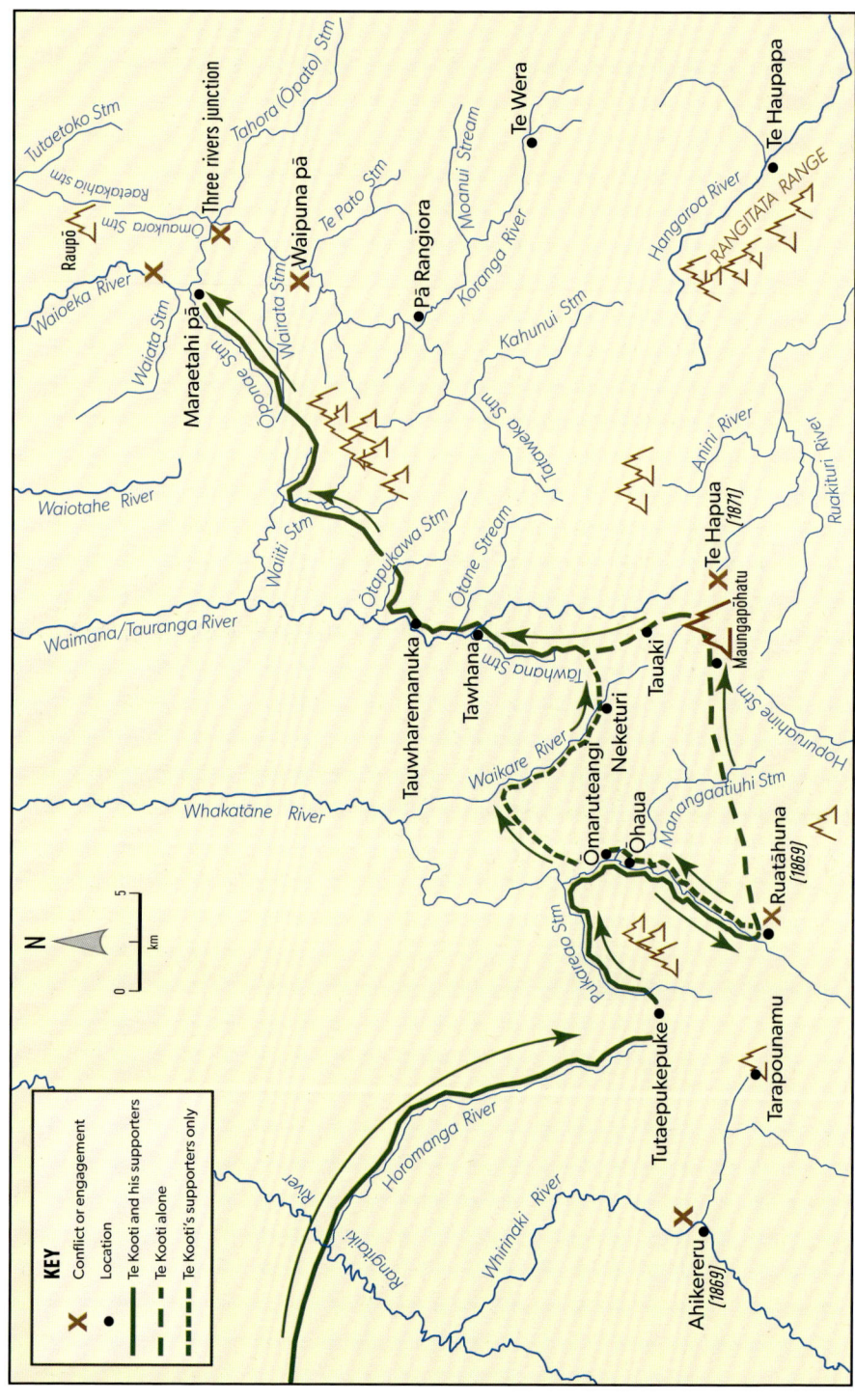

Detailed map of routes taken by Te Kooti and his supporters in February 1870 as they traversed across Te Urewera from west to east to reach Maraetahi pā. (See pp. 50–53, 221–25.)

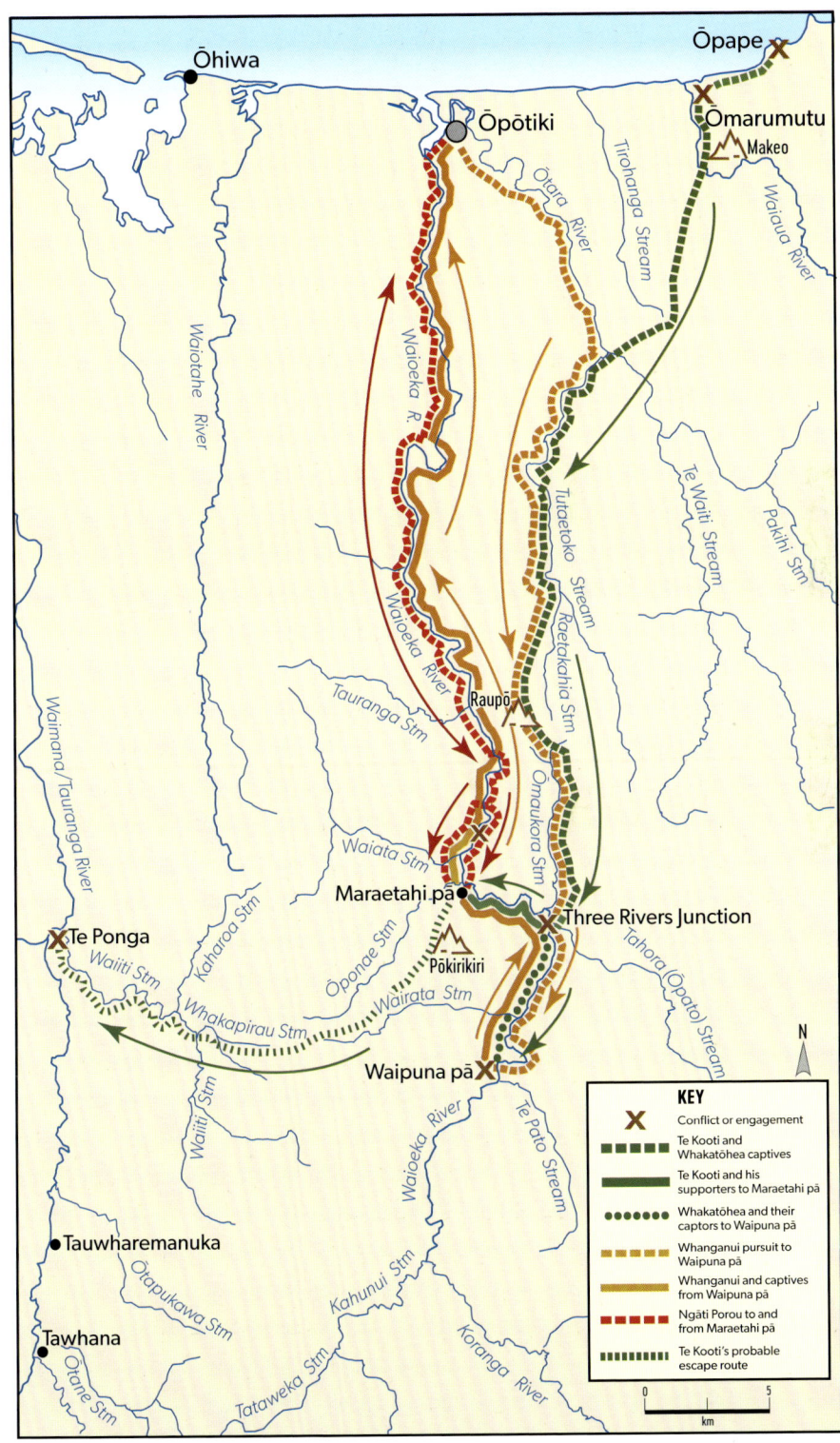

Map showing routes followed by Te Kooti and his pursuers after the abduction of the Whakatōhea communities at Ōmarumutu and Ōpape in March 1870. (See pp. 66–68, 225–30.)

ABOVE *Ōpape marae and kāinga, March 2021.*
Harvey Brunt drone image

RIGHT *Whakatōhea people leaving Ōpape pā and streaming away west along the beach towards the Waiaua river mouth.*
Stu Spicer

ABOVE *Mid Tutaetoko valley looking south — Ōmaukora valley is beyond the highpoint at the centre of the image. The blue arrow indicates the direction of flow in the stream. The dotted line shows the route followed by the Whanganui Contingent in pursuit of Te Kooti. (See pp. 122–23.)*
Chris Gray collection, October 2021

TOP *The view to south of the Ōtara River flats. The Ōtara River is to the left and Tutaetoko valley is at centre right. Ōpōtiki is just out of view at centre right. (See p. 122.)*
Harvey Brunt drone image, March 2021

LEFT *The author and Mark Law heading south up the Tutaetoko Stream towards the Raupō ridgeline (at centre of image).*
Chris Gray collection, October 2021

Raetakahia Stream looking north. Te Kooti's people, Whakatōhea from Ōpape and their Whanganui pursuers ascended the ridgeline to left just past the end of the clearings in the distance. The Bay of Plenty is just visible in the far distance. Ōpape lies on the coast, just beyond the high point to the centre right. (See pp. 123–26, 237–39.)
Stu Spicer collection, July 2022

Raupō ridgeline that Te Kooti's people, their Whakatōhea captives and their Whanganui pursuers traversed en route from Tutaetoko Stream to Ōmaukora Stream.
Stu Spicer collection, July 2022

Waioeka River from south of Raupō peak — Mark Law and Chris Gray with a similar view as that recorded by Samuel Austin: 'when the moon showed out we could see the silver stream below us and could not get at it …'
(See pp. 125, 237–38.)
Author collection, October 2021

Chris Gray and Mark Law on the Raupō ridgeline looking south to Ōmaukora valley, which was the route taken by Te Kooti's people, Whakatōhea from the Ōpape reserve area and their Whanganui pursuers.
Author collection, October 2021

DESCENT FROM RAUPŌ RIDGE INTO ŌMAUKORA

ABOVE *The creek junction in the Ōmaukora Stream where the Whanganui advance party at last obtained a drink of water after spending 26 hours traversing the Raupō ridgeline. They finally descended from a highpoint on Raupō ridge and followed down to the spur marked with the dotted yellow line.* (See pp. 126–27, 238.)
Harvey Brunt drone image, March 2021

LEFT *Looking downriver at Wairata, or Austin's 'three rivers' junction. It is formed by the junction of the Waioeka River, Ōmaukora Stream and Tahora (Ōpato) Stream. The dotted lines show how Te Kooti's group divided. His party moved downriver to Maraetahi pā, while Whakatōhea and their captors moved upriver to Waipuna pā. The site of the day-long ambush by some members of the Whanganui Contingent on 25 March 1870 was probably set on the clear terrace on the true left of the Waioeka River, which is now in grass and marked here with a red cross.*
(See pp. 127, 133–34, 238.)
Stu Spicer collection

LEFT *The view in March 2022 looking south upriver from the top of the elevation just south of modern Wairata, or Samuel Austin's 'three rivers' junction. This is the likely view Whanganui scouts would have obtained by climbing a tree to get a view above the canopy. The probable location of Waipuna pā is marked with the yellow arrow just this side of the central high points on the skyline. The Te Pato Stream catchment is just visible in sunlight to upper left, beyond the cleared spur to upper left. Nikau Flat hut is beyond the craggy ridgeline in the upper centre. (See pp. 127–29.)*
Stu Spicer collection

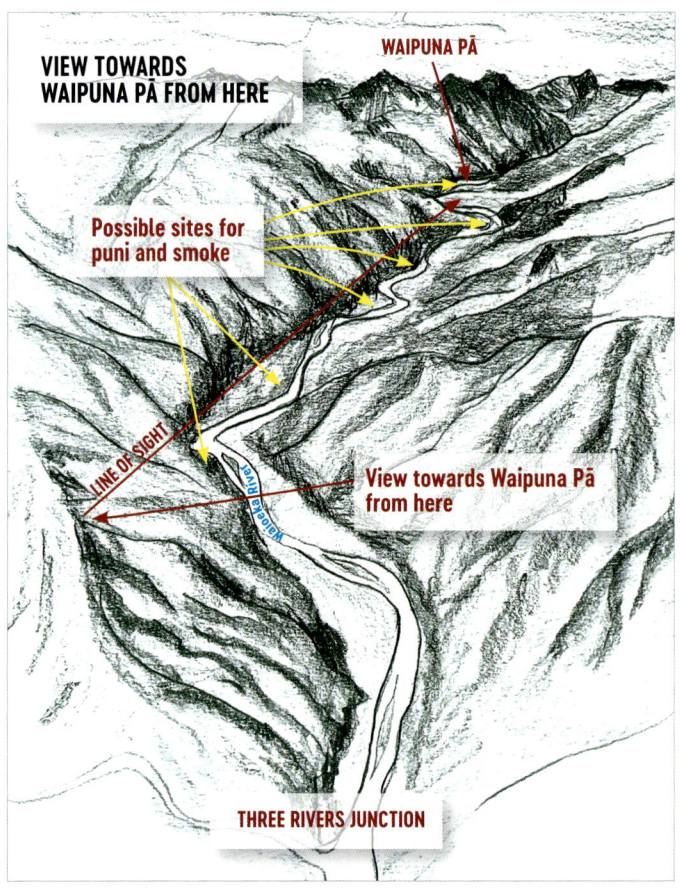

LEFT *Artist's aerial impression of smoke from puni upriver, applying sightlines available to the south from the high point above 'three rivers' junction. (See pp. 128, 242–44.)*
Stu Spicer

Te Piahana Tiwai.
Auckland Museum
PH-1969-33-13

Wiremu Kingi Tutahuarangi of Ngāi Tai.
Ref: 1/2-237012-F, Alexander Turnbull Library, Wellington, NZ

One mitigating factor was perhaps the moon state at the time. It is possible with modern computer software applications to ascertain hours of daylight and moon states, which show that on 20 March 1870 the moon rose at 7.52 p.m.; it was a three-quarter full moon, with full moon having occurred on 18 March.*

Austin's diary entries commence on each morning of 18, 19 and 20 March respectively with the words: 'Fine again', 'A fine morning', and 'Fine again'. It is therefore reasonable to assume that those three days would have had clear skies. A three-quarter moon would have provided a reasonable level of visibility on the evening of 20–21 March, as the Whanganui Contingent moved across the open farmed country of the Ōtara River flats. Visibility would have become reduced as they entered the more enclosed and bushed Tutaetoko valley, but even on those much narrower and smaller river flats the lunar state would have assisted them all the way to dawn, as the moon did not drop below the horizon until about 8.30 a.m.

A LONG PURSUIT

From Austin's diary the route taken by the force can be relatively closely tracked. He refers to their crossing twice what he describes as the 'Opotiki River', which must have been the Ōtara River.** He then continues:

> … after this we struck right into another River running S.E. This one we followed, crossing and re-crossing it untill 10 a.m. when we halted for brekfast. After brekfast we fell in and marched again, still crossing and re-crossing this river. At 2.30 p.m. the countary began to get more open and the hills not so high, or steep. At 4.30 p.m. we came to where the Hau Haus had halted and cooked their food. Marched on and at 6.30 p.m we came to where the Hau Haus had camped for a night. We got some potatoes hear and we camped hear for the night. This place is pretty clear. We came about 15 miles to day. It is a frightful road, we are about 25 miles from Opotiki. Now the name of the [river] we are going up is the Tutae Toka River.***

These few sentences disguise what would in modern terms be described as a truly extraordinary effort. They had started marching in the dark at 10 p.m., after half of them had already walked some 20 km that day. Now here they were

---

* Here the author must acknowledge a deep debt of gratitude to Harvey Brunt, a retired engineer from Auckland, who shares a keen interest in New Zealand history and has researched the daylight hours and moon states for these crucial three days from 20 to 23 March.

** The Ōtara River flows into the Waioeka at Ōpōtiki, but elsewhere in his diary Austin repeatedly refers to that river as the 'Ōpōtiki River'.

*** The name on modern topographical maps for this large stream is the Tutaetoko.

searching for food before a meal and camping at 6.30 p.m. the next day. As the sun set at 5.58 p.m. that day, with darkness falling at 6.18 p.m., they would have had to set up camp in the dark, because the moon did not rise that night until 8.31 p.m. With a pause only for breakfast, they had been travelling continuously for over twenty hours, and had covered about 40 kilometres over rough terrain. Yet as events had proven before, and were to prove time and again during the concluding parts of this expedition, such efforts were apparently accepted as being relatively routine.

Orders for such extraordinary efforts continued to be observed over the following days without challenge or query, an indication of the dedicated loyalty that both Te Kēpa and Topia Turoa had inculcated in their men, and the respect they were given. Indeed, that dedication to duty and observance of orders was to be thoroughly tested on each of the following two days. After this long and taxing day on 21 March, the men were ordered to fall in at 3 a.m. the next morning to prepare for another day's march. At 3 a.m. it would still have been dark, with sunrise not occurring until about 5.45 a.m. The moon state at that early hour of the morning would have been close to three-quarters full and it would still have been high in the sky, so that would have assisted till dawn. The moon's effect on visibility may have been limited that morning, however, even in the open riverbed. Austin's diary entry for 22 March began: '22nd Dull morning and very heavy fog.' The diary continued:

> Had our brekfast at 3 a.m. fell in and marched at 3.30 a.m. once again with the expetation of reaching where Te Kooti is at about 11 or 12 o'clock. We are still keeping in the Tutae Toka river, and had to do so for about 4 miles when we took to another creek and followed this one for 3 or 4 miles when we came to the spur of a large hill and another creek.

This creek, which flows into the Tutaetoko Stream on its western side, is the Raetakahia Stream, which flows parallel to the Waioeka in a south to north direction. A saddle at its head connects over into the Ōmaukora Stream, which flows in the opposite direction, north to south. In due course the Ōmaukora flows into the Waioeka River far to the south.

A VERY TESTING RIDGELINE MARCH

For the Whanganui, the challenge now was to negotiate the ridgeline system they had chosen to ascend on the western side of the Raetakahia Stream, in the belief that it would link over into the Ōmaukora Stream.

The planning behind this route and its choice can be found in a report written some weeks later by Henry Clarke, after he had interviewed both Whanganui and Ngāti Porou rangatira:

> I ought to explain here the lines of march of the two columns. Major Kemp was joined by the Chief Wiremu Kingi, of the Ngaitai, and a considerable number of the Whakatohea, who happened to be absent with the Whanganui when Te Kooti made the raid upon their settlements at Opape.
>
> These counselled Major Kemp to advance on Maraetahi (the pa said to be occupied by Te Kooti and his followers in the Waioweka River), by the gorge formed by the Opotiki River;* after ascending which for a considerable distance, to strike a leading spur of the watershed range which separates the Waioweka and Opotiki Rivers, and to advance along its summit.
>
> The reasons given for this line of march were, that the almost insurmountable difficulties of the Waioweka would be avoided, and all the Hauhau settlements could be turned before the attacking party would be discovered. This route was much the longest, and would take a longer time to traverse.
>
> Major Ropata decided to take the more direct way of the Waioweka River, as he had no time to lose if he was to take part in the fight which it was anticipated would take place at Maraetahi.[91]

Clarke's description of 'a leading spur of the watershed range which separates the Waioweka and Opotiki Rivers, and to advance along its summit' slips readily from the tongue, but in heavy bush country with numerous spur ridges running off to the side of the 'main' ridge the choice of direction to link to the correct ridgeline is not easy (see Appendix 3 for recent investigation of these areas). It is, of course, quite possible that a reasonable guide to the route may have been left by the recent passage of Te Kooti's group of up to 100 supporters and their return with the 218 Whakatōhea.

Austin's diary entry on 22 March makes it plain that while the ascent was difficult, they were able to reach the top of the range by late afternoon, and soon after had notice of the proximity of their quarry:

> We took to the spur of this hill there being a creek on each side of the spur. This was a difficult spur to get up in some parts, one had to pull the other up. When we got to the top it was a narrow ridge. It was 5 p.m when we got to the top and shortly after the advance guard passed word to the main body that they had seen smoak some distance a head. Several of the men went up some of the large trees

---

* As noted above, the Ōtara River on modern maps.

and they seen some huts. Shortly after they heard chopping, as if cutting wood. We moved on until dark when we halted for the night and we could not get a drop of water. And after such a day's march as we had it was frightful to be all night without water, we could not get a drop anywhere. We could hear it running about 3 or 4 hundred feet below us and when the moon showed out we could see the silver stream below us and could not get at it. Guards etc as usual all quiet.

It is almost certain that the huts seen and the sounds of chopping heard that night were located at Maraetahi pā as no other sites of occupation were recorded in that area of the gorge that year. Moreover, the pā location is directly below the line of the ridge west of the Raetakahia along which the column was moving. The highest point on that ridgeline is called Raupō, and it is in direct line of sight to points downriver from Maraetahi. This fits with Austin's reference to seeing the waters of the Waioeka shining like silver away in the distance below.*

Once again, Austin's account somewhat understates the tribulations the group were subjected to that day. After travelling for over twenty hours the previous day, they had woken at 3 a.m., and now at about 5 p.m., with night falling at 6.16 p.m., they had finally stopped. This after a 15-hour day involving an initial significant climb of about 400 metres, followed by many hundreds of metres of ascents and descents along an undulating ridgeline in heavy bush. To make things even worse, they were now benighted up on that high ridge with no water, and being in enemy territory many of them then had to take turns standing watch as sentries for stretches likely to have lasted for two hours. (There is no fixed or recognised 'rule' for the duration of sentry watches as the circumstances will vary depending on risk level, size of force, topography and cover, amongst other factors. However, it is common for sentries to be set in twos, with relief staggered by one being relieved at a time ensuring one man is always fresher than the other. Two hours is evidently a common duration for any one man.)

Yet these two days of extraordinary effort were to be but the prelude to a climactic period that extended well beyond a 24-hour day.

DESCENT INTO THE WAIOEKA AND A SIGHTING

The start to the new day did not augur well for Austin's advance group, with thirst continuing to torment them:

---

* A photograph from one of the few open places on that ridge today is in the colour photos on A6, lower left. It shows the type of view down to the Waioeka in places from the Raupō ridge, and the distance they were from the silver reflection of the river they would have seen, which was so tantalising to the thirsty men.

23rd Fine again. As we had to encamp in two divisions last night it was 6 a.m. before the rear division came up. The reason that we camped in two divisions was the rear division found water and halted where it was and the advance party could find none. So we had to halt where we were and wait for the rear party to come up or we would have marched at 3 a.m. and with this delay it was 8.30 a.m. before we could march, and the advance party was now without water for 19 hours and it is a dense bush and very warm weather.

Again, the traverse along this steeply undulating ridgeline would not have been easy. It would almost certainly have included an ascent and descent up and over the high point of Raupō at 674 metres, and ended with an even steeper descent from about 640 metres down to 200 metres at the upper junction of the Ōmaukora. Austin's diary records:

> About 12 noon we got to a creek and after being 26 hours without a drop of water we now halted and had our brekfast, composed of water, sugar and biscuits, we were not allowed to light any fires. When we got to the bottom of the spur there [were] two creeks, we took the largest one, the which is Maukoro and we kept to it, there is a little flat land hear but very little.
>
> After marching untill 1.30 p.m. we halted for a short time to give the scouts time to look about, as we are now

Artist's impression of Samuel Austin and a Whanganui toa quenching their thirst in the Ōmaukora Stream headwaters after 26 hours without water.
Stu Spicer

on Te Kooti's track. It appears it was down the Maukoro River that Te Kooti came when he left Opapa pa. We again moved on and came to where Te Kooti had camped for a night. 3 p.m. we then pushed on, we had to keep in the river, some times the water was up to our waists. At 4 p.m. we came to the Junction of (3) rivers, two beside the one we came down, the others were the Waiwaka and Tetahora. The advance guard seen a pa or village about one and a half miles from the junction of the rivers.

Austin's 'Waiwaka' is the Waioeka River, and his 'Tetahora' was called the Tahora at that time. On modern topographical maps it is now called the Ōpato Stream. The location of the junction is known today as Wairata.

Austin's description of the scouting tactics of the 'advance guard' used by the contingent raises two possibilities as to how the scouts came to see the pā or village that he describes as being about one and a half miles away. It must be borne in mind that at that time all of this country was heavily bushed right down to the banks of the Waioeka. Moreover, in that area the Waioeka has high banks, commonly 5 to 10 metres or more in height.

It is unlikely that the scouts would have travelled in the riverbed during the day, for the obvious reason that they would have been exposed to the view of any enemy walking along a bush terrace track above. They would also have stayed well off to the side of any riverside track, back in the bush, to avoid surprise discovery by the enemy. Their travel through untracked bush, as they attempted to find a way through without making any noise, all the time keeping their eyes and ears keenly aware for any human movement or sounds, would have been extremely slow.

It therefore seems highly unlikely that they would have had time to scout out as far as one and a half miles in advance of the main group and then bring news back one and a half miles. It is far more likely that they would have been doing exactly what Austin described them doing the day before up on the Raupō ridge, which was climbing trees at high points to obtain a view well ahead, and looking for signs of human habitation such as clearings, huts, pā, puni (temporary camps) or smoke from cooking fires.

Immediately above the junction of the Tahora (Ōpato) Stream and the Waioeka there is a very obvious relatively high point (immediately above the old Wairata school building) which they would have seen as having the potential to provide a clear viewpoint up the valley.

The image on page A8 of the first colour section in this book shows the view that can be obtained from that point today, although it is somewhat misleading as in those days the now green pasture terraces would have appeared as flat areas of heavily bushed terraces. A likely contemporary view is depicted in the colour sketch at the bottom of A8. Scouts would have been able to estimate the distance to the first column of smoke they saw coming from the nearby pā as about one and a half miles. This discovery would have enabled them to reconnoitre the pā more closely, and plan the best method of attack.

A SERIES OF SEVEN NIGHT-TIME ATTACKS

When the exciting news of the sighting was received, the men of the contingent had already been walking for about eight hours. They would now probably have had about two hours of rest in preparation for the attack on the pā while the scouts were sent forward to carry out a closer reconnaissance. Austin and his men would have had a chance to eat and prepare for an assault before the scouts returned with their more detailed intelligence. His diary entry for 23 March continued:

> A halt was called hear so as the place could be reconnitirid after which was done I was sent in charge of (100) one hundred men (See AP.D.) of all ranks.* At 6.30 p.m. we stole quietly up to the pa and entered it, we got (10) women and children, but they would not give us any information as to the whereabouts of Te Kooti. We moved on to another settlement where we got (5) more women and children and two (2) men.

Today there is a small, deeply entrenched pā site in heavy bush cover just over a kilometre from the junction of the Waioeka and the Tahora (Ōpato) on the true right side of the Waioeka River.** The unnamed pā site is protected by deep trenches dug on its eastern, northern and western sides, with the southern side being protected by a virtually vertical riverbank.*** Its location suggests it may well have been the small occupied pā spotted from the hillside directly above.

The attackers obviously waited until just after nightfall, which occurred

---

* 'AP.D' refers to the diary's Appendix D, which is no longer with the diary.

** That is, the right side when one is facing downriver, the 'true' way for the river flow.

*** This impressive pā site was shown to the author and Harvey Brunt in 2020 by Murray and Anne Redpath and their son Dale. It is located in high regenerating tawa and rewarewa bush to the left of the first vehicle track down to the Waioeka past the Wairata bridge. It is not obvious at all from outside despite being immediately adjacent to that access track, and it is next to where a gravel pile used to be situated. Nor is it readily visible from the riverbed, as the riverbed side is a steep rock face. At the time of writing (2022) that rocky face had a deep pool below it, although in low flow the riverbed there is dry either side of the pool.

about 6.15 p.m., before launching their first assault in the Waioeka valley at 6.30, as Austin recorded. The moon did not rise that night until 10 p.m. Given that the moon would have provided some illumination only for the later attacks that night, it can be reasonably assumed the earlier attacks must have relied on firelight from each puni. If the old pā site below the hill was the first location attacked, the next obvious site for another puni or camp settlement with ample flat land for planting crops appears to have been the next terrace, about 400–500 metres away from the pā site. Fires at a puni there would have been clearly visible from the pā site across the broad sweep of a major bend in the river, as well as from the high point earlier described.

From there on a series of terraces, interspersed with spur ridges descending from the east, are today in pasture. Small parts of the terraces close to the river would have been ideal locations to clear for small puni with adjacent māra (gardens), with ready access to river water. The contingent now proceeded to attack each of these puni in turn.

Te Kēpa's later report to Donald McLean described the orders he gave at the junction of the Tahora and the Waioeka after receiving the initial reports of the scouts:

> ... we sent out the scouts; they discovered the enemy encamped. At night I sent forward 120; the officers were Paora, Tapa, and Uruteangina, also Austin, a European. They rushed that camp, and captured all that were in it — eight, four women and four children. After that, I sent out 200, under Mei and Wiremu Kingi;* they got to another encampment, and took the whole. After that the party went out again; another attack was made, and all were taken; after that another and so on ...[92]

In his report, Te Kēpa states that this series of attacks all occurred after nightfall on 23 March. Austin's diary provides the only other detail available as to the sequence of the attacks and their outcome:

> The next place we got one (1) man, two women, & two (2) children. Next place ten (10) women and one (1) man. Next place two (2) women and three (3) children. The next place two (2) men and two (2) children. Next place six (6) men and two (2) women. Four of those men the natives tomahawked as they were belonging to Te Kooti and had taken part in the Poverty Bay murders. One of them had an open gun shot wound in his shoulder.

---

* Te Kēpa identified these two rangatira as Te Meihana of Ngāti Pukeko and Wiremu Kingi Tutahuarangi of Ngāi Tai, later in his report singling them out for praise.

By the end of this series of attacks the Whanganui Contingent had taken one small pā and six puni. Austin records that in total four men had been killed, and 50 taken captive, of whom 12 were men and 38 were women and children. For the occupants of these puni the shock of the assault must have been stunning, as numbers of heavily armed men suddenly burst into their whare or wharau (huts or temporary shelters). Austin makes no mention of any casualties among the Whanganui, an indication of the sudden and overwhelming nature of each of the attacks.

THE ADVANCE ON WAIPUNA PĀ AND ITS CAPTURE

As this series of attacks still revealed no sign of either Te Kooti himself or the Whakatōhea captives, Te Kēpa must have been increasingly wondering where they were located. (The mystery about the exact location of Waipuna pā continues today. Finding a credible location of the actual pā site was one of the most vexing tasks involved in the research for this book, as discussed in Appendix 3.)

Then, just before dawn on 24 March, Te Kēpa received fresh news of major significance from his scouts. The scouts must have very cautiously approached right up to a pā in the dark close enough to see Kereopa and Hakaraia, because Te Kēpa in his later report to William Fox stated: '… when a messenger came to me from Austin, then I sent out 300, because I heard that Kereopa the eye-eater, and Hakaraia the son of Satan, were there. Then that pa, Waipuna, was surrounded.'[93]

The assault on Waipuna pā took place after a whole night of action by the Whanganui Contingent. The walking time alone in daylight to cover the distance from Wairata to Waipuna pā is about three hours, if following the line of the bends of the river or on riverside tracks. But the Whanganui Contingent would have taken far longer than three hours to cover that distance, for a number of reasons: the need to follow either a riverside track or the bush along the riverbank in the dark; the delays inherent in moving a long column of around 450 men in single file, supplemented by, in the end, 50 reluctant prisoners; the need to move quietly at all times, both with scouts out front and to approach each puni extremely carefully to take its occupants by total surprise; and the time required to plan each attack and order appropriately sized forces forward.

The approach to Waipuna pā itself would also have required time and great caution. Crossing the river in the last hour of darkness was obviously hazardous. Even if by then the moonlight was illuminating the exposed riverbed rocks to some extent, it would have been impossible to gauge the depth of the water. The scouts must have very cautiously approached right up to the pā in the dark to have been able to see Kereopa and Hakaraia. Finally, having surrounded the pā in the dark, the contingent settled down to await dawn to launch its assault.

Austin's description of the taking of the pā is brisk:

> 24th After marching all night we came to where the main body was and as soon as it was light we made arrangements to attack the pa.* Just as we moved forward a rebel was seen to run toward the pa, a young native took a tomahawk out of my hand and followed him and tomahawked him before he got to the pa. The Hau Haus had just begun their prayers, we rushed in to the pa. Kereopa and Hakaraia were hear, Kereopa got away, Hakaraia was killed. We killed thirteen (13) men and never fired a shot, and we took in this place two hundred and sixty two (262) men, women and children prisoners.

The capture of the pā, occupied as it turned out to be by about 280 people, and involving a surprise assault by approximately 450 of Te Kēpa's men, would have resulted in scenes of considerable noise and confusion. Te Kēpa later described the scene succinctly in his report to Premier William Fox: 'Then that pa, Waipuna, was surrounded and a general attack was made; it was like a mob of horses racing.'[94] During the confusion some managed initially to get away, the most prominent of these being Kereopa.

THE TOMAHAWK

Today the brutality of war conducted by tomahawk, as described by Austin, can seem shocking. But it has to be seen against a background in which European cavalry used heavy sabres as their standard weapon — whether at Te Tarata near Ōpotiki in 1865; in the Crimean War or the Civil War in the United States of the 1860s; as late as the battle of Omdurman in the Sudan in 1898; and even at times during the First World War. Sabres inflicted wounds as deep and savage as any inflicted by tomahawk. In an age in which close person-to-person combat still sometimes occurred, brutality during military clashes was common.

Notwithstanding, Te Kēpa's own reports, written on 30 March to Premier William Fox and to the Minister of Defence Donald McLean, were somewhat sanitised. The more detailed of the two reports was that made to William Fox. It described the assault on Waipuna pā in matter-of-fact terms:

> The pa was taken; 18 were killed. Of Te Kooti's own force 35 were taken prisoners, 44 women, 30 children. The prisoners of the Whakatohea tribe, who had been

---

* Austin is here referring to the fact that there were more of Te Kooti's people living at Waipuna ('the main body') than at Maraetahi.

taken by Te Kooti, were retaken by me in this pa — 45 men, 77 women, and 74 children. The total number, counting the living and the dead, is 323. The chief who was killed was Hakaraia the son of Satan, of Ngaitapuika. Timoti, who commanded the vessel when they came from Chatham Islands, and Hakopa, a cousin of Te Kooti, were killed. The Chief whose life I spared was Wiremu Kingi of Turanga; the only man who escaped was Kereopa the eye-eater. All these camps, including the pa, were taken in one night.

In the morning I sent out a party to look for Kereopa, the eye-eater; 200 went out. After two days they returned.[95]

Kereopa was not located and escaped west into the Urewera.

One issue that arises in relation to the tomahawk killings is whether they occurred during the actual fighting or later as executions of captured prisoners. The only accounts now available do not provide much definitive guidance on this issue. James Cowan, however, certainly seems to regard some of the killings as executions of political prisoners. Cowan also asserts that a well-known Pākehā scout, Tom Adamson, was with the Whanganui Contingent, and that Adamson 'took a ruthless hand in the execution of the principal prisoners'.[96] This assertion has not been able to be verified from any other source, however, and Cowan himself provided no reference so its truth is doubtful. Adamson's name is not mentioned at all in Austin's detailed diary, or in contemporary accounts by Te Kēpa, Topia or Clarke.

Moreover, in Austin's own petition years later when he sought financial support from the government, and where he detailed all the engagements he was involved in during the New Zealand Wars, he stated that he was the only Pākehā with the Whanganui Contingent in the Waioeka: 'Was present and in command of the natives at the taking of Waipuna Pa where Hakaraia was killed and 20 others of the rebels. … I was the only European present in the engagement.'[97]

PURSUIT

The assault on Waipuna pā was followed up immediately by patrols seeking to capture any others who had managed to flee. Austin's diary described the outcome:

At 12 o'clock we again shot one man, this was the first of the firing. (The tomahawk did the work) and we took 4 prisoners. Shortly after we took another man and four (4) women prisoners. About 2.30 p.m. we got two (2) more men. The name of the pa we took and killed Hakaraia in was Waipuna (I got the flag hear that flew at Gate Pa when General Cameron attacked it in 1865.) It is about 8 miles from Tetahora river.

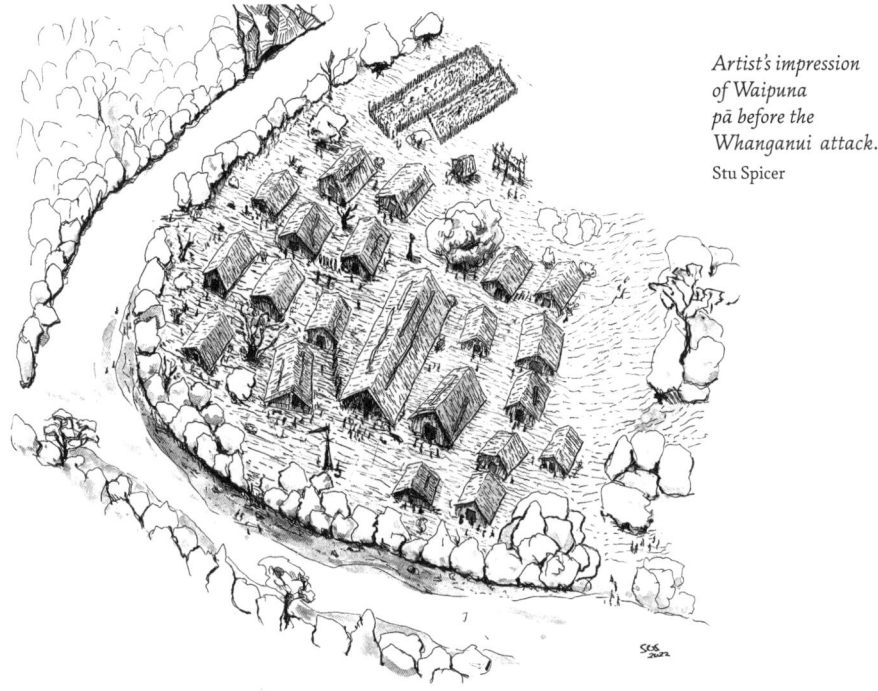

Artist's impression of Waipuna pā before the Whanganui attack.
Stu Spicer

... (8) eight of the men killed last night and this morning were belonging to the party who came from the Chatham Islands and took part in the Poverty Bay murders. At 7 p.m. I had taken (325) prisoners and there was killed 14 men. It came on to rain at 7.30 p.m. so we took shelter in a settlement and I had to pig into a hut with 100 of the prisoners ...

By the time Austin 'pigged' into the crowded whare that night, the contingent had been engaged in marching or fighting for 35 hours without sleep.

A DAY-LONG AMBUSCADE

Austin's diary for the following day records that while the ope Te Kēpa sent out to hunt down Kereopa failed, another ope was a success.

Austin records that an 'ambuscade' of 100 men was set up soon after dawn at the mouth of 'the gorge'. This was probably immediately downriver from the Ōmaukora junction, or perhaps on the terrace opposite and above it on the western side, where Te Tahora pā was noted by surveyors in the late 1890s. His diary entry reads: '25th Fine again but dull. A party comprised of 100 men went out at daylight to lay an ambuschade as Te Kooti's men are expected to come up the gorge.'

The river below Waipuna pā is an area of the Waioeka valley with large terraces on both sides. In that approximately 8-km stretch the river has broad, open riverbed areas with reasonable crossing places all the way down to the Ōmaukora junction. It is only downriver from the junction that the valley walls close in and the riverbed becomes more confined again, such as to be described as a 'gorge'.

The ambush proved to be very successful. Austin recorded that ten men were captured at 10 a.m., and another three at 11 a.m., 'two of them bleeding from wounds they had received'. These recent wounds suggest these men may well have been members of the picquet or its supporting force who were wounded in the early firing exchanges at the Te Karoro Gorge, discussed in the following chapter. At 11.30 a.m. four more men were captured, 'but the natives at once tomahaked them as they were some of Te Kooti's men from the Chatam Islands.' In the early afternoon one more man and one woman were captured, and they, Austin recorded, 'informed us that the natives under Ropata & Capt Porter had taken Te Kooti's pa and burned it.' At 4 p.m. the ambush group 'took one more man prisoner'. For the Whanganui Contingent,, 25 March had been a very successful day.

OUTCOME OF THE WHANGANUI ATTACKS

By nightfall Austin recorded that a total of 18 men had been killed over the previous two days and one night. Fourteen had been killed during the night of 23 March and the morning of 24 March, with four more killed on 25 March. Of those, only one had been shot, the rest being tomahawked.

According to Austin's figures a total of 196 Whakatōhea men, women and children had been released at Waipuna pā on 24 March. He also records a total of 125 of Te Kooti's people had been captured at this stage — 109 on 23–24 March when the seven puni were taken and Waipuna pā was captured, and 16 more on 25 March.

There was plainly some residual suspicion about where the loyalties of the Whakatōhea lay. As a result, it was decided that a combined total of 323 captives would all now have to accompany the 451 men of the Whanganui Contingent as they headed downriver to link up with Ropata's Ngāti Porou.

The passage of this column — totalling some 774 men, women and children — down the Waioeka would have taken quite some time under any circumstances. In the current situation, however, they would have had scouts out front, and the advance companies would have been on guard to try to pick up any further refugees from the Ngāti Porou attack on Maraetahi pā. This, in addition to negotiating the physical challenges such as deep river crossings, would have made the passage downriver particularly cautious and slow.

7

NGĀTI POROU ASSAULT MARAETAHI PĀ

Ngāti Porou had left Ōpōtiki to ascend the Waioeka River in the early evening of 22 March, Porter's diary recording their departure at 5 p.m. A dramatic description of a militarily very efficient Ngāti Porou ascent of the Waioeka can be found in the report of Henry Clarke, the civil commissioner in Tauranga, written after their return:

> Nothing could exceed the spirit of the Ngatiporou. They were undaunted by the gloomy prospect held out by some of those Natives who had encountered the difficulties of the Waioweka river, and were determined at all hazards to co-operate with the Whanganui.
>
> Every kainga on the route was approached with caution, and dispositions made to surround them, but in every instance they were found to have been deserted for a considerable time. The advance of Major Ropata's column met with no resistance till it reached within a short distance of Maraetahi.[98]

The level of the river must have been very low for the trip to be achieved at all, as it involves constant river crossings, and in the lower reaches of the gorge the flow is augmented by the contributions of many significant upstream feeder catchments. A newspaper report from Ōpōtiki dated 13 April supports this assumption, observing of the summer season in 1870:

The expedition has been remarkably lucky in the weather. We have never had such a continuance of fine weather; the consequence being the wells are all dry, and the only water to be got is half mud. However, the crops are all right; and most of the potatoes, of which there are hundreds of tons, are very fine.[99]

The first day of the Ngāti Porou expedition would not have required river crossings, and Porter did not refer to any problems with this stretch. The lower reaches of the river ran through open flats, where travel would have been mostly on the flat eastern terraces. The next day, however, they entered the gorge, where the depth of the water was sometimes troubling, as Porter recorded: '23rd March.— Our march to-day has been up the bed of the Waioeka Gorge, the water in many places being up to the armpits.'

The diary entry for 23 March continues: 'We are encamped to-night close to Kairakau, the scene of one of the fights in 1865, which has not been visited since. We shall take it to-morrow.' Unfortunately the diary as it was published in the *Appendices to the Journals of the House of Representatives* has no entry for 24 March and the following diary description is not dated, but it can be reasonably assumed that Kairakau pā was entered on 24 March.* Porter's entry for what must have been that day begins:

> Went in advance with Te Aowera, and getting to Kairakau, we found that it had been abandoned some few days previous. We stayed here for dinner, and found large quantities of kumaras, pumpkins, &c. Our track still lies through the river bed, which is very difficult, the rocks being large and slippery.[100]

If, as seems most likely, Kairakau pā was near the stream now known as the Mangaoira, the camp on the night of 23 March would probably have been at or near to modern Matahanea.

The timing and nature of the 'dinner' that Porter describes being taken at the abandoned Kairakau pā also helps to establish the column's progress on 24 March. At that time the word 'dinner' connoted our modern lunch, while the evening meal would be described as 'tea'. As the meal included kumara and

---

* Doubtless, as with numerous other such occupation sites up and down the Waioeka, memory of its location faded with the passage of time. Much the same occurred with Waipuna pā. It can be reasonably assumed, however, to have been in the locality of the high point called Kairakau which is shown on the C.A. Baker 1888 survey plan called Tahora No. 2 Plan. The high point named Kairakau was marked on that plan as being south east of the high point Puke nui o raho which was marked on old maps, and still is marked on modern maps. On modern topographic maps Kairakau appears to now be called Maungawhiorangi. It lies to the south of the Mangaoira Stream. Oral discussions with Derek Kingi of Ngāti Ira in September 2022 suggest that Porter's Kairakau pā was at the location known now to Ngāti Ira as Pararakau pā. It was located on the first terrace south of the Mangaoira Stream, and was used as a source of tānekaha.

pumpkins, it is reasonable to assume it must have been cooked. It makes sense that this would have occurred at Kairakau, as Ropata would have anticipated that by the end of that day's travel they would be so close to Maraetahi pā that fires could not safely be lit for fear of providing warning of their arrival.

Porter's diary entry confirms the increasing concern about fire lighting after leaving Kairakau, and that they must have overnighted very close to Maraetahi pā:

> We have been expecting to hear firing, as Kemp should have reached Maraetahi ere this. We suppose he must have fallen in with Te Kooti's trail, and followed elsewhere. We attack Maraetahi in the morning. We have heard much of its strength from the Wakatohea guides, who tell us that the Kawanatanga could not reach it in 1865. Although it is raining now we cannot light fires, lest the enemy should see the smoke.

This coincides with the rain that Austin recorded drove him on the night of 24 March to 'pig in' with a hundred others in a large whare upriver at Waipuna pā after its capture that day by Whanganui.

THE ASSAULT ON MARAETAHI PĀ

For any details of the assault on Maraetahi we must once again rely on Lt Porter, who left various accounts of these events: his initial handwritten diary, submitted to his senior officer, Lt Col St John, on 31 March, the day after Porter's return to Ōpōtiki; an accompanying handwritten letter; a report sent to Donald McLean on 28 April, later published in the *AJHR*; and an account that appeared in the series of articles he wrote for the *Poverty Bay Herald* in 1897. While these various accounts of the assault are consistent in most respects, there are some important differences between the earliest accounts and those that followed.

The first of these accounts, being written contemporaneously with the events, would usually be regarded as the most reliable. Lt Porter gave this to Lt Col St John at Ōpōtiki on 31 March, the day after he returned there; St John then forwarded it to his superior officer, Lt Col Lyon, at Auckland. Never published, the letter is now held in the National Archives,[101] and states:

> I have the honour to forward for the information of the Defence Minister the details of the Expedition of Ngatiporou to Waioeka — and the fall of Maraetahi pa on the 25th inst. On that date early in the morning when in the narrowest part of the gorge where the track passed under an immense perpendicular rock our advance was fired into by an outlying picquet of the enemy some 20 in number.

Our men did not shrink but surged on and returning the fire most effectually and driving the enemy before them. One rifle and three guns left behind them in their hasty retreat fell into our hands. This position taken up by the enemy was where they depended solely upon the defence of their pa. There being no other approach. Our hasty advance however completely disconcerted them as we met another kokiri coming to relief of the picquet who in turn were compelled to retire to the pa. Turning a bend in the river we came in sight of the pa and could see the Hauhaus running about from whare to whare. We kept up a steady fire and advanced upon the pa which lay on the opposite side of the river and very high above us. The enemy then retreated to a hill in rear of the pa and kept up a fire upon us but doing little damage. Our casualties being one wounded.

Seeing so few men in the pa and the resistance being so feeble we thought it was the Whakatohea alone who occupied the place. We still pressed on and within two hours from picquet attack we were in possession of the pa and the enemy gone.

Some men were at once in pursuit. Rapata and a greater part of the men remained in the pa still under the impression we had been opposed to Whakatohea alone. At night we were undeceived by a woman of that tribe coming in having bolted back from Te Kooti — she stated that Major Kemp at some place distant in rear had taken all Whakatohea prisoners among whom was her husband. ...

The woman reports Kooti to have had 67 men in the pa at time of attack ...

Porter's published diary entry, which he did not send to McLean until 28 April, was subtly different. It changed the story from his original handwritten version, reducing the time between first encountering the picquet to taking the pā from two to one and a half hours. In this published 1870 account, however, he still said that the picquet opened fire first:

The details are as follows: — Getting to the narrowest part of the gorge, where the track passes under an immense perpendicular rock, our advance was fired into by an outlying picquet of the enemy. Our fellows did not shrink, but pressing on returned the fire most effectually, driving the enemy before us. Two of the Hauhaus were here wounded, and are now prisoners. One rifle and three guns were left behind in their hasty retreat. The part of the gorge where the picquet attacked was that on which the enemy depended solely for the defence of the pa, as if properly defended it was almost impassable, and there was no other approach.

... We still pressed on, and in less than one hour and a half from the time of the picquet's attack we were in possession of Maraetahi Pa, the resting-place of Te Kooti. The enemy had gone.[102]

Twenty-seven years after these events, the now Lt Col Porter wrote in one of the articles for the *Poverty Bay Herald* about the actual approach and assault on Maraetahi pā. By now he had further changed his story. In this account, he had Ngāti Porou surprising the picquet by opening fire on them; further reduced the time between firing on the picquet and arrival at the pā to just one hour; and asserted that a 'large number of prisoners' were taken by the attackers, removing his earlier factual report that 'The enemy had gone.' His 1897 account read:

> At daylight on the 23rd the advance guard surprised the sentry of the enemy's outlying piquet at a part of the gorge narrowed in between steep rocky cliffs with deep rapid water between. This was really the gate of the enemy's position, upon which they depended to successfully repel attack. The sentry being disposed of, a rush was made up the rock, and the piquet of twenty men surprised and the position won. The firing at this spot alarmed the pa, but Ropata pushed over the cliff and descended to the river bed beyond, directly in front of the pa, which now stood out clear and bold 300 yards in front built upon a sloping tongue of land at the junction of the Waioeka and Waipuna Rivers. The attacking party had to advance up the river bed with little or no cover except what the boulders afforded. Some of the men hanging back, Ropata, although himself fully exposed, rushed forward with his toko toko (Alpine stock). Nearing the pa, the attacking party divided right and left, that to the right under the narrator and the left Ropata. Under cover of the banks a heavy fire was poured into the pa from both flanks. Only about an hour had elapsed from the time of the attack upon the piquet when a number of men and women could be seen escaping up the hills from the rear of the pa. Ropata then ordered the kokiri,* and the pa, with a large number of prisoners and large quantities of food, etc, fell into the hands of the force. During the attack Te Kooti had a narrow escape. Being recognised when upon the ridge of a whare, he was fired at, and the bullet struck just underneath his feet.[103]

Despite the changes as to events, in terms of general topography his descriptions fit reasonably well with the physical land forms at and near the Maraetahi pā. However, he does not make it clear in any of his accounts that the gorge where the firing first occurred is about 2 km downriver from the pā.

The Whakatōhea name for the gorge is Te Karoro a Tamatea — the seagull or parrot of Tamatea —Tamatea being the eponymous tipuna or ancestor of Ngāti Ira

---

* A kōkiri can in this context mean a charge.

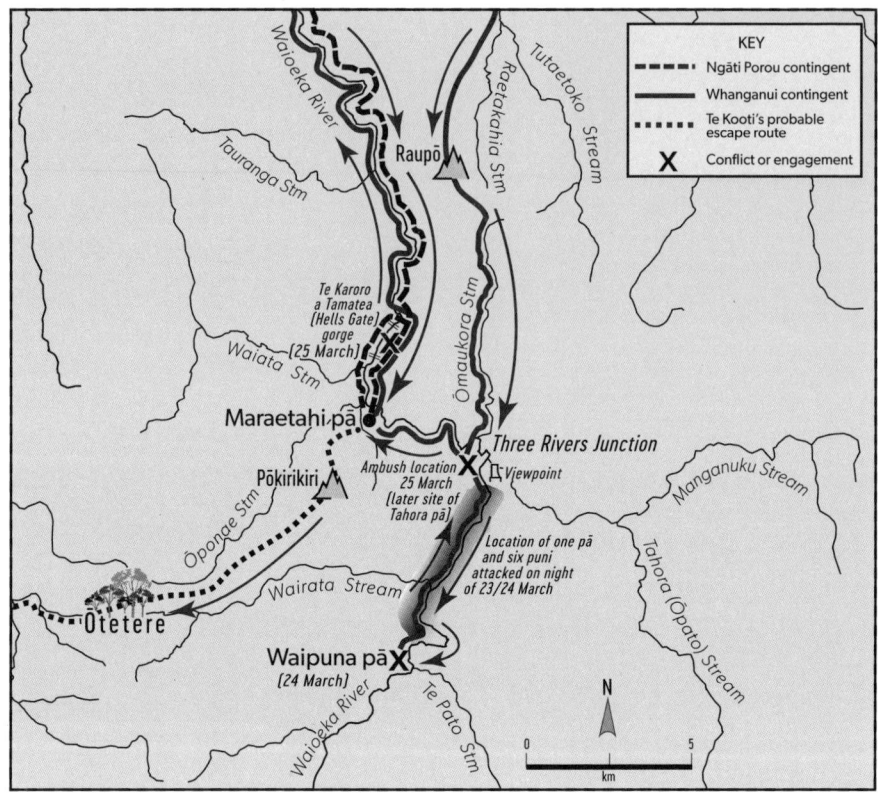

Map showing routes taken and engagement locations for Whanganui and Ngāti Porou in late March 1870 and Te Kooti's probable escape route to the west.

hapū of Whakatōhea.* The Pākehā name for the gorge, which is still used on the modern topographical map, is Hell's Gate. Its waters are very deep, and it is studded along its length by huge rocks. At its narrowest point, rocky bluffs rise above the water on both sides. On the true right, or the left-hand side facing upriver (the side on which Ngāti Porou approached), the forbidding bluffs continue for one to two hundred metres, with sections of rock wall that are almost vertical. The topography above these rock faces remains steep, but by climbing much higher up in the bush it would have been possible to bypass the gorge. On the true left, however, above the steep riverside bluffs a high terrace area can be utilised to bypass the gorge.

---

* In his book *Te Waimana: The Spring of Mana*, at p. 63, Jeffrey Sissons quotes from the Native Land Court evidence of Mini Tamapaoa, who described the 'Karoro' as being Tamatea's parrot in the Tahora No. 2 Block case. A.C. Lyall, in *Whakatohea of Opotiki*, at p. 51, describes in some detail the background to a translation of 'Karoro' as Tamatea's seagull, said to be named by Tamatea after a red and white stone at that location which resembled a seagull.

Based on Porter's 1897 account, and that of Tuta Nihoniho of Ngāti Porou, it was in this forbidding blocking position that they encountered the picquet, and the extra supporting men of Te Kooti's, which Porter termed a kōkiri in his initial unpublished report of 31 March.

According to Tuta Nihoniho's account, Ropata sent Porter across the river with a group of about fifty men. To effect a crossing they would have had to drop back some distance to where the gorge ran out to shallower water. Having crossed at that point, they would have been able to return on the elevated bush terrace above the gorge on the true left or western side. Once opposite the picquet, it would have been possible to fire at the members of the picquet from across the river. Nihoniho expressly confirms the need to cross the river below the gorge, and the engagement of the picquet across the river from the west bank. The translation provided by James Cowan misses some crucial context from the original te reo Māori version, so both are provided here:

Te Karoro a Tamatea (Hell's Gate) gorge — scene of Te Kooti's picquet and supporting kōkiri (dashed circle) firing downriver at Ngāti Porou, with other Ngāti Porou (dotted circles) on the high terrace to right of sketch firing across the river at the picquet.
Stu Spicer

... po toru a Ngati-Porou e haere ana ka tae ki Marae-tai, i reira te apiti o te awa. Kei reira nga heteri a te Hauhau e kati ana mai. Katahi ka whakahoki e Ngati-Porou e wha maero ki muri, katahi ka pikitia e nga tangata e rima tekau, ma runga i nga maunga, ma roto i nga ngahere haere ai, me te whakapiri kia eketia te wahi e nohoia mai ra e nga heteri a te Hauhau. Ko te matua a Ngati-Porou i waiho tonu i te taha o te awa; no te ritenga atu o te rima tekau ra ki nga heteri a te Hauhau e noho ra, katahi ka puhia, ka mate etahi, ka oma etahi ma ro ngahere, ka watea hoki te apiti hei pikitanga ake mo te matua. Heoi ano ko te aranga ake o te matua, haere te waha o te pu, te waha o te tangata. Kotahi tonu te kokiritanga atu, ka horo te pa, ka rere a Te Kooti me nga morehu.

Ngati-Porou entered the Waio-weka River and reached Marae-tai in a three days' march. There, at a narrow pass, Hauhau sentries were posted, preventing any advance. Ngati-Porou then fell back down stream, and fifty men clambered over the ranges and through the forest, advancing warily to gain the place occupied by the Hauhau look-out men. Meanwhile the main body of Ngati-Porou remained by the river. When the party of fifty came opposite the Hauhau look-out men, they fired upon them, killing some, while others escaped into the forest; thus the pass was opened for the passage of the main body. So the main body now advanced, the voices of guns and men being now heard. The pa was taken at the first charge, Te Kooti and others escaping.[104]

In the original te reo Māori version Nihoniho states that the blocking 'heteri', or sentry force (Porter's 'picquet'), was encountered at the 'apiti', or gorge (not a 'pass', as in Cowan's translation). Nihoniho then says a group of 50 Ngāti Porou 'ka whakahoki e Ngati-Porou e wha maero ki muri', or dropped back four miles to cross the river and re-emerge through the bush on the other side, from where they opened fire on the picquet. Strangely, Nihoniho's reference to 'wha maero' (four miles) was not translated by Cowan.

The distance of four miles (6.4 km) is almost certainly incorrect. To have dropped back so far in broken, steep bush country then returned on the other side, a total of eight miles or 12.8 kilometres, would have taken at least three or four hours. Porter's initial account makes it plain that the time lag was less than that. Moreover, to locate a crossing it would not have been necessary to drop back four miles, since there are suitable places much closer than that to the gorge.

It is probable that, as Austin appears to have done in his diary on a number of occasions, Nihoniho was giving a return distance, that is the 50 men dropped back about two miles (3.2 km) then returned on the opposite side of the river.

Moving at a rapid pace that would have taken about two hours, which fits well with Porter's original handwritten account of 31 March, where he recorded: 'We still pressed on and within two hours from picquet attack we were in possession of the pa and the enemy gone.'

As the picquet and its support force withdrew under the fire of the Ngāti Porou who had crossed the river, Ropata and his men would have been able to climb into the bush above the bluffs then descend to the riverbed at the upriver end of the gorge, as both Porter and Nihoniho later confirmed.

Upstream of the gorge there were still just under 2 km of river to be covered before the place where it turns to the east or left, from where the pā site is clearly visible on the opposite side of the river. At that point the river banks are not so confined by solid rock banks and a reasonable crossing is possible of the river bed, particularly in the lower-flow conditions that existed in late March, 1870. Once across the river Ropata would have ordered the kōkiri or charge on the pā itself but on entry they would have found 'the enemy had gone'.

LACK OF FORTIFICATION AT MARAETAHI PĀ RENDERS IT INDEFENSIBLE

The landform on which Maraetahi pā was situated is a long spur that runs down to form a sharp bend in the river. On the upriver side the spur falls very sharply into the river, while on the downriver side it has a gentler face, sloping down into a small catchment. In evidence at the Supreme Court in Wellington at the trial of some of Te Kooti's men in late June 1870, several witnesses mentioned the lack of fortification at the pā site. Miriama Okiakia, who was one of the pā occupants at the time of the attack, was reported to have said:

> The place belonged to the Whakatohea, whose chief was Hera. It is a hilly settlement, but had not been fortified at all. The Ngati Porou under Ropata attacked Te Kooti there, and I was taken by the Wanganuis under Kemp and Topia. I was caught above Tahora at Waioeka. The prisoners were all caught at Waioeka.[105]

Similarly, Piahana Tiwai, the Whakatōhea rangatira with Te Kēpa's Whanganui Contingent, stated at the hearing:

> I went with Kemp's force to Tahore. I was sent in the same party with Austin to Ripawa, where we captured a lot of prisoners, and then went towards Tahore ... Te Kooti and his men were at Maraetahi. We went down to Maraetahi with the prisoners taken at Tahore and Ripawa. It was not fortified. There was a large church there.[106]

Wiremu Kingi Te Paia from Tūranga stated in evidence at that same hearing: 'Nothing was done to the fortification at Maratahi while I was there.'[107]

Even without having to overcome any fortifications, the difficult approach and the assault of the pā took about two hours. That time would have enabled most of Te Kooti's and Hira Te Popo's supporters to grab some food and flee up the ridges at the back of the pā, as suggested in several of the accounts of these events.

The early warning conveyed to the occupants of the pā by the shooting at Te Karoro (Hell's Gate) was confirmed by Hoani Te Paiaka, the Whanganui rangatira who was related to Topia, but also had Tūhoe and Arawa whakapapa. He was at the gorge when it was attacked, and later, on 20 May, surrendered with 44 others to Gilbert Mair at Fort Galatea (Waikaramuramu). In his statement Te Paiaka said: 'All his [Te Kooti's] best men were killed at Waioeka, and he himself would have been taken, but I gave the alarm when surprised by Ngatiporou at Te Karoro.'[108] The warning and the opportunity thus provided for Te Kooti to escape was confirmed in more detail in the statements his wife Huhana Tamati gave to Porter in August:

> At daylight soon after this information was received we heard firing in the direction of the picquet. ....Te Kooti then gave the word for the whole to retreat. We ran away, after crossing the creek and when at the top of a hill we waited to rest.[109]

As soon as Maraetahi had been taken it seems that a few of the Ngāti Porou set out in pursuit, climbing up the steep spurs above the pā, with possibly some others going up the Waioeka River. Initially, however, neither Ropata nor Porter gave orders for fighting patrols to head out in pursuit. According to Porter's published diary account, this was because Ropata seemed to doubt the significance of his opposition:

> Ropata and a greater portion of the men remained behind, still being under the impression that it was Whakatohea alone who occupied the pa, although we found many things that led us to suppose that Te Kooti had been there lately, such as blank cheques, &c.[110]

In military terms, when compared to Te Kēpa's assault on Waipuna pā, the attack on Maraetahi pā appears to have had significant tactical deficiencies, not only in the course of the assault itself, but also in the lead-up and the immediate aftermath.

TACTICAL DEFICIENCIES ON ROPATA'S PART

The first point of tactical criticism that must be made is that Ropata does not appear to have sent out scouts to reconnoitre the approaches to Maraetahi pā as Ngāti Porou were approaching the difficult Te Karoro Gorge. Instead, his forces seem to have encountered a picquet of some sentries who were able to fire at them first, followed by a relieving kōkiri or force to support the picquet who also opened fire on them.

This sustained exchange of heavy fire occurred about 2 km from the pā, where it would have been heard, as Huhana's statement made clear, giving the occupants plenty of time to escape. Porter's initial report stated that it took two hours from the time of that exchange of fire with the picquet until Ngāti Porou actually took possession of the pā. By that time all the occupants had gone, except the one man who climbed on the whare and fired at them.

In contrast, Te Kēpa's own report and Austin's diary display the great emphasis that Te Kēpa placed on scouts always being out front, or climbing trees to gain views well ahead. These tactics, coupled with their careful and purposeful night-time approaches, and close-quarter reconnaissance, ensured they avoided blundering into Te Kooti's own scouts or sentries. As a consequence, each of the eight assaults made by the Whanganui Contingent over the night of 23 March and dawn of 24 March achieved total surprise and the great majority of the Waipuna pā occupants were captured. That was possible because Te Kēpa had received early warning from his scouts of the existence of each of the puni and the pā attacked. Moreover, Te Kēpa had ensured the puni and the pā were surrounded at night before, in the final major assault, a dawn attack achieved the vital element of surprise. In contrast, at Te Karoro Gorge it was Ngāti Porou who were surprised, and the occupants of Maraetahi warned of their approach.

A further point of contrast at Te Karoro Gorge was the delay caused by the need to send a party down the river to cross to the opposite bank, then return to fire across at the picquet. And even after the picquet had been suppressed, an advance of 2 km was still needed to round the point and assault the pā. All of these potential problems could have been discovered and resolved by prior reconnaissance and observation. Different methods of approach using higher ground could have been devised and carried out to bypass the gorge and achieve surprise.

In his report of 18 April, Henry Clarke tried to cast Ropata in the best possible light in terms of his careful tactics, stating that as Ngāti Porou advanced up the Waioeka: '[e]very kainga on the route was approached with caution, and dispositions made to surround them, but in every instance they were found to have been deserted for a considerable time.'[111] If this was the case, then it is hard to fathom why Ngāti Porou did not exercise similar caution as they made the crucial final advance on Maraetahi pā. This was the very pā where Te Kooti was expected to be found. Moreover, their Whakatōhea guides would have warned them of the difficulties in attempting to pass through Te Karoro Gorge on the eastern side only.

The lack of caution in the final advance is particularly difficult to understand given that Porter's diary entry before 25 March makes it clear that they knew they were in the vicinity of Maraetahi pā: 'We attack Maraetahi in the morning. We have heard much of its strength from the Wakatohea guides, who tell us that the

Porter's account of firing on Te Kooti personally

In his published diary Porter told a rather strange story about Te Kooti that is difficult to reconcile with Huhana's account.

Huhana had described how after hearing the shooting Te Kooti and his close group of wives and soldiers immediately crossed a creek and withdrew up the hills behind the pā, while an unnamed Whakatōhea woman had told Porter that Te Kooti had initially gathered a group of his men and sent them out to support the picquet.

Porter's published account of the events as Ngāti Porou entered the pā stated:

> Te Kooti at last was completely deserted by his men, and left alone to defend the pa. While we were advancing in the morning, after nearly all the firing had ceased, a man got up on the top of a whare and called out to us, 'Ko Wanganui tenei.' He then fired three times at us. I and Eru Rangiwaha ran up and fired two shots at close range at him, but little thought at that time it was Te Kooti himself. Every man now is greatly exasperated to think how narrowly the rebel escaped us.[112]

It does seem both extremely strange and unlikely that Te Kooti would have exposed himself in that risky manner, or that he was completely deserted. After all, he had plenty of time to observe the advance of the hundreds of Ngāti Porou, and to withdraw rapidly up the ridge behind the pā with his wives and others, which is what Huhana said he did. Porter's own handwritten contemporary unpublished account of 31 March did not include any evidence as to why he later concluded the man involved was Te Kooti. This suggestion simply does not ring true.

Kawanatanga could not reach it in 1865.' They had also taken care not to light fires, further evidence that they knew they were near Maraetahi.

It is notable that Porter's contemporary diary account does not give precise numbers of those captured or killed during the assault phase, and nor did his later newspaper article. The only casualties he recorded in the published diary account were two wounded among the picquet: 'Two of the Hauhaus were here wounded, and are now prisoners. One rifle and three guns were left behind in their hasty retreat.'

In his handwritten initial account Porter had stated: 'We still pressed on and within two hours from picquet attack we were in possession of the pa and the enemy gone.' Even in his published diary account he concluded his description of the assault: '... in less than one hour and a half from the time of the picquet's attack we were in possession of Maraetahi Pa, the resting-place of Te Kooti. The enemy had gone.'

Topia Turoa was denigratory of the Ngāti Porou attack at the conclusion of his report to McLean: 'Friend, I think we should have taken Te Kooti, if it had not been that Ropata attacked the pa in which he was at the time. I think if I had had the storming or taking of the position we should have captured that man (Te Kooti).'[113]

Major Te Kēpa was more generous on the issue of Ropata's tactics in his report to Premier William Fox, but stressed the lack of scouts:

> Major Ropata's force killed one, they took one man and a woman; so that they accounted for three. They made the attack on Te Kooti's pa; they came upon it suddenly, and not having sent scouts. Some of them say that the lot in front were dull fellows; had it been Major Ropata's own hapu, some of the enemy would have been caught. That is all that is to be said. Sufficient.[114]

THE WHANGANUI AMBUSH NEAR ŌMAUKORA JUNCTION

The outcome for some of the survivors who fled upriver from Maraetahi pā was not good. Having probably been part of the picquet and its supporters, they would have been closely pursued as they fell back towards the pā. They would not have had time to climb up to the pā without being exposed to the fire of hundreds of pursuing Ngāti Porou, and their only hope may have been to try to escape up the riverbed.

They were not captured by Ngāti Porou, but were picked up by the ambuscade Te Kēpa had ordered to be set near the Ōmaukora junction (described in Chapter 6). It will be recalled that the ambuscade throughout the day of 25 March resulted

in the killing of four men, and the capture of fifteen men and one woman.*
Thus, the only major success in inflicting casualties on the day was not achieved
by the 330 Ngāti Porou who actually assaulted the pā. Rather, it was achieved by
100 Whanganui waiting in ambuscade some five or six kilometres up the river.

OUTCOMES OF THE PURSUITS

There is no suggestion in Porter's diary entries on the day of the assault, or
the following day, that the few pursuers who used their own initiative actually
captured anyone. The nearest any of them came to success was recounted later
by Huhana in her statement about what occurred when the group with Te Kooti
stopped on the ridgeline above the pā for some food:

> While we were sitting down eating, I, Te Kooti and three other of his women, two
> men of the government people came. They fired at us. The whole of the soldiers
> ran away at once leaving only three men with Te Kooti.
>
> Te Kooti cried out for them to charge these two men but they would not listen,
> and ran away, leaving the whole of their swags behind them.[115]

It was not until the day after the attack on the pā that Porter recorded a strong
pursuit patrol finally being ordered out: '26th March.— At daylight, 120 men
started out to endeavour to follow the trail of Te Kooti.' On 27 March, he was able
to record only some very limited success on the part of the pursuers:

> 27th March, Sunday.— The 120 men out yesterday returned, bringing three
> prisoners, and report having killed one man. They followed the track of some
> thirty men as far as Te Punga. At Waimana learned it was the Urewera of Te Kooti
> returning to Ruatahuna, and hearing from one of the prisoners that Te Kooti
> had not gone in that direction, they returned. At dark a man came in to give
> himself up, and reports himself as one of a picquet of ten men sent by Te Kooti to
> reconnoitre our camp. He says that Te Kooti has taken refuge in a potato clearing
> some distance in rear of this place; that he has with him twenty men and a few
> women. It is too dark to-night to go out, but at daylight 300 men will start to
> endeavour to catch him.

Those 300 men sent out on 28 March were in two strong patrols, one of Ngāti
Porou and one of Whanganui. They were recorded by Porter as having returned
on 29 March, after failing to make contact with any of Te Kooti's supporters.

* Austin's diary again has a total figure of those captured which it is not possible to reconcile with the detailed figures he recorded. His total figure for those captured was 18.

Austin's diary does record that an earlier Whanganui patrol sent out by Te Kēpa on 27 March from Maraetahi returned at 1 p.m. having captured one prisoner.

Austin also described in two diary entries, on 28 and 29 March, Ropata's wish to execute some of the worst of the prisoners taken by Whanganui. On 28 March: '... one of the prisoners which we took turns out to be as bad as Te Kooti's self. Ropata wants to shoot him and (3 or 4) three or four others but Kemp will not allow it until he writes to the Government on the subject ...' And on 29 March:

> We have one of the Rev. Wm. Vaulkners murders [murderers] and (3) three of the verry worst characters of the Pverty Bay murders. We will have to keep a sharp look out for them, the guards has orders to shoot the first one who attempts to escape, either man or woman. Ropata wants to shoot them at once but Kemp will not allow it as it was his men that took them prisoner. He says that he will wait until he hears from the Government.

ROPATA AND PORTER INSPECT MARAETAHI PĀ

After the capture of Maraetahi pā on 25 March, Ropata, Porter and most of their men appear to have focused on what they could discover from the pā buildings and layout. They were clearly impressed by the garden areas. A woman who had been in the pā, and returned on the night of the attack, told Porter that Te Kooti 'had only sixty-seven men with him in the pa at the time of attack'. He continued, 'We found very large quantities of food planted here, some five acres of "taro," and many acres of maize, &c. It is the largest Native plantation I ever remember to have seen.' However, it was the pā buildings that most impressed:

> It appears that Te Kooti left men here last year, after his escape from Ngatapa, to plant food, and to build him a church, as after he had visited the King and Taupo he would return here, his atua appointing this his place of rest, saying the Kawanatanga would never reach here. We found a splendid new church built for him. It was eighty-four feet in length, and thirty feet wide, beautifully finished. It was covered from end to end with two large kiakia mats, plaited crosswise.*
> Along the centre of each there were scriptural names worked in red wool, in letters six inches in depth. Te Kooti had only the opening service in his church some few days before we attacked the pa. He then had again assured his people that the Kawanatanga would never reach there. A pretty little carved house was

---

* Porter's 'kiakia' should read 'kiekie', a plant commonly used for finer weaving.

also destroyed by us, which had been built for Te Kooti's own private abode. Altogether we destroyed forty-two whares, many of them large ones.[116]

Austin recorded that all buildings, including the church, were burnt.

THE DESCENT OF THE WHANGANUI FROM WAIPUNA PĀ TO MARAETAHI

On 26 March Austin recorded the departure of the Whanganui force from Waipuna pā, with the 323 occupants of the pā as prisoners. The departure was marked by the burning down of the whare at the pā.

It must have taken quite some time to organise the departure of such a huge combined body, totalling some 770 people. Unlike the Whanganui's normal very early departure times, on this morning it was 8 a.m. before they were under way:

> 26th Fine again. Under orders to march. The reason we remained hear so long was to cut off Te Kooti's retreat and his men as we expected that Ropata would follow them up. We fell in and marched at 8 a.m. in the following order: Numbers 1, 2, & 3 companys in advance, the Whakatohi prisoners next, the prisoners belonging to Te Kooti came next with a guard of 50 men, I was in charge of them. Our orders were to shoot anyone who attempted to escape. No's 4, 5 & 6 companys in the rear.

After three to four hours' travel they would have arrived at modern Wairata, or what Austin described in his diary as the junction of the three rivers. From there, the further downriver they progressed the slower and more drawn out the column would have become, as the river entered a more confined stretch of gorges, with deeper, swifter crossings until they reached Maraetahi pā about six kilometres downriver. Downriver from the 'three rivers' junctions the size of the flow, and depth of crossings in the Waioeka, would have markedly increased in a river gorge. Furthermore, the level of caution would have continued to rise as they progressed downriver, as they would have been on the lookout for more refugees fleeing from Ropata's attack on Maraetahi. As Austin recorded, that is exactly what occurred: 'On our way down the advance guard shot (4) four men. We arrived at a place called Maraetoi about 2 p.m. all safe. Ropata had just arrived so we halted and camped hear for the night. Guards mounted etc. as usual.'

The now combined force of the Whanganui Contingent's augmented party and the Ngāti Porou stayed on at Maraetahi for four days, during which time the pursuit patrols described above were conducted. The only other event of significance that occurred during that time was the burning of all the buildings at Maraetahi pā by

Austin on 28 March. This followed the sending out of a strong patrol on 27 March, in the hope that the burning action would trigger Te Kooti to return prematurely to Maraetahi. Austin described the rationale of the burning at that stage:

> 28th A dull morning. As soon as the force got well into the bush last night 100 men was sent back. This morning I fell in all the prisoners and then set fire to all the huts and marched away. The man that was taken prisoner last evening said that Te Kooti would come down hear as soon as we left this place. (So this was done as a blind to draw him. We have burned all the huts we came across yet.)

The attempt to draw Te Kooti out did not succeed.

While Austin does not mention where the column stopped for the next two nights, it seems likely to have been just downriver from the pā site. Both his and Porter's diaries for 30 March state that their respective forces left Maraetahi that day for Ōpōtiki.

DESCENT OF THE WAIOEKA

By this time, the combined forces of the 450 members of the Whanganui Contingent and the 330 Ngāti Porou* had been swollen by at least 340 or 350 prisoners and released Whakatōhea. It simply was not possible for over 1100 people to survive any longer on the limited food supplies available at Maraetahi. Moreover, the physical condition of both the Whanganui and Ngāti Porou had been further degraded by the marches inland, and the post-attack patrols, coming as they did after such a long period of bush campaigning for both contingents. The pursuit of Te Kooti, whose whereabouts were still unknown, would have to be abandoned for the time being.

The first to depart from Maraetahi was an advance party of Ngāti Porou led by Porter. It comprised a small group of picked men, and they moved rapidly, as Porter's diary recorded. However, maintaining such a speed took its toll:

> 30th March.— I, with fifty men, started in advance this morning at 5 o'clock, to come on to Opotiki, leaving the main body to come on with prisoners. We made the journey very quickly to-day, doing that in eleven hours which took us two days and a half to do before. Many of the men were knocked up completely, and were compelled to remain behind. Seven men only, out of the fifty who started with me, reached Opotiki the same night.[117]

---

* Forty men had been left behind at Ōhiwa, as they were too badly injured or ill to join the Waioeka expedition.

Austin's experience was not dissimilar:

> 30th Fine morning. We fell in and marched at daylight for Opotiki, the Ngataporous marched in front and we brought up the rear with the prisoners. We were glad to get a shift out of this place and get to where we could get some provisions. About 9 a.m. I left the main body with (12) men and pushed on for Opotiki which we reached at 5 p.m. all safe after a frightful march of about 40 miles down a lead of a gorge or river. We had to cross and re-cross said river about 150 times and at each crossing we were up to our waists in water, and in some cases we had to take each others hands when crossing or we would have been swept off our feet the stream ran with such forse.

Porter's diary entry for 31 March recorded that the main bodies of Ngāti Porou and Whanganui arrived at Ōpōtiki together:

> 31st March.— Ropata, Kemp, and the main body came in about 5 o'clock this evening. I had rations all ready for them. I have selected the worst of the male prisoners to await their trial. All anxiously expecting the Defence Minister's arrival.

RECOVERY OF TE KOOTI'S GUNPOWDER SUPPLIES

For a small group of Ngāti Porou under Ropata, one final action was required before they could rest. Ropata had heard talk among the prisoners that a sizeable cache of gunpowder had been secreted by some of the Whakatōhea for Te Kooti near Ōpōtiki. Henry Clarke outlined the following events in his report of 28 April:

> After the return of the expeditionary forces to Opotiki, Ropata ascertained from some of the prisoners that there was a considerable supply of ammunition in the mountains at the back of Opotiki, kept there at the desire of Te Kooti for future use in his operations on the coast of the Bay of Plenty. By threats he managed to obtain guides to conduct his men to these concealed stores.* They returned to Opotiki shortly after our arrival with eight quarter-casks of loose powder; but not satisfied with this, Ropata still pursued his inquiries, and found that there was a further store of twelve casks, and the place of concealment was known only to one individual, a person named Eru Nopenope confined with thirty-six other prisoners in the redoubt.

---

* It is notable that in this era the report of Ropata using 'threats' against a prisoner drew no official comment, let alone condemnation. In the modern military such an action would lead to an investigation by the legal department of the New Zealand Defence Force, and potential prosecution for abuse of a prisoner's rights not to speak other than to give their name, rank and number.

Eru, under a strong escort of Ropata's men, guided them to the spot, many miles in the forest, and the whole stock was brought in, together with a bag of ready-cast bullets. The whole loss to the enemy was, therefore, twenty quarter-casks of powder, and a bag of bullets.[118]

The recovery of such a large amount of gunpowder was a major loss for Te Kooti, whose resources were now even further degraded following the events in the Waioeka. He was now left not only undermanned, but also short of gunpowder. Ropata later reported to McLean, after the surrender of Hira Te Popo: 'I then enquired what the strength of his force was. They said fifty, but they are without powder and caps, not very many guns; but even those, of what use are they without powder and caps? The whole fifty are not supplied with guns.'[119]

The lack of resources was serious enough to lead Te Kooti to make yet another difficult and lengthy foray out from the upper Waioeka to Uawa (Tolaga Bay) in July, in an effort to replenish supplies of both men and munitions. The raid on Uawa was unsuccessful, however, and led to the capture of Te Kooti's wife Huhana and others of his supporters.

In effect, the Waioeka engagements of late March 1870 had broken Te Kooti's power, and his ability ever to resurrect it. From that time on his supporters were so reduced in number that he was in reality an unsettling risk to good order rather than a major threat to peace in the new colony.

TE KOOTI'S MOVEMENTS AFTER HIS ESCAPE FROM MARAETAHI

Very few details are known about the route Te Kooti took after the fall of Maraetahi, and much of what is known requires an interest in the rather complex Te Urewera topography. What follows is a limited summary; a closer consideration of his possible routes can be found in Appendix 2.

In her first statement about the attack on the pā, Huhana described the relative ease with which they escaped. She told of the warning they had received the night before the attack, that there was a government force upriver, so if the pā was attacked from downriver the obvious escape route would be up into the bush-covered ridges behind the pā, rather than up the river. Huhana confirmed that was the route they took:

> The night before we were attacked at Maraetai two women and a man came and told us the government people were approaching by the rear. At daylight soon after this information was received we heard firing in the direction of the picquet. Te Kooti called to all the soldiers to fall in and collect upon the hill at the back

Huhana Tamati.
Binney, Judith Te Tomairangi o te Aroha (Dame), 1940–2011. Ref: PAColl-9928-46, Alexander Turnbull Library, Wellington, NZ

of the pa. We saw the government people approaching and many of Te Kooti's soldiers were inclined to run away. Te Kooti then gave the word for the whole to retreat. We ran away, after crossing the creek and when at the top of a hill we waited to rest.

It is unclear which ridgeline Huhana is referring to in this statement. The most obvious ridge or spur was immediately behind the pā. However, Te Kooti would have known that that ridgeline in a southerly direction would take them back over to the upper Waioeka at its junction with the Wairata Stream; that is, downriver from Waipuna pā and the government forces there. In high-river freshes he had probably used that ridgeline to access the Te Pato Stream area, where Waipuna pā was located. It is much more likely that Te Kooti and his few close followers would have climbed up to the high point of Pōkirikiri, southwest of the pā. From Pōkirikiri, the main leading ridge heads west for many hours before ending up in the Waimana/Tauranga River catchment.

Huhana described a number of hard travel movements over the following days into and out of the Tataweka Stream, and back down to Waipuna pā and the puni downstream, where they buried a number of bodies. She also described what seems to have been perhaps the start of a journey towards Ruatāhuna before they encountered some government 'soldiers' in the Otane Stream, in the Waimana catchment. That led to a panic withdrawal, again probably back up the high ridge over into the Tataweka.

If the Tataweka was their ultimate destination that day, even though its headwaters are probably at least 12–15 hours' travel from Maraetahi using the ridgelines, that was not unrealistic. Te Kooti and his supporters would have been desperate to put as much distance as possible between themselves and the hundreds of Ngāti Porou they had seen streaming up the river towards Maraetahi pā. In addition, they faced the threat of a further major force upriver, whose whereabouts and direction of travel were unknown. In the previous two years Te Kooti and his people had repeatedly marched extremely long distances in steep bush country. They had shown their capability for rapid travel in such conditions only two months earlier, when they had probably used the same Pōkirikiri route to reach Maraetahi from Tawhana pā.

The only other piece of direct evidence about Te Kooti's movements in the days after his escape from Maraetahi comes from Hoani Te Paiaka, in the statement he gave to Gilbert Mair two months later, on 21 May. Te Paiaka's statement was considered by Mair to be an accurate source of intelligence, for reasons he outlined in his covering letter:

> I enclose a statement made to me by Hoani Te Paiaka. It contains definite information as to Te Kooti's whereabouts. Te Paiaka is a chief of the Ngatihau, a near relative of Topia's, and is also related to the Arawa. His mother, too, was an Urewera woman — a sister of Paerau's. He appears to exercise considerable influence over the Urewera.[120]

In his statement, Te Paiaka said:

> The Urewera would not go with Te Kooti to Waioeka. I went with ten; two were killed, and the rest came back with me to Ruatahuna on the 27th April. We left Te Kooti a few days before. He was then at a place called Te Pato; it is a small stream

that branches off to the left from Waioeka, just above Maraetahi and near Te Tahora. Te Kooti told me that he intended to make that place his head-quarters. The food was carried from three small clearings about Te Tahora. Te Kooti told the Natives to be careful of their food, as that was all they had to depend upon till the spring. Te Kooti is now either at Te Tahora or Te Pato. He says if he is pursued he will go up to the very source of the Waioeka, and trust to pigs and honey to live on, or go on to Whanganui-o-Parua, the eastern arm of Waikaremoana Lake. ...

About a week after the fight, I came back with Te Kooti from Te Pato, and he gave orders to his men to go and bury the dead. I went with them and saw these men put in their graves. Te Kooti then went back to Pato, and I told him I would leave him, as I had lost faith in his Atua. I then came to Ruatahuna.[121]

Te Paiaka finally emerged from Te Urewera months later, in the Rangitaiki valley to the west, where he and 44 others surrendered to Gilbert Mair.

OUTCOMES OF THE FALL OF MARAETAHI

Although this event was later trumpeted in the press as a striking success, Ropata himself did not view either the assault on Maraetahi pā or its immediate aftermath that way. A sense of despondency was evident not only in Ropata's later repeated requests to execute some of the worst characters among the Whanganui's prisoners, but also in his own report to McLean, written at Ōpōtiki on 1 April.

In contrast to the detailed reports that Ropata sometimes provided to McLean after Urewera expeditions, this one was very short. In his report Ropata expressed a sense of regret verging on the surprisingly apologetic:

> I have one word to say to you, which is this: Pray come down and see us Ngatiporou, notwithstanding that you maybe disappointed at our not securing Te Kooti. The proverb says, 'It is a work to which one may return again.' What could we do, owing to the difficult nature of the country? Had Te Kooti escaped when we attacked the pa, then there would be good cause for disappointment; as it was, he kept to the open bush, and before we could overtake him, your people had become exhausted with the fatigue of climbing or going up and down the precipices of this rough country.
>
> Captain Porter will give you all the particulars of this expedition.*[122]

---

* In this report Ropata has accorded Porter a promotion to 'Captain', which would not have been within his power to grant. Porter's own reports at that time, and those of other senior officals, accord him the rank of Lieutenant only.

Even in his account written many years later in te reo Māori, Ropata dealt with the attack on Maraetahi pā in a generalised manner in just five lines.[123] These five lines gave no details other than recording that Maraetahi was attacked, and that the survivors dispersed. Ropata did not mention the difficulties encountered at the gorge below the pā at all. He did record that no member of the Kāwanatanga force was killed, but then merely concluded by saying:

> Hei te mutunga o te mahi ki reira, ka hoki ki Ōpōtiki, e ono rau e whitu tekau te ope; e rua rau o Te Whakatohea i whakaraua ai i Te Kooti ka tae ki Opotiki, a ka noho te ope ki reira.

This can be translated as:

> After that task was completed we returned to Opotiki. There were six hundred and seventy in the force and two hundred Whakatohea who had been captured by Te Kooti who were returned home to Opotiki, and the force stayed there also.

In fairness to Ropata and his Ngāti Porou, when assessing the wider strategic value of the capture of Maraetahi pā, sight must not be lost of the impact on the morale of Te Kooti and his followers of being hounded out of their main winter refuge. They had lost all their buildings and, even worse, all their gardens had been destroyed, just before the start of winter. Moreover, the loss of the two pā meant that all his closest followers had dispersed.

Of even greater long-term significance was that as a result of the losses at the Waipuna and Maraetahi pā, Te Kooti had lost mana with Tūhoe, Hira Te Popo and his Ngāti Ira, and also with Whakatōhea generally. These were the hapū and iwi that had previously been his greatest sources of support. Hoani Te Paiaka, the Te Atihaunui rangatira, had been one of Te Kooti's more prominent supporters. His decision to leave Te Kooti after these events is one more example of Te Kooti's loss of mana.

In the long term, these outcomes contributed significantly to the government's strategy of undermining support for Te Kooti and cutting him off from the resources he so badly needed — men, ammunition, accommodation, refuge and food — particularly through winter. Yet in terms of directly wearing down his manpower by assaults that inflicted serious casualties or took large numbers of his supporters as prisoners, the Ngāti Porou attack on Maraetahi pā had extremely limited success.

In detailing the attack on Maraetahi pā and the following patrols, even Porter's later published account recorded only two of Te Kooti's men being wounded and captured by Ngāti Porou during the exchanges with the picquet on 25 March; in fact none at all were killed, wounded or captured during the actual taking of the pā on 25 March; and only one was killed and three captured by a later Ngāti Porou patrol on 26/27 March. This summary accords with the evidence Porter was reported as giving at the trial of those prisoners prosecuted in the Supreme Court at Wellington later that year:

> I was attached to Ropata's expedition in March, 1870, when we went to Maraetahi. We were fired into by a picket of Hauhaus in the Waioeka Gorge, about a mile from the pa. We drove the picket, and saw some Hauhaus retreating, while a fire was kept up from the pa, and a hill little to the left. We only captured two prisoners — none of the men in the dock. I saw all of these men brought in prisoners by the Wanganuis.[124]

Whanganui had released or taken prisoner 323 people in eight assaults over the night of 23 March and the morning of 24 March, leading up to and including the capture of Waipuna pā; 16 more prisoners were captured in the ambuscade near the Ōmaukora junction on 25 March; and one more prisoner was taken in a pursuit patrol after the fall of Maraetahi pā on 27 March, making a grand total of 340. In addition, they had killed a total of either 21 or 25 men, including the well-known rangatira Hakaraia.* Hoani Te Paiaka put the total figure of those killed even higher, at 30.[125] In contrast to Ropata's force, through their actions Whanganui directly reduced Te Kooti's manpower.

---

* Again in terms of numbers killed Austin's diary defies logical reconciliation between detailed accounts of numbers killed on each occasion and totals he provides of those killed at various stages. The additional four men killed on 26 March do not seem to have been added to his total.

PART 3
THE CONTINUING AFTERMATH

8

THE END OF THE CAMPAIGN AND THE DEVELOPMENT OF A MYTH

By the end of March the combined forces were all back in Ōpōtiki, and in his diary Austin records the high spirits of the whole expedition as the men awaited the arrival of the Minister of Defence, Donald McLean. But he contrasts that with the poor physical state of the Whanganui force, and the cold conditions that they now had to endure:

> 31st Fine morning but the men are all very stiff after the march yesterday. Some of the natives had their feet frightfully cut, the road was through stoans and some verry large ones at that, all the way with the exception of about (2) miles or so. They will want a day or twos rest before they can do anything. The remainder of the forse arrived to day with the prisoners at 4 p.m. all right. …

> 3rd … we have not had any parades since our return as the men has been engaged all their time in building huts for themselves as we have no tents.

> … when he [McLean] comes we expect the order for Wanganui again as we have no clothes I have only a shawl no trousers and only one shirt no boots and as winter has set in hear it is frightfull there is frost every night and some days it is 12 oclock before the white frost has disappeared off the ground in the mornings

there is not one of us but has a cold and the doctor in charge of this post has no medicine so we have to bear it as best we can ...

4th ... there was a great war dance hear today there was about 1500 men and women took part in it all of whom were nearly naked and before it was over it nearly ended in one party shooting the other it took Kemp and Wi Kingi all they could do to prevent it the Ngatiporous said that they were superior to all natives in New Zealand the Arawas and Wanganuis would not stand that and from words it nearly came to blows. But after some little time it was settled to all appearance and they were friends again but it put an end to the war dance which was the most disgusting I have ever seen I have seen many a war dance but the like of this one I have never seen for smut. ...

A report in the *Otago Daily Times* of 7 May quoted an account that it said had been published in unidentified 'Auckland papers', which emphasised, among other things, the run-down physical condition of the Ngāti Porou and Whanganui men:

> The question of another expedition into the Uriwera country was discussed, but the natives — especially those of Major Ropata's division — were so very footsore — boils and sores having broken out on the legs and feet of many of them, and the season having become excessively cold in the mountain regions of the Uriwera country — it was decided to send the natives back to their homes.[126]

Meanwhile, as the senior rangatira of Whanganui, Ngāti Porou and Ngāi Tai awaited McLean's arrival they wrote their reports to the minister. Those of Ropata, Te Kēpa and Topia Turoa have been well quoted earlier; Te Kēpa was also fulsome in his praise of his allies from Ngāi Tai, Ngāti Awa and Ngāti Pukeko. In concluding his report to McLean, he singled out some of their rangatira:

> Mr. McLean, I wish to bring under your notice the good doings of the Chief Wiremu Kingi, of the Ngaitai Tribe; of Kerei Kawakura, of the Ngatiawa; both behaved well. Also the Ngatipukeko Tribe, headed by their chief Te Meihana: they all did their work equally well. This finishes my report.[127]

Wiremu Kingi Tutahuarangi's own report of 1 April was very matter of fact, but it concluded with an expression of his ongoing and longstanding concerns about his neighbours the Whakatōhea:

> Those of the Hauhaus who were killed in the attack by us there were nineteen;

those who were taken prisoners, men, women, and children, altogether there were 300. I will say no more just now to you.

My friend, my heart is grieved for the proceedings of these people, the Whakatohea. I should be glad if these people were removed to some other place, lest if they should remain here they may again escape and join the Hauhaus, and the blame be laid upon me and my European friends at Opotiki.[128]

Wiremu Kingi's concern about Whakatōhea loyalties was shared by McLean, Clarke and Ropata, and would be addressed after McLean's arrival. It was heightened by Porter's discovery at Maraetahi of a letter purportedly written to Te Kooti by the Whakatōhea rangatira Te Ranapia, which suggested that Whakatōhea had provided Te Kooti with munitions. However, those who knew Te Ranapia's handwriting said the letter did not seem to be in his hand. The issue plainly needed to be addressed with Te Ranapia, which happened when McLean arrived in Ōpōtiki on 8 April, having been delayed after the steamer on which he and Clarke were travelling broke down and had to return to Auckland for repairs.

What was not contained in Wiremu Kingi's formal report was the completely different appreciation he had developed as a result of working alongside Te Kēpa during the Waioeka assaults. In his report of 18 April, Henry Clarke recorded Wiremu Kingi's views as expressed to him on the 8th at Ōpōtiki:

Wiremu Kingi, chief of the Ngaitai, who has been serving under Major Kemp ever since the Whanganui came to the Bay of Plenty, told me that he had served under Pakeha colonels and majors, but none of them would compare with Major Kemp; and he concluded his remarks by saying, 'That is a man of judgment, and one I would follow to death.'[129]

CONSEQUENCES OF THE RONGOPAI WITH ERU TAMAIKŌWHA

The issue of Te Kēpa's judgement would be addressed by McLean when he arrived in Ōpōtiki, having earlier come into question when the minister learned of the rongopai that Te Kēpa had entered into with the Tūhoe rangatira Eru Tamakōwha. McLean was keenly aware that throughout the country opposition settler voices, and some newspapers such as the *Otago Daily Times*, viewed this unauthorised action by Te Kēpa as proof that the Fox and McLean government had lost control of the campaign in pursuit of Te Kooti. Tamaikōwha was regarded by the Pākehā community as having led a campaign of terror against settler farmers in the Ōhiwa/Waioeka areas for some years without suffering any effective retribution. The timing of Te Kooti's raid on Ōpape, coming hard on the heels of the news of Te Kēpa's rongopai with Tamaikōwha, could not have been worse for McLean politically. It was not until 8 April, however, when they met at Ōpōtiki, that McLean and Te Kēpa came face to face and there was an opportunity to address the issue.

It seems logical that McLean might have considered it likely that Te Kēpa's and Ropata's joint actions over the last few weeks had changed the political situation dramatically. After all, now McLean could point to the capture of the two pā at Waipuna and Maraetahi, the release of all the Whakatōhea captives taken by Te Kooti, and the killing or capture of many of Te Kooti's closest supporters, including Hakaraia. It is probably a mark of the level of personal affront that McLean still felt in response to the rongopai that he seems to have been dismissive of Te Kēpa's explanation. Indeed, he seemed unwilling to engage with Te Kēpa at all either on that issue or on potential land confiscations facing Whanganui.

In his report of 18 April, Henry Clarke described the nature of the very brief exchanges between the two men (and Clarke's choice of words to describe Tamaikōwha itself demonstrates the pressures McLean was facing from the Pākehā community): 'Major Kemp also entered into some explanation of his truce with the notorious murderer Tamaikōwha, but was told that he had acted on his own responsibility, without the sanction of the Government.'[130]

It was not very long, however, before McLean realised just how sensible Te Kēpa's action had been. First, the rongopai meant Te Kēpa and the government received a flow of information about Te Kooti's general location in the Waioeka through Tamaikōwha, and that enabled Te Kēpa and the Whanganui to head off into the upper Waioeka area to search for him. Second, it removed from the reckoning a rangatira who was potentially a major supporter of Te Kooti, and with it the necessity to commit forces to searching the whole of the Waimana.

Third, it provided very timely protection for Tamaikōwha from Ropata Wahawaha and his Ngāti Porou, who were about to surge down the Waimana from Maungapōhatu to attack him and his people in the lower Waimana; the rongopai thus ensured that peace reigned in this major Urewera catchment and a dangerous foe was pacified. Finally, it was to save Tamaikōwha and his people from the pressures being exerted on all other Urewera tribes to abandon their lands and come out of the Urewera if they wished to avoid attack.

McLean's realisation of the wider benefits of the rongopai was demonstrated by his approach on the far western side of Te Urewera. In late February, and all through March and April, McLean was holding back Captain Gilbert Mair and Captain George Preece and their two Arawa Flying Columns from pushing aggressively into Te Urewera. He restrained them because, increasingly, it appeared from their reports that they were likely to achieve by negotiation the surrender of most of the Ngāti Patuheuheu and Ngāti Whare from the western areas of Te Urewera, and even of some of the major Tūhoe rangatira from the Ruatāhuna area. As these negotiations progressed, and some major rangatira led their people out of the western Te Urewera bush country to surrender, it became plain that Tūhoe, and their allies such as Ngāti Whare and Patuheuheu, had been swayed by the rongopai agreed between Te Kēpa and Tamaikōwha.

The fact that even Ropata had honoured the rongopai as he and his Ngāti Porou descended the Waimana from Maungapōhatu had also obviously made an impression on the Tūhoe rangatira. It is quite clear that as the surrender negotiations advanced very cautiously, but promisingly, Te Kēpa's actions had provided Tūhoe rangatira with some confidence that they would receive fair treatment from Crown officers or officials. The result was that they started to consider beginning the difficult resolution of the Crown–Tūhoe conflict.

LT COL ST JOHN'S ATTACK ON TAMAIKŌWHA

On 23 April, at this critical stage in the negotiations with central and western Tūhoe rangatira, Lt Col St John at Ōpōtiki heard that Eru Tamaikōwha and some of his relatives, relying on the rongopai, had descended the Waimana. They were reported as staying at the Whakarae pā, on the Nukuhou River near Ōhiwa harbour, just southwest of Kutarere. This old location known as Whakarae was later called Matakerepū pā; modern Whakarae pā is well up the Waimana River, by its junction with the Waiiti Stream.

In fact, Tamaikōwha's purpose in coming down the Waimana to Whakarae was to send his son to Ōhiwa with letters intended to confirm that the government was honouring the rongopai he had entered with Te Kēpa. In these, Tamaikōwha asserted that the rongopai was being observed on his side, and that he was not supporting Te Kooti, but each letter threatened that if further invasion of his lands occurred he would fight back.

St John was aware that the government had never sanctioned Te Kēpa's rongopai and, seemingly basing his decision on that fact, resolved to lead a lightning

Lieutenant-Colonel J.H.H. St John.
Ref: 1/2-028459-F, Alexander Turnbull Library, Wellington, NZ

raid on Whakarae in an attempt to capture Tamaikōwha and his people. He made no effort to obtain advice or agreement from the government before launching his raid. The results were to prove disastrous, both for the state of negotiations with Tūhoe, and for St John personally.

Although the raid was staged in darkness, the approach of the attackers was detected and Tamaikōwha and all his people were able to escape, with three exceptions. One of Tamaikōwha's sons, with a young companion, was detained at Ōhiwa after delivering his father's letters, but the worst result was that Tamaikōwha's elderly uncle Tipene was killed. (Tamaikōwha was later to build a wharenui at Tauwharemanuka and name it Tipene in honour of his uncle.)

The entirely predictable result of St John's raid on Whakarae and the killing of Tipene was a deep sense of outrage among all Tūhoe rangatira — and of course, particular outrage and deep hurt for Tamaikōwha, who felt personally betrayed by the killing of his uncle and the detention of his son. His feelings would have been exacerbated by the fact that his son had actually been sent from Whakarae into Ōhiwa to convey the letters intended to ensure the government was adhering to the rongopai. Instead, as he justifiably now saw it, the government's response was to reject the rongopai, without informing him of that decision. Even worse, the rejection took the form of a treacherous attempt to capture or kill him and his people.

As a result of McLean's angry reaction to the news of the attack, Tamaikōwha's son and his friend were released in late May, which may well have helped to restrain Tamaikōwha from turning back to his former more aggressive actions and seeking retribution. But reaction to the raid and the killing of Tipene went well beyond Tamaikōwha, having an immediate effect on the negotiations with Tūhoe, as their rangatira lost all trust in the good faith of the government.

MCLEAN'S REACTION TO THE ATTACK

McLean was plainly furious when he read St John's report on 7 May. His reaction was immediate and decisive:

> Auckland, 7th May, 1870.
> I have to-day received your letter of the 26th ultimo, reporting that you had made an attack upon the Chief Eru Tamaikowha, during the time he was on a visit to Wakarae, and in communication with the Arawa stationed at Ohiwa.
> ... The course you have taken is not only likely to endanger the safety of the settlements at the Bay of Plenty, but also to impress the Natives with the conviction that an act of treachery has been committed by an English officer.

I cannot, therefore, too strongly deprecate your action in this instance, which leaves me no alternative but to remove you from the command at Opotiki.

You will, therefore, be good enough to hand over charge of the district to Major Mair, who has been instructed to assume the duties with which you have been intrusted at Opotiki.[131]

As it turned out, however, St John did not receive McLean's letter for some weeks, as by the time it reached Ōpōtiki he had already left to carry out McLean's and Ormond's earlier orders to pursue Te Kooti up in the Waipuna and Maraetahi pā areas. This expedition, led by St John and Wiremu Kingi Tutahuarangi of Ngāi Tai, left Ōpōtiki on 12 May.

ST JOHN AND WIREMU KINGI'S EXPEDITION INTO WAIOEKA

It must have come as shattering news to St John when he emerged from the bush after nearly two weeks of extremely hard effort to learn that he had been summarily dismissed from his command by a letter written five days before he had headed into the hills. Notwithstanding, on 24 May he dutifully wrote a full report to McLean, describing the travails of his expedition with Wiremu Kingi.

While St John may have been a headstrong man, he was obviously also a physically tough one, as were all those with him on such a challenging winter trip:

... I gathered together a Native force for the purpose of clearing the Waioeka, in pursuit of Te Kooti. William King, of Ngaitai, got together his men, and Te Hata's and Matenga's [both rangatira of Whānau a Apanui], whilst I obtained the Ngatipukeko and Whakatāne. The force assembled was larger than I intended, ... but the Natives did not like going in less numbers.

Unfortunately the weather turned bad. I started on the 12th, and on the 15th the rain commenced, and the rivers rose. I had taken the Tutaitoko track, and on arriving at Raepawa it was as much as we could do to cross half the force over to Tahora.

We decided upon falling back to Maraetahi to economize our provisions, and wait for the subsidence of the flood, I taking the right bank, and Wi Kingi the left. On the 17th we both got to Maraetahi. I had seen no traces, but King had seen tracks leading up the river.

The flood was still such that we could not communicate, and here we were obliged to remain for six days. Scouting parties were sent out, who reported the other fords to be even worse than this.

Attempts to bridge the stream by felling trees at narrow places failed; huge ratas and rimus being swept away like straws. At last Taniora, of Motu, hit on a very good plan. By tripods lashed together and connected with poles a sort of bridge was formed, by which we were enabled to cross the river — here some forty yards wide, and for half that distance four feet deep, with an awful current.

By this time we had been ten days out, under almost incessant rain. The rivers were rising, and the information I received was to the effect that once the winter flood had begun, it would not go down again.

It was with great reluctance that I gave in at last to the unanimous ideas of the Natives, and turned homewards.

To get back we had to find our way as best we could through the bush, and it took us three days to accomplish the march Mr. Porter did in one.

The Whakatōhea, who had a sick man on a litter, had to come on by slow marches, and the rear is not even yet in.[132]

It is not possible to confirm the numbers of men on this expedition as no record was kept, but it must have been large. There were contingents from Ngāi Tai, Whānau a Apanui, Ngāti Pukeko, Ngāti Awa and some Whakatōhea as well as settler volunteers.

This was the last expedition to head up the Waioeka in direct pursuit of Te Kooti and any Whakatōhea supporters. After Hira Te Popo's surrender on 17 June, no further Whakatōhea lived up the gorge for some years.

FINAL GOVERNMENT FORAYS INTO THE WAIOEKA AND MOTU AREAS

In July 1871, Ngāti Porou under Ropata and Porter descended the Waioeka in the closing stages of their third invasion of the Urewera, during which they visited the unoccupied Maraetahi pā site.

Then, in October 1871, Porter and a group of 65 Ngāti Porou, Ngāi Tai and Whakatōhea travelled up the Waioeka once more to the site of the still unoccupied Maraetahi pā. From there they headed west to the Waimana as they took resupplies back to the Waimana from Ōpōtiki during the course of Ropata's last invasion of Te Urewera.

Another expedition into the upper Motu area, adjacent to the upper Waioeka, was conducted by Wiremu Kingi Tutahuarangi of Ngāi Tai. He entered from Tōrere for a month in April and May 1871, coming out at Tūranga (Gisborne). Tutahuarangi encountered no sign of Te Kooti or any of his people. In fact, there was no contact at all with any of Te Kooti's people in the upper Waioeka or Motu River headwaters on any of these occasions.

NGĀTI POROU RESPONSE TO CRITICS OF 'MĀORI-ONLY' POLICY

All of Ngāti Porou's efforts in Te Urewera had involved repeated, strenuous travel with inadequate food supplies. In conjunction with Whanganui in the Waioeka these efforts had resulted in a significant reduction of Te Kooti's mana and the dispersion of his forces. In the end, under this constant pressure in their own homelands, Tūhoe rangatira withdrew their support for Te Kooti.

However, in the eyes of many Pākehā detractors such as Colonel Whitmore (who had led earlier conventional military pursuits of Te Kooti, and had been in command at Ngātapa), Ropata had always just failed actually to kill or capture Te Kooti. Disparaging comments kept circulating in the media, and orally, to the extent that on 16 July 1870 Ngāti Porou rangatira felt compelled to issue a rare public statement in response. It was published in the *Wellington Independent* on 23 July, under the heading 'MAORI REPLY TO EUROPEAN SLANDERS'.

(TO THE EDITOR OF THE INDEPENDENT.)

[Translation.] Wellington, July 19,1870. Sir,— We, the people of the Ngatiporou tribe, publish this that you, the Europeans and the Maoris, may know our thoughts in respect of fault-finding statements which have been published, and which we have seen.

It is stated that the Government have done wrong in entrusting the whole conduct of affairs [with regard to fighting] to the Maoris. We on our part say to you, whoever you are, who made that statement, that your opinion is not correct; for our faith with you, the Europeans has not been broken. You commenced by introducing Christianity, we embraced that; next, the law, we took fast hold of that, and continued during the year 1865 up to this present year 1870 …

We say that a hard-faced man is not the one to pacify others, but a man of a generous disposition will succeed. Now, we object to European officers giving orders to the Maori soldiers; let the Europeans be over their European soldiers, and let the Maoris have their own Maori officers; but notwithstanding that division both are under the one law, and both are working for one object, and there is one authority over all the work that we are together engaged upon.

There is no reason why Colonel Whitmore — a European officer — should curse Major Ropata as he has done. Ropata is not jealous of him; if there is any such feeling it is on his side. We, the Maoris, have not yet been able to discover the magnitude of your European ideas — they may be large, or they may be otherwise. For Colonel Whitmore, we have acted together, cease, you and your supporters from acting as you have done; do not attempt to draw either pakeha or Maori into your foolish ways of thinking. …

Friends,— You who are our sincere friends, work out a system, that shall be alike beneficial to Whitmore and the Maoris, so that we may live united together, and governed by one law, with one idea and one object in view — that of peace and happiness. — From your friends,
CAPTAIN HOTENE,
MOKENA KOHERE,
IHARAIA HOUKAMAU
MAJOR ROPATA WAHAWAHA

THE CREATION OF THE MYTH OF A MAJOR NGĀTI POROU SUCCESS

The later myth that developed — that Ngāti Porou had played the leading role in the events in the Waioeka in March 1870 — has its genesis in the way Porter fudged the record in his published diary entry for 26 March, the day following the fall of Maraetahi pā:

26th March.— At daylight, 120 men started out to endeavour to follow the trail of Te Kooti. In the afternoon Kemp and Topia, with our men out since yesterday, returned, bringing in 303 prisoners, who were escaping from here and fell into their hands. Nineteen of the enemy were killed since the attack upon the pa, many of them falling unawares into the hands of the Wanganuis, when followed by our men in the rear. Hakaraia is amongst the killed; Kereopa, Karanama, and Kaiwhatu, narrowly escaped in the confusion of taking so many prisoners. It was horrible to see the manner in which some of the dead were hacked about. One man was partly in and partly out of the river, his head was smashed to atoms, and the brains floating about upon the water.[133]

This account, which was published in the *Appendices to the Journals of the House of Representatives*, can only be described as markedly misleading in the impression it conveys.

For a start, the statement that Kemp and Topia arrived 'bringing in 303 prisoners, who were escaping from here and fell into their hands' was factually wrong, as Porter would have well known by the time he wrote up his diary. The very next sentence in the published version of his diary was also fudged: 'Nineteen of the enemy were killed since the attack upon the pa, many of them falling unawares into the hands of the Wanganuis, when followed by our men in the rear.'

The phrase 'since the attack upon the pa' leads the reader to believe that the 19 men were killed after the fall of Maraetahi pā, and the sentence suggests that the victims were being pursued by Ngāti Porou before being killed by them, with others 'falling unawares into the hands of the Wanganuis'. Porter knew the reality was that the Whanganui had killed all those men well upriver from Maraetahi. There is simply no mention at all in Porter's published diary of the successful Whanganui attacks, nor is any mention made of the existence of Waipuna pā, or its capture by Whanganui. Yet, inexplicably, this version of events on 26 March quickly became the basis of the 'official' version when Porter's account was adopted, and corrupted even further by Henry Clarke in his report to the Under Secretary of the Native Department dated 18 April. It is important to record that Clarke wrote his report after he had met in Ōpōtiki with both the Whanganui Contingent and later the Ngāti Porou and Porter.

While Porter's inaccuracy lay primarily in his apparently deliberate omission of any mention of Whanganui successes before or at Waipuna pā, Clarke took matters further in a manner that is startling in its combination and confusion of the two pā assaults at Waipuna and Maraetahi. This despite the fact that he must have known from his discussions with Whanganui that the two attacks had occurred on separate days.

Once again the lack of any mention of the Whanganui attack at Waipuna pā, and the capture by Whanganui of almost all of the hundreds of prisoners, are the most notable features of Clarke's contrived and misleading report:

> When the party neared Maraetahi the enemy were seen from the tops of the trees to be pursuing their usual avocations, and it was proposed by Topia to make an attack, but this was opposed by Kemp and Wiremu Kingi, their object being to turn Maraetahi. When this was done a descent was made, and so well timed was the movement that Kemp's advance guard of picked men struck the bed of the river just as Ropata surprised the picquet, as before related. The flying picquet fell in with this party, and were all taken prisoners.
>
> Major Kemp then ordered all his people to advance, and guided by the Whakatohea of his force, took possession of all the roads and passes, so that the greater portion of the enemy were intercepted in their flight from the Maraetahi Pa, and fell an easy prey to Kemp's men. The only resistance offered was by Te Kooti's own followers, twenty of whom, including the well-known old chief Hakaraia, were killed, without a serious casualty on the side of our people, two only being slightly wounded. Te Kooti, however, with between twenty and thirty men, escaped; and it is asserted by the prisoners that he has now only seven of the Chatham Islanders with him, all the rest having been killed or taken prisoners. All the Whakatohea brought away by Te Kooti from Opape were retaken, one of their number being killed. The notorious Kereopa managed to elude his pursuers from the fact that he was not recognized in the confusion occasioned by the affair.

Old Hakaraia was attempting to escape, but being well known to many of the Whanganui was shot down, and recognised by the Bay of Plenty Natives, who composed part of the attacking force.

Both forces united, and after a brief rest, with 325 prisoners including the retaken Whakatohea, returned to Opotiki.[134]

A CATALOGUE OF FACTUAL ERRORS IN CLARKE'S REPORT

Even a brief analysis of the errors in Clarke's report shows how factually wrong it was. For example:

> ... so well timed was the movement that Kemp's advance guard of picked men struck the bed of the river just as Ropata surprised the picquet, as before related. The flying picquet fell in with this party, and were all taken prisoners.

The Ngāti Porou attack on Maraetahi pā occurred early on the morning of 25 March, when most of the Whanganui were some 13–14 km away, at Waipuna pā. Only 100 of the Whanganui took up an ambush position that day at about the junction of the Waioeka and the Ōmaukora, approximately 5–6 km upriver from Maraetahi. The main body of the Whanganui Contingent did not arrive at Maraetahi until the afternoon of the following day, 26 March. The members of the picquet, or their supporting kōkiri, may well have been the men picked up in the Whanganui ambush at or about the Ōmaukora junction on 25 March, but as noted above, that occurred some 5–6 km upriver from Maraetahi. They were not captured by an advance party of Whanganui linking up with Ropata. The two forces did not link up until the following day, 26 March.

> ... Major Kemp then ordered all his people to advance, and guided by the Whakatohea of his force, took possession of all the roads and passes, so that the greater portion of the enemy were intercepted in their flight from the Maraetahi Pa, and fell an easy prey to Kemp's men. ...

This statement verges on fantasy. Neither Major Kemp nor any of his men were involved in taking possession of 'all the roads and passes' from Maraetahi. Nor were the 'greater portion of the enemy' who fled from Maraetahi intercepted by Kemp's forces. Most in fact got away up the bush-covered ridges behind the pā. On 26 March, as the Whanganui Contingent moved downriver from Waipuna to Maraetahi, they killed just four people who were fleeing from Maraetahi and captured none. The reason for this outcome was that there were so few present to intercept by then.

> The only resistance offered was by Te Kooti's own followers, twenty of whom, including the well-known old chief Hakaraia, were killed, without a serious casualty on the side of our people, two only being slightly wounded.

Hakaraia was not killed at Maraetahi on 25 March, but the day before at Waipuna, 13–14 km away. Nor were 20 killed at Maraetahi. Only two were wounded near there, 2 km away at Te Karoro Gorge.

> All the Whakatohea brought away by Te Kooti from Opape were retaken, one of their number being killed.

None of the Whakatōhea taken from Ōpape by Te Kooti were retaken at Maraetahi pā on 25 March. All those events occurred the day before, at Waipuna pā.

> The notorious Kereopa managed to elude his pursuers from the fact that he was not recognised in the confusion occasioned by the affair. Old Hakaraia was attempting to escape, but being well known to many of the Whanganui was shot down, and recognised by the Bay of Plenty Natives, who composed part of the attacking force.

Neither Kereopa nor Hakaraia, nor the Whanganui, were at Maraetahi at the time of its fall on 25 March. Kereopa had already escaped the Whanganui assault on Waipuna pā the day before. Hakaraia had been captured at Waipuna on 24 March, and tomahawked there, not shot.

In most of his reports, Henry Clarke was particularly careful to be accurate. In this report he was far less than accurate — his account of the attack on Maraetahi pā was so contrived, and so compounded with events at Waipuna events, as to be almost nonsense. Clarke's inaccuracies were particularly harmful because of his official position — as the civil commissioner at Tauranga his mana was very high. His account of events became an integral part of the official published record.

OTHER INACCURACIES IN PORTER'S DIARY ACCOUNT

The effect on the historical record of this series of inaccuracies was probably exacerbated by Porter further fudging his account of the events at Maraetahi by concluding his entry for 26 March in the published version of the diary in a dramatic and grisly manner: 'It was horrible to see the manner in which some of the dead were hacked about. One man was partly in and partly out of the river, his head was smashed to atoms, and the brains floating about upon the water.'[135] If Porter indeed saw such a sight on 26 March, rather than hearing a description of it, he can only have seen it many kilometres distant from Maraetahi. That is because all of the tomahawk killing was carried out by Whanganui well before they headed downriver from Waipuna on 26 March to reach Maraetahi.

Porter's entry for 26 March began with the words, 'At daylight, 120 men started out to endeavour to follow the trail of Te Kooti.' However, his entry for the following day makes it plain that the 120-man patrol actually headed uphill and inland from Maraetahi to the west, and crossed over to the Waimana catchment. In other words, on 26 March there was no Ngāti Porou patrol up the Waioeka River that Porter could have been with, or where he could have seen the grisly sights he described in the diary account he forwarded to McLean.

Moreover, in the entry for 27 March, Porter refers to 'they' rather than 'we', which suggests he was definitely not with the group of 120 men who had headed out west on the follow-up patrol the day before:

> 27th March, Sunday.— The 120 men out yesterday returned, bringing three prisoners, and report having killed one man. They followed the track of some thirty men as far as Te Punga. At Waimana [they] learned it was the Urewera of Te Kooti returning to Ruatahuna, and hearing from one of the prisoners that Te Kooti had not gone in that direction, they returned.

It appears far more likely that if Porter did indeed personally observe the bodies of some of those who had been tomahawked, it would have been when he was part of one of two strong patrols, comprising 150 men each, who were sent out two days later. On that day, 28 March, he uses the word 'we', which suggests he was indeed on one of those patrols:

> 28th March.— We started this morning in two parties of 150 men each, the one of Wanganui and the other of Ngatiporou. We travelled over some very bad places, being afraid to keep the direct track lest we should meet some of Te Kooti's scouts, and they give him the alarm.

In the entry for 29 March, he included the following observation:

> When, returning, in the bed of the creek where the dead Hauhaus were, we found a number of them buried, and others half-eaten by dogs; also two dogs hanging upon a tree close by, evidently done by the Hauhaus.

That would appear to suggest that it was on 29 March, not on 26 March, that he saw tomahawked bodies in the riverbed. They were not at Maraetahi as his earlier entry suggested. They were either 6 km upriver at the ambush site, or 14 km away at Waipuna pā.

PORTER'S DIARY — CONTEMPORARY, OR AMENDED LATER?

The inaccuracies in the 26 March entry in Porter's published diary confirm that many parts of it were creatively crafted at a later date. Weight is lent to this conclusion when the entry for 26 March in the published diary is compared with that in his original handwritten report, which he handed to Lt Col St John on 31 March after his arrival at Ōpōtiki. It was this handwritten report that St John sent on to Lt Col Lyon in Auckland. In this first report there is no reference at all to his seeing tomahawked bodies in the riverbed or being with a patrol that day:

> 26th March
>
> 120 men of Ngatiporou out to follow the track of Te Kooti. In the afternoon Kemp and Topia arrived bringing with them 303 prisoners of Whakatohea and Te Kooti's people captured on escaping from here — Maraetahi. Whakatohea were taken some distance in rear of Maraetahi. Kereopa Kanama Kaiwhatu managed to escape in the confusion of taking so many prisoners.
>
> 27th
>
> Men out have returned …[136]

This evidence of a redrafting of his diary for potential publication, and other examples given earlier, gives rise to considerable circumspection as to the accuracy and overall contemporary nature of Porter's published diary. The redrafting process could also go some way to explaining how the published diary strangely omits any entry for 24 March on the approach up the Waioeka River.

Porter submitted his diary for publication to the Minister of Defence on 28 April, nearly a month after he had returned to Ōpōtiki from Maraetahi. In his covering letter, written from Tūranganui (Gisborne), he made it plain that the version he was forwarding was not in its original form:

> Sir - I have the honor herewith to forward a copy of my rough diary kept during the march of Ngatiporou expedition through Urewera country. It has not been carefully copied. I therefore leave it to your Honor to excuse all corrections and alterations.

Yet despite the inaccuracies and omissions in Porter's diary, and the omissions and even contrived fabrications in Clarke's report, they became part of the official history of the 1870 Waioeka events. Both were published on 7 July 1870 in the *Appendices to the Journals of the House of Representatives*. In contrast, Austin's clear and thorough contemporary diary of the actions of the Whanganui Contingent was not published at all in the official records. (It needs to be borne in mind that

Lieutenant Porter was an officer and Austin an NCO; that mattered a great deal in those days.)

However, Major Te Kēpa's report and that of Topia Turoa were published in the 1870 *Appendices to the Journals of the House of Representatives*. Each of these reports included details of significant matters that make a mockery of Porter's and Clarke's accounts. For example:
- the captures and killings during the assaults on seven pā or puni;
- the major assault on Waipuna pā;
- the capture of nearly all the prisoners by Whanganui;
- the release of all the Whakatōhea during the final assault at Waipuna pā; and
- the killing of all except one of the men killed by both forces.

With the exception of the four men killed at the ambush site near the Ōmaukora junction on 25 March, and the four men shot on 26 March during the Whanganui descent of the river to Maraetahi pā, Te Kēpa's and Tūroa's reports made clear that all these events occurred well before the attack on Maraetahi pā. Their reports made it plain that all those outcomes were achieved by Whanganui and their allies, and not by Ngāti Porou. (Even the eight men killed later on 25 and 26 March were of course also killed by the Whanganui, not Ngāti Porou.)

Given that these two separate reports were written by two well-respected Whanganui rangatira, Te Kēpa and Topia Turoa, both of whom held the rank of major in the New Zealand militia, it is hard to comprehend how the newspapers of the time did not pick up on the serious inaccuracies and distortions apparent in Porter's and Clarke's reports.

NEWSPAPER REPORTING OF THE EVENTS IN THE WAIOEKA

In fact, the accounts that were recorded in the official reports by Porter and Clarke appear to have provided the basis of the information that most of the newspapers picked up and effectively repeated as the accurate version of events. That Porter's version of events was spread very early on is highlighted by a diary entry made by Lt Herbert Way at Maketū. Way was the man in charge of provisioning the Arawa Flying Columns inland at Kaiteriria, and other government forces along the Bay of Plenty, using a seven-horse team to carry the supplies and ammunition. On 4 April, just days after the Waioeka events, Way wrote in his diary:

> Arrived at Maketu at sundown. Trooper Kelly arrived from Opotiki with despatches for Tauranga. Major Ropata has had a fight with Te Kooti up the

Waioeka Gorge. He took 31 prisoners & killed 17. Ropata has got all the
Opape natives back, except a few that Te Kooti and Kereopa took with them.
Hakaraia is killed.

The lack of any mention at all of Te Kepa, Topia Turoa and the Whanganui Contingent suggests strongly the base source must have been Porter.

The newspapers similarly expressed excited admiration for the achievements of Ropata and his Ngāti Porou, both in bold headlines and in the text in their columns. Only occasionally did some of the newspapers provide passing recognition of the role of Te Kēpa and Topia Turoa and the Whanganui Contingent. It is intriguing, however, to note that the media adulation of Ropata and Ngāti Porou commenced well before Porter's and Clarke's reports were published on 7 July.

Before addressing the increasing adulation expressed in the media for Ropata's achievements in the Waioeka, the point needs to be made strongly that there is no evidence that Ropata himself was ever involved in self-promotion in the media, or with officialdom at the expense of other rangatira. The only report he made with regard to the Waioeka events was succinct and to the point, and as observed earlier, if anything it even had a tone of apology for the failure to capture Te Kooti. Moreover, Ropata did not speak English at all, and he would not have appreciated the nature of the media attention he was receiving, or its inaccuracy as to the Waioeka events.

The first manifestation of this focus on Ropata Wahawaha came two days after the arrival at Ōpōtiki on 31 March of over 1100 people – pursuers, prisoners, and the released Whakatōhea. The *Daily Southern Cross* of 2 April published an account that immediately highlighted Major Ropata as leading an assault on Maraetahi pā, with Major Kemp in a secondary supportive role of capturing fugitives:

Important Native Intelligence
DEFEAT OF TE KOOTI
19 Killed and 300 prisoners
HAKARAIA KILLED

The government received a despatch from Opotiki yesterday, which contained the following important news:

On the 25th of March Major Ropata attacked the Maraetai pa, and captured it after an hour's engagement.

Owing to the slight resistance offered Ropata did not think Te Kooti was present; which was actually the case. The garrison abandoned the pa after an hour's fighting, the fugitives falling into the hands of Major Kemp, who was marching down, after taking all the Whakatoheas up the river.

The total number of killed on the enemy's side is 19; prisoners taken, over 300. No loss reported by Major Ropata.

Te Kooti has escaped with about 20 followers. His track lay towards the Waimanawa; but he must have doubled back, as a following party reached Te Ponga, and found the Urewera had all deserted him. Rakuraku and others have also got off; but Hakaraia is killed.

The whole of the force and the prisoners were expected in Opotiki on April 1.[137]

Thus, already by 2 April, no mention was being made of the seven puni assaults on the night of 23-24 March by Te Kēpa and his Whanganui, or the capture of Waipuna pā on 24 March. To any reader of this article it would also appear that it was Ropata's men who had killed Hakaraia, not Whanganui.

It is worth noting that the source of the article was a 'despatch' to the government, without the source being identified. However, in the same edition of the newspaper another major story provided an insight as to who may have been the source of the 'despatch'. At page 3 appeared the following paragraphs:

… Today we publish the gratifying news that Te Kooti was defeated with heavy loss, in killed and prisoners, on the 25th ultimo, by the force under Major Ropata's command. The chief Hakaraia, who kept the Tauranga district in trouble for the last four years, was amongst the slain.

Particulars of the action, which was fought inland of Opotiki, in the Urewera country, were brought by Lieutenant Porter, who was with Ropata's party. The details will be found in another column.

This would appear to be the most damaging blow struck against the rebels during the war. It is no slight discouragement to Te Kooti, to find himself so severely beaten by Ropata; and the loss of Hakaraia cannot be supplied. …

Ropata has marched through it, capturing two pas, and taking in all 350 prisoners. Major Kemp, another native chief, has likewise behaved well in this affair; …

It may be that for some reason McLean himself, either on his own or in conjunction with Porter and Clarke, was also a source of material that increased the press adulation of Ropata. A strong pointer that way appeared on 7 April when the *Wellington Independent* newspaper printed the following story:

LATEST TELEGRAMS.

DEFEAT OF TE KOOTI BY ROPATA.

19 OF THE ENEMY KILLED, AND 300 TAKEN PRISONERS.

(FROM OUR OWN CORRESPONDENT.)
NAPIER, Tuesday, 5th.
Ropata attacked Te Kooti in the Urewera country, and defeated him, killing 19 of the enemy, and taking upwards of 300 prisoners. Hakaraia, one of the murderers of the Rev. Mr Volkner, is amongst the killed; but the arch-miscreant Te Kooti, with about 20 men made his escape.

The following telegram from Mr M'Lean has been received by the Government:—
Major Ropata attacked Te Kooti's position in the Urewera country. The fighting against the pa lasted an hour, and 19 of the enemy, including Hakaraia, were killed; 300 were taken prisoners by Ropata and Kemp. Te Kooti, with twenty followers, escaped.
The prisoners were to be at Opotiki yesterday (Friday).
Except the worst characters, I propose to place some under Kemp and Topia.
I leave again for the East Coast to-night or Monday.[138]

While McLean's telegram did make two brief references to 'Kemp', it commenced with the statement that only referred to Ropata: 'Major Ropata attacked Te Kooti's position in the Urewera country.'

To be fair to McLean, when he sent that telegram he had not spoken with Te Kēpa and Topia Turoa, or with Ropata, as he did not arrive at Ōpōtiki until 8 April. He did not, therefore, know on 5 April that Te Kēpa's Whanganui had attacked Waipuna pā and taken almost all of the prisoners, released the Whakatōhea, and done almost all of the killing. The only information he had to hand at that stage was the handwritten report of Lt Porter and Lt Col St John's earlier letter of 30 March. Nonetheless, the effect of his telegram was reflected in the heading 'DEFEAT OF TE KOOTI BY ROPATA', with no mention of Kemp.

This kind of excessive adulation for Ropata's achievements in the Waioeka was to continue. Numerous such stories appeared in a wide range of newspapers throughout New Zealand in April and May 1870. The general tone of these reports ensured that Porter's myth grew to 'reality' as time went by. One of the reasons for this was perhaps Porter's willingness to seek out the news, while Te Kēpa, Topia Turoa and the Pākehā Austin, and for that matter Ropata himself, did not. Evidence of this can be found in Austin's own diary, when the *Star of the South*, which was taking the Whanganui Contingent back home, called at Napier on 14 April. It was also carrying the prisoners who had been committed for trial in Wellington.

Austin's account is illuminating:

> 14 (April) ... Lieut Conlne Whitmore came on board today and showed me some newspapers and he wanted me to tell Kemp and Topia that Mr McLean had put this into the newspapers that Ropata had done all the work and the Wanganui natives had done nothing. This I knew was false and I refused to tell Kemp and Topia and Coln Whitmore got into a rage with me because I would not do as he told me. He had nothing to do with us and I refused point blank he then done his best to tell them himself the natives only laughed at him and pointed to the prisoners and told him to ask them who it was that took them ...

While obviously the Whanganui rangatira and Austin were all personally comfortable with the facts as they were known to them, in retrospect more politically aware people might have seen Porter's action as a ploy to establish a basis for greater recompense for Ngāti Porou from the government. This observation is pure surmise, as we will never know Porter's reasoning, but it is difficult to perceive any other reason for his obfuscation of the facts, other than possible embarrassment at being surprised at Te Karoro Gorge and enabling Te Kooti and his people to escape.

Lieutenant-Colonel George Whitmore.
Davis, William Henry Whitmore, 1812–1901.
Ref: PA2-0604, Alexander Turnbull Library, Wellington, NZ

The picture painted over the next month, as article after article, and headline after headline, reinforced Porter's myth, demonstrates that the significance of capturing the print media was as important in those days as the capture of television and online news is today.

Some of the examples that follow show how that pattern developed, but the first illustrates just how egregiously inaccurate the reporting was. Once again suspicion must fall on McLean as the source of this palpably incorrect account. This headline in the *Daily Southern Cross* of 6 April gives all credit to Ropata, and the story itself contains a hopelessly inaccurate description of Topia's report to McLean:

ROPATA'S VICTORY — FURTHER PARTICULARS.
We understand that a letter from the chief Topia was received by the Hon. the Native and Defence Minister yesterday. Topia confirms the previously published account of Ropata's victory; as to the death of Hakaraia and off 18 others of the enemy; and he states the number of prisoners at 325.[139]

In fact, what Topia Turoa had written to the Defence Minister was nothing like that at all. Rather, his report read:

Opotiki, 30th March, 1870.
Friend, salutations to you. Now listen. On the 20th day of March my war-party advanced on Waioeka. On the night before the 24th we came up with the Hauhaus at their first settlement. At 8 o'clock at night I attacked another of their positions. There were four men with me. We took it and took all the people prisoners, eight in number, principally women and children. On the same night we pushed on and attacked another position, and took all hands. From there we pushed on to the station occupied by Hakaraia, and here we caught Hakaraia and Wiremu Kingi. Kereopa escaped, but Hakaraia was killed — there were eighteen killed in all. The prisoners belonging immediately to Te Kooti, including men, women, and children there, were eighty-six, and including those belonging to the Whakatohea who were there, in all 218 persons, taken by Te Kooti. The whole of the killed and wounded and prisoners amounted in all to 323.
...
Friend, I think we should have taken Te Kooti, if it had not been that Ropata attacked the pa in which he was at the time. I think if I had had the storming or taking of the position we should have captured that man (Te Kooti).[140]

At this distance in time it is impossible to establish how or why such a level of inaccuracy could have been passed on to the *Daily Southern Cross*, or whether

McLean himself was responsible. But regardless of who was involved in pushing the Porter/Clarke myth, it continued to spread quickly throughout the country, as just a few more examples demonstrate:

Oamaru Times, 15 April 1870, headline: 'MAJOR ROPATA'S VICTORY', and text:

> ... we may safely congratulate the Colony upon a signal success against the rebels — not the Colony only, but specially the Native forces under Ropata, to whom the sole credit appears to be due. ... But, dead or alive, thanks to Major Ropata and the Friendly Natives under his command, his power for mischief has been greatly weakened.

Otago Witness, 16 April 1870, headline: 'ROPATA'S VICTORY'
Evening Post, 16 April 1870, headline: 'ROPATA'S RECENT SUCCESS'
Wellington Independent, 30 April 1870, headline: 'ROPATA'S CAMPAIGN IN THE UREWERA COUNTRY', and text:

> Moving with wonderful celerity, Ropata followed like a bloodhound on Te Kooti's track, travelling, it is said, night and day. Te Kooti was over a week in advance, yet in three or four days Ropata overtook him far away in the Uriwera wilds, at the pa Maraetahi. After an hour's fight during which Te Kooti lost the noted Hakaraia leader and 18 men, Ropata stormed the pa in very gallant style. Bursting out in all directions, the Hauhaus fled for their lives, but to finally get clear there appears to have been but one outlet, the bed of a river. In this direction it had been arranged that Kemp should advance to support Ropata, or secure fugitives if Ropata succeeded in forcing them to retire. The result was, by these judicious arrangements, that between them Ropata and Kemp netted 350 rebels and murderers.

The story continued to run. As late as 2 June, by which time Whanganui rangatira should have been interviewed by the newspapers, the *Wellington Independent* ran a story (which it attributed to the *Hawkes Bay Herald*) with the headline 'ROPATA AND HIS EXPEDITIONS', and the words: 'We learn from an eye witness that Ropata's advance on Waioeka to attack Te Kooti was a plucky affair.'

By now the Porter myth really did have a life of its own, and in time Porter was to reinforce it further — resulting in later historians being misled.

9

THE IMPACTS OF WAR

One of the most direct impacts of war, which tends to linger well after the last shots are fired, is the taking of prisoners. In campaigns such as this Waioeka one, the problem arises as to what is to be done with those prisoners.

Initially, as discussed earlier, Ngāti Porou left about fifty prisoners at Ōpōtiki while they conducted their operation up the Waioeka. The next identifiable group of prisoners brought down to Ōpōtiki were the more than 320 taken by Whanganui as they assaulted the seven puni and Waipuna pā on the night of 23–24 March, and over later days. These prisoners fell into three distinct categories:
› The Whakatōhea captives who were taken from Ōpape by Te Kooti,
› Te Kooti's fighting men, and
› The women and children who were family of those fighting men, or were otherwise supporters of Te Kooti's.

In his official report of 18 April, Henry Clarke recorded what then happened to Te Kooti's fighting men:
> On the 9th and the 11th instant, the witnesses against the prisoners (thirty-five in number, said to be of Te Kooti's immediate party) underwent a preliminary examination, and thirty-two of the prisoners were committed under 'The Disturbed Districts Act, 1869,' to take their trial for various offences under that

Act. The other three, being boys, were placed in Ropata's charge. ...

Thirty-one of the prisoners were shipped on board the 'Star of the South' on the 11th instant, together with the whole of the Wanganui expeditionary force.[141]

It seemed that the government had learnt from its mistakes, after its cavalier treatment in exiling the captives taken after the siege at Waerenga a Hika in 1865 to Wharekauri (the Chatham Islands) without trial. It had been a hard-earned lesson.

The women and children among Te Kooti's supporters were accorded different treatment, as Clarke also recorded:

> Just before embarkation the Hon. The Native Minister revisited the camp of the Wanganuis to give his decision regarding the women and children under the charge of Topia, about whom there had been several warm discussions amongst the allies.
>
> Mr. McLean explained that the Government did not consider women and children in the light of prisoners, and that, therefore, the women might elect with which of their relatives amongst the loyal Natives they would remain, the only condition being that they did not return to the disaffected Natives. The decision was acquiesced in and carried out, the chief part of the women choosing to remain under the charge of Wiremu Kingi, of the Ngaitai, a sufficient evidence of the estimation in which that influential young chief is held by the Natives generally.

OUTCOMES FOR WHAKATŌHEA

While many hapū were part of the grouping described simply as Whakatōhea, the actions of Hira Te Popo's Ngāti Ira are made relatively distinct in the historical documentation over the period from 1865 to 1870. This is partly because of the relatively high profile Hira Te Popo always maintained, and also because the responses of Ngāti Ira under his leadership had often been quite distinct from those of most other Whakatōhea hapū. Te Ūpokorehe also were often differentiated in the various reports, but it is not always so easy to discern from historical documents the differing actions of the more eastern hapū of Ngāti Rua, Ngāi Tamahaua, Ngāti Patu and Ngāti Ngāhere, which in general were described generically as Whakatōhea.

Of course, the confiscation of their lands, and being compelled to live together in the Ōpape reserve area at the eastern end of the rohe, also meant the individual hapū were not always separately acknowledged. Once more, however, Te Ūpokorehe were separated out as they were confined to the Hiwarau reserve, further to the west at Ōhiwa.

Given the outcomes of the land confiscations and the compulsion to live at Ōpape, it may be surprising to many Whakatōhea uri (descendants) of the other hapū, apart from Ngāti Ira, that in February 1870 many of their younger fighting men had actually decided to join up with the Whanganui Contingent against Te Kooti. As described earlier, however, over time relations had thawed with their Pākehā and Te Arawa occupiers in Ōpōtiki and Ōhiwa, and limited trade and other social relationships began to develop.

The first overt signs of a reluctant acceptance of the realities of that enforced lifestyle appeared when the Whakatāne and Ōpōtiki districts were threatened as Te Kooti's raids came nearer after 1868. Hira Te Popo's alliance with Te Kooti in 1869 had cast a shadow of suspicion in the minds of government officials about Whakatōhea loyalties, a feeling accentuated by the realisation that Whakatōhea people at Ōpape were making visits to their Ngāti Ira relatives at Maraetahi pā. For the latter part of 1869, however, when Te Kooti was in the Taupō and King Country areas, the fact of these earlier visits does not seem to have raised undue concerns.

The pressure rose a notch when Te Arawa established their base redoubt at Ōhiwa and started regular horseback patrols out to Ōpape and beyond in 1869. It then ramped up further when Te Kēpa and Topia and part of their Whanganui Contingent arrived and set up their base camp on the beaches east of Ōhiwa harbour on 11 February 1870. Their fighting men initially numbered some 200 men, augmented about two weeks later with the arrival of another 159 Whanganui who had been left inland at the Tapapa camp by the Mamaku ranges. That many fighting men, particularly when increased even further by the Ōhiwa force of about 60 Te Arawa, and the volunteer settler forces of about 40 men at Ōpōtiki, would have appeared formidable to Whakatōhea at Ōpape and Ōmarumutu, who could muster at most about 60 fighting men.

Similarly, the government forces would have seemed to Whakatōhea to be overwhelming for Te Kooti, despite his having the support of Hira Te Popo and his Ngāti Ira (whose fighting men probably numbered about 40 or 50 at most). Te Kooti was believed to have about 100 to 120 fighting men with him, and a similar number of supporting women and children. When it became clearer, in late February 1870, that Te Kooti had returned to Maraetahi pā, it must have become apparent that decisions would have to be made as to where Whakatōhea loyalties lay.

It was probably not too surprising that when government officers approached the Whakatōhea to join with the Whanganui Contingent, and weapons were offered for their own defence against Te Kooti, their rangatira Tiwai and Te Ranapia

Looking north down the Waioeka with Samuel Austin's 'three rivers' junction in view at modern Wairata. To the right of centre is the spur the Whanganui scouts are most likely to have climbed to obtain a view south up the Waioeka. (See pp. 127–28, 242–44.) Stu Spicer collection

Waioeka River looking north, over probable Waipuna pā site at terrace bend opposite junction with Te Pato Stream centre right. The seven pā or puni sites attacked on the night of 23/24 March lay downriver from Waipuna pā to the 'three rivers' junction. (See pp. 128–30, 241–43.) Harvey Brunt drone image

LEFT *The probable position of the Waipuna (Raepawa) pā site on a bend in the Waioeka opposite Te Pato Stream junction at lower centre. (See pp. 130; 235–37, 239–40.)*
Author collection

LEFT *An enlarged section of the photograph above showing likely whare sites to the left and centre of the terrace, with garden demarcation lines to the right. (See pp. 239–41.)*
Author collection

LEFT *Whare excavations at the probable Waipuna pā site are visible beside the track to Te Pato Stream. Chris Gray is by the track that leads down from the terrace to Te Pato Stream junction.*
Author collection

Nikau Flat hut on the Waioka River, a few hours walk upriver from Te Pato Stream junction. (See pp. 235–36, 239.)
Harvey Brunt drone image, March 2021

The Waioeka River in relatively low flow conditions immediately below Te Pato Stream junction. (See p. 149–50, 241.) Stu Spicer collection

LEFT *The Waioeka River immediately north/downriver from Te Karoro a Tamatea (Hell's Gate) gorge. The size of the person indicated with the yellow arrow provides scale for the depth and width of the river at that point. Ngāti Porou had to drop further down the river to make their crossing. Blue arrow indicates the direction of river flow.*
(See pp. 141–43.)
Stu Spicer collection

OPPOSITE *Looking upriver at the Te Karoro a Tamatea gorge. Te Kooti's picquet opened fire on Ngāti Porou from one of the bluffs at left (true right of the river, indicated by yellow arrow). Ngāti Porou had to drop back downriver to cross so they could fire across from an elevated terrace position (top right). Red arrows show their positions.*
(See pp. 137–43, 145–46.)
Stu Spicer collection

ABOVE *Maraetahi pā (circled area), looking south-west. Ōpanae Stream is at right with an unnamed creek that is likely where Te Kooti, his wife Huhana and others crossed when they fled from the pā (left of the building that lies to the right of the dotted line and is marked by a tall tree). They would have ascended the peak that is Pōkirikiri (red cross). A long ridgeline leads away to the west to the Waimana/Tauranga catchment.*
(See pp. 153–56, 225–27, 245–49.)
Harvey Brunt drone image

Maraetahi pā. The 42 whare and the large whare karakia (church) were most likely on the spur-line below the group of dead standing pine trees. The garden area that exceeded five acres was most likely located below to the right, as shown on the sketch below.
Harvey Brunt drone image

A modern artist's impression of Maraetahi pā before the Ngati Porou attack.
Stu Spicer

ABOVE *View north down the Waioeka River. The Maraetahi pā site is marked with a yellow cross. Te Karoro a Tamatea gorge is marked with a red cross. The yellow dotted line indicates Te Kooti's probable escape route.*
Stu Spicer collection

LEFT *A typical Te Urewera misty scene in the Waioeka catchment. This image was taken at the Wairata Stream.*
Stu Spicer collection

ABOVE *The large, flat elevated Ōtetere kererū 'food basket' area for Ngāti Ira. The Wairata Stream catchment area is upper left and the Ōpanae Stream valleys are at centre and right. The Waimana/Tauranga River lies beyond the skyline ridges. This was the likely route linking Maraetahi pā to the Waimana. The dotted line is the probable escape route followed by Te Kooti. (See pp. 155, 224–28, 245–49.)* Stu Spicer collection

ABOVE *Looking north down the Waimana/Tauranga River at the junction of the Tauranga River (centre left) and Waiiti Stream (bottom right) at modern Whakarae. Te Punga/Te Ponga hill (marked with the yellow cross), with current pine cover, sits above the junction. In the far distance lies modern day Waimana township, with the Bay of Plenty beyond. (See pp. 112, 117, 127, 227.)* Stu Spicer collection

LEFT *Mark Law, Eugene Hunia and author, October 2022, on the ridgeline between Ōponae and Wairata streams heading west towards Whakapirau Stream headwaters in the Waimana catchment. (See pp. 245–49.)* Chris Gray collection

accepted. Yet it was very significant that the majority of their younger fighting men also agreed to join the Whanganui Contingent. Thirty-four of these men accepted government engagement and went to Ōhiwa, where Austin records them arriving on 22 February. Although some fighting men were left with Te Ranapia at Ōpape, and they were also issued with weapons by the government, the reality was that the ability to fight off any raid by Te Kooti disappeared with their 34 young men to Ōhiwa.

The firming of relationships with government forces was suddenly thrown into chaos by Te Kooti's raid less than two weeks later, on 7 March. As discussed earlier, Te Ranapia's and Tiwai's initial reaction to that raid was to write a letter of complaint to Henry Clarke, as the government's civil commissioner at Tauranga, expressing their anguish at what had happened to their communities at Ōpape and Ōmarumutu. They also expressed their willingness to join any expedition to free their relatives, and in fact had already done just that with their men. It was plain from this correspondence, and the action of joining Te Kēpa's expedition, that Te Ranapia had not only not aligned himself with Te Kooti, but he and some of the fighting men still at Ōpape had actually campaigned against him.

Nevertheless, suspicion arose among the Crown officers about Te Ranapia's allegiance. On 30 March, when Lt Col St John received Porter's oral report on Maraetahi and reported to his superior officer Lt Col Lyon, he stated: 'Mr. Porter has a letter signed by Ranapia showing the complicity of the friendly Whakatohea inas much as it amounts [to] a present of ammunition and cap.* ... Besides this I presume some investigation will take place about Ranapia's complicity.'[142]

The 'investigation' into Ranapia's alleged complicity with Te Kooti had to await the arrival of McLean and Clarke at Ōpōtiki on 8 April and their meeting with the Whanganui Contingent. Clarke's report provides the detail of Ranapia's response, and also reveals Clarke's personal animosity towards Whakatōhea, which needs to be borne in mind when reading the report:

> This settled, the serious charge brought against the Whakatohea, of complicity with Te Kooti, had to be considered. The principal evidence against them was contained in certain letters found at Maraitai purporting to be signed by the Chief Ranapia and two others; and I beg to refer you to former correspondence on

---

* There is a difference between the original of this letter by St John, which is held by National Archives, and the published version in the *Appendices to the Journals of the House of Representatives*. In the original handwritten letter the wording appears as it does here, with the word 'to' missing, and the singular use of 'cap'. In the published version it reads, 'inasmuch as it *announces* a present of ammunition and caps.' The word 'amounts' is hard to read in the original, however it clearly has a crossed letter 't' in it, so it is far more likely to be 'amounts' than 'announces'.

this subject, in which I endeavoured to show that it was inadvisable to entrust the Whakatohea indiscriminately with Government arms.

The Hon. the Native Minister addressed the Whakatohea in terms of strong disapprobation for the duplicity shown by some of them, but he at the same time expressed a willingness to believe that the complicity complained of emanated from a few individuals, and not from the tribe generally. That it had been a matter of deliberation with him whether they ought not to be either removed altogether from the district or be disarmed.

Ranapia pleaded for himself. He said he was quite innocent of the charge brought against him. He recounted the services he had rendered to the Government against the Hauhaus. He reminded Mr. McLean that, when Opape was attacked by Te Kooti, he succeeded in making his escape, carrying with him all the arms and ammunition intrusted to his keeping by the Government, and asked whether it was likely, if he favoured Te Kooti's designs, he would have done so? The Whakatohea who were with Te Kepa and the Wanganuis also pleaded the services they had rendered. They stated that most of Te Kooti's men who were killed in the late expedition to Waioeka met their death at their hands, and that they thought this was sufficient evidence that they did not sympathize with his cause.

These statements deserved consideration, and the Hon. the Native Minister told them that certain members of the tribe were suspected on very good grounds, and that a very careful watch would be kept on them. That Ropata Wahawaha should be intrusted to look after them, and also that the Chiefs Wiremu Kingi, Te Tatana, and Te Hata, who were living much nearer to their settlements than Ropata, would be required to visit them occasionally, and that they should all live in one pa, and not, as heretofore, scatter themselves over the country. Ropata then addressed the Whakatohea. He told them that he accepted the responsibility, and that if he heard of any misbehaviour on their part he would himself punish them. Wiremu Kingi also spoke, and told the Whakatohea plainly that he did not feel altogether safe with such troublesome neighbours, but that he and his friends were willing to carry out the wishes of Mr McLean, not that he was very sanguine that any great good would result.[143]

It must have rankled with Whakatōhea to be told that their longstanding adversary, Wiremu Kingi of Ngāi Tai from Tōrere, was to be their close 'keeper'. Clashes between Ngāi Tai and Whakatōhea over their common boundary, relating to the area between Tarakeha and Haurere Point to the east of Ōpape, had been longstanding and hereditary. Wiremu Kingi's statement 'not that he was very sanguine' as to the outcome of the leniency shown to Whakatōhea by McLean was indicative of his lack of enthusiasm towards his Whakatōhea neighbours.

The fact that their more distant 'overseer' was named as Ropata of Ngāti Porou would also have rankled. Ngāti Porou were an iwi with whom Whakatōhea had engaged in major fighting in 1834, during the Musket Wars, as part of a taua of Mātaatua iwi who sought to bring succour to Whānau a Apanui when they were besieged by Ngāti Porou at Toka a Kuku pā at Te Kaha.

The other rangatira identified by McLean as having a supervisory role over Whakatōhea were Te Tatana Ngatawa and Te Hata, who were both of Whānau a Apanui. Te Tatana was from Maraenui, near the mouth of the Motu River, and Te Hata was from Raukokore. It is likely that their involvement would not have been resented as strongly, given the past close relationship between Whakatōhea and Whānau a Apanui during the 1834 siege at Te Kaha.

Moreover, it is highly likely that Te Ranapia personally, and Whakatōhea generally, were relieved that McLean appeared reluctant to accept allegations of complicity with Te Kooti and therefore took no action against them other than the imposition of loose 'oversight' by the specified rangatira. Although Clarke's report did not record this fact, a later report by J.H. Campbell, the Resident Magistrate for Waiapu, recorded that McLean also agreed that Whakatōhea could retain the government weapons with which they had been issued.[144] This concession suggests that some level of friendly relationship and trust between Whakatōhea and the government was maintained.

Campbell's report came nearly a month after McLean and Clarke had been at Ōpōtiki. He described what he saw on an inspection trip of Māori communities around Tai Rāwhiti, from Ōhiwa travelling around the eastern Bay of Plenty into Waiapu:

> At Opotiki a part of the Whakatohea tribe, numbering fifty men, besides women and children who were lately brought in by Rapata and Kemp, chiefs of the Ngatiporou and Whanganui tribes, were being detained. They are allowed to retain their arms upon Rapata pledging himself for their future good conduct. The remainder of this tribe, to the number of forty men, are still at a settlement up the Waioeka Gorge, about two day's march from Opotiki. Messengers were sent by them a few days ago for the purpose of ascertaining the intentions of their friends at Opotiki towards Te Kooti, before deciding upon their future course of action. The reply which has been sent to them, together with a letter from Lieut-Colonel St. John, warning them of the danger they incur by exhibiting any leaning towards Te Kooti, will probably have the effect of inducing them to come in and surrender to the Government.

> From all the friendly tribes, however, along the coast I hear strong doubts expressed of the prudence of placing any reliance upon them, and all regret that they have been left in possession of their arms. The day previous to my leaving Opotiki the portion of the tribe which had been detained there were permitted to return to their settlements at Opape and Omarumutu, about five miles distant, on account of the labour and difficulty of conveying their food so great a distance. They have pledged themselves to assist Lieut.-Colonel St. John in capturing Te Kooti in the event of his returning to Waioeka. ...
>
> The threat of Rapata to the Whakatohea of speedy retribution in the event of their proving faithless, is the best guarantee for their future good behaviour.

Campbell's report later re-emphasised the stressed nature of the relationship between Ngāi Tai and Whakatōhea:

> At Torere, thirteen miles south of Opotiki, is the stronghold of Wiremu Kingi and the Ngaitai. This tribe has ever proved loyal, although strong efforts were made by Te Kooti to gain them over. They number sixty good fighting men, soldierly, well-disciplined, and obedient to their chief. Wiremu Kingi will keep a close watch upon the actions of the Whakatohea, towards whom he bears little love.[145]

From Campbell's report, and another by Captain G.P. Walker, sent from Ōpōtiki in mid April, it appeared that regular interchanges were occurring throughout April and May 1870 between Whakatōhea on the coast and their Ngāti Ira relations in the upper Waioeka. Walker, who was temporarily in command at Ōpōtiki while Lt Col St John was visiting Whakatāne, made his report on 16 April, just over two weeks after the return of Whakatōhea from Waipuna pā. This makes clear that it was open knowledge that regular communications were still occurring between Whakatōhea at Ōpape and those under Hira Te Popo who were probably then living at a pā at Tahora:

> The people now living at Maraetahi consist of about 40 souls, the remnant of the Whakatohea, and they are reported as being ready to come in, provided they are assured of personal safety. Under these circumstances, I have advised that they be written to by their friends here, which no doubt will have the effect, together with Colonel St. John's letter, of inducing them to surrender. I have told the Whakatohea, in the event of their holding any intercourse with the emissaries of Te Kooti, to endeavour to induce them to lay down their arms, under a promise of being allowed to return to their people with the sanction of the Government.[146]

In a report of 19 April, Lt Col St John specifically mentioned using those links to communicate with Hira Te Popo and Paora (Ua a te Rangi):

> I opened a communication with them, knowing that for some time past Paoro has been anxious to surrender, and sent to them by Tiwai a letter stating that if they helped us to apprehend Te Kooti, their past offences would be forgiven. At the same time I sent by their hands a letter to Hera Te Popo to the same effect, and the chiefs of the Whakatoheas wrote also to him.[147]

In summary, then, while the other Whakatōhea apart from Ngāti Ira had suffered major disruption to their lives, and very real hardships in the travel and living conditions they had had to endure, the outcome finally remained relatively neutral for them after the dramatic events of March and April 1870.

The impression that a relatively tranquil period was commencing at last in Ōpotiki was probably reflected in the government decision to scale back significantly the garrison force there. This was reported in the *Wellington Independent* on 30 April:

> The garrison of Opotiki is done away with, instead of it, a small scouting party of six men, half European and half native, is to be continually on the move to give timely notice of any desperate attempt which might be made by Te Kooti with a view of obtaining ammunition and guns, of which he is very short.[148]

This more peaceful outcome still left Whakatōhea with ongoing grievances arising from the breaches of the Treaty of Waitangi that they had endured after the Crown invasion of 1865. These issues still remain unresolved today.

HIRA TE POPO AND NGĀTI IRA

For Ngāti Ira, the impact of war in the immediate aftermath of the events of March 1870 very much depended on the reactions of Hira Te Popo, and the Crown officers and officials who dealt with him.

One of the most significant consequences of the attacks on the Waipuna and Maraetahi pā by Te Kēpa, Topia and Ropata was the rupture they caused in the relationship between Ngāti Ira and Te Kooti. Ngāti Ira had voluntarily offered refuge to Te Kooti when he was besieged at Ngātapa in the opening days of January 1869, and he had fled to Maraetahi on his escape from Ngātapa pā later that month. He had brought with him his new faith, which would fall on receptive ears among the Ngāti Ira who gathered to hear him preach. When, later in 1869, Te Kooti had made his major foray to the west, he had left instructions for the building of the huge whare karakia at Maraetahi pā that was completed just after his return in March 1870. That whare was formally opened just before the Ngāti

Porou attack on Maraetahi. Just two weeks earlier, Te Kooti had staged his raid on Ōpape and Ōmarumutu, which resulted in large numbers of Whakatōhea being taken to Waipuna pā, within a comfortable day's walk of their Ngāti Ira relatives at Maraetahi. So by 23 March, the last day before the assaults commenced on Waipuna and Maraetahi pā, in the eyes of Hira Te Popo and his Ngāti Ira people their relationship with Te Kooti must have seemed to be increasingly positive.

There is a possibility, though, that just prior to the attack on Maraetahi pā Te Kooti himself had been upset by the actions of some Whakatōhea. Hoani Te Paiaka, the Whanganui supporter of Te Kooti who provided an account of his involvement with Te Kooti to Captain Gilbert Mair, had told Mair on 21 May:

> Te Kooti got away from Maraetahi with nearly one hundred men, but they left him on account of his anger, because Te Hira and others killed a man called Ruka (a nephew of Te Kooti's), because he took another man's wife.
>
> Te Kooti was heard praying that some evil might befall all his people for killing Ruka. A short time after this occurrence, they were attacked at Maraetahi, and the people said it was through Te Kooti's cursing them ...[149]

However, there is no other sign that these events had affected Whakatōhea's devotion to Te Kooti before the attack.

What a difference a few days can make when the heavy hand of war strikes. By nightfall on 25 March, Hira Te Popo and his people were scattered in the steep bush country of the Waioeka, desperately hiding from the forces of some 800 men comprising Ngāti Porou, Whanganui, Ngāti Awa and Ngāti Pukeko, Ngāi Tai, and even some Whakatōhea of other hapū.

It is impossible to be precise about the numbers of Ngāti Ira who regathered in the days after the government forces withdrew downriver following the burning of Maraetahi pā, and who later developed Te Tahora pā.* However, judging by the numbers who later came out of the bush to surrender at Ōpōtiki, there were probably only about 60–70 Ngāti Ira still in the bush up the Waioeka Gorge with Hira Te Popo after the government forces withdrew.

The first indications that Hira Te Popo and his people might be open to persuasion to come out of the bush and surrender were reported in April. On the

---

* Tahora pā was subsequently constructed and occupied opposite the junction of the Waioeka with the Tahora (modern Ōpato) and the Ōmaukora. That pā did not exist in mid-May 1870, when Wiremu Kingi Tutahuarangi and Lt Col St John led their combined force down each side of the river from Waipuna until they reached Maraetahi. Tutahuarangi's force went down the river on the true left bank, and he recorded seeing only some footprints before reaching the old location of Maraetahi pā. St John's force on the true right bank encountered no sign of anyone. The survey of the Tahora No.2 block, which occurred in 1888, still noted the location of Te Tahora pā.

15th, Captain Walker reported to Lt Porter, who he would have known was about to re-enter the Urewera with Major Ropata to continue the search for Te Kooti, entering from the East Coast side once again:

> Opotiki, 15th April, 1870.
> One of the Whakatoheas has just come in from Maraetahi. He says Te Kooti has gone to Waikare, so you are safe to fall in with him.* This news is reliable.
> Te Kooti is in hopes of being reinforced there, and his intention is to come down to the Waiaua in May, and take away the Whakatohea. The messenger came down with thirteen of the Ngatiporou (Hauhaus), to sound the Whakatohea. He fell in with our scouts (Whakatohea), and of course is detained here. To-morrow they will be communicated with, with a view to induce them to come in. Mr. Campbell, R.M. of Waiapu, is here.
> P.S.—Te Kooti left Maraetahi on the 9th, with thirty Urewera and ten of his own men. There are now at that place about forty men, mostly Whakatohea.[150]

Walker's report to McLean the next day expanded on this sudden development and is quoted above in relation to the communications between Whakatōhea at Ōpape and those at Maraetahi.[151] St John followed up promptly on his return to Ōpōtiki; his report of 19 April is quoted above in respect of the means used to send communications to Hira Te Popo through the agency of Tiwai, one of the Ōpape rangatira. His report concluded with the response from Tiwai:

> Yesterday Tiwai returned. He had seen the two chiefs, who started off at once back to Hera. They expressed themselves very glad at the chance of coming in, and promised to use their best exertions with Te Hera. Should the latter not consent, they stated that to purchase their pardon, they would lead the Whakatohea friendlies on to Te Kooti's resting place, from which hint it is supposed that Te Kooti has not left for Waikare.
> The intelligence of the movements after the defeat corroborates that previously given. I expect Hera's answer on Thursday.[152]

The official correspondence, particularly between Major William Mair and his superiors McLean, Clarke and Ormond, shows that all of them held Hira Te Popo in some regard. He and his people were known not to have been involved in the killing of Carl Volkner, and their withdrawal back into the Waioeka Gorge seems to have earned Hira a grudging respect from his adversaries among Crown officials and officers.

---

* In contemporary documents 'Waikare' usually referred to Lake Waikaremoana, not to the Waikare tributary of the Whakatāne River.

John Davies Ormond.
Collection of Hawke's Bay Museums
Trust, Ruawharo Tā-ū-rangi, 2519

For some months, however, while it was still suspected that he might be providing succour to Te Kooti, there was still the intent to attack him and his people, as much as Te Kooti himself. Hence the instruction referred to by McLean in his 7 May letter to St John, which he began by recording his dismay that St John had not followed 'the verbal instructions I gave you at Opotiki', namely to go up the Waioeka Gorge to capture Te Kooti and his few followers there.

Moreover, those verbal instructions had been followed up in a report by J.D. Ormond, the General Government Agent at Napier, who wrote to St John instructing him expressly in a detailed manner:

Napier, 31st April, 1870. [sic]

... it is believed Te Kooti is still hiding with a small force in Waioeka Gorge, and the Government are desirous that an endeavour should be made to follow him. From the information given by the Urewera, it would appear that, shattered as Te Kooti's force is, he is still meditating mischief, and it is most desirable that every endeavour should be used to deal with him before the winter regularly sets in.

I have therefore, by direction of the Government, to request you will at once take the necessary steps to get an expedition started to thoroughly scour the Waioeka country.[153]

Plainly at that stage, in the eyes of both McLean and Ormond, Hira Te Popo and his Ngāti Ira people would be swept up in the 'thorough scouring' of the Waioeka Gorge, if they were still supporting Te Kooti. However, the May expedition conducted by St John and Wiremu Kingi found no sign of Te Kooti or Hira Te Popo in the course of its own rather desperate winter traverse of the Waipuna and Maraetahi pā areas. The hope then continued to grow among government officials and serving officers in the field that Hira Te Popo might indeed decide to surrender and come out with his people.

On 21 May, the reliable Hoani Te Paiaka described those now living at Te Tahora pā (near modern Wairata): 'Hira te Popo, Te Iki, and eighteen or twenty of the Whakatohea are at Te Tahora. They have left Te Kooti by this time. They were mostly old men, and badly armed.'[154]

Gilbert Mair added a note in a wide-ranging report he made on 23 May from Te Teko to H.T. Clarke at Tauranga as to the importance of persuading Hira Te Popo to come out of the bush:

> I am of opinion that some of the surrendered Whakatohea could be made use of in bringing out Te Hira Te Popo, and some of his people, and in inducing them to show us where Te Kooti is hiding. An expedition of 100 to 150 men would be quite sufficient to take up the Waioeka in search of him. They should all be well clothed and shod.[155]

Despite his brother Gilbert's suggestion, Major William Mair had a more subtle means in mind of communicating with Hira. This means was traversed by Wepiha Apanui of Ngāti Awa when he and other Ngāti Awa rangatira met with McLean at Whakatāne on 25 May. Quite some weight can be given to Wepiha's account because while he was seeking to disprove to McLean rumours that he himself was a supporter of Te Kooti, he was at the same time very frank about his hereditary enmity with Whakatōhea — he just had the complication to cope with that his wife Maraea was Whakatōhea! Her Whakatōhea whakapapa led in the end to Wepiha Apanui travelling up the Waioeka to meet with Hira personally, as noted in William Mair's record of the May meeting of Ngāti Awa rangatira with McLean at Whakatāne. Mair reported Wepiha as saying:

> When I was at Ohope I never saw any Hauhaus; I had a difference with my old people, and then I went to live on my wife's land at Opotiki. I built houses there and cultivated; the Hauhaus of Waioeka were related to me through my wife, and they heard from the Whakatohea at Waiaua, that I was living at Opotiki; then Hira Te Popo wrote letters and sent messengers to me. Nothing was concealed from Major Mair; we both wrote to Hira, urging him to surrender. After a time

I went to Waioeka to see Hira; he would not come out, he was ashamed. I said, promise that no evil shall come to us; and he said, if you make Waioeka tapu, no harm shall go to Opotiki from here, and I will keep you informed of everything. Major Mair approved of this, and when Dr. Pollen came to Opotiki, he agreed that Waioeka should be tapu.* Hira kept his word, and informed me about Te Kooti. Major Mair has the letters.[156]

William Mair would appear to have used Wepiha Apanui as his conduit for letters to Hira that he referred to in a report he sent to the under-secretary of the Native Department on 27 May:

> There are very few of the Whakatohea now in the bush, the only men of consequence being Hera Te Popo, Paora Te Ua o te Rangi, and Te Iki; I have caused letters to be written to the two former which I have reason to hope will induce them to submit.[157]

It was with a mixture of relief and delight, then, that on 21 June William Mair was able to write to the government advising that Hira Te Popo had surrendered:

> Opotiki, June 21st, 1870.
> I have the honor to report for the information of the Government that, on the 17th instant, Hira Te Popo, and the greater portion of his hapu (Ngati-ira), viz., thirteen men, eleven women, and ten children, making a total of thirty-four, submitted at this place. The remainder of the hapu were engaged in searching for some women who were missing, and may be expected in shortly.
>
> The submission of this well-known chief is an event of very great importance, and will, I have no doubt, produce a very marked effect upon the Urewera. Although never taking any active part in their operations, he has nevertheless been viewed by the King party as one of their greatest supporters in these parts, and his defection from their ranks, coupled with the destruction of their rendezvous in the Waioeka, will prove a severe blow to their cause. At the same time his accession to our party will be a great gain, as he is a man of considerable ability, and of good character. He has kept aloof from us hitherto, because the other chiefs of the Whakatohea made their peace with the Government without any reference to him — who had not shared in their offence, and his pride prevented him from following in their track. Even now he expresses a wish to have as little to do with them as possible.[158]

---

* Dr Daniel Pollen was a member of the government at the time.

Ropata supported William Mair's appreciation of Hira's mana in a report he provided to McLean on 26 July, after he travelled to Ōpōtiki by sea to fulfil his obligation to check on Whakatōhea and report to McLean. In so doing he met with Hira and Paora Ua a te Rangi. It is plain that the conclusions Ropata drew from his exchanges with Hira Te Popo and Paora would have influenced the final decision by the government to treat Hira and Ngāti Ira with restraint:

> I have also seen Te Hira Te Popo, and Uaaterangi. I have addressed these men in a friendly and conciliating spirit, and I was at the same time impressed with a good opinion of their bearing.
>
> I enquired of these two, how it was that they and their tribe came in so quickly? They replied, 'We were afraid of being attacked by the Government forces, who are now going through, and subduing the length and breadth of the land, and we also believed that it was owing to the suspension of the operations during the winter season that we have been saved, and that when the summer season came in again, we should run great risk of being taken and killed. Another reason that induced us to come in and surrender was that the lives of all the prisoners had been spared under your merciful treatment. Hence it was that this remnant of the Whakatohea has come in and surrendered. If it be true that yours is a mission of friendship to these tribes, then let your clemency be great towards them under the laws of the Queen, so that we may be spared. Our evil and stupid proceedings have ceased to be; we shall never return to them again. When we joined Te Kooti's rebellion we believed at the time that the salvation of the people was in that direction, but instead of that we have found it to be the reverse. We have nothing further to say to you on the occasion of this your appearance amongst us.'
>
> After this was over, I then enquired of them as to what led to their separating themselves from Te Kooti, and Te Kooti from them?
>
> Paora te Uaaterangi and Hira Te Popo said, in reply— 'The reason that led to our separation was this: Te Kooti had ceased to incite the Natives in his cause; he discovered that his own schemes and devices had failed and broken down, and that the Natives, his allies, were deserting him in all directions.'
>
> I then enquired of them as to what the particular error was on Te Kooti's side that induced them to separate from him.
>
> Paora and Te Hira replied— 'The chief causes was the frequent deaths amongst his followers, and the frequent desertion of the men. He (Te Kooti) had also stated, or led the people to believe, that his own God had the power of destroying his enemies, and we waited to see whether his God had the power of destroying the forces against him, but we found it to be all a false statement, and that instead of the Government forces

falling into his hands, it was, on the other hand, we who suffered the loss, and then it was that we determined to separate from him, for we reasoned thus: if we stay with him we shall die; and if we go, we cannot fare worse: the risk is equal.'[159]

The advice of William Mair, Gilbert Mair and Ropata seems to have hit home with Donald McLean, and no steps were taken to prosecute Hira Te Popo and his Ngāti Ira people who had surrendered.

Ngāti Ira have since occupied a small area of land at Ōpeke, where they still have their home marae at the mouth of the Waioeka Gorge. They, too, still have to resolve with the Crown their claims in respect of the Treaty breaches they have suffered.

TRIAL OF PRISONERS

Thirty-one prisoners were shipped to Wellington for trial, arriving there on 15 April. They were brought up for trial before Mr Justice Johnston in the Supreme Court (now the High Court) on Monday 27 June, the witnesses against them having arrived by ship from the East Coast a few days before. The principal charge faced was that of waging war against Queen Victoria — treason — for which the punishment on conviction was death.

The *Wellington Independent* of 28 June provided a very detailed description of events during the first two days' hearings.[160] The evidence relating directly to the Waioeka events was detailed in the edition of 30 June, commencing with Wiremu Kingi Te Paia, the Tūranga rangatira captured at Waipuna pā. Extracts from Te Paia's long statement are quoted in Chapter 3.

The newspaper account of Wiremu Kingi Te Paia's evidence was dramatic, because of the fact that he was arguably one of Te Kooti's more aggressive supporters, but now he was giving evidence against others who had been less involved:

Mr. Allan, in defending the prisoners, hurled the bitterest invectives at this witness, denouncing him as being all that is base and unprincipled. The Counsel made a most impassioned harangue. Of course, as he had no rebutting evidence on behalf of the prisoners, and as the witnesses for the Crown made out a very strong case, Mr. Allan had a delicate and difficult task. He acquitted himself, however, with great ability.[161]

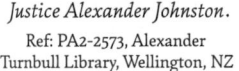

Justice Alexander Johnston.
Ref: PA2-2573, Alexander Turnbull Library, Wellington, NZ

Despite the seriousness of the trial, a moment of light-hearted relief occurred as Wiremu Kingi was giving evidence:

> An amusing instance of ignorance of the usages of Courts was furnished by Wiremu. When he was in the box, he was asked if he recollected the presence of a certain prisoner in the Waioeka Gorge, but in some sort of doubt about the matter, he quickly asked the prisoner 'Were you there?'[162]

Other witnesses included Piahana Tiwai, the Whakatōhea rangatira who had accompanied the Whanganui Contingent on the Waioeka expedition, Samuel Austin and Thomas Porter. It is notable that in his evidence Porter did not claim that Ngāti Porou killed any opposing forces, and he was recorded as stating 'We only captured two prisoners.'[163] Charges against two of the older men, Karanama and Hopa, were withdrawn, but all the others were found guilty. The prisoners were tried and sentenced in groups of five.

Mr Justice Johnston's sentencing comments reflected the severity of the penalty the prisoners faced on conviction on a charge of treason. However, perhaps surprisingly in those days when attitudes towards 'rebellious' Māori were generally uncompromising, the judge also expressed the hope that there might later be some mitigation of the penalty by the government.

The *Wellington Independent* published the sentencing report under the headline 'HIGH TREASON':

> Sat 2 July ... After hearing the evidence against you, the jury have found that you were guilty of fighting against the Queen's Government. You know that according to your own views of right and wrong you deserve to be punished with death. The law of England, under which you live, punishes with death those who commit this offence; and when a person has been found guilty of it, in a court of justice, the judge has no choice, but must pronounce the sentence which the law awards. But, according to the English Constitution (or ritangi), the Queen herself, advised by the proper officers, has power to alter the sentence pronounced by law. I said that you were convicted by a jury; but the truth was, that after considerable evidence had been given, you admitted your guilt, but the case is exactly the same. However, I feel very sure that no one of you will lose the life which has been so justly forfeited by law; and that your sentence will be changed into one which will be as little severe and afflictive to you as the ends of justice will permit. And I have no doubt that the Government will take the trouble to inquire who are more and who are less guilty, and act accordingly. The sentence of the Court upon each of you prisoners — this sentence which I have told you I am obliged to pass — is that you each shall be taken to the place of execution, and be there hanged by the neck until you are dead.[164]

The judge's comments were deliberately framed to exert pressure on the ministers forming the government, but later that month more pressure came to bear on the government from an even more unlikely source than Mr Justice Johnston. Ropata Wahawaha concluded his report to the Minister of Defence, following his meeting with Hira Te Popo and Te Ua, with some unexpected views on the fate of the convicted prisoners:

> I said to them, 'Will not the Urewera come out and surrender?' They replied, that if they hear that we are spared, and in safe hands, they will all come out. I then thought thus: the final destination of the prisoners now at Wellington will influence the movements of those people who are now wandering about in the bush. I say, then, let those people be brought down and set at liberty ...[165]

Ropata's recommendation of mercy for the prisoners in Wellington would almost certainly have come as a considerable surprise to McLean, as he knew how merciless Ropata himself had often been to prisoners in the field. He had seen an example of that attitude during the Waioeka events in March, when Ropata had sought permission from Te Kēpa and Topia to kill some of their prisoners. Now Ropata was recommending leniency toward those very prisoners. McLean's pithy response to Ropata followed on 4 August: 'The decision of the Government is not yet finally arrived at as to the prisoners now in gaol here, only that they are not to be hung. You will hear more about this soon.'[166]

The harsh wording of the statute governing the crime of treason in 1870, specifying as a mandatory matter the terms of the sentence to be imposed, assisted the prisoners in this case, just as it had a major influence on the outcome the previous year, when 70 of Te Kooti's followers were tried after the fall of Ngātapa. In each case the judge was Justice Johnston. He found himself required by an archaic law to solemnly intone the following barbaric sentence to the prisoners:

> You shall be drawn on a hurdle to the place of execution, and be there hanged by the neck till you are dead; and afterwards your head shall be severed from your body; and your body shall be divided into four quarters, which may afterwards be disposed of according to law.

Governor Bowen, reporting on the trial and its outcome to the Secretary of State for Colonies on 11 January 1872, recorded:

> 4. ... The Judge, with my sanction, stated on each occasion that this sentence would not be carried out in its terms ...
>
> 6. Not one of the thirty prisoners recently convicted was clearly proved at his trial to have taken an active part in the Poverty Bay massacre, or in the other equally

heinous atrocities of Te Kooti and Titokowaru. Consequently, it was determined by myself and my Ministers, in the Executive Council held yesterday, to commute, in accordance with the opinion of Mr. Justice Johnston, the capital sentences in every case to various terms of penal servitude or imprisonment. The principle which we have laid down for our guidance from the beginning is that, looking to the circumstances of this country, sentences of death will not be inflicted for rebellion against the Queen's authority alone, unless such high treason is accompanied by murder in cold blood, or some other atrocity.[167]

Governor Sir George Ferguson Bowen.
Puke Ariki New Plymouth
PH02012-0162

After representations were made on their behalf by Te Kēpa directly to the governor, the prisoners were actually released in January 1872, meaning they served sentences of about 21 months.*

Governor Bowen explained this action in his report to the Secretary of State for Colonies:

> 8. ... I have, with the advice of my Ministers, determined on remitting the remainder of the punishment of the fifty-eight (58) Maoris who were still (several having been previously released) in confinement at Dunedin, under the sentences passed upon them for rebellion by the Supreme Court in 1869 and 1870 ... The conduct of these men while in gaol has been good; and when I was last month at Wanganui, Te Kepa (Major Kemp) and the other loyal chiefs who had taken them in action, addressed me to the effect that these prisoners had been sufficiently punished, and that they (the loyal chiefs) would be responsible for their peaceable behaviour for the future if released. Mr. McLean and his colleagues in the Ministry were decidedly of opinion that it would be safe and politic to grant this petition, and the remaining prisoners will consequently be set at liberty forthwith. It is satisfactory to be enabled to report that at the end of this month no Maori will be under confinement for any political offence.

LONGER-TERM IMPACTS ON TE KOOTI

After he had withdrawn from the Waipuna and Maraetahi pā areas, Te Kooti is believed to have waited for a regathering of his supporters at his Te Wera base, in the uppermost headwaters of the Waioeka River system, in the upper Koranga

---

* Judith Binney, in *Redemption Songs*, says, 'The prisoners were all released by governor's clemency in 1873' (p. 600, fn. 44). Unusually for her, she provides no reference to any document in that regard, and the date she provides is out by more than a year.

branch. While that refuge could be expected to offer him a degree of security over the winter of 1870, he would have been keenly aware of the need to supplement his supplies of weapons and ammunition, and manpower, after his losses at Waipuna and Maraetahi. His desperation led him to make the last of his aggressive raids — this time on Te Aitanga a Hauiti, at Uawa on the East Coast, at the end of July 1870. The attack failed miserably, and while Te Kooti and some of his followers escaped, they lost a number of weapons and even more supporters were captured, including his wife Huhana Tamati. Te Kooti headed back for Te Urewera far worse off than he had been before the raid.

For the next two years he was hounded as a refugee rather than a real threat, being constantly harried throughout the Urewera. A number of his camps were discovered and attacked, as were the pā of those suspected of supporting him. Once again, these pursuits were carried out by Māori forces accompanied by just a few Pākehā officers. From the east, Ngāti Porou under Ropata Wahawaha made repeated forays; from the north came Wiremu Kingi Tutahuarangi of Ngāi Tai; from the south and particularly at and around Lake Waikaremoana, Ngāti Kahungunu; and from the west Te Arawa and some Ngāti Awa in the two Arawa Flying Columns based respectively out of Kaiteriria (Rotokākahi) and Te Teko.

It was not until August 1871 that the Arawa Flying Columns under Gilbert Mair and George Preece were actually able to track down Te Kooti himself, at his Waipaoa River puni in the eastern Urewera, in the massive Ruakituri catchment. The following month a Ngāti Porou column under Captain Porter attacked him at a campsite known as Te Hapua, just east of Maungapōhatu. Te Kooti himself miraculously survived both these attacks, but he lost more men and supporters at each of these locations. By that time large numbers of Tūhoe hapū had either come out of Te Urewera and surrendered, or had actively joined his pursuers.

The long, drawn-out pursuit was to last until mid May 1872, when for the last time Te Kooti slipped out of the Urewera to the southwest. He was able to move off into the sanctuary of the Kingitanga, where King Tāwhiao now also regarded him as a refugee rather than a threat and was prepared to let him live under his protection with that status. Te Kooti continued to reside there in safety as a refugee until he was pardoned by the government in 1883 as part of its process of making a binding peace with the followers of the Māori King.

In short, then, it is proper to observe that the events in the Waioeka in March 1870 destroyed Te Kooti's hopes of ever leading a major force to victory against the government. With the exception of the 'pinprick' raid on Uawa in July 1870 he was never again able to threaten other communities, Māori or Pākehā.

10

THE FRUITS OF WAR — AND THE LAST WORD TO TE KOOTI

Following the Waioeka campaign, the reports of the rangatira involved demonstrate a high level of pride, despite the escape of Te Kooti and Kereopa there. These feelings were based on the destruction of Te Kooti's two refuge pā; the release of the Whakatōhea captives; the killing and capture of so many of Te Kooti's followers; and the sheer physical hardship and effort each contingent had exerted to achieve those results.

Nevertheless, the failure to capture Te Kooti or Kereopa had taken the gloss off the outcome, and was not offset by the killing of Hakaraia, notwithstanding his seniority and the respect he had been accorded among Kingite and Paimārire or Ringatū Māori. Te Kooti and Kereopa were the two main causes of concern for the government, and the only two fugitives for whom major monetary rewards had been posted. Their escape meant that the rewards offered for their capture or killing — £5000 for Te Kooti, £1000 for Kereopa — were unable to be claimed.

Both Ngāti Porou and Whanganui pressed for other recognition of their efforts in tangible ways. Negotiations commenced as soon as McLean met with the rangatira at Ōpōtiki on 8 April 1870. It is fair to say that for once the Māori rangatira were negotiating with a grateful government; McLean was genuinely impressed with the hardships they had undergone and appreciative of the results of their attacks, and his views were shared by all senior officials, including Premier William Fox.

As a reward for their efforts, both Whanganui and Ngāti Porou asked the government to promise that their lands would not be subject to further confiscation. This was agreed, and the promises were soon formalised, first by McLean to Ropata, under a formal memorandum, and not long after by Fox to Te Kēpa and Topia Turoa, in this case by written agreement confirming a past oral promise.

PROMISES OF RELIEF FROM THE THREAT OF LAND CONFISCATIONS

NGĀTI POROU

McLean had sailed from Tauranga to Ōpōtiki in the company of Henry Clarke on board the *Sturt*, which together with the *Rangatira* also took Ropata and his Ngāti Porou aboard to return them to the East Coast. Clarke recorded what occurred both at Ōpōtiki and in the formal exchanges during the process of return of the Ngāti Porou contingent in his report of 18 April. On landing at Ōpōtiki on 8 April McLean and Clarke had first visited the Whanganui encampment, where they saw the physical effects of the hard months-long campaigning on the young men. They then moved over to the other side of the town where the Ngāti Porou were camped. Clarke's report conveyed both the high spirits and the physical effects that the Ngāti Porou were still exhibiting eight days after emerging from the bush:

> From the Whanganui the Native Minister proceeded to the camp of the Ngatiporou, on the opposite side of the town. He was received with the same demonstrative welcome. The speeches were very much to the same effect as those of the Whanganui chiefs. A greater number of these people were suffering from festering sores than the Whanganui,— not to be wondered at when it is remembered that they had marched, with but little rest, over perhaps the roughest country in New Zealand. ...
>
> The Ngatiporou were thanked by the Native Minister for the good service they had rendered, for having given practical proof of the accessibility of the Urewera country, and especially for the successes at Waioeka, which were mainly due to their activity and perseverance.[168]

The formal commitments were made by McLean as he, Clarke, Ropata and the Ngāti Porou contingent continued the journey back to the East Coast. Clarke recorded:

On the night of the 12th we anchored in Hicks' Bay. Early next morning the Native Minister, accompanied by Ropata, visited the Chiefs Te Iharaira, Houkamau, and Mokena. The question of the land lying between Hicks' Bay and Tologa Bay, over which the Government had put in a sort of claim, was discussed, and Mr. McLean told them that in consideration of the good conduct of the tribe, and the great service they had rendered to the Colony, he would, on the part of the Government, relinquish, with certain small reservations, all claims to the lands.*
A memorandum was written to that effect, and an agreement signed by the Natives as to their particular obligations under the arrangement.[169]

Notwithstanding this formal concession by the Crown, which in reality meant that it would no longer seek to acquire wide swathes of land under the East Coast Land Titles Investigation Act 1866, Ropata remained wary. He was plainly cognisant of the fact that Ngāti Porou willingness to continue to hunt down Te Kooti was the only real bargaining power they had to ensure the settler government did not use the legislation that already existed, or similar confiscatory legislation, at some time in the future. Clarke's report continued with a reference to the commitment expressed by Ropata:

> Here also Ropata gave a short account of his march through the forest of Maungapowhatu and up the Waioweka Valley, and also intimated that it was his intention to organize another expedition of picked men for the object of beating up Te Kooti's quarters, supposed to be somewhere near Waikare Moana, and of getting in the rest of the Ngatikowhatu hapu. ...
> From Hicks' Bay we steamed for Mataahu, Ropata's residence in Open Bay,** and, after landing the Natives,*** returned to the Bay of Plenty the same evening.[170]

WHANGANUI

The government did not delay in making a similar commitment to Whanganui, removing the threat of further land confiscations in recognition of the military efforts of the Whanganui Contingent. McLean had hinted at Ōpōtiki that some

---

* Clarke's reference to 'a sort of claim' on the part of the government is a classic understatement with regard to the threat of confiscation posed to Ngāti Porou ever since the East Coast Land Titles Investigation Act had been passed in 1866.

** An English name used in the past to refer to Waipiro Bay. Mataahu took its name from a high point between Waipiro and Wharepongo bays. Ropata's home pā of Akuaku was located on the flats to its south.

*** This reference to 'Natives' rather than only to Ngāti Porou will have been made as Ropata's prisoners taken before and at Maungapōhatu were also dropped off with Ropata. In his 1923 book on Ropata, Porter records all the prisoners Ropata had been holding at Mataahu were released at the end of 1871. (page 41.)

Premier William Fox.
Photographer unknown.
Ref: PA2-2495, Alexander
Turnbull Library,
Wellington, NZ

formal reward was to come the way of Whanganui, but he must have decided to leave that to the premier to deal with. That would have been logical, as it was Fox who had personally led the government's negotiations with Topia Turoa back in December 1869, when Topia had agreed formally to join Te Kēpa's contingent with his own force.

It was quite an issue to decide how to deal with a rangatira of Topia's mana, who had effectively changed sides, and who otherwise would have been regarded as 'rebellious' in terms of the confiscation legislation. Doubtless Topia's actions over recent months and weeks, and his oral assurances direct to McLean, had reassured the government.

Clarke's report conveyed the terms of Topia's statements at Ōpōtiki:

The Chief Topia Turoa, whose name has lately been prominently associated with the Wanganui force in pursuit of Te Kooti, took an opportunity of explaining to the Native Minister the reasons and motives which had induced him to follow the course he had lately adopted. He admitted that he had been a King's man and a leader of that party; that he had advocated that cause, because he hoped that it would lead to light and the advancement of the people of the Island; but after having followed the road he had chosen, he had discovered that it brought him to greater darkness. He was now trying another road, and had taken part with those he had formerly opposed, in the punishment of crime and outrage; and it very much depended upon the action of the Government whether he continued to follow the road upon which he had now entered, and which he hoped would bring him to the light he was so anxious to obtain.

Mr. McLean replied to Topia, thanked him for his assistance in suppressing crime and murder, and said that he trusted he would not be disappointed in his expectations of obtaining that light he was now seeking.[171]

The Whanganui Contingent had travelled back to Whanganui on the *Star of the South*, which made short calls at the ports of Napier and then Wellington, where the 31 prisoners were offloaded to face trial. Unfortunately, William Fox was not in Wellington when the vessel called there, but very shortly after, on 16 April, he wrote personal letters of gratitude to both Te Kēpa and Topia Turoa.[172] Each letter refers to promises made at the opening of the Te Aomarama wharenui at Ōhinemutu, on the Whanganui River, on 1 December the previous year. At that time Topia had formally agreed with Fox in person that he would join with Te Kēpa in the pursuit of Te Kooti, and in return Fox had promised that no further confiscations of Whanganui land would occur.

In particular, the letter to Topia Turoa emphasised that the assurances made at Te Aomarama were a 'permanent word':

To: Topia Turoa
Chief of the Tribes of the Upper Whanganui
Dunedin, April 16, 1870.
My friend, you and I conversed together face to face in the Aomarama. The word which was proclaimed on that day is a permanent word. You have driven forth that pest (Te Kooti), and quenched his power.

I have heard of your deeds at Tuhua, at Tapapa, at Opotiki, and at all the other places from whence you have driven Te Kooti.

Our work now is to be a work of peace. Let me know your thoughts on this subject, as you made known your thoughts at Ranana and at the Aomarama.

I rejoice greatly that you and your people have returned to Whanganui. Convey to your people the thanks of the Government for the services they have rendered. This is all.
From your friend,
William Fox.

The letter to Te Kēpa was similar:
To: Major Kemp
Dunedin, April 16, 1870.
Salutations. I am sorry that I was not at Wellington on your arrival at that place. I

have, however, heard of all your good works, of your fights, and of the capture of prisoners by you. That man Te Kooti is defeated, and his evil deeds are defeated. Your feet, and the feet of Whanganui have trodden him down. You have fulfilled the promise which you made in the Aomarama. My belief is that the war is now over; let us turn our thoughts, you and I, to works of peace. This is all.
From your friend,
William Fox.

For both Whanganui and Ngāti Porou, these formal assurances that there would be no confiscations were the primary reward that they had always sought and hoped for. However, given Te Kooti's escape, the issue of the monetary reward remained unresolved.

Ropata for one was willing to continue the pursuit of Te Kooti in Te Urewera, as he did repeatedly over the next two years in conjunction with the Arawa Flying Columns and other Ngāti Kahungunu forces. Whether or not his actions were influenced by thoughts of the reward will never be known, but the following year Ropata's continued efforts did receive some direct monetary reward — relating not to Te Kooti but to Kereopa.

THE REWARD FOR KEREOPA'S CAPTURE

After his escape from Waipuna pā Kereopa had made his way west through Te Urewera and over into the upper Whakatāne River, where he finally settled at Te Roau, a small kāinga near the modern Ōhaua o te Rangi marae. This is two to two and a half hours' travel down the Whakatāne River from the road-end north of Ruatāhuna. In those days with no road it would have taken more like three or three and a half hours to walk there from Ruatāhuna.

Kereopa lived quietly at Te Roau, having no further direct involvement in any action against the government, until 18 November 1871, when he was captured by a Tūhoe guide, Te Whiu Maraki, who was leading a Ngāti Porou patrol in search of him. Lt Porter delivered Kereopa to Napier and uplifted the £1000 reward, taking it back for division among Ngāti Porou at Kohimarama, the redoubt they had built at Ruatāhuna.* Te Whiu and each Ngāti Porou man involved in Kereopa's capture and delivery to Napier received £10, and the officers £25.[173] Kereopa was tried, convicted and hanged at Napier on 5 January 1872.

---

* Kohimarama meaning 'Gather the months'. Another redoubt, built at Maungapōhatu, was called Kohi a Tau, meaning 'Gather the years'. When Ngāti Porou finally left Te Urewera in December 1871, Tūhoe destroyed both redoubts as loathed symbols of their oppressors.

ACCOLADES AT HOME FOR WHANGANUI

The arrival home of the Whanganui Contingent in late April 1870 was a major event that was marked by the government and local iwi in a most colourful manner. After the hardships the men had endured, one imagines that they would have greatly appreciated these festivities. The members of the contingent had been absent for nearly five months, during which they had been out of communication for sometimes weeks at a time, with their home people not knowing how many casualties they might have suffered. They had endured arduous travelling conditions and been involved in many engagements. They were clearly tired but very proud by the time they reached Whanganui.

The colourful and boisterous scenes at a hākari (feast) on the day of their arrival in Whanganui were fitting of the occasion, and the equally colourful account of the event bears repetition:

> Our native contingent under Majors Kemp and Topia (is the latter a Major?) returned to us from their East Coast campaign yesterday. The steamers St Kilda and Storm Bird came up the river clad in bunting, amid any amount of rifle shooting and triumphant yells from the braves on board. The natives landed in two detachments, and were crossed to Putiki in the punt in relays of 80 and 90 at a time. The Government had provided refreshments for them at the pa, and their own friends had roasted an ox for the occasion, not to mention pigs and other comestibles. The war dance was struck up. Majors Kemp and Topia were naturally the observed of all observers — the former gorgeous in ribbons, the latter equally gorgeous in paint — one side of the face entirely blue and the other side entirely red. Our representative in Parliament, Mete Kingi, Esq., M.H.R. also was lightly attired, wearing only a slight shawl round his loins and his intellectual cranium, no doubt in consequence of his distinguished position, covered by a rusty bell-topper. Further dress he had none. Governor Pipi, the most demonstrative and good-natured of Maoris, was resplendent in all the glory of a mat, probably of a couple of stones weight. The Maori ladies apparently were not expected to take part in this saltatory demonstration; they were no doubt reserving their strength for another occasion; but two or three of them, fired and incited by the agility and most horrible facial contortions of their lords could not possibly remain quiescent, and joined in the movements. The dance was to be repeated on Friday at the Market Place, between 11 and 12 o'clock in the forenoon, when there was a general invitation to the pakeha to be present.[174]

SWORDS OF HONOUR

The final fruits of the Waioeka campaign for the victors were to be personal to Te Kēpa and Ropata Wahawaha. On 20 June, in a highly formal ceremony held at the Mount Cook Barracks in Wellington, the two rangatira were presented with Swords of Honour by the governor acting on behalf of the queen, along with one presented to another Ngāti Porou rangatira, Mōkena Kōhere, for his displays of loyalty in earlier fighting against the Paimārire.

In his speech the governor also recognised Topia Turoa's support for Te Kēpa:

> You have been ably and bravely assisted by your friend Topia Turoa, on whom also a mark of the approval of the Queen's Government will be hereafter bestowed. Te Kepa here is your sword. It bears on the blade this inscription 'Given by Queen Victoria to Te Kepa for his unfailing loyalty and valor.' May you long wear it in wealth and honour.[175]

Ropata and Mōkena received similar plaudits:

> To you, Ropata and Mokena, I now present in the name of the Queen these swords, which also bear your names and similar inscriptions with that presented to Te Kepa. Your tribe, the Ngatiporou, have rivalled the Wanganui in loyalty to the Crown, in goodwill to your English neighbours, and in gallantry in war.

THE RINGATŪ RELIGION

Ironically, the long-term 'victor' in the Waioeka in a spiritual sense must be Te Kooti himself, or at least his legacy.

During the years of war, and in the lengthy periods of refuge and peace that he was to enjoy after escaping to the King Country in 1872, Te Kooti increasingly developed his prophetic style of religious thought, writings and waiata. The religion he established came to be termed Te Hāhi Ringatū, or simply Ringatū (the Upraised Hand). Te Kooti finally died peacefully in 1893 at Ōhiwa, very close to the scene of the events described in this book, but his religion has survived, and still has major strongholds today among many Māori. Ringatū adherents are found particularly among Ngāi Tūhoe of Te Urewera, but its following is spread throughout the Bay of Plenty, all East Coast and Rotorua areas, and in many other areas. As at the 2018 Census, 12,336 people identified as adherents of Te Hāhi Ringatū.

Of particular interest in the context of this book is the large number of Whakatōhea people in, or with whakapapa to, the Ōpōtiki area who adhere to Ringatū. The irony lies in the fact that the uri (descendants) of the very people who were compelled to accompany him on that long, tough trek into the headwaters of the Waioeka now follow the religion of which Te Kooti Arikirangi was the founding prophet.

In large part such widespread support for Te Hāhi Ringatū developed because after Te Kooti was pardoned, on 13 February 1883, he embarked on a dedicated and sustained peace-making effort. This involved visiting all the areas in which he had conducted his military activities. Despite heated opposition to his visits by some in both Māori and Pākehā communities, he was surprisingly successful in calming past grievances during that long campaign of peaceful tours. As he travelled, the word of Te Hāhi Ringatū spread.

One area where he met particularly strong opposition, however, was Tūranga (Gisborne), his own rohe. Memories of the Matawhero killings in 1868 were still too raw among many in both the Māori and Pākehā communities here. When Te Kooti continued, despite opposition, to lead a large number of his supporters on a march from Ōpōtiki to Tūranga in 1889, they were restrained en masse in the lower Waioeka and prevented from continuing with him. Te Kooti himself turned aside and crossed over to the west into the upper Waiotahe valley, where he was arrested by members of a hastily assembled militia force from the Gisborne and East Coast areas.

Two of the men heavily involved in Te Kooti's arrest were none other than Thomas Porter, now a Major, and Ropata Wahawaha. Unlike his arrest in 1866, on this occasion Te Kooti was brought before a court and tried. He was convicted on a charge of unlawful assembly but was not imprisoned. Notwithstanding his conviction, the government was anxious to ensure Te Kooti was provided with land on which to live, away from his home area, so as to avoid further conflict. It was an approach the government had been pursuing with him for some years after his pardon in 1883. In 1891 a landlocked block of some 600 acres (approximately 243 ha) at Te Wainui, near Ōhiwa harbour, was selected, after earlier attempts to locate him at Ōrākau in the Kingitanga had failed. Te Kooti lived there for the last few years of his life, although he continued to travel extensively, actively promoting the Ringatū religion until his death.

The rapid spread of the Ringatū word after Te Kooti's pardon in 1883 occurred against a background of ongoing aggressive and widespread acquisition of Māori lands for Pākehā farm settlement. To achieve its aim of Pākehā settlement the Crown used a range of techniques that the Waitangi Tribunal has repeatedly found were in breach of the guarantees provided under the Treaty of Waitangi and the duty they imposed to actively protect Māori land and not pursue its acquisition.* The consequences of land loss by confiscation, and even more broadly by other nefarious practices on the part of the Crown, have been devastating for generations of Māori as they have lost their homelands and their ability to support themselves using their own resources.

Even worse were the devastating cultural effects of the loss of marae and communal living areas because of dispersion of Māori from their hereditary lands, and the suppression for many generations of their language — te reo Māori — in the education system. The result, as the Waitangi Tribunal has found, again repeatedly, was widespread and longstanding socioeconomic deprivation, coupled with serious cultural devastation.

One passage alone out of the massive Te Urewera report of 2017 summarises the outcome of these wilful Crown Treaty breaches succinctly:

> ... massive land loss; cultural and linguistic marginalisation, especially within the education system; and lack of political and economic power. These three factors, as well as numerous lesser factors, were well within the Crown's sphere of influence and were in fact often the direct result of Crown action.[176]

This background, in the Bay of Plenty and Te Urewera, and elsewhere, provided fertile ground in which Te Kooti was readily able to spread his 'new' word of salvation, and in which it continued to be spread after his passing in 1893. The result was a high level of success in 'capturing' a Ringatū congregation in the Ōpōtiki area.** The following that Te Kooti sought and failed to achieve by abduction, coercion and aggressive war in 1870, he 'won' in the long run by spiritual appeal.

---

* There are now numerous Waitangi Tribunal reports on historic claims that have reached these findings, and their acceptance by the Crown has led to historic settlement packages and legislation, usually involving formal Crown apologies for the Treaty breaches. A classic recent example of this type of report, which relates to areas affected by some of the events described in this book, is the very detailed 2017 Te Urewera report, some eight volumes.

** One notable exception is the Tōrere area among Ngāi Tai, where the Anglican religion prevails.

EPILOGUE

THE EFFECT OF THE PORTER 'MYTH' ON THE HISTORICAL RECORD

Te Kooti's abduction of almost the whole of the communities of Whakatōhea from the pā at Ōpape and nearby Ōmarumutu in March 1870 involved the taking of some 218 men, women and children. This disparate group, which would have included aged kaumatua and kuia and very young children, was forced to walk for three days back into the Urewera over extremely difficult terrain. Once arrived at the site of what would become Waipuna pā, they then had to construct whare to protect them from the harsh climate, to forage for food, and begin to establish gardens. It was an even tougher repetition of the forced movement of people from Tūranganui (Gisborne) to Ngātapa pā that had occurred in late 1868. The only comparable actions during the New Zealand Wars were the Crown's forced movement of massed numbers of Māori prisoners, with or without trial.

Yet the recorded history of the events around the Ōpape abduction has been marred by inaccuracies, and in recent years the whole episode has almost dropped out of the record. Many of the inaccuracies that have become embedded in the records can be traced back to what I have earlier referred to as the Porter 'myth', based on errors — or 'amendments' — in Lieutenant (later Lt Col) Thomas Porter's published record of these events. Porter's blurring of the facts about the assaults before and at Waipuna pā and those at Maraetahi pā has led to a catalogue of books, including those by eminent historians, in which the two locations are confused, or success is attributed predominantly, or even solely, to Ropata and Ngāti Porou at Maraetahi.

James Cowan's comprehensive and widely read history of the whole of the New Zealand Wars, published in two volumes in 1922 and 1923, provides a detailed description of some of these events in the Waioeka in 1870.[177] Unfortunately, Cowan's account contains a number of errors that were clearly influenced by the Porter 'myth', which may in turn have led to their being picked up by later writers.

One example relating to Whakatōhea history is A.C. Lyall's *Whakatōhea of Opotiki* (1979), in which the Whanganui Contingent's attacks on the seven puni at Waipuna and the pā there are not mentioned at all; nor does Lyall acknowledge these sites as even existing. Rather, he wrote of Maraetahi in a manner that can only have been heavily influenced by Porter's 'myth':

> [Maraetahi] was a particularly strong position, but fell to a Ngati Porou rush with the firing of only a few shots. Keepa (Kemp) had by this time fought his way to a commanding position in the rear of Maraetahi, but could not bring fire to bear for fear of inflicting casualties on the Whakatohea prisoners from Opape. A combined assault finally overwhelmed the position in which Ngati-Ira were numbered amongst the defenders. Both Te Kooti and Kereopa were present at the time and both escaped. About a hundred Hauhaus were captured and nineteen were either killed or summarily executed on the river beach below.[178]

Similarly, Ranginui Walker's *Ōpōtiki-Mai-Tawhiti* (2007) makes no mention of the Whanganui attack on the seven puni, or Waipuna pā. Walker wrote only a few lines about the attack on Maraetahi pā, again with major inaccuracies plainly based on Porter's 'myth':

> Here the track was narrow, and easily held against a large force. Ngāti Porou caught the sentry napping and twenty guardsmen were driven back. Maraetahi was taken, but again Te Kooti escaped with sixty-five men and some women. He left behind twenty dead and thirty-five men, women and children captured.[179]

Walker states correctly that Te Kēpa arrived at Maraetahi pā only the following day with the released Whakatōhea, though wrongly placing the release of the Whakatōhea at Wairata: 'The next day Major Kēpa arrived with his force after taking Wairātā and freeing the Whakatōhea prisoners from Ōmarūmutu …'

As noted in Chapter 5, Judith Binney deals in considerable detail with some aspects of the Waioeka events, at times including errors that can be traced back to Porter's accounts. In *Redemption Songs: A Life of Te Kooti Arikirangi Te Turuki*, she includes a number of uncharacteristic errors about the locations of some of these events — for example attributing 19 killings to Ngāti Porou at Maraetahi, most of which actually occurred the day before about 14 kilometres upriver at Waipuna at the hands of Whanganui.[180]

I, too, found myself struggling to reconcile the published accounts when writing *Kūpapa: The Bitter Legacy of Māori Alliances with the Crown* (2015). On the one hand there were the apparently authoritative and detailed accounts by Porter and Clarke, which portrayed the events as having happened at Maraetahi; and on the other hand the relatively circumspect accounts by Te Kēpa and Topia Turoa relating to a location called Waipuna. I was uncomfortable with the outcome that I felt compelled to write, naively accepting the accuracy of Porter's and Clarke's accounts.[181] I struggled, too, to work out exactly where Waipuna pā was located, being led astray on that particular issue by Judith Binney's assertion in endnote 31 for p. 214 in her book *Redemption Songs* that Te Kēpa called 'the main pa Waipuna, which was also the name of the nearby river'. The only use of 'Waipuna' in relation to a river was by Porter, in his 1897 *Poverty Bay Herald* account when he said Maraetahi pā was '… at the junction of the Waioeka and Waipuna Rivers.' Porter's error in memory, 27 years after the Maraetahi Pā assault, plainly misled Judith Binney. The only junction at Maraetahi is of the Waioeka River and the Ōponae Stream.

The difficulties that I had in reconciling the varying accounts, however, particularly nagged. That was why I kept in mind Barbara Mabbett's references in her book on Samuel Austin, and why, several years later when I finally had time available, I undertook the task of reading Austin's diaries, with Barbara's assistance. The analysis of those diary entries, coupled with crucial investigations on the ground, enabled me to reconcile the differences between the various accounts. It is Porter's fudging of the two entirely separate events of the attacks on Waipuna and Maraetahi that has led to the inaccuracies in later histories.

In addition, however, some recent histories of the New Zealand Wars have inexplicably reduced focus on these events in the Waioeka to a level where they have dropped out of the narrative altogether. For example, Danny Keenan's *Wars Without End: New Zealand's Land Wars — A Māori Perspective*, first published in 2009 and republished in 2021, makes no reference at all to these Waioeka events. Similarly, Vincent O'Malley's *The New Zealand Wars: Ngā Pakanga o Aotearoa* (2019) does not mention these Waioeka events in any way, either in the text or on the relevant map.*

---

* The map at p. 210 of Vincent O'Malley's *The New Zealand Wars* is captioned: 'Map 10: This map shows localities and sites of major conflicts during the pursuit of Te Kooti, 1868–72.' The map is entirely blank as to the Whakatōhea rohe. It does not identify Ōpōtiki, Ōpape or the later engagement locations at Waipuna pā and Maraetahi pā in the Waioeka. Yet in other areas it identifies a number of locations where the casualties inflicted and numbers engaged were far smaller than those in the Waioeka.

One other relatively recent history, Peter Maxwell's *Frontier: The Battle for the North Island of New Zealand* (2000), demonstrates the worst possible outcome of the fallacies based on Porter's 'myth'. It provides the following completely erroneous description of events at Maraetahi after the fall of the pā:

> Now the long suffering Ringatu faced a second ordeal. One judge, jury, and executioner — Te Kooti, had been replaced by another — Ropata.
>
> The Ngati Porou chief felt inclined to institute a mass execution, but softer voices prevailed.
>
> A compromise was struck — 19 men identified as those closest to Te Kooti were led to the riverbank, then forced to stand in line, following which, at Ropata's nod, the Ngati Porou ran in with their tomahawks to split each man's skull in turn. The men were killed sequentially, man by man until the entire row lay crumpled on the gravel.
>
> The dead were picked up by the wrists and ankles and carried across the shingle, and slung out into the current like sacks of grain to tumble downstream through the gorge from which their killers had just emerged. Many bodies became trapped among the rocks, or washed into back eddies where they circled until they grounded in the shallows.
>
> Ropata considered those deaths to be a minimal result for the efforts of the preceding weeks — there were a number of captives over whom he expressed doubts, but in the end he allowed himself to be placated.

As this book has shown, no one was shot or tomahawked, at or after the fall of Maraetahi pā. Porter himself recorded that by the time Ngāti Porou reached Maraetahi pā, two hours after the engagement two kilometres downstream at Te Karoro Gorge, 'The enemy had gone.'

Yet notwithstanding that hard fact, Maxwell's account continues:

> Porter, a lone pakeha amid almost 800 victorious warriors, witnessed the executions. Later he was moved to write of the stoicism with which the Ringatu men met their fate — ranged up with imminent death staring them in the face, they awaited the blow ... without a word of beseechment, and not a tremor visible on their features.

Quite simply, none of this ever happened.

There were no people at Maraetahi pā to be executed by the time Porter and Ngāti Porou arrived. For that reason Porter did not recount being present at any such execution there.

Ngāti Ira still suffered severely at and after Maraetahi from the actions of this new Crown invasion of their rohe; the destruction of Maraetahi pā meant they had lost their longstanding refuge pā with all its whare and gardens, leaving them badly exposed in the rapidly approaching winter. They were left with no gardens or permanent place of occupation. The effects on them, then, were that rather than facing executions or capture, they were dispersed in the bush in harsh conditions. It was Te Kooti's whakarau who suffered the executions or capture well upriver.

It would be unfortunate, though, if Ngāti Ira's understanding of the events at Waioeka, and particularly at Maraetahi pā, where their people were living in March 1870, was to be influenced by such erroneous accounts.

Many recent histories, including Keenan's and O'Malley's, have very properly highlighted egregious Crown actions such as the forced movements by ship of Māori prisoners. This makes the absence in those histories of any mention of a similar movement compelled by Te Kooti, and one involving great hardship, as was inflicted on the Ōpape and Ōmarumutu communities, that much more noticeable.

Another factor that makes the increasing disappearance from memory of these events all the more perplexing relates to the large numbers involved in the various forces and the casualties inflicted. Te Kooti himself appears to have been accompanied by about 80 to 100 fighting men when he arrived at Ōpape and Ōmarumutu. At Maraetahi pā there were probably another few score of his supporters, together with perhaps a similar number of Hira Te Popo's Ngāti Ira people of Whakatōhea. And, of course, at Waipuna pā there were in addition the 218 Whakatōhea captives who were at the heart of these events, together with another 100 to 120 of Te Kooti's followers guarding them or living at the puni and pā downriver towards modern Wairata. Te Kooti's pursuers in Te Kēpa's and Topia Turoa's Whanganui and combined forces numbered about 450 men, and Ropata Wahawaha's Ngāti Porou force comprised another 330.

These were significant numbers of combatants on both sides. When the combined columns of pursuers, prisoners and the victims of the abduction finally descended the Waioeka River after both Waipuna and Maraetahi pā had fallen they would have numbered over 1100 people.

Moreover, the casualties inflicted and the numbers captured, both at the time of the abduction and particularly during the follow-up assaults two to three weeks later, dwarfed many other events in the New Zealand Wars that have been given a much higher profile in recent histories. About twenty-five more of Te Kooti's people were killed in the later response attacks. Another 31 or 32 were captured and later tried in the Supreme Court at Wellington. Another fifty or so who had been taken prisoner were taken to the East Coast until the end of 1871. In addition, and of most significance for Whakatōhea, all their 218 people who had been forcibly taken from the Ōpape reserve area were returned to their coastal pā and kāinga.

The omission of these major events in more recent histories has resulted in the loss of significant historical memory for Whakatōhea, Whanganui, Ngāti Porou and Ngāi Tai, as well as Ngāti Awa, Te Arawa, Whānau a Apanui and Ngāi Tūhoe.

DIFFERENT TREATMENT OF THE TWO STAGES OF THE NEW ZEALAND WARS?

One reason why this has occurred may be that the focus of most of our more recent histories of the New Zealand Wars has been on the Crown invasions in north Taranaki, Waikato and Tauranga that were launched by British Imperial troops between 1860 and 1864. This has perhaps led to a loss of sight of the significance of some of the major events that occurred from 1865 to 1872, which were fought by settler militia and allied Māori forces opposing Māori who dissented against the settler government.* Māori reactions to Crown and settler government invasions, at the time and later, and land confiscations by the Crown, resulted in the rapid spread of the Paimārire religious movement, followed by Titokowaru's and Te Kooti's campaigns. That led in turn to large areas outside north Taranaki, Waikato and Tauranga becoming involved in conflicts during this later period. These included the whole sweep from south Taranaki and the Whanganui area up into western Taupō and the central Volcanic Plateau, including the Taupō and Rotorua areas and into the Kaimai ranges behind Tauranga; through the Urewera and into the upper Motu area in the Bay of Plenty; and most of the major Tai Rāwhiti catchments from the East Cape down to and including Hawke's Bay.

The effects of the warfare in these huge areas were just as unsettling to the predominantly Māori communities within them as the earlier campaigns had been in the north Taranaki, Waikato and Tauranga areas. Moreover, these later events saw further significant Treaty breaches by the settler government, with widespread land confiscations carried out in south Taranaki, the eastern Bay of Plenty and Hawke's Bay, and threats of confiscations on the East Coast.

---

* In his two-volume history *The New Zealand Wars*, published in 1922–23, James Cowan gave approximately equal treatment to the two periods. The period 1845–64, which involved British Imperial troops, is addressed in Volume 1, while Volume 2 covers 1864–72, when the New Zealand settler government had control of operational military activity.

A major difference between these two periods of warfare, 1860–64 and 1865–72, was that in most of the latter period the settler government increasingly relied on Māori forces, since British Imperial troops had been withdrawn from offensive operations by the end of 1864. These Māori forces, who have come to be called kūpapa, fought alongside the forces of the settler government for a variety of reasons, which were mostly about maintaining tino rangatiratanga (untrammelled customary authority) in their own rohe, although in many cases they were deployed in areas outside those rohe. In addition, some Māori were resistant to the new religions, partly because of their loyalty to the Anglican, Wesleyan or Roman Catholic churches. After 1865, an additional driver was the desire to avoid being branded as 'rebellious' by the settler government if they did not actively oppose leaders such as Titokowaru and Te Kooti, and thereby having their own lands confiscated.

This complex history of the relationships between various Māori iwi/hapū, and between Māori and the Crown in the Ōpōtiki/Waioeka area, deserves to be fully told. And with respect to the Ōpape abduction and the later events in the Waioeka, Porter's 'myth', which has badly misinformed part of that history, needs to be exposed.

APPENDIX 1
FOOD AND OTHER RESOURCES

FOOD RESOURCES FOR THE WHAKATŌHEA CAPTIVES

One of the most puzzling questions about Te Kooti's capture of the 218 Whakatōhea people at their coastal homes and their forced relocation about 45 km inland in heavy bush country was just how he anticipated their survival in terms of food.

Porter noted that at Maraetahi pā there were extensive gardens covering about five acres (2 ha) planted in taro and many more acres in corn, and doubtless the ubiquitous potato. However, it is also likely that in March 1870 there were about 150 people living at Maraetahi. Porter recorded a woman coming into the pā the night before it fell who said there had been 67 men there, and there were clearly many more women and children also.

Upriver from Austin's 'three rivers' junction at modern Wairata there are extensive flat river terraces, which if cleared of bush would have provided room for more garden areas for the seven puni sites attacked by the Whanganui. Unfortunately, none of the contemporary documents comment on the size of gardens at those locations, although Hoani Te Paiaka did state that after the fall of Maraetahi some food was taken back to Te Pato: 'The food was carried from three small clearings about Te Tahora.'

At what is believed to be the Waipuna pā location four lines of garden stones show that an extensive area may have been cleared for planting there. While 262 people were captured there by Whanganui, they had arrived only about ten days earlier and were reliant on food from Maraetahi. Winter was approaching and at that elevation, and that far inland, potatoes and corn could not have been grown before the onset of winter.

Bush foods were the only other source of nutrition. These included a mixture of birds, such as kākā, kererū, kākāriki, whiō and even kiwi, all of which would have been prolific then; tuna (eels) and freshwater kōura in the rivers and streams; kiore (Polynesian rat); some limited supplies of bush honey; the pith of nikau and tī kōuka (cabbage tree), both of which are present, but in limited quantities; and other berries such as hīnau and tawa. Pikopiko shoots and other plant foods such as kareao (supplejack) tips were also in limited supply. (Porter mentioned that at Maungapōhatu, Tūhoe foods included 'birds, rats, and a small mountain-grown blue potato'.)

In fact, all the plant-based bush foods would have been available in only limited quantities, and gathering enough would have been very time-consuming. Bird snaring also required high levels of skill and a lot of time to gather sizeable quantities.

It may well be that the promptness of the Whanganui response to the seizure of the Whakatōhea saved them from severe privation over the forthcoming winter. They had lost their major coastal resource of seafood and their coastal gardens, and might have struggled to find sufficient bush foods to survive if the Maraetahi supplies turned out to be inadequate. Starvation was a real prospect.

SUPPLIES FOR TE KOOTI'S PURSUERS

The food supplies provided to Ngāti Porou and Whanganui, or more accurately, their shortages, have been highlighted throughout this text. So just what food was supplied to these expeditions?

In one of his earlier newspaper articles, published in the *Poverty Bay Herald* in 1897, Porter provided some useful details of the food and ammunition issued to the men:

> The provisioning of the Natives was simple — a bag of biscuits was supplied to every two men, also to each 4 lbs of bacon, 4 lbs of sugar, and 1/2 lb of tea ... In addition to the items mentioned, each man carried 100 rounds of ammunition, so that with arms, rations, etc. no man carried less than 80 lbs weight. This, however, became lightened as the march continued ...[182]

Similarly, Austin's diary quite often mentions issues to the Whanganui Contingent of biscuits and sugar, usually interspersed with complaints of shortage, and descriptions of desperate efforts to find food either by fishing, bird-catching or digging up old potato beds. Sometimes instead of biscuit he mentions issues of flour that the men cooked up into some form of 'biscuit', probably damper.

SHELTER

Shelter would also have been a major issue. In several localities, such as at Ōhope, Austin's diary entries make it clear that Whanganui had no tentage at all. Shortly after their arrival at Ōhope on 5 February it rained, and Austin recorded on the 7th: 'Under Orders to go into the Bush after Te Kooti but as it was raining so heavy we did not go. We are in a most frightful state, no tents, nothing but Blankets to shelter us.'

And on 11 February, after landing at Ōhiwa once again: 'It came on to rain shortly after landing and rained for the remainder of the day. We were fortunate to find some good Huts hear as we had no tents with us ...'

According to Porter, however, Ngāti Porou seem to have been more fortunate, with calico tent sheeting being provided to them:

> In the first instance no camp equipment was required. For tentage two yards of double-width unbleached calico was served out to each man to carry. When camp was pitched, long frames constructed of light saplings lashed together verandah shape were quickly erected. The calico sheets were then stretched, overlapping a little, along the top, pegged to the ground in rear, the front being so fastened as to form a sloping verandah shelter. Beneath the whole length of front fires were lit if required, the men resting with their feet towards it. Thus on an average twenty sheets afforded shelter for sixty men lying down with rifles ready at their sides.[183]

For the Whakatōhea travelling inland under Te Kooti's guard, it would have been necessary to construct wharau or temporary huts in the late afternoons. These were usually made of tree fern leaves spread over rapidly constructed sapling frames. Once they had arrived at Waipuna, and with winter soon to be upon them, they would have set to urgently to construct more substantial whare. The large number of people in the pā, in excess of 260, would have meant that much could be achieved in a short time, both gathering materials and in actual construction.

Usually those whare were constructed by digging out some soil, which was piled around the excavated area to ensure rainwater could not flow in. The outer edges of the sapling structure of sloped roofing, descending from a central ridgepole, extended far enough to ensure that water from the roof dripped outside the piled-up soil, leaving the occupants dry within. Roofing and, if present, low walls could be thatched to a considerable thickness from a range of materials, depending on what was available. Strips of tōtara bark, parts of the raupō plant, flax leaves and stalks, tī kōuka leaves, tree-fern fronds, tussocks and similar plants that might shed water rather than absorb it, were all used at times.

Porter provided a description of the warmth that could be obtained within such simple whare at Maungapōhatu, which was probably true of bush whare anywhere: 'Their houses were Whare Punis, partly below and above ground, and with doors and windows closed embers were burned inside until each house became almost an oven.'[184] Typical whare construction of the time can be seen in the photograph of Tamaikōwha's pa at Tauwharemanuka on page 112.

APPENDIX 2
TE KOOTI'S TE UREWERA ROUTES IN FEBRUARY AND MARCH 1870

Readers with a connection to or knowledge of Te Urewera may find it of interest to consider in some detail aspects of the routes Te Kooti and his supporters likely followed after the events of February and March 1870. Te Kooti undertook many long, hard marches in 1869 and 1870, and to a lesser extent in 1868 and 1871. Of these, the colossal efforts that he and his followers undertook in Te Urewera in February and March 1870 stand out. Each trek involved quite extraordinary route marches across very tough terrain within amazingly short periods of time.

The first part of this appendix addresses their escape from Gilbert Mair and his Te Arawa force in February 1870 as they traversed from the Horomanga River to Ruatāhuna, and thence to Maraetahi pā in the Waioeka. This journey was made in only about two weeks, over increasingly tough country. As very few detailed records remain, this account necessarily relies on educated suggestions as to the exact route followed, particularly in its latter stages.

The second part addresses events that are even less well documented, that occurred after the capture of Maraetahi pā in March 1870. It attempts to determine just where Te Kooti is most likely to have gone in the following days to evade his pursuers. Once more that mystery requires calculated guesswork, much of it based on physical investigation of the terrain, as described in Appendix 3.

FEBRUARY 1870
HOROMANGA TO RUATĀHUNA

It was recorded by Lt Gilbert Mair that Te Kooti and his followers had fled from his attack at Lake Ōkaro, southeast of Rotorua, in the dark on the night of 7–8 February 1870. The next day or so would have been absorbed in traversing the tussock-covered Kaingaroa Plains to the Rangitaiki River, to cross it at the Horomanga ford — a distance of over 40 kilometres.

It is known the group had some wounded with them, so travel would have been slow.[185] It is reasonable to assume they took two days to reach Te Urewera, arriving late on 9 February. One wounded man, Hohepa, died in the Horomanga valley, but his body was taken for burial up to the Tutaepukepuke pā, on the large clearing at the head of the Horomanga. Even though they had some horses with them to carry the wounded, it would probably have taken the whole day for all of them to ascend the Horomanga and climb up to Tutaepukepuke clearing. Taking into account the wounded, it is more likely to have taken two days, as there were about 250–300 people involved at that stage.

From Tutaepukepuke they would have descended into the Pukareao Stream and followed it down to the Ōkarika Stream, which flows into the Whakatāne River. At that location they had to turn south and head upriver to ascend to Ruatāhuna. As a large group, with limited food, and slowed by young children and older people, it is likely all that travel took them another two, or probably three, days to reach Ruatāhuna from the crossing of the Rangitaiki at the Horomanga junction.

In the statement he gave to Porter and St John in April 1870, Wiremu Kingi Te Paia described the route taken to the crossing of the Rangitaiki, and the run-down condition of Te Kooti's people by that stage: 'We crossed it at the Horomanga ford, and followed up that gorge until we got to Omaruteangi. ... If it had been Ngatiporou following us we must all have been killed, as we moved along very slowly, from hunger and fatigue.'

Ōmaruteangi was a kāinga of the fiercely independent Tūhoe rangatira Kereru Te Pukenui. The missionary William Colenso, who passed through it in 1843 during his Urewera traverse, described it as being on the east bank of the Whakatāne River near a junction with a major stream coming from Maungapōhatu. That description best fits the Manangaatiuhi Stream, and in that case would place the kāinga of Ōmaruteangi at or about the location of the modern Ōhaua o te rangi marae.*

If one allows for three to four days' travel from the Rangitaiki valley to Ruatāhuna, that means they would not have arrived there until 12 or 13 February. It appears that they had been recovering at Ruatāhuna for only a few days before receiving news from the ope that had set out to attack the Runanga redoubt, that government forces were on the way to Te Urewera.

TRAVERSE FROM RUATĀHUNA TO THE WAIMANA/TAURANGA RIVER

The hurried departure by Te Kooti's supporters from Ruatāhuna would have involved another descent down the Whakatāne River past Ōmaruteangi to the

---

* About 4–5 km downriver from Ōhaua marae the old Tūhoe route that descends the Pukareao and Ōkarika streams hits the Whakatāne River on the true left. That route is now a marked track.

Wharau range, which lies to the Whakatāne River's east and links over to the Waikare catchment. If one allows for, say, three days at Ruatāhuna, that would mean they were fleeing north on or about 16 or 17 February.

A very old Tūhoe trail from the mid Whakatāne River over to the Waikare tributary runs from the location of the previous Tawhiwhi hut up the Mangatawhero Stream before ascending onto the Wharau range.* After traversing north the route descends the Motumako Stream, past the previous Takurua Hut, to join the Waikare River at the Waikarewhenua clearings. As Te Paia said that they then reached Neketuri, which is in the upper Waikare River, they must have turned upriver at Waikarewhenua. The walk from Waikarewhenua to Neketuri up the Waikare River would have occupied most of a day. That stretch of the Waikare is beautiful but it involves countless river crossings — most easy, but not all, and passes the previous Otanetea Hut.

Neketuri was a kāinga located just downriver from the previous Taurawharona Hut location. From Tauaki pā an old Tūhoe trail descended for about an hour north to the Waikare at Taurawharona, before ascending a long, steep, undulating ridgeline over to the mid Tawhana Stream in the Waimana catchment. In 1870 it would have been common to intercept the old route from Tauaki pā at Neketuri. The traverse took most of a day, involving an initially steep and then long, undulating ascent of over 500 metres to a high point of about 850 metres above sea level, before the equally long descent into the head of the Tawhana Stream. It would then have taken about another two hours to reach the junction of the Tawhana Stream with the Tauranga River, where the valley opens out at the beautiful site of the Tawhana pā. This pā was within the rohe of Eru Tamaikōwha.

The walk from Ruatāhuna to Tawhana pā would have taken about three days at least, so by the time they reached Tawhana it must have been about 20 or 21 February. It was probably somewhere during this stage, before or at Tawhana, that Te Kooti himself caught up with his followers, as described in Chapter 3.

TAWHANA PĀ TO MARAETAHI PĀ

It will be recalled that Te Paia concluded his account of this major traverse in very simple terms by saying that having reached Tawhana pā: 'we descended the river, and after two nights on the road reached Waioweka'. There are two most

---

* During the hut-building for the government's deer-culling operations, huts were constructed at Tawhiwhi in the Whakatāne, Takurua in the Motumako, and Otanetea and Taurawharona on the Waikare River. They were linked by a marked track. After the text for this book was written, DOC agreed to a proposal by Te Uru Taumatua to destroy all these good huts. At the time of publication, the long-term future of other Te Urewera huts is uncertain.

plausible options as to the route they may have taken, but as Whakatōhea scouts from Maraetahi pā had joined them to lead the way it is likely they would have taken the most direct route. Te Paia noted the arrival of the Whakatōhea in his statement:

> I forgot to mention that while in Ruatahuna Te Kooti wrote to Waioweka, telling the Whakatohea to be prepared for his coming, and to send some people to Opotiki as scouts. Aporo took the letter. Some of the Whakatohea then came to visit us; among them was Pera (now a prisoner here).

The most direct route involved continuing downriver past both Tawhana pā and Tauwharemanuka pā, which was Tamaikōwha's principal pā, located just upstream from the major Ōtapukawa junction. This junction is about 6 km downriver from Tawhana pā. A route leads up the major Ōtapukawa side stream for a few kilometres then climbs up onto a leading spur that heads north and then east over into the upper Waiiti Stream.*

From further down the central Waiiti Stream, which is broad and easy going, it is possible to climb steeply from the Whakapirau sidestream up onto the high ridgeline that heads east. This undulates along through the Ōtetere food basket area to link directly to the east right through to Maraetahi over the high Pōkirikiri feature, just behind and to the west of Maraetahi itself. Guidance for most of that route could be provided by keeping the Ōponae Stream catchment always to the north of the ridgeline, and the Wairata Stream to the south. Whakatōhea had sent guides to meet Te Kooti and his people, and they would have been very familiar with this route. Following that route it would have taken most of one day from Tawhana to reach the Whakapirau junction with the Waiiti. The next day would have been a long, hard day on the ridges before descending to Maraetahi pā.

The direct route had its complications in finding and following the long ridgeline to the south of the Ōponae Stream to go direct to Maraetahi, but the detailed local knowledge of the Whakatōhea scouts would have enabled them to find their way and greatly reduce the distance they had to travel. (In kōrero tuku iho evidence of oral history given before the Waitangi Tribunal in 2022 a Ngāti Ira witness, Derek Kingi, described how this area south of the Ōponae was regarded as a major food basket for Ngāti Ira, and was known as Ōtetere. Ngāti Ira knew it as the last or largest area in which miro berries ripened, and as a

---

* This ridgeline on the western side of the upper Waiiti forms part of the kōkako restoration area where until recent times a major recovery of the kōkako population was achieved by some very dedicated DOC and Tūhoe staff. An associated offshoot of that recovery also saw a major growth in the whio population in the Waiiti catchment.

flocking place for kererū. It had the advantage of being a large flattish elevated bush area.)[186] This direct ridgeline route above the Ōponae Stream would have been feasible in two very long days, which is all Te Paia said they took from Tawhana to Maraetahi. Again, though, this would have been possible only for very tough people who were prepared to walk 10 to 12 hours a day.

Another less direct route from Tawhana pā existed, but it would not have been any easier. About a kilometre downriver from the pā is the junction of the Tauranga River and the Ōtane Stream. From there another old Tūhoe route leads up the Ōtane Stream for seven or eight kilometres to another very high ridgeline, rising to over 900 metres above sea level, which leads over to the Tataweka Stream in the Waioeka catchment.

The Tataweka Stream flows northeast down a very gentle, open course to meet the Kahunui, a major headwater of the Waioeka. From there, apart from one short stretch of gorge comprising very large rocks, a very long walk in low river conditions (as might be expected in mid February), would have taken them to the junction of the Kahunui River with the Koranga River, at modern Koranga Forks. It is here that these two rivers join to form the Waioeka River itself.

In low river conditions it would just be possible to travel from Tawhana pā to reach the Koranga Forks junction via the Ōtane/Tataweka route in one long day involving 10–14 hours' walking. The next day's travel would have involved an easy start for an hour in the Waioeka, followed by at least two more lengthy and difficult stretches of river gorge, which would have brought them after a massive day-long effort to Maraetahi pā.

MARCH 1870
LIKELY ESCAPE ROUTES AND MOVEMENTS OF TE KOOTI AFTER HIS ESCAPE

In her first statement, Te Kooti's wife Huhana described the attack on Maraetahi, and both the relative ease with which they escaped and the time they had to do so. Forewarned of a government force upriver, Te Kooti and his people's obvious escape route if attacked from downriver would be up into the bush-covered ridge behind the pā. Huhana confirmed that was the route they took:

> The night before we were attacked at Maraetai two women and a man came and told us the government people were approaching by the rear. At daylight soon after this information was received we heard firing in the direction of the picquet. Te Kooti called to all the soldiers to fall in and collect upon the hill at the back of the pa. We saw the government people approaching and many of Te Kooti's

soldiers were inclined to run away. Te Kooti then gave the word for the whole to retreat. We ran away, after crossing the creek and when at the top of a hill we waited to rest.

There is a very small catchment to the immediate west of the pā site, and it is possible that they initially ran into the bush there, crossed the bed of the creek and ascended the bush-covered ridge behind the pā. As the ground conditions were very dry at the time, however, it is unlikely that this catchment would have had running water in it. In fact, the spur they would have ascended links up anyway with the main ridge directly above the pā, which also descends a different spur on the eastern side of that very small catchment into the pā site.

The main ridge behind Maraetahi pā ascends quite steeply from the pā site for about 200 metres to an initial high point where the two spurs join. There it flattens out for a short distance before again ascending another 350 metres or so to a high point at 581 metres. While following that first ridgeline option immediately behind the pā in a southerly direction would have taken Te Kooti and his wives and few men well clear of Maraetahi pā, it would have brought them back to the Waioeka River below Waipuna pā, at the junction of the Wairata Stream and the Waioeka. Te Kooti would have realised that to descend the Wairata Stream back to the Waioeka would place him at real risk of encountering this government force as it descended the main Waioeka River. For all these reasons that ridgeline running south seems unlikely to have been the route.

(Today a vehicle track essentially follows along that ridgeline and finally descends from the top of the ridge at its southern end down into the farmhouse block of Murray and Anne Redpath at the end of Redpath Road, adjacent to the Wairata Stream.)

There was an alternative route, which involved crossing a larger, unnamed creek between the pā site and the main Ōponae Stream. This creek actually flows into the Ōponae about a hundred metres before its junction with the Waioeka. If that was the creek Huhana was referring to, which seems much more likely, then after crossing the creek the spur on the other side would have taken them up to a high point called Pōkirikiri at 789 metres. Today, a farm track runs part of the way up that spur. From Pōkirikiri, a major, well-defined ridgeline runs west past the head of the Ōponae Stream towards the Waiiti catchment, which flows into the Waimana/Tauranga at modern Whakarae pā. Te Kooti would have reasoned that following this route to the west led to safe refuge in the Waimana valley, whereas heading south up the Waioeka would take them towards an enemy party.

As discussed in Chapter 7, for that reason it seems likely that Te Kooti and his few close followers would have climbed up to Pōkirikiri and continued west along the main leading ridge for many hours, heading through the Ōtetere area to the Whakapirau Stream. That would have taken them into the Waiiti Stream in the Waimana/Tauranga River catchment. From there they could have gone up that river to the Ōtane catchment, before later coming back over into the headwaters of the Tataweka Stream, which flows into the Waioeka much further up past the Waipuna pā.

Lt Col St John, in his report of 30 March, described what Porter believed to have been Te Kooti's initial escape route: 'His travel lay towards the Waimana but he must have doubled back as a following party reached Te Ponga and found the Urewera had all deserted him.'

Te Ponga was on a spur located near modern Whakarae pā, in the Waimana catchment at the Waimana/Tauranga junction with the Waiiti. This lends weight to the Pōkirikiri ridge escape route as that would have taken them almost directly to Te Ponga. Moreover, it was likely the reverse of the route they had followed to reach Maraetahi. The 'following party' that St John was referring to was the Ngāti Porou pursuit patrol that went out on 26 March and returned on 27 March. Porter's diary records that the patrol had gone to 'Te Punga' in the Waimana valley:

> 27th March, Sunday.— The 120 men out yesterday returned, bringing three prisoners, and report having killed one man. They followed the track of some thirty men as far as Te Punga. At Waimana learned it was the Urewera of Te Kooti returning to Ruatahuna, and hearing from one of the prisoners that Te Kooti had not gone in that direction, they returned.

Ropata Wahawaha's later account, in te reo Māori, of the pursuit of Te Kooti referred to that route being followed the next year by a number of his Ngāti Porou.

Huhana's second statement provides a further clue that this may have been the route taken. In her statement of 8 August she said that after fleeing from Maraetahi pā, 'We went on to Taweka a branch of Waioeka, and in the morning we came to the main stream of Waioeka to an old puni where we found 3 bodies that had been killed by the Government. Winiata Hakitara, Harapeta Kepatu & Te Kerehama Te Kauau.'

The reference 'Taweka' is presumably to Tataweka Stream, which is a significant sidestream of the upper Waioeka. It is linked by an old Māori route (still marked roughly as a track) over to the Ōtane Stream, a very considerable distance up the Waimana/Tauranga River. As described earlier, the Tataweka flows into the Kahunui well upstream of the major Kahunui/Koranga junction that forms the Waioeka River itself.

As noted earlier, if the Tataweka was their destination that day, that route should not be surprising even though it would have taken at least 12–15 hours, possibly even longer, to reach the Tataweka headwaters from Maraetahi using the ridgelines.

Te Kooti and his supporters would have been desperately anxious to put as much distance as they could between themselves and the hundreds of Ngāti Porou they had seen pouring along the river towards Maraetahi pā, let alone the threat of the unknown numbers of the government force upriver. Moreover, they had demonstrated time and again over the previous two years their capacity for rapid travel over extremely long distances in rugged, heavy bush country — including recently, when they probably used the Pōkirikiri route to reach Maraetahi from Tawhana pā.

Today, that amount of travel from Pōkirikiri heading west to the Waimana along an initially steep then undulating, bush-covered ridgeline, or on a mixture of ridgeline and riverbeds, might seem extreme. To Te Kooti and his people it would have been achievable, particularly when spurred all day by fear of deadly pursuit.

In her statement on 5 August Huhana described their later descent of the Waioeka River from the Tataweka (her reference to Raipawa is to the same pā as Waipuna):

> When the place was cleared of the government people we collected together again and started to Raipawa where the main body had been sent, when we got there we found it unoccupied.
>
> We saw three bodies lying dead, the names of them were Kareama, Hape te Kipatu, and Winiata; they were from the Chatham Islands & Turanga. We buried them and went to the Waioeka stream where we found three more dead bodies and that of a woman. ... We buried them.

Both of Huhana's statements lend some support to the likelihood of their initially fleeing as far as the Tataweka. Moreover, her account of later events also makes it clear that Te Kooti took refuge when threatened, either in the Tataweka catchment or in the next catchment to the west, the Ōtane, which flows into the Waimana/Tauranga River. In both accounts she described how after a few days Te Kooti had gathered about 20–30 supporters and moved back down to Waipuna pā (or Raipawa in Huhana's statements), and on down to the Tahora (modern Ōpato), where they buried the bodies. She then said, in her second statement:

Te Kooti told off 20 soldiers to go & follow the Government up to endeavour to rescue their prisoners. When they arrived at Maraetahi they saw the Government people and one of their party a Whakatohea escaped to the Government party. When they found that this man had escaped they returned to Te Taora.

This second statement then made reference to Te Kooti with two of his wives heading for the mouth of a creek called the Ōtane. A descent into the Ōtane may have followed a route from the Tataweka, which in more recent times has been marked as a track linking the headwaters of the Tataweka and the Ōtane. Huhana described these events, some of which occurred some days later and involved the Ōtane, in both her statements:

On 5 August she said:
When we got to the top of the hill Te Kooti with a few men descended to the bed of the stream, and when he got down saw some of the government people who were out chasing him. Four of them beckoned to him, he came to them; Te Kooti knew they were government people and told those with him to run away at once. He then followed. I was there and ran away leaving all our things behind; we very narrowly escaped.

And on 8 August:
When we had gone some distance, he, with his two women Horinia and Honia went towards the mouth of the creek called Otane. When Te Kooti reached the bank he saw two of the Government soldiers on the other side of the river, they beckoned to him. He returned to us & told us that the Government were there. We fled leaving all our food. We ascended a very high hill & slept there. In the morning we went on until we reached another branch of Waioeka we remained there three days & then returned down the Waioeka stream.

Her statement then continued by describing another scouting visit to the 'Marakoro near Tahora' ('Marakoro' likely being a misspelling of Ōmaukora). From there, she told how they moved well up the Waioeka to 'Parangiora' (again, probably a reference to the Rangiora pā site, or Pā Rangiora, which Te Kooti is known to have established well up in the Koranga headwater of the Waioeka). She then said that they wintered at 'Te Weranga', another locality in the headwaters of the Koranga, known today as Te Wera.

The only other piece of direct evidence as to Te Kooti's movements in the days after his escape from Maraetahi came from Hoani Te Paiaka. In his statement, with reference to the days after the fall of Maraetahi pā, Te Paiaka said:

> ... the rest came back with me to Ruatahuna on the 27th April. We left Te Kooti a few days before. He was then at a place called Te Pato; it is a small stream that branches off to the left from Waioeka, just above Maraetahi and near Te Tahora ... Te Kooti is now either at Te Tahora or Te Pato.
>
> About a week after the fight, I came back with Te Kooti from Te Pato, and he gave orders to his men to go and bury the dead. I went with them and saw these men put in their graves.* Te Kooti then went back to Pato, and I told him I would leave him, as I had lost faith in his Atua. I then came to Ruatahuna.

Te Pato Stream has a short but tight gorge immediately above its junction with the Waioeka, opposite which the Waipuna pā site was established. Passage is possible through the gorge, but the boulders are so big that travel is slow. However, the gorge can be bypassed on narrow rock benches on the true right, and today an easy track is marked along those benches. A little distance above the gorge the valley widens into a series of bushed terraces on each side of the stream.

The existence of the gorge in Te Pato Stream would have given Te Kooti a sense of protection as the gorge and the track running just above it would have made for an easily defensible position, not dissimilar to Hell's Gate (Te Karoro a Tamatea) below Maraetahi. Yet it seems from Huhana's statement that this position was not secure enough for him, and that Te Kooti spent the winter at either or both of Pā Rangiora and Te Wera up the Koranga River. His forces may have been beaten and dispersed at two locations in the mid Waioeka catchment, but the extreme upper river reaches, which were even more difficult for his pursuers to reach, may have given him a sense of safe refuge.

---

* Te Paiaka did not name the men who were buried. The only account recorded was given by Huhana Tamati, who named some of those she assisted in burying or saw. (Her statements are recorded in handwriting, which is sometimes difficult to read, and the Pākehā records may also have made misspellings. Her two statements have different spellings.)

APPENDIX 3
FOLLOWING IN THEIR FOOTSTEPS

The immediate problem faced in researching this book was the general loss of historical memory about many of these events and places. In particular, there was a lack of readily available information about even the location of the large pā described variously as Waipuna and Raepawa. So, too, was there a lack of readily available information about the routes that Te Kooti and his supporters followed when heading into Maraetahi from the direction of Ruatāhuna; the routes he took on his way to and from his attack on Kōkōhinau pā from Maraetahi; and the routes he took in travelling to and from his attack on the pā at Ōmarumutu and Ōpape.

This last route, back from Ōpape with the Whakatōhea captives, was integrally linked with the possible location of Waipuna pā. But that location was not recorded on any archaeological record, nor marked on any map or old survey plan. This was not too surprising, as it was probably only occupied for about two weeks at most before being captured by the Whanganui Contingent and burnt to the ground. If one takes 7 March as the date the Ōpape and Ōmarumutu captives started walking inland from the coast, and allows say three days for them to walk in to the Waipuna site, that means the construction of the whare would have commenced on about 10 or 11 March. The pā was burnt down on 26 March, and there is no apparent oral or written knowledge of it ever being reoccupied as a pā site. Memory of its location seems to have just disappeared.

As described in the main text, the answers to some of the uncertainties lay in a close analysis and comparison of the accounts of one of Te Kooti's wives, Huhana Tamati, and those of Wiremu Kingi Te Paia and Hoani Te Paiaka, but most reliably in the contemporary diary record of Samuel Austin. Without Austin's detailed daily account of events it is highly unlikely this book could have been written. His diary provided the basic key to the route to Waipuna pā being up the Tutaetoko, then into another stream, the Raetakahia, before ascending a very high ridge and finally heading down into the Ōmaukora Stream. Austin also provided distances between locations in the Waioeka itself.

It is all very well having various snippets of tantalising information as to locations of rivers as at 1870. These often have different modern names, or use of the old names has simply been discontinued and lost. What really became the key to unlocking the areas of doubt was to go to the places involved and check out on the ground the reality or otherwise of certain conclusions that seemed feasible on paper. So began a series of trips from 2020 to 2022 into the Waioeka and Waimana areas as part of a process of proving, or disproving, on the ground where particular locations or routes were.

TUTAETOKO AND RAUPŌ RIDGE ROUTE FROM ŌPAPE TO WAIPUNA PĀ

The place to start was the route Te Kooti took when he brought the Ōpape captives back to the Waioeka, as that route was also followed by the Whanganui Contingent and later by St John and Wiremu Kingi. Moreover, in each of these cases it led the group to head up the Waioeka River to Waipuna pā.

An intriguing early find was that on the NZ Topo50 App map (on the version showing purple Department of Conservation land boundaries) an old surveyed road line showed up. It went up from the Raetakahia Stream, which flows into the Tutaetoko River, and over the Raupō ridgeline, descending into the Ōmaukora Stream, which flows south into the Waioeka. The surveyed road line was just down from the ridgetop on the eastern or Raetakahia side.

Chris Gray at the stream junction in the Ōmaukora Stream where the Whanganui advance party at last obtained a drink of water after spending 26 hours without water traversing along the Raupō ridgeline. They finally descended from the skyline peak in the distance behind.
Author's collection, October 2021

Since most old surveyed road lines followed either stock routes or Māori trails, this seemed a good place to start searching on the ground. In March 2020, Dave Stallworthy and Stu Spicer of Whangārei accompanied me into Brills Bivvy in the Raetakahia valley for some days as we walked the riverbed below the hut down past the Raetakahia junction, and up the steep ridge behind the hut. On that trip we twice pushed south along the ridge for a short distance but did not quite make it up to the Raupō high point. We did leave some red tape where we hit the ridgeline.

That trip established a number of interesting points. First, that no physical road line was ever constructed, nor any benched track for stock on the old surveyed road line. The ridge was uniformly steep and bush-covered all the way up, and still bush-covered along the main ridge. Second, from that point above Brills Bivvy the ridgeline was narrow, and at the top it clearly demarcated between the Raetakahia on the eastern side and the Waioeka River on the west, as Austin had described. Third, the

ABOVE *A typical rata tree on the flank of the Raupō ridge above the Raetakahia Stream, March 2020. Author providing scale*. Stu Spicer collection

TOP *Stu Spicer in typical bush cover on Raupō ridgeline, March 2020.* Author collection 'undulations' along the ridgeline were significant enough to make it impossible to see a saddle below as one descended hundreds of feet before hitting a saddle and starting up the next stretch of the ridge. That meant it would be difficult to be sure you were descending the main ridgeline and not wandering off down a side-spur.

Finally, that initial trip showed that the climb up was a slog, and would have been very hard going for the young children and older people from the Ōpape community who might have been forced to walk along the ridge.

HELICOPTERS AND DRONES

During that March 2020 trip we were helicoptered into Brills Bivvy by Luke Lamont of Whakatāne-based Kāhu NZ, via an overflight of Maraetahi pā to enable us to obtain photos there and at Wairata (or 'the three rivers junction', as Austin termed the Wairata area, being at the junction of the Ōmaukora, Tahora/Ōpato and Waioeka rivers). Because of Covid-induced delays, it was not until a year later, in March 2021, that I flew over the upper Waioeka area in a small Robinson helicopter with Mark Law of Kāhu NZ. Mark has a deep interest in the history and geography of the region, and this was an overflight of various points of historic relevance all over Te Urewera.

By that time I had completed much of the research for this book, which had raised other issues, such as how the Whanganui Contingent knew of the existence of the puni sites upriver from the junction of the three rivers, and their possible locations. My research had also drawn my attention to the number of contemporary accounts that described Te Kooti's attachment to the Te Pato Stream area. The map shows that Te Pato Stream connects by a lowish bush saddle over to the Moanui Stream, providing a possible escape route or an alternative route in high flood conditions to the upper Koranga River, which is a major tributary of the Waioeka. I knew Te Kooti had refuge pā or puni locations at Pā Rangiora and at Te Wera on the upper Koranga River, so he would have valued alternative access to that area.

During that March 2021 flight Mark hovered over the junction of Te Pato Stream and the Waioeka to allow me to take photos up Te Pato towards that low saddle. The bottom segment of one of those photos happened to capture an elevated but flat protruding terrace on the west bank of the Waioeka above the Te Pato junction. At the time I did not pay any attention to the terrace, but its inclusion in the photo was later to prove crucial. We then flew up the Waioeka before heading west.

The next day, together with Harvey Brunt of Auckland, a retired engineer of keen intellect (nowadays redirected at informing himself and others about New Zealand's history by droning historic sites for a fascinating series of YouTube videos he posts under the name Kiwi Codger), I met up with Murray and Anne Redpath and their son Dale at the end of Redpath Road. From there we travelled through Murray's brother Bob's farm to drone two large terrace areas on two separate large bends of the Waioeka River, one about 2 km downriver from the Te Pato junction and the other at the junction.

After that, from a site near the bush edge, Harvey was just able to fly the drone about 4 km upriver to sit above the ridgeline opposite the Nikau Flat Hut and take an image from there. We then moved to drone the upper Ōmaukora Stream and Raupō ridge areas. Harvey and I then droned the Wairata area, the Maraetahi pā site, the Tutaetoko mouth and Ōtara River area, and from over the sea back facing south into the Ōpape and Ōmarumutu areas. Many of those drone images provide the illustrations for this book.

WAIPUNA PĀ LOCATION

Austin's diary suggested two different possibilities for the location of Waipuna pā. In his entry for 24 March, he provided a specific distance from Te Tahora River to Waipuna pā: 'The name of the Pa we took and Killed Hakaraia in was Waipuna ... It is about 8 miles from Tetahora River.'

The distance of 8 miles converts to 12.8 km, or close enough to 13 km. After consulting some surveyors in Blenheim, Tony Hawke and Phil Morton, I used Google Earth mapping to measure the riverbed distance from the Tahora (modern Ōpato), and found that 12.8 kms ended almost exactly at Nikau Flat Hut, well up the Waioeka. (Later, more accurate measurement, has shown the riverbed distance to Nikau Flat Hut from the modern Ōpato or Te Tahora junction to be 12.3 km.)

I had last been to Nikau Flat in October 1987, and as I recalled it the area around the hut was stony, very steep, and bush-covered out the back, with the hut occupying a relatively small terrace. It seemed highly unlikely to have had room for enough whare sites to house over 260 people, including one large whare with room for 100 people. Moreover, it was located south of a very steep feature on the opposite eastern side of the river, so in winter would be an exceptionally cold place to live.

Furthermore, the river entered gorges both below and immediately above Nikau Flat, making crossing in high-flow conditions difficult if not impossible in 1870. (Nowadays there is a clearly marked and largely benched track, well above the river downstream of Nikau Flat Hut on its west or true left side.) In 1987, because the river was in a highish fresh, (a 'fresh' signifies a high flow that is not quite at flood level), and I was on my own, making crossing risky with a very heavy pack, I had had to cross a swingbridge that was there at that time (this was later washed away). I then had to make the very long, steep climb of some 550 metres up to the opposing ridgeline to follow it south towards the Koranga Forks Hut.

Nikau Flat therefore seemed an unlikely site for Waipuna pā, but it could not be discounted on my memory of 35 years earlier, particularly as Austin's statement was so definite. As it turned out, I had not initially placed enough significance on Austin's diary entry for 30 March, two full pages later, when they had arrived back at Ōpōtiki after descending the Waioeka River all the way from Waipuna. In that entry, Austin had written: 'The Distance from Opotiki to where Hakaraia was killed is, by this Road, some 70 miles and a bad road it is.'

When I reconsidered that distance of '70 miles' (113 km) after measuring the distances to Nikau Flat, this 30 March entry brought me up with a start. I knew the main State Highway from Ōpōtiki to Gisborne basically followed the Waioeka Gorge all the way up to Matawai. When I looked up the road distance from Ōpōtiki to Matawai (which is well to the southeast of Waipuna), I found it was not 70 miles, but only 44.5 miles, or 71.5 km. That led to a rough calculation using Google Maps to find the approximate distance by river from Ōpōtiki to the likely site of Waipuna pā, which turned out to be about 55 km, or roughly 35 miles. (Later, more accurate riverbed measurement has shown the distance from Waipuna pā to Ōpōtiki to be only 50.1 km.) If Austin was in fact using a return distance to arrive at 70 miles, that immediately raised the question: where would a return distance of 8 miles take one, being 4 miles (6.4 km) from the three rivers junction? The answer, when measured on Google Maps, was almost exactly to the junction of the Waioeka and Te Pato Stream.

The question then was on which side of the river? It could only be on the western side, because as the colour photo in this book (BII, top image) shows, the area of the Te Pato Stream mouth is extremely steep, and the start of the stream above the junction is in a gorge for about half a kilometre. Other factors that impacted on the relocation arose out of the fact that the pā was in existence for a period of only 14–16 days. Austin's diary entry on 28 March says that as they were leaving Maraetahi pā, 'We have burnt all the huts that we came across as yet.' Therefore the pā would have existed only from about 10 or 11 March, when the Whakatōhea prisoners arrived, until it was burnt down on 26 March.

Thus, all memory of the pā's location had been lost. Even the surveyors who conducted the first surveys of the Waioeka River in this area in the late 1880s and 1890s did not note its location on either their survey plans or in their field notes. Significantly, their field notes record that their physical chain measurements were taken down the eastern side of the river, so they may not have noticed the pā site's dug-in remains, such as they were, on the western side. That is because at the Te Pato junction the terrace on which the pā would have been located is much higher than the river edge on the Te Pato side.

RAUPŌ RIDGE AND NIKAU FLAT WALKS

In October 2021, after more Covid-19 delays, Mark Law and Chris Gray, both ex-special forces soldiers, agreed to accompany me to try to walk the bush-covered ridge from the Tutaetoko catchment via the Ōmaukora to the Waioeka River. As it turned out, this required all their bush navigation skills.

We walked from the end of the Tutaetoko valley road up the riverbed for an hour or so before meeting the junction with the Raetakahia Stream. From there a benched track continued for about 15–20 minutes before striking the ridge between two streams, just as Austin's diary described. The western stream at that junction was the very one that the old surveyed road line mentioned on page 232 followed up. Austin had described how they got to that point as follows:

> We are still keeping in the Tutae Toka river, and had to do so for about 4 Miles when we took to another Creek, and followed this one for 3 or 4 Miles when we came to the spur of a large Hill and another Creek.
>
> We took to the spur of this Hill there being a Creek on each side of the Spur. This was a difficult Spur to get up in some parts, one had to pull the other up. When we got to the top it was a narrow ridge. It was 5 p.m. when we got to the top …

We had difficulty at one steep location trying to link from that spur ridge, which basically runs northeast to southwest, to the one that runs northwest to southeast over the high point of Raupō to head further on south to the Ōmaukora. (For me personally, it was with a sense of relief that at about lunchtime we located the red tape marker that I had left at the northern point of the Raupō ridge seven months earlier.) In the afternoon we did have repeated concerns, while we made the long descents on undulations in the bush along the top of the ridge, as to whether we were still on the main ridgeline or descending a side-spur. Finally, however, we reached a series of small clearings on the western side of the ridgeline above the Waioeka that were evidently the remains of clearing for grazing. From there we could see down into the Waioeka, much as Austin had described in his diary entry for 22 March:

> Shortly after the Advance Guard passed word to the Main Body that they had seen Smoak some distance a head. Several of the men went up some of the large trees and they seen some Huts. Shortly after they heard chopping, as if cutting wood. ... and when the moon showed out we could see the silver stream below us and could not get at it.

Shortly after began the long, steep descent east into the Ōmaukora valley. We were intrigued to find we were then in cut-over but still high-canopy bush, following very steeply down an old bulldozed logging track all the way to the junction of two creeks in the bed of the Ōmaukora Stream, just as Austin had recorded.

For us, a stop for a drink of water at the junction of these two headwaters of the Ōmaukora provided pleasant relief from the jarring of knees on the long descent of some 450 to 500 metres — for Austin's advance Whanganui party it must have been like salvation after 26 hours without water. From there we followed the stream down for a few more hours to arrive in heavy rain at Geoff and Rebecca Redpath's house by the Waioeka at Wairata — the three rivers junction point in Austin's diary. According to Chris Gray's fancy watch we had travelled 25.5 km in 10.5 hours, and had gained 1350 metres of elevation over the day.

Virtually all the time we were up on the ridge, we all felt amazed at the toughness of the Whakatōhea community in completing such a hard traverse, particularly taking into account the diverse range of ages and physical abilities within the group. They may have had the luxury of time and taken three days, or even more, to make the whole trip from Ōpape or Ōmarumutu to Wairata (Austin noted two overnight campsites that Te Kooti had stayed at), but we had only done the harder part of the trip, without the 25-kilometre preliminary stage they had also walked from Ōpape up to the end of the modern road.

Mark Law and the author in October 2021 at the 'three rivers' junction at Wairata after walking 25.5 kms along Tutaetoko stream, Raupō ridgeline and Ōmaukora stream in the footsteps of Te Kooti's people, Whakatōhea from Ōpape and their Whanganui pursuers.
Chris Gray collection

The trip also illustrated just how determined Te Kooti and his people must have been even to contemplate taking that route out to Ōpape, knowing that on their return they would have to shepherd a whole community of people of all ages. And for the Whanganui Contingent, while they may have had the advantage of following in the footsteps of about 300 people, being without water for 26 hours on such a trek would have been an added severe hardship.

NIKAU FLAT HUT TERRACE AS POSSIBLE SITE FOR WAIPUNA PĀ

Two days later, and after one night of incredibly heavy rain that made the Waioeka a brown, swirling and uncrossable maelstrom, Chris Gray and I headed off to Nikau Flat Hut for a night — essentially to prove a negative, that it could not logically have been the site of Waipuna pā. And we were soon convinced of that.

The gorge below the hut was long, and impressive in the fresh. In 1870, in those conditions, without a benched track above the river, it would have been impossible to negotiate in higher flows. The flooded sidecreeks alone, such as the Wairata, were tricky enough for us, and we had to wait for one day after finding we could not even safely cross the Wairata Stream by the end of the road.

The Nikau Flat Hut area was much as I remembered it from 1987. In the flooded conditions it was not possible to move up past a bluff above the hut. The hut terrace was too small to house 250–300 people plus the very large garden areas they would have needed. In addition, the ground was stony and not conducive to gardening at all.

The Whanganui Contingent faced the added difficulties and tensions of travelling at night. There was the additional need for scouts to be out in advance, travelling extremely slowly and quietly so as to locate each of the seven puni sites and the pā without being detected, then for attacking forces to be assigned to capture the occupants of each site by stealth. It would easily have taken from 6.30 p.m., when the first attack occurred, till dawn at about 6 a.m. the following morning to advance quietly on each of the seven puni and capture them in turn, then to move on and surround Waipuna pā, without disturbing any of the occupants.

What can definitely be said from walking those areas is that after carrying out all the attacks on the puni there would not have been time to go on through another length of river gorge for 4.5 km to the Nikau Flat Hut terrace in the one night.

FORTUITOUS DISCOVERY OF THE WAIPUNA PĀ SITE

The trip to Nikau Flat hut was not solely negative in outcome.

As we walked along the farm road to head into the bush, Chris suggested that we should go over the few hundred metres to the Te Pato junction so that I could gain a feel for its setting. Initially I demurred, as the pack already felt heavy, and it seemed an unnecessary diversion off our route to the bushline when the Waioeka was in such high flood and we could not cross to the Te Pato. But Chris prevailed, and I am glad he did.

When we got to the terrace area opposite the Te Pato mouth we had to move through an electric fence. As we did so I commented to Chris how close to the ground Geoff Redpath's cattle had grazed the terrace, as the grass was very short. As we then moved across the terrace we both began to notice a series of depressions that appeared quite regular in their size and layout. To my eyes, after having walked over numerous pā sites in the past, they looked exactly like old whare sites.

The pā had of course been constructed as a long-term place of residence, which would provide accommodation against a cold and wet Urewera winter. Its whare would have been carefully dug in and prepared, and constructed with that long-term purpose in mind.

We both took photographs, with the aim of being able to show the width and depth of the depressions. Once back home in Blenheim I showed my wife Margy the photos, telling her that I intended to use them in the book as physical proof that we had located Waipuna pā. She responded that she and anyone else looking at those photos would say they just looked like photos of a paddock, and that they proved nothing. A shattering response.

A few days later I was despondently explaining all this to an old friend, Pete Anderson, a retired vet with a good sense of country. He asked to see the images. Like Margy, he was unimpressed, but asked if I had tried blowing up the aerial shot of the terrace opposite the Te Pato taken from the helicopter eight months earlier. So, as we both watched, I enlarged the image on the computer. We were amazed to see that as the image was enlarged not only the regular lines of the old whare sites started to stand out, but also four distinct straight lines to the south that I had not noticed before.

The next day I visited the respected archaeologist Dr Atholl Anderson, who then lived near Blenheim, and he agreed to look at the aerial image. As he enlarged it on his computer screen, he immediately commented that it showed evidence of being a major site of Māori customary occupation. He said that he had formed that tentative view on the basis of the pattern of obvious regular whare site depressions and their size, as well as the four lines off to the south. Atholl explained that they were similar to the lines demarcating garden areas, which were usually formed by stones that were removed as a pā site was developed. He showed me diagrams of other archaeological digs where similar lines of garden stones could be seen next to sites where there were whare depressions.

The ability to observe whare sites and lines of garden stones at this site is itself somewhat fortuitous, given the high likelihood that the farmer, Stuart Redpath, the father of Murray and Bob Redpath, had ploughed the terrace in the 1950s or 1960s when he bought his first bulldozer.

There was also a large amount of luck in the timing of this find, as both when the helicopter photo was taken in March 2021 and when Chris Gray and I walked the site in October that year, the grass was grazed well down — by sheep on the first occasion, and cattle on the second. When, in February 2022, Dave and Lynda Stallworthy, Stu Spicer and I returned to go up the Te Pato, so that I could walk back from Waipuna to the Wairata Stream along the riverbed, we found the grass on the terrace was long and the whare sites were almost impossible to see.

RECORDING DISTANCES IN 1870

The mystery as to why Austin may have recorded return distances to Waipuna pā in his diary, or for that matter how he could have achieved any sort of accuracy at all as to distances in rough bush or river conditions, was resolved by a suggestion from Chris Gray. He pointed out that as an experienced NCO from his British Imperial Army days, Austin would have been very used to counting his paces, and in fact may have been relied on to do so. This was a recognised military way of maintaining some idea of distances travelled before the days of GPS.

Chris's suggestion was confirmed in later discussions with another retired officer friend, Graye Shattky from Alexandra. Graye had served on operations in the 1960s in Borneo and Vietnam as an infantry platoon commander, and in Vietnam as a special forces patrol commander. He confirmed that in all those roles he and one of his NCOs would always count and record their paces as a critical means of verifying distances covered in jungle conditions for navigation purposes. He was firmly of the view that as an experienced NCO Austin would almost certainly have followed that practice. Contemporary special forces officers have also confirmed that on occasion that same practice of counting paces is still utilised by their patrols to simulate situations of GPS denial.*

---

* GPS denial occurs when enemy electronic jamming renders GPS equipment useless to the soldier on the ground.

To verify Austin's times and distances from modern Wairata (his three rivers junction) to Waipuna pā, in February 2022 I walked that route in different ways. For the stretch of river from the three rivers junction to the Wairata Stream at the road end, the terraces are so level on each side that even in 1870 travel would almost certainly have been on tracks on the terraces for that stretch. For that section, then, I twice walked along the road, which is beside the river all the way to the Wairata Stream.

Then from the suspected Waipuna pā location I walked the Waioeka riverbed back to the road end at the Wairata Stream, crossing and recrossing the river as I went. This is a beautiful river walk, with only some of the crossings being a bit tricky. A generous allowance in daylight to cover the total distance of 7.8 km would be 2.5–3 hours, or less for fit people younger than the 73-year-old author.

Walking all these areas also demonstrated that the military skill and the endurance of those in the Whanganui Contingent was truly extraordinary for them to achieve what they did in one night. This is particularly so when one takes into account their being fatigued after having walked all the previous day. It was an achievement that would be inspirational to our own modern special forces.

This was not the only feature that was at a level comparable to modern special forces' operations. The whole of the extended approach marches leading up to the Waioeka events, and those events themselves, had repeatedly involved what would be called 'deep penetration' special operations in modern terminology. The Whanganui and Ngāti Porou contingents were completely on their own once they headed into the bush, and were entirely self-reliant for supplies and their own defence. Their operations were covert and unknown to their opposition, enabling complete surprise, as long as careful scouting was consistently carried out. Furthermore, the country they had to cover was difficult in the extreme. It was bush-covered, steep and rugged, pushing all those involved to their physical limits. And after all those travails, they were required to carry out a number of operational assaults to achieve their objectives. Finally, they were very effective in dispersing significant groupings of opposing forces, all at limited cost in logistical supply to the government. The operations they performed could not have been undertaken by conventional forces of their time.

All those traits and characteristics are common with modern special forces operations, which are usually described as being focused, often discreet operations of an unorthodox and frequently high-risk nature that are beyond the current capability of conventional forces. And of course their opponents, such as Te Kooti, displayed very similar characteristics themselves in their guerrilla style of warfare, which was carried out with extraordinary determination and hardiness.

POTENTIAL LOOK-OUT SITE AND MARAETAHI PĀ

One of the common aspects of Austin's and Porter's diary entries is that whenever they were in doubt as to route finding, or trying to spot the smoke of enemy fires, their men would climb high trees to get a view above the canopy. Often they recorded that the trees they climbed were rata, presumably since they have many-branched, twisting trunks that make them easier to climb than other trees, as well as the fact that they grow to an impressive height. Both Gilbert Mair and George Preece recorded similar practices by their Te Arawa men in Te Urewera.

On that basis it seemed to me that a force like the Whanganui Contingent, on arriving at the major three rivers junction, would be very keen to get a view up the valley ahead, or downriver, if they saw anything of interest down there. The only way to do that would have been to select a high point likely to provide a view up and down the river. At Wairata there are two possibilities that would place scouts centrally in the valley, in line for an upriver and downriver view.

The first is a protruding spur that lies between the Ōmaukora and the Tahora (modern Ōpato), on the northeastern side of the Waioeka and the modern state highway in the Ōmaukora valley. However, if that high point was ascended it would soon have been apparent that the opposing ridge to the south, on the western side of the Waioeka, has a very high protruding spur that is too high to allow views past it to the south.

The second, stronger possibility is the high point at 286 metres on modern topographical maps, on the long descending spur immediately above and to the southeast of the Tahora/Ōpato and Waioeka junction. From that point it is obvious that clear sight lines are available up and down the valley. Another factor that supports this particular high point as being most likely is that of course even to have reached a 'junction' of three rivers they would have had to move upstream from the Ōmaukora/Waioeka junction to the meeting at modern Wairata of the Waioeka and what Austin called the Tetahora (now called the Ōpato). Crossing that river would have placed them right at the base of this high point at modern Wairata (south of the old schoolhouse).

When Mark Law and I flew up the Waioeka in March 2021 we hovered above each of those points, and that is exactly what we observed. The view upriver from the Ōmaukora high point was obscured by the spur running down from the ridge on the western side. The view from the Wairata high point was excellent for 6 km up the river, and it also gave a view that showed the Waioeka entering a gorge downriver from the Ōmaukora junction.

This finding was confirmed by some view-shaft maps provided to me by Simon Anderson of Whakatāne, which showed on a topographic map what areas could be seen from those locations. With that background knowledge, Stu Spicer, Dave and Lynda Stallworthy and I climbed the Wairata high point on two different days in February 2022 to take photos, one of which appears in this book (see colour page A7).

Particularly after those two visits in varying weather conditions, I believe that the Whanganui scouts would have climbed a tree to obtain the view above the canopy, which Austin described on 23 March: 'At 4 p.m. we came to the Junction of (3) Rivers, two beside the one we came down, the others were the Waiwaka and Tetahora. The Advance Guard seen a pa or Village about one and half miles from the Junction of the Rivers.'

The only way such a view could have been obtained from the three junctions area in heavy bush would have been from a tree above it. From there the smoke of cooking fires at about that time in the afternoon would have been clearly visible for many kilometres up the river, as the photo and sketch on colour page A8 demonstrate. Subsequent more accurate measurement has shown that direct line of sight to be 6 km.

LOCATION OF PUNI SITES

In Chapter 6, reference is made to the first site attacked possibly being the old pā site to the southwest of the high point just referred to. It is notable that in his diary entry of 23 March, Austin referred to this first site as a 'pa or village': 'The advance guard seen a pa or village about one and a half miles from the junction of the rivers ... At 6.30 p.m. we stole quietly up to the pa and entered it ...' In contrast, Austin described most of the other six puni that were attacked that night as 'a settlement' or 'places', except for Waipuna itself, which he also described as a 'pā'.

In March 2021, Harvey Brunt and I were taken by Murray Redpath and his family to inspect a well-preserved pā site located about 1.1 km from the junction of the Tahora/Ōpato with the Waioeka. It is highly likely that the main body of the Whanganui waited at that junction while the scouts climbed the spur to obtain the view they did.

This pā site is hidden away from the immediately adjacent road by the dense foliage of the trees around and within it. Deep entrenchments are still well preserved on three sides, while the other, river side would have been protected by the sheer rock face above the river. This site is located at about the distance from Austin's 'three rivers junction' to meet the descriptions he gave.

As mentioned earlier, from there another possible puni site would have been obvious directly across a very wide bend in the river. After those first two puni were taken it would have been a matter of following very cautiously in the dark, with the help of moonlight, the likely line of a track linking these seven puni sites and Waipuna pā. Any firelight at the puni would have helped in the final identification of their location, the approach and the attack. Still, it is just not possible now, and never will be, to locate where those other puni may have been on the way upriver to Waipuna pā.

MARAETAHI ISSUES

The location of Maraetahi pā is recorded in the national register of archaeological sites, so its location is certain. In addition, there has been a partial archaeological assessment of the site as part of the commercial forestry consenting processes on adjacent land. It is not signposted, which is possibly not that surprising as from the state highway it has all the appearance of the devastated landscape caused by commercial forestry activity — including, as at 2021 and 2022, old trimmings, a log-loading site, forestry roading and replanted pines, as well as some dead standing pines above the pā site.

The site of the 42 whare Porter recorded as being contained in the main pā has not been planted in commercial forestry and that small area retains some native cover, as the colour photos taken from the drone show. As those images also make clear, it is not an historic site of which we can be proud as a nation. The sheer scale of the commercial forestry activity overwhelms the small area of native cover.

One of the major unknowns with this site is whether or not the stream that Huhana said she, Te Kooti and his other wives and close supporters crossed as they fled from the oncoming Ngāti Porou is the obvious very small catchment to the immediate west of the pā location. That very small catchment runs directly down into the Waioeka.

The other possibility is that what they crossed was the larger stream over the next spur to the west, which flows into the Ōponae Stream, just a hundred metres up from the Ōponae junction with the Waioeka. As explained earlier, I believe the stream Huhana was referring to was this larger one, with the spur on its western side leading up to the high point of Pōkirikiri. Following the ridgeline west from that high point would have taken them to the Waimana/Tauranga catchment. As described in Appendix 2, that was likely the ridgeline used by Te Kooti when they arrived at Maraetahi from Ruatāhuna in mid February 1870.

These assessments meant, of course, that another trip was necessary to verify that the ridgeline route from Maraetahi up to Pōkirikiri and down to the Whakapirau/Waiiti streams area could be traversed in a day. I had written to

Chris Gray and Mark Law back in April 2022 to see if they would be interested in helping me to change one word in the book from 'appears' to 'is', in the phrase stating that 'it appears possible' to use a particular ridgeline route between the Waimana and the Waioeka. In other words, would they be interested in helping me demonstrate whether this route was possible? They both said 'yes'. Mark said he also wanted to bring along Eugene Hunia, another ex-Special Forces chap from Ōpōtiki. We decided to do the trip when flows in the Waiiti (a tributary of the Waimana) were likely to be lower and when the days were longer. This meant making the trip in early summer. We expected to be able to make the journey in one longish day.

Eugene Hunia and the author at the Kaharoa/Waiiti Stream junction the day after walking from Pōkirikiri to this location at the end of October 2022.

Chris Gray collection

On 29 October 2022 we were driven part-way up the Pōkirikiri ridge in the Waioeka valley, to begin climbing at 7 a.m. It rained lightly most of the day and our limited clothing was soaked by that evening. The going was reasonable but still required much effort for most of the day, with route finding the main challenge: it slowed us down considerably, particularly on the very long descent as there was no track until we hit the Whakapirau that flows into the Waiiti. Time was running out for us to complete the journey without being caught out overnight. But it looked like we were on the point of proving that the route was indeed possible.

At about 8.30 p.m. in the Whakapirau Stream we parted company with Mark in pitch darkness. His partner Chanal was waiting in a car to pick us up in the Waimana, which he said he thought was only about two and a half hours away if we went fast. I responded that my legs were completely shot and added that I was starting to stumble and fall repeatedly. I said I intended to stay for the night in what I knew as Sonny Biddle's whare at the Kaharoa junction. (It comprises a rough canvas slung over a long pole.) Chris and Eugene decently agreed to stay with me as the older bloke, while Mark took off to jog-run the rest of the way out in the dark to the Waimana River road.

Mark left us his fast cooker, and also advised us that there was actually a tidy little DOC hut, the Kaharoa hut, set back quite a way in the bush from the junction, opposite Sonny Biddle's whare. As it was left for biodiversity staff, it was not marked on the map but he described generally where we could look for it.

We followed the Whakapirau down to the Waiiti, and continued on down the Waiiti, crossing it back and forth in the dark as we walked with head-torches. We finally reached the Kaharoa junction at 9.30 p.m., with light rain falling all the time. (Chris' watch later showed we had walked for 15.5 hours, climbed 1315 metres and covered 21.7 kilometres during the day.)

I then had to say to the others that I was so lacking in energy that I could not contemplate climbing around in the bush in the dark looking for the DOC hut. I was content to just cross one last time and stay in Sonny Biddle's whare. However, the other two still thought we should try to find the hut. So we decided I should just stay put while they looked for it, though I had to turn off my head-torch as it was running out of power. Chris suggested I give them 20 minutes out and 20 back, so I should turn my head-torch back on after 40 minutes. I lay in the dark in the gentle rain while the others pushed off. After about 20–30 minutes I saw their lights flashing, so I turned mine back on, and they approached with the very welcome news that they had found the hut — how, I will never know, as the route to it was not obvious, had seen little if any recent use, and was unmarked.

The hut was a purler, with two bunks (but four mattresses), a wood-burning stove, a full gas bottle and a covered dry outside area for our wet gear. It even had a food cupboard with milk powder, tea and cordial (which Chris quickly heated on the cooker for a warming drink, followed by hot tea). As for a meal, I had four Milkshake lollies to share and, for myself, four sardines remaining in a tin — two for dinner and two for breakfast. The others were similarly well equipped for a feast.

Eugene got the fire going and soon the hut was toasty. Chris generously lent me an Icebreaker singlet he had managed to keep dry, and with dry overtrousers from my day-pack I was pretty comfortable, though none of us had a sleeping bag. It poured heavily from time to time, and constantly rained for the rest of the time.

Meanwhile, unbeknown to us Mark was still in the bush, about two hours away, having decided at 10.30 p.m. that he was not going to get out that night; he figured by that time Chanal would have given up on us anyway. He spent a miserable night under two different tawa trees, having to shift when the drips from the first one became too much. Mark had no food — his last morsel being one of my battered Milkshake lollies eaten in the afternoon. He got going again at about 5.30 a.m., still in the dark, and ran out to the road, where at 7 a.m. he was relieved to see Chanal driving towards him. They went back to Whakatāne. As he knew by then the rivers would be flooded, they took off in one of the helicopters he operates to see if they could help.

Meanwhile, in the Waiiti we got going in steady rain at about 7 to find the first river crossing discoloured and flooded as we crossed at the Kaharoa junction. We looked across at Sonny Biddle's rather rough tarpaulin whare — and I silently thanked DOC that we had not had to spend the night there. (This incident is a reminder of how important DOC huts in remote places are for emergencies like ours.) After the junction with the Kaharoa the crossings got deeper and trickier from the larger volumes of water as we passed each tributary. It was slow going as we tried to locate safe crossing points with safe exits to where we hoped the track would be. In crossing I was placed in the centre with Chris and Eugene on each side linking arms with me while I held on firmly with both hands to a wooden pole. That worked well, even in the higher flows.

Then about 9.15 am we heard a chopper heading upriver but it did not see us as we were climbing over quite a high point in the bush. We moved on down to the river, and crossed again. Chris was in the bush with Eugene and I was out in the river when the chopper passed back over us heading downriver. Again we were not spotted.

We continued to do a few more crossings as the bush closed in on us, right down to the river's edge on each side. During one crossing I could feel the water high up my back and starting to lift us. I leaned back, saying we needed to try to pull back. Quietly-spoken Eugene, for the only time, said tersely in my ear, 'Go with the flow Ron — just go with the flow,' which we did, as we bounced off our feet a few times and got across.

But then we finally reached a spot where the river was deep and swift between high banks. We moved some metres back upriver where we thought we could just get across, but it looked possibly too deep and swift on the other side. I said to the others I thought we could hold onto the rock face there to make our way down to a possible exit point. (Chris' watch later showed we had walked 7.97 kilometres that morning to reach this point.)

We started crossing and were about 15 metres out into the flow when we suddenly heard the chopper again heading upriver. We looked up, waving, and it swung around — they had seen us! It turned out that, luckily, Mark had taken Chanal along as another set of eyes, and it was she who spotted us.

I was thinking that we would have to make a number of crossings back upriver to get to an open area where the chopper might be able to land, but in the few seconds I had to think that it was descending in tight circles. We scooted back to the bank and into the bush edge as it was clear Mark was going to land in the river. He had to make a tricky manoeuvre under an overhanging tree, then he settled the helicopter down in about a foot of swift-running water. (He told me later that as he came down he could see an area where the flow was shallower and thought he could put it down there.)

The others told me to go first, and Chris told me later that Eugene said he should try to get a photo of the scene as I was heading out to the chopper. But it all happened too quickly as we moved through the shower of spray the rotors were throwing up and clambered aboard. Mark slowly piloted the chopper a little out of the river and moved backwards to avoid the overhanging tree before starting to spiral up and out of the gorge. It was a seriously impressive demonstration of pilot skill and courage.

So ended a most entertaining trip. And so, too, was I able to change the word 'appears' to the word 'is' in the book!

One uncertainty about the Maraetahi site that will never be answered is just where the five-plus acres of taro, corn and potatoes that Porter described could have been. The ridgeline above the pā site has a wide terrace that could be about the right size. Alternatively, and possibly more plausibly, gardens of that size may have been in the area to the west of the pā site where the forestry roading and log-loading area have now changed the land form.

The final uncertainty about the Maraetahi site that needed exploring was the difficulty posed by the gorge downriver from Maraetahi at Te Karoro a Tamatea. Porter's self-serving, varying descriptions as to the time between Ngāti Porou encountering the picquet of sentries here and the capture of the pā needed clarification on the ground. I believed from Tuta Nihoniho's account that it must have required some Ngāti Porou to fall back downriver, cross the river and then come back up to fire across at the picquet. And so it proved.

On visiting the site it is clear that a party moving upriver on the true right or east bank, the side where the state highway now runs, would strike a sheer rocky area of about 100 to 200 metres in length that could readily be defended by just a few men. We know from Porter that the picquet that surprised them here was soon reinforced by another kōkiri or group. As the colour photo of the gorge shows, for Ngāti Porou to overcome that resistance at such a difficult point they would have had to do what Tuta Nihoniho said and go downriver to cross. Once they had crossed and come back up the western bank they could have fired across and down on the picquet, as Stuart Spicer's sketch (page 141) shows.

Opposite the Maraetahi site it is possible to drive down a rough track to the river and look across at the pā site. From that point as one looks downriver it is possible to see many hundreds of metres of riverbed before the next bend in the river, and Te Karoro a Tamatea Gorge starts much further around that next bend and downstream of the Waiata Stream junction. In other words, the gorge is not immediately below Maraetahi pā at all, as Porter's accounts imply, but rather about 2 km from it. In the Supreme Court trial of some of the prisoners Porter himself confirmed that, stating, 'We were fired into by a picket of Hauhaus in the Waioeka Gorge, about a mile from the pā.'

So even once Ngāti Porou got past the gorge they still had 2 km to travel to reach the pā. All of that clearing of the gorge and then movement up to the pā would have taken at least two hours, if not more.

Certainly that time lapse from when the first heavy firing commenced would have given more than enough time for Te Kooti and all those in the pā to grab some food and leave. The members of the picquet and their reinforcements would have had less time, but still enough to get away up the river where they later met with the Whanganui ambuscade. That explains why Porter was compelled to record that when Ngāti Porou reached the pā: 'The enemy had gone.'

APPENDIX 4
PORTER'S QUESTIONABLE RELIABILITY

Long after completion of the manuscript for this book, I was planning another Urewera trip for a different purpose when I happened upon some historical notes relevant to the issue of Lt Col Porter's questionable reliability. On 4 October 1921 Captain Gilbert Mair wrote to James Cowan,* commenting on a range of issues relating to Cowan's draft text for a chapter in his book on the New Zealand Wars that recounted the events of the attack by the Arawa Flying Columns on Te Kooti in the Waipaoa River in August 1871. The attack was led by Mair and Captain George Preece, with Preece also writing to Cowan about his text. Mair's comments to Cowan reflect the same conclusions I reached in relation to Porter's inaccuracies about the Waioeka events, as well as other situations. Mair wrote:

> ... Ngati Porou speak very bitterly of the manner in which Porter claimed much of the kudos Ropata Wahawaha was entitled. They totally deny Porter's cock & bull story about the crucified Ngati Porou dead at [? torn off the corner of page 3 of the letter] or Tore a Tai or wherever it was, also his graphic attack on ['a' ? again torn off] place up the Waioeka resulting in the capture of 8 rebels — fighting men — Those found there were the helpless Whakatohea, principally women and children whom Te Kooti, with the connivance of two or three of their disloyal chiefs, had inveigled away up the Waioeka to escape being destroyed by Te Kooti in his threatened attack on and final destruction of the Europeans and loyal natives. Poor old Porter, had a good military record which it was quite unnecessary to supplement by making statements utterly contrary to facts. He gave Preece no credit for his extraordinary march along Ngatiporou trail after our attack at Waipaoa. Porter was on the wrong scout and only Preece's arrival enabled him to carry out his attack on T.K. at Ruahapu in which 3 women and 2 men were slain, though T.W.P. makes it appear that a large number were 'done out'. These exaggerations are on a par with his fictitious account of his defence of an A.C. post at the foot of the Ruahine ranges inland of Napier, where nothing of the kind ever occurred. However, it is now too late to overtake these misstatements besides the adage *de mortius nil nisi bonum.*** I have nearly forgotten the correct rendering.

---

* National Library MS0096 Folder 6.

** The full Latin phrase is *de mortuis nil nisi bonum dicendum est* ('of the dead nothing but good is to be said'). Porter had died the previous year at the age of 77, on 12 November 1920.

GLOSSARY

hapū	(noun) subtribe; (adjective) pregnant
Hauhau	common terminology for a follower of the Paimārire religion
hui	meeting
iwi	tribe
kāinga	village or settlement
kaumātua	an older person
kāwanatanga	depending on context can mean the settler government or the Crown
Kingitanga	the Māori King movement; loosely used in some historical documents to refer to the King Country
kōkiri	depending on context can mean a charge or a small force
kuia	an older woman
kūpapa	a name accorded to Māori who fought alongside the Crown for their own reasons
manaakitanga	hospitality
māra	garden
marae	traditionally, the courtyard for a complex of main buildings at a pā
mōkihi	a raft for crossing rivers, lakes or lagoons, usually made of bundles of dry flax stalks
niu	a very tall pole erected by the Paimārire sect for their ceremonies which were often conducted around it
ope	a group, company or section of a taua, contingent or column
oriori	traditional song, lullaby
pā	a customary area of occupation, commonly but not always fortified
Paimārire	the religion established by Te Ua Haumēne
puni	camp or temporary cluster of whare
rangatira	chief or leader
rangatiratanga	authority
rohe	customary district or area
rongopai/rongo pai	in the context of the events in this book a truce or peace agreement (more commonly a reference to the four Gospels). In contemporary usage peace is translated as maungārongo
tangi/tangihanga	mourning and burial ceremonies
taua	war party
te ao Māori	the Māori world
Te Hāhi Ringatū	the Ringatu Church established by Te Kooti
te reo Māori me ona tikanga	Māori language and its surrounding tikanga or customs
tikanga	Māori customs and practices which can vary from hapū to hapū
tino	the utmost
uri	descendant(s)
waka	a canoe or boat
whakapapa	bloodlines or common genealogy
whakarau	Māori captives on Wharekauri (the Chatham Islands) who became Te Kooti's followers
whānau	family
wharau	a temporary shelter
whare	a house
whare karakia	a church or building for prayers
wharenui	a meeting house

SELECT BIBLIOGRAPHY

PUBLISHED DOCUMENTS AND OFFICIAL PUBLICATIONS
Appendices to the Journals of the House of Representatives, New Zealand 1855–1872 (AJHR)
Papers Past, 1870–1914, https://Papers Past | Newspapers Home (natlib.govt.nz).

UNPUBLISHED DOCUMENTS
Anonymous, Maori account of the campaign against the Hauhau on the East Coast, 1865–1870, copied by A.S. Atkinson, MSS 1187:6A, Alexander Turnbull Library (ATL).
Austin, Samuel, Diary 1844–1870, Accession No. 1992.1422/2, Queen Elizabeth II Army Museum, Waiouru.
——, Undated petition seeking support, Accession No. 1992.1422/1, Queen Elizabeth II Army Museum, Waiouru.
Kingi, Derek, 31 May 2022, Ngāti Ira kōrero tuku iho oral history to Waitangi Tribunal North East Bay of Plenty Inquiry, https://www.youtube.com/watch?v=Gd6olxZxH0s
Nihoniho, Tuta, Translation of a Narrative of The Fighting On The East Coast 1865–1871, http://www.enzb.auckland.ac.nz/docs/Nihoniho/pdf/niho1003.pdf.
Porter, Lt. T.W., Report 31 March 1870, to Lt. Col St John, National Archives (NA), AD1 70/2762.
Soutar, M., *Ngati Porou Leadership: Rapata Wahawaha and the Politics of Conflict*, DPhil thesis, January 2000, Massey University.
Tamati, Huhana, Statements 5 & 8 August 1870, NA AD1 70/2668 & 70/2635.
Wahawaha, Ropata, ATL, MS-Papers-0072-39E, Best, Elsdon, 1856–1931: Papers — War narrative of Rapata Wahawaha.

SECONDARY PUBLISHED SOURCES
Aikman, L., *Opotiki's Upper Ōtara valleys (Tutaetoko, Te Waiti, and Pakihi) — A collection of memories and history*, self-published, Opotiki, 2020.
Andersen, J.C. & Petersen, G.C., *The Mair Family*, A.H. & A.W. Reed, Wellington, 1956.
Belich, J., *The New Zealand Wars and the Victorian Interpretation of Racial Conflict*, Penguin, Auckland, 1988.
Best, E., *Tuhoe*, Board of Maori Ethnological Research, New Plymouth, 1925.
Binney, J., *Redemption Songs: A Life of Te Kooti Arikirangi Te Turuki*, Bridget Williams Books, Wellington, 1995.
——, *Encircled Lands*, Bridget Williams Books, Wellington, 2009.
Chapple, L.J.B. & Veitch, H.C., *Wanganui*, Hawera Star Publishing Co. Ltd, Hawera, 1939.
Clark, P., *'Hauhau': The Pai Marire Search for Maori Identity*, Auckland University Press & Oxford University Press, Trentham, 1975.
Cowan, J., *The New Zealand Wars and the Pioneering Period*, Vols 1 & 2, Government Printer, Wellington, 1922 & 1923.
——, *Sir Donald Mclean*, A.H. & A.W. Reed, Wellington, 1940.

Crawford, J. & McGibbon, I. (eds), *Tutu Te Puehu: New Perspectives on the New Zealand Wars*, Steele Roberts, Wellington, 2018.
Crosby, R.D., *Gilbert Mair: Te Kooti's Nemesis*, Reed Publishing NZ Ltd, Auckland, 2004.
——, *Kūpapa: The Bitter Legacy of Māori Alliances with the Crown*, Penguin, Auckland, 2015.
Elsmore, Bronwyn, *Like Them That Dream: The Maori and the Old Testament*, Tauranga Moana Press, Tauranga, 1985.
Featon, J., *The Waikato War & Te Kooti's Expeditions*, Brett Printing and Publishing Co. Ltd, Auckland, 1923 ed.
Finlay, N., *Sacred Soil: Images and Stories of the New Zealand Wars*, Random House, Auckland, 1998.
Gascoyne, F.J.W., *Soldiering in New Zealand being Reminiscences of a Veteran*, T.J.S. Guildford & Co. Ltd, London, 1916.
Grace, J. Te H., *Tuwharetoa: A History of the Maori People of the Taupo District*, A.H & A.W. Reed, Wellington, 1959.
Green, D., *Battlefields of the New Zealand Wars: A Visitor's Guide*, Penguin Group, Auckland, 2010.
Gudgeon, T.W., *Reminiscences of the War in New Zealand*, H. Brett, Auckland, 1879.
——, *Defenders of New Zealand*, H. Brett, Auckland, 1887.
Hamilton-Browne, Col. G., *With the Lost Legion in New Zealand*, T. Werner Laurie, London, n.d.
Hocken, Dr T.M., *The Early History of New Zealand — Being a Series of Lectures Delivered Before the Otago Institute: Also a Lecturette on the Maoris of the South Island*, Dunedin, 1914.
Keenan, D, *Wars Without End: The Land Wars in Nineteenth-century New Zealand*, Penguin Group, Auckland, 2009.
King, Michael, *The Penguin History of New Zealand*, Penguin Group, Auckland, 2003.
Lambert, T., *Story of Old Wairoa and the East Coast of New Zealand*, A.H. & A.W. Reed, Auckland, 1925.
Lyall, A.C., *Whakatohea of Opotiki*, Reed Books, Auckland, 1979.
Mabbett, B., *For Gallant Service Rendered: The Life and Times of Samuel Austin*, Steele Roberts Aotearoa, Wellington, 2012.
Mackay, J.A., *Historic Poverty Bay and the East Coast, N.I., N.Z.*, J.A. Mackay, Gisborne, 1949.
Mair, G., *Gate Pa*, Bay of Plenty Times, Tauranga, 1926.
Mair, G. & Preece, G., *Te Kooti Expeditions*, as Appendix to J. Featon, *The Waikato War*, Brett Printing and Publishing Co. Ltd, Auckland, 1923.
Maxwell, P., *Frontier: The Battle for the North Island of New Zealand 1860–72*, Celebrity Books, Auckland, 2000.
Newman, K., *Beyond Betrayal*, Penguin Group, Auckland, 2013.
O'Malley, V., *The Great War for New Zealand: Waikato 1800–2000*, Bridget Williams Books, Wellington, 2016.
——, *The New Zealand Wars: Ngā Pakanga o Aotearoa*, Bridget Williams Books, Wellington, 2019.
O'Malley, V. & Armstrong, D., *The Beating Heart*, Huia Publishing, Wellington, 2008.
Porter, T.W., *The History of the Early Days of Poverty Bay: Major Ropata Wahawaha, The Story of his Life and Times*, The Poverty Bay Herald Company Limited, Gisborne, 1923.
Prickett, N., *Landscapes of Conflict*, Random House, Auckland, 2002.
——, *Fortifications of the New Zealand Wars*, Dept of Conservation, 2016.
Pugsley, C. (ed.), *Scars of the Heart: Two Centuries of New Zealand at War*, David Bateman, Auckland, 1996.
Ross, W.H., *Te Kooti*, Collins, Auckland, 1966.

Roxburgh, Irvine, *The Ringatu Movement: A Phenomenological Essay on Culture Shock in New Zealand/ Aotearoa*, rev. edn, Cadsonbury Publications, Christchurch, 1998.

Ryan, T. & Parham, B., *The Colonial New Zealand Wars*, Grantham House Publishing, Wellington, 1986.

Sissons, J., *Te Waimana – The Spring of Mana: Tuhoe History and the Colonial Encounter*, University of Otago Press, Dunedin, 1991.

Stafford, D.M., *Te Arawa: A History of the Arawa People*, A.H & A.W. Reed, 1967.

———, *Landmarks of Te Arawa*, Vols 1 & 2, Reed Publishing, Auckland, 1994 & 1996.

Walker, R., *Ōpōtiki-Mai-Tawhiti: Capital of Whakatōhea*, Penguin, Auckland, 2007.

Wells, P., *Journey to a Hanging*, Random House, Auckland, 2014.

Whitmore, G.S., *The Last Maori War in New Zealand under the Self Reliant Policy*, Sampson Low, Marston & Company, London, 1902.

Wilson, Ormond, *War in the Tussock*, Government Printer, Wellington, 1961.

Wright, M., *Two Peoples, One Land: The New Zealand Wars*, Reed Publishing, Auckland, 2006.

Young, D., *Woven by Water*, Huia Publishers, Wellington, 1998.

WAITANGI TRIBUNAL REPORTS

He Maunga Rongo: Central North Island Report, WAI 1200, 2008.

Ngati Awa Raupatu Report, WAI 46, 1999.

Te Urewera Report, WAI 894, 2017.

Turanga Tangata Turanga Whenua Report, WAI 814, 2004.

The Whanganui River Report, WAI 167, 1999.

ACKNOWLEDGEMENTS

I am indebted to Barbara Mabbett for her assistance in relation to the diaries of Samuel Austin, without which this book could probably not have been written. In addition, a number of other people provided invaluable assistance with research, either accompanying me on various trips into Te Urewera or providing me with information. In particular, I wish to thank:

Stuart Spicer of Whangārei and Andrew Walter of Auckland, for providing me with company on an extended three-week trip in 1987, which formed the base to my geographical knowledge of the Waioeka, so crucial for this book, and sparked Stuart's interest in the intrigue of that valley, leading to his later sketches and images which now adorn this book. These sketches are of particular value since no contemporary photography or sketches are available of the Waioeka sites or events. They also reflect that Stuart has personally walked much of the country involved to gain experience of the conditions his sketches have captured.

Dave and Lynda Stallworthy, and Stu Spicer, of Whangārei for further trips on the ground, walking parts of the routes involved and for photos;

Chris Gray of Wellington, Mark Law of Whakatāne and Eugene Hunia of Ōpōtiki for accompanying me on various walks in the footsteps of the Whakatōhea and Te Kooti, and for providing photos, helicopter inspections, helpful advice and good company;

Harvey Brunt of Auckland for skilful drone footage, moon-state advice, and informative input on a range of issues;

Murray and Ann Redpath and their son Dale, of Wairata, for assistance and advice on the ground in their remote 'backyard';

Geoff and Rebeccca Redpath, and Bob Redpath, all of Wairata, for permission to access, initially by vehicle and later on foot, some locations on their upper Waioeka lands, and in the Ōmaukora valley;

Bob and Mary Redpath for their hospitality;

Dave Lunn of Ōponae for providing access to the route Maraetahi to the Waimana and transporting us up his farm track;

Peter Anderson of Blenheim for particularly helpful discussions as to the possible location of the Waipuna pā site;

Dr Atholl Anderson, for archaeological advice with respect to the image of the Waipuna pā site;

Pete Shaw of Pohokura, Hawke's Bay, for providing local contacts and sharing his wealth of Te Urewera knowledge;

Simon Anderson of Ōhiwa for local knowledge and the provision of sight lines up the Waioeka from high points near Wairata;

Lynda Walter of Whakatāne for sharing her detailed knowledge of archaeological records of the Waioeka;

Tony Hawke and Phil Morton of Blenheim, for very helpful information as to early surveys of the area and advice on how to use Google maps to measure river distances;

ACKNOWLEDGEMENTS

Tā Pou Temara for his careful confirmation and correction of the translations of parts of Ropata Wahawaha's and Tuta Nihoniho's narratives;

Andris Apse of Ōkārito for photographic advice;

Graye Shattky of Alexandra for helpful comments on an initial draft;

Peter McBurney of Auckland for providing some helpful older survey plans, and for general discussion on a range of issues;

Deborah Riddell of Tōrere for arranging permissions for image use;

Wilson, Suzie and Eria Isaac of Maraetaha for providing accommodation and warm hospitality;

Mike and Kay Houlding of Mount Maunganui, Chanel Haggart and Mark Law, and Lewis and Renay Jones of Whakatāne, and Chris and Nadine Gray in Wellington similarly as to accommodation and warm hospitality;

And some other current military acquaintances who know who they are, and who provided valuable practical advice and assistance.

Information from iwi sources as to locations, and the adherence to the Ringatū religion, came willingly from people such as:

Te Ringahuia Hata, Te Rua Rakuraku and Derek Kingi of Ngāti Ira;

Nadine Gray of Wellington;

Merehira Wills of Renwick, Marlborough; and

Sam Gibson of Gisborne.

I also wish to particularly thank Peter Dowling of Oratia Books, who has been supportive of the book from its initial conception. Peter's agreement to publish this book is a mark of his commitment through Oratia Books to ensure that New Zealand's history is recorded.

For the very clear cartography I wish to thank Jonette Surridge;

For the editing of the book I am indebted to both Susan Brierley and Peter Dowling, with later input by Mike Bradstock.

For the design of the book and management of its publication process I am similarly indebted to Sarah Elworthy and Carolyn Lagahetau respectively.

I thank Tā Joe Williams who, despite his pressured time, has provided a foreword. He has a deep knowledge of the historical significance of Te Kooti, and he and his partner Gillian Warren have walked in reverse one of the routes I consider Ngāti Porou likely to have followed on their way into Maungapōhatu. It is fitting that one of Gillian's images of that maunga appears in this book.

Finally, I wish to thank my wife Margy. She has been particularly helpful with the design of the Powerpoint presentation that I developed for the purposes of this book. Margy always advocates for the capturing of any aspect of the Māori history of Aotearoa, and she has been encouraging and supportive throughout. However, I suspect she regards my real interest as being merely to enable even more trips to Te Urewera for 'ground-truthing' purposes.

ENDNOTES

1 DIFFICULT YEARS FOR WHAKATŌHEA
1. Dr T.M. Hocken, *The Early History of New Zealand — Being a Series of Lectures Delivered Before the Otago Institute: Also a Lecturette on the Maoris of the South Island*, p. 278.
2. Bronwyn Elsmore, *Like Them That Dream: The Maori and the Old Testament*, p. 71.
3. See Chapter 5, 'A Universal Phenomenon', in Irvine Roxburgh, The Ringatu Movement: A Phenomenological Essay on Culture Shock in New Zealand/Aotearoa, 1998, pp. 28–33.
4. Waitangi Tribunal, *Ngāti Awa Raupatu Report*, WAI 46, 1999, p. 60.

2 TE KOOTI'S RELATIONSHIP WITH WHAKATŌHEA
5. *AJHR*, 1870, 1A–8B, No. 53, 2 April 1870, pp. 26–27, Statement by Wiremu Kingi Te Paia.
6. Ibid.
7. *AJHR*, 1870, 1A–8B, p. 65, Encl. to No. 88, Statement made by Hoani Te Paiaka.
8. *AJHR*, 1870, 1A–8A, p. 74, Letter 18 February 1870, Defence Minister to Lt Col McDonnell.
9. *AJHR*, 1870, 1A–8B, p. 3, Letter 19 February 1870, Defence Minister to Ropata Wahawaha.
10. *AJHR*, 1870, 1A–8B, p. 4, Letter 3 March 1870, Defence Minister to Majors Kemp and Tōpia.
11. *AJHR*, 1870, 1A–8B, p. 3, Letter 19 February 1870, Defence Minister to Ropata Wahawaha.
12. *AJHR*, 1870, 1A–8B, p. 3, Letter 18 February 1870, Defence Minister to Mohi Tureirei.

3 TE KOOTI'S ARRIVAL AT MARAETAHI AND THE RAID ON ŌPAPE
13. *AJHR*, 1870, 1A–8B, No. 53, p. 29, 2 April 1870, Statement by Wiremu Kingi Te Paia.
14. Ibid.
15. Ibid., pp. 29–30.
16. Ibid., p. 30.
17. Ibid.
18. *AJHR*, 1870, 1A–8B, p. 65, Encl. to No. 88, Statement made by Hoani Te Paiaka.
19. *Auckland Star*, 6 June 1914, p. 16.
20. *Wellington Independent*, 30 June 1870, p. 5.
21. *AJHR*, 1870, 1A–8B, p. 64, Encl. in No. 70, Diary of Lt T.W. Porter 28 February to 31 March 1870.
22. *AJHR*, 1870, 1A–8B, p. 10, no. 25, Report 11 March 1870, Major William Mair to H.T. Clarke.
23. *AJHR*, 1870, 1A–8B, p. 10, No. 26, Report 13 March 1870, Major Kemp to the Defence Minister.
24. *AJHR*, 1870, 1A–8B, No. 53, p. 30, 2 April 1870, Statement by Wiremu Kingi Te Paia.
25. *AJHR*, 1870, 1A–8B, Sub-Enclosure 2 to Enclosure 2 in No. 44, Letter 17 March 1870, Te Ranapia Waihaku and Piahana Tiwai to H.T. Clarke.
26. *AJHR*, 1870, 1A–8B, p. 10, Enclosure in No. 25, Report 7 March 1870, Captain Walker to Major W. Mair.
27. *AJHR*, 1870, 1A–8B, p. 11, Enclosure No. 1 in No. 27, Report 7 March 1870, Capt Walker to Lt Col Fraser.
28. *AJHR*, 1870, 1A–8B, p. 11, Enclosure No. 2 in No. 27, Message 7 March 1870, Capt Walker to Ōhiwa and other settlements.
29. *AJHR*, 1870, 1A–8B, p. 9, No. 25, Report 11 March 1870, Major W. Mair to H.T. Clarke.
30. *AJHR*, 1870, 1A–8B, p. 11, Enclosure No. 3 in No. 27, Report 8 March 1870, Capt Walker to Lt Col Fraser.
31. Statement of Huhana Tamati, 5 August 1870, to Major Charles Westrup, NA AD1 70/2668; Statement of Huhana Whakarau [Tamati], 8 August 1870, to S. Locke, NA AD1 70/2635.
32. *Daily Southern Cross*, 1 April 1870, p. 7.
33. *AJHR*, 1870, 1A–8B, p. 22, Encl. 3 in No. 44, 18 March 1870, Letter Wiremu Kingi Tutahuarangi to Major Mair.
34. Statement of Huhana Tamati, 5 August 1870, to Major Charles Westrup, NA AD1 70/2668.
35. *AJHR*, 1870, 1A–8B, p. 25, No. 49, 30 March 1870, Report Major Kemp to the Premier William Fox.
36. *AJHR*, 1870, 1A–8B, p. 30, 2 April 1870, Statement by Wiremu Kingi Te Paia.
37. *Wellington Independent*, 30 June 1870, p. 5.
38. Ibid.

4 WHANGANUI'S DETERMINED COMMITMENT
39. *AJHR*, 1870, 1A–8A, p. 4, No. 2, Report 29 October 1869, Lt Col T. McDonnell to J.D. Ormond.
40. Waitangi Tribunal, *The Whanganui River Report*, 1999, WAI 167, p. 155.
41. *AJHR*, 1870, 1A–8A, p. 13, No. 28, Telegram 7 December 1869, Premier Fox to J.D. Ormond.
42. *AJHR*, 1870, 1A–8B, Enclosure in No. 77, 14 January 1870, Report Major Kemp to Lt Col McDonnell.
43. *AJHR*, 1870, 1A–8A, No. 75, 13 January 1870, Letter Tōpia Tūroa to the Premier W. Fox.
44. *AJHR*, 1870, 1A–8A, p. 30, No. 77, 14 January 1870, Telegram 8.45 p.m., Lt Col McDonnell to J.D. Ormond.
45. *AJHR*, 1870, 1A–8A, Enclosure 2 in No. 78, p. 31, 16 January 1870, Letter Hitiri Paerata to Te Kapa and Te Perenara.
46. *AJHR*, 1870, 11A–8A, p. 40, No. 119, 21 January 1870, Report Lt Col McDonnell to Defence Minister.
47. *AJHR*, 1870, 1A–8B, p. 3, No. 4, Letter 19 February 1870, Defence Minister to Major Kemp.

48 *AJHR*, 1870, 1A–8A, p. 74, Letter 18 February 1870, Defence Minister to Lt Col McDonnell.
49 *AJHR*, 1870, 1A–8B, p. 4, No. 7, 4 March 1870, Report Major Kemp to the Defence Minister.
50 *AJHR*, 1870, 1A–8B, pp. 9–10, No. 25, 11 March 1870, Report Major Mair to H.T. Clarke, Civil Commissioner.
51 *AJHR*, 1870, 1A–8B, p. 10, No. 26, 13 March 1870, Report Major Kemp to Defence Minister.
52 *AJHR*, 1870, 1A–8B, p. 12, No. 28, 16 March 1870, Report Wiremu Kingi to Major Mair.
53 *Evening Post*, 19 March 1870, p. 2.
54 *AJHR*, 1870, 1A–8B, p. 19, Enclosure 1 in No. 11, Letter 15 March 1870, H.T. Clarke to Lt Col McDonnell.
55 *AJHR*, 1870, 1A–8B, pp. 21–23, Enclosure 2 in No. 44, Report 19 March 1870, Lt Col McDonnell to H.T. Clarke.
56 *AJHR*, 1870, 1A–8B, pp. 21–23, Sub-encl 1 to Enclosure 2 in No. 44, Report 19 March 1870, Lt Col McDonnell to H.T. Clarke.
57 *AJHR*, 1870, 1A–8B, p. 21, Sub-Enclosure 2 to Enclosure 2 in No. 44, Letter 17 March 1870, Te Ranapia Waihaku and Piahana Tiwai to H.T. Clarke.
58 *AJHR*, 1870, 1A–8B, pp. 18–19, No. 44, Report 20 March 1870, H.T. Clarke to the Under Secretary, Native Department.
59 *AJHR*, 1870, A1–8B, No. 41, p. 45, Lt Porter to Minister of Defence.
60 *Auckland Star*, 6 June 1914, p. 16.
61 *Poverty Bay Herald*, 24 August 1897, p. 3.
62 *AJHR*, 1870, 1A–8B, p. 32, No. 56, 18 April 1870, Report by H.T. Clarke, Civil Commissioner to the Under Secretary, Native Department.

5   NGĀTI POROU TRAVERSE TE UREWERA

63 *AJHR*, 1870, 1A–8B, No. 3, 19 February 1870, Letter Defence Minister to Major Ropata Wahawaha.
64 *AJHR*, 1870, 1A–8B, p. 8, No. 19, 19 February 1870, Letter Mr. Locke, R.M., to the Premier.
65 *AJHR*, 1870, 1A–8B, p. 8, No. 21, Major Westrup to the Hon. the Defence Minister.
66 *AJHR*, 1870, A–8B, No. 41, 21 March 1870, Letter Lt Porter to Minister of Defence.
67 *AJHR*, 1870, 1A–8B, p. 42, Enclosure in No. 7, Diary of Lt T.W. Porter.
68 Ibid. [Porter as above]
69 Ibid., p. 43.
70 Ibid., pp. 42–43.
71 *Poverty Bay Herald*, 21 August 1897, p. 3.
72 *AJHR*, 1870, 1A–8B, p. 43, Enclosure in No. 7, Diary of Lt T.W. Porter.
73 Ibid. [Porter p 43]
74 Ibid., pp. 44–45. [Porter]
75 *AJHR*, 1870, 1A–8B, p. 41, Encl. in No. 70, 28 April 1870, Report Lt Porter to the Defence Minister.
76 Ibid.
77 *Poverty Bay Herald*, 21 August 1897, p. 3.
78 *Auckland Star*, 6 June 1914, p. 16; Lt Col T.W. Porter, *The History of the Early Days of Poverty Bay: Major Ropata Wahawaha N.Z.C., M.L.C. — The Story of His Life and Times*, Poverty Bay Herald, Gisborne, 1923.
79 *AJHR*, 1870, 1A–8B, p. 44, Encl. in No. 70, 28 April 1870, Report Lt Porter to the Defence Minister.
80 ATL, MS-Papers-0072-39E, Best, Elsdon, 1856–1931: Papers — War narrative of Rapata Wahawaha.
81 Judith Binney, *Encircled Lands: Te Urewera 1820–1921*, p. 162.
82 *AJHR*, 1870, 1A–8B, p. 32, No. 56, Report 18 April 1870, H.T. Clarke to Under Secretary, Native Department.
83 Ibid, p. 34.
84 James Cowan, *The New Zealand Wars*, Vol. 2, p. 413.
85 *AJHR*, 1870, 1A–8B, p. 45, Encl. in No. 70, Diary of Lt T.W. Porter 28 February to 31 March 1870.
86 *AJHR*, 1870, 1A–8B, pp. 17–18, No. 41, Report Lt T.W. Porter to the Minister of Defence.
87 *AJHR*, 1870, 1A–8B, p. 45, Encl. in No. 70, Diary of Lt T.W. Porter.
88 T.W. Porter, *The History of the Early Days of Poverty Bay: Major Ropata Wahawaha N.Z.C., M.L.C.*, p. 37.
89 T. Lambert, *Story of Old Wairoa and the East Coast*, 1925, p. 655.
90 *AJHR*, 1870, 1A–8B, p. 45, Encl. in No. 70, Diary of Lt T.W. Porter.

6   WHANGANUI CAPTURE WAIPUNA PĀ

91 *AJHR*, 1870, 1A–8B, No. 56, pp. 32, 33, Report 18 April 1870, H.T. Clarke, Civil Commissioner, to the Under Secretary, Native Department.
92 *AJHR*, 1870, 1A–8B, p. 25, No. 48, Report 30 March 1870, Major Kemp Te Taitokokiteuru to Donald McLean.
93 *AJHR*, 1870, 1A–8B, p. 25, No. 49, Report 30 March 1870, Major Kemp Te Taitokokiteuru to the Premier Mr. Fox.
94 *AJHR*, 1870, 1A–8B, p. 25, No. 49, Report 30 March 1870, Major Kemp Te Taitokokiteueu to the Premier Mr. Fox.
95 *AJHR*, 1870, 1A–8B, p. 25, No. 49, Report 30 March 1870, Major Kemp Te Taitokokiteueu to the Premier Fox.
96 James Cowan, *The New Zealand Wars*, Vol. 2, p. 416.
97 Samuel Austin, undated petition seeking support, Waiouru Museum Accession number 1992.1422/1. (The concluding sentence of the petition refers to 25 years having passed since the events recited, which began at 1865, so the likely date was about 1890.)

7   NGĀTI POROU ASSAULT MARAETAHI PĀ

98 *AJHR*, 1870, 1A–8B, No. 56, pp. 33, 34, Report H.T. Clarke, Civil Commissioner, to the Under Secretary, Native Department.
99 *Wellington Independent*, 30 April 1870, p. 6; the report quoted was sent from Ōpōtiki and dated 13 April 1870.

100   AJHR, 1870, 1A–8B, p. 45, Encl. in No. 70, Diary of Lt T.W. Porter, 28 February to 31 March 1870.
101   Diarised report letter 31 March 1870, Lt Porter to Lt Col St John, NA AD1 70/2762.
102   AJHR, 1870, 1A–8B, p. 41, Encl. in No. 70, Diary of Lt T.W. Porter.
103   Poverty Bay Herald, 24 August 1897, p. 3.
104   'Narrative of the fighting on the East Coast, 1865-71: with a monograph on bush fighting / by Tuta Nihoniho of Ngāti-Porou ... Nga pakanga ki Te Tai Rawhiti, 1865-71: me nga korero mo uenuku / na Tuta Nihoniho o Ngāti-Porou', Dominion Museum, Wellington, 1913, p. 13 (te reo), p. 40 (transl.). Accessed at ENZB - 1913 - Nihoniho, T. Narrative of the Fighting on the East Coast - Nga Pakanga ki Te Tai Rawhiti, pp. 4-19 (auckland.ac.nz).
105   Wellington Independent, 30 June 1870, p. 5.
106   Ibid.
107   Ibid.
108   AJHR, 1870, 1A–8B, p. 65, Encl. to No. 88, Captain Gilbert Mair to H.T. Clarke.
109   Statement of Huhana Tamati, 5 August 1870.
110   In the original official published version of Porter's diary in the Appendices to the Journals of the House of Representatives the phrase 'blank cheques' is used. That looks to be a printing error, with Porter meaning 'bank cheques', presumably made out to Te Kooti.
111   AJHR, 1870, 1A–8B, p. 33, No. 56, Report H.T. Clarke to Under Sec Native Dept.
112   AJHR, 1870, 1A–8B, Encl. to No. 70, p. 46, Diary of Lt T.W. Porter.
113   AJHR, 1870, 1A–8B, No. 50, Report 30 March 1870, Tōpia Tūroa to the Defence Minister.
114   AJHR, 1870, 1A–8B, p. 25, No. 49, Report 30 March 1870, Major Kemp Te Taitokokiteueu to the Premier Mr. Fox.
115   Statement of Huhana Tamati, 5 August 1870, to Major Charles Westrup, NA AD1 70/2668.
116   AJHR, 1870, 1A–8B, p. 46, Encl. to No. 70, Diary of T.W. Porter.
117   AJHR, 1870, 1A–8B, p. 46, Encl. in No. 70, Diary of Lt T.W. Porter.
118   AJHR, 1870, 1A–8B, No. 56, pp. 33, 34, Report H.T. Clarke, Civil Commissioner, to the Under Secretary, Native Department.
119   AJHR, 1870, 1A–8B, p. 94, No. 121, 26 July 1870, Report Major Ropata to the Defence Minister D. McLean.
120   AJHR, 1870, 1A–8B, No. 88, Report 23 May 1870, Captain Gilbert Mair to Mr Clarke, Civil Commissioner.
121   AJHR, 1870, 1A–8B, p. 66, Encl. to No. 88, Statement made by Hoani Te Paiaka.
122   AJHR, 1870, 1A–8B, No. 51, Report 1 April 1870, Major Ropata to the Defence Minister.
123   ATL, MS-Papers-0072-39E, Best, Elsdon, 1856–1931: Papers — War narrative of Rapata Wahawaha pp. 29-30.
124   Wellington Independent, 30 June 1870, p. 5.
125   AJHR, 1870, D–No. 37, p. 3, Return of the Killed and Wounded of the Colonial Forces and of the Rebels Killed, Captured, and Surrendered from the 28th June, 1869. This official return included Te Paiaka's figure of 30 killed.

8 THE END OF THE CAMPAIGN AND THE DEVELOPMENT OF A MYTH

126   Otago Daily Times, Supplement, 7 May 1870, p. 5.
127   AJHR, 1870, 1A–8B, p. 24, No. 48, Report 30 March 1870, Major Kemp to Defence Minister.
128   AJHR, 1870, 1A–8B, p. 26, No. 52, Report 1 April 1870, Wiremu Kingi to Defence Minister.
129   AJHR, 1870, 1A–8B, p. 35, Report 18 April 1870, H.T. Clarke to the Under Secretary, Native Department.
130   Ibid., p. 31.
131   AJHR, 1870, 1A–8B, p. 40, No. 67, Letter 7 May 1870, D. McLean as Defence Minister to Lt Col St John.
132   AJHR, 1870, 1A–8B, p. 67, No. 93, Report 24 May 1870, Lieut.-Colonel St John to the Defence Minister.
133   AJHR, 1870, 1A–8B, p. 46, Encl. in No. 70, Diary of Lt T.W. Porter 28 February to 31 March 1870.
134   AJHR, 1870, 1A–8B, p. 33, No. 56, 18 April 1870, Report H.T. Clarke to Under Secretary, Native Department.
135   AJHR, 1870, 1A–8B, p. 46, Encl. in No. 70, Diary of Lt T.W. Porter 28 February to 31 March 1870.
136   Diarised report letter 31 March 1870, Lt Porter to Lt Col St John, NA AD1 70/2762.
137   Daily Southern Cross, Vol. XXVI, Issue 3935, 2 April 1870, p. 4.
138   Wellington Independent, Vol. XXIV, Issue 2977, 7 April 1870, p. 2.
139   Daily Southern Cross, 6 April 1870, p. 2.
140   AJHR, 1870, p. 25, No. 50, Report 30 March, 1870 Tōpia Tūroa to the Hon. the Defence Minister Mr McLean.

9 THE IMPACTS OF WAR

141   AJHR, 1870, 1A–8B, p. 34, No. 56, 18 April 1870, Report H.T. Clarke to Under Secretary, Native Department.
142   Original letter from Lt Col St John to Lt Col Lyon, NA, AD1 70/1190. Published in AJHR, 1870, 1A–8B, No. 10, 1870, p. 17.
143   AJHR, 1870, 1A–8B, p. 34, No. 56, 18 April 1870, Report H.T. Clarke to Under Secretary, Native Department.
144   AJHR, 1870, A16, pp. 9, 10, No. 8, Report 4 May 1870, J.H. Campbell R.M. to Under Secretary, Native Department.
145   Ibid. [Campbell report]
146   AJHR, 1870, A1–8B, p. 36, No. 57, Report 16 April 1870, Capt. G.P. Walker to Minister of Defence.
147   AJHR, 1870, 1A–8B, p. 36, No. 58, Report 19 April 1870, Lt Col St John to Minister of Defence.

148 *Wellington Independent*, 30 April 1870, p. 6.
149 *AJHR*, 1870, 1A–8B, p. 65, Encl. in No. 88, Statement made by Hoani Te Paiaka.
150 *AJHR*, 1870, A1–8B, p. 51, Sub-Enclosure to Enclosure 4 in No. 77, 15 April 1870, Extract from Captain Walker's Letter to Lieut. Porter.
151 *AJHR*, 1870, A1–8B, p. 36, No. 57, Report 16 April 1870, Capt. G.P. Walker to Minister of Defence.
152 *AJHR*, 1870, 1A, p. 36, No. 58, Report 19 April 1870, Lt Col St John to Minister of Defence.
153 *AJHR*, 1870, 1A–8B, p. 51, Enclosure 3 in No. 77, 31 April 1870, Letter J.D. Ormond to Lt Col St John.
154 *AJHR*, 1870, 1A–8B, p. 65, Encl. in No. 88, Statement made by Hoani Te Paiaka.
155 *AJHR*, 1870, 1A–8B, pp. 64–65, No. 88, 23 May 1870, Report Captain G. Mair to H.T. Clarke.
156 *AJHR*, 1870, A16, p. 9, Encl. no. 1 to No. 7, Notes of a Meeting of Ngatiawa Tribe at Whakatāne, May 24th and 25th, 1870.
157 *AJHR*, 1870, A16, p. 8, No. 7, Report 27 May 1870, Major William Mair to Under Secretary, Native Department.
158 *AJHR*, 1870, 1A–8B, pp. 88–89, Enclosure in No. 112, 21 June 1870, Report Major W.G. Mair to H.T. Clarke.
159 *AJHR*, 1870, 1A–8B, p. 94, No. 121, 26 July 1870, Report Major Ropata to Minister of Defence.
160 *Wellington Independent*, 28 June 1870, p. 2.
161 *Wellington Independent*, 30 June 1870, p. 2.
162 Ibid., p. 4.
163 *Wellington Independent*, June 30, 1870, p.5
164 *Wellington Independent*, 5 July 1870, p. 3.
165 *AJHR*, 1870, 1A–8B, p. 94, No. 121, 26 July 1870, Report Major Ropata to Minister of Defence.
166 *AJHR*, 1870, 1A–8B, p. 94, No. 122, 4 August 1870, Letter Minister of Defence to Major Ropata.
167 *AJHR*, 1872, 1A, pp. 48–51, 11 January, 1872, Report Governor G.F. Bowen to Secretary of State for Colonies.

10 THE FRUITS OF WAR — AND THE LAST WORD TO TE KOOTI

168 *AJHR*, 1870, 1A–8B, p. 31, No. 56, Report 18 April 1870, H.T. Clarke to the Under Secretary, Native Department.
169 Ibid., pp. 34–35.
170 *AJHR*, 1870, 1A–8B, p. 35, No. 56, Report 18 April 1870, H.T. Clarke to the Under Secretary, Native Department.
171 Ibid., p. 31.
172 *AJHR*, 1870, 1A–8B, p. 63, No. 83, Letter 16 April 1870, The Premier William Fox to Major Kemp; *AJHR*, 1870, 1A–8B, p. 63, No. 84, Letter 16 April 1870, The Premier William Fox to Tōpia Tūroa.
173 James Cowan, *The New Zealand Wars*, Vol. 2, p. 456.
174 *Wanganui Chronicle*, 21 April 1870, as quoted at page 4 of the *Wellington Independent* of 23 April 1870.
175 *Wellington Independent*, Vol. XXV, Issue 3009, 21 June 1870, p. 8.
176 Waitangi Tribunal, *Te Urewera Report*, 2017, WAI 894, Vol. 8, p. 3761.

EPILOGUE

177 James Cowan, *The New Zealand Wars*, Vol. 2, pp. 414–17.
178 A.C. Lyall, *Whakatohea of Opotiki*, p. 166.
179 Ranginui Walker, *Ōpōtiki-Mai-Tawhiti: Capital of Whakatōhea*, p. 120.
180 Judith Binney, *Redemption Songs: A Life of Te Kooti Arikirangi Te Turuki*, pp. 209–17 and 222–24.
181 Ron Crosby, *Kūpapa*, pp. 415–21.

APPENDIX 1: FOOD AND OTHER RESOURCES IN 1870

182 *Poverty Bay Herald*, 21 August 1897, p. 3.
183 *Auckland Star*, 6 June 1914, p. 16.
184 *Poverty Bay Herald*, 21 August 1897, p. 3.

APPENDIX 2: TE KOOTI'S TE UREWERA ROUTES IN FEBRUARY AND MARCH 1870

185 See Mair's account to James Cowan in *The New Zealand Wars*, Vol. 2, p. 543.
186 31 May 2022, kōrero tuku iho oral history, accessed at https://www.youtube.com/watch?v=Gd6olxZxH0s.

INDEX

Page numbers in **bold** indicate illustrations.
f/n = footnote

A
Adamson, Tom 132
Akuaku 119 f/n, 203 f/n
Allan, Mr (barrister) 196
Alexandra 241
Anderson, Atholl 240
Anderson, Pete 240
Anderson, Simon 243
Anglican church 210 f/n, 217
Anini River 107, 108
Apanui, Maraea 193
Apanui, Wepiha 193, 194
Aporo (Māori King's representative in the Whanganui) 76, 77
Aporo (Te Kooti's supporter in Te Urewera) 53, 224
Appendices to the Journal of the House of Representatives 117, 136, 137, 169, 174, 175, 185 f/n
Arapera 54
Arawa Flying Columns and Tumunui **45**, 163, mid 1870-72 events 200; fruits of war 206; following in their footsteps 243
Armed Constabulary 44, 46, 69, 71, 73
Atiamuri 80
Auckland 27, 29, 30, 101, 137, 162, 165, 174, 234
Auckland Star 96, 113, 114, 116
Austin, Sgt Samuel and McLean's decision 46; Whanganui Contingent raid up the Waimana 57, 58; Ōpape raid 61; post-Ōpape raid events 66, 67 f/n; Dec 1869-Feb 1870 engagements against Te Kooti 70-72, 74, 75, 75 f/n, 76, 77, 79, 79 f/n, 80, 81, 81 f/n, 82, 83; Waimana/Tauranga raid 85, 86; news of & reaction to Ōpape raid 87, 89, 92, 94, 96, 98; Ōhiwa meeting of Te Kepa & Ropata 118, 119; Whanganui pursuit 122, 122 f/n, 123-30; assault on Waipuna pā & aftermath 131, 131 f/n, 132-34; Maraetahi pā 137, 142, 143; tactical comparison Maraetahi & Waipuna attacks 145; post-Maraetahi events 148 f/n, 149-52, 158 f/n; events after return to Ōpōtiki 160; myth of Ngāti Porou success 174, 175, 178, 179; outcomes for prisoners & Whakatōhea 185, 196, 197; effect of the Porter 'myth' on historical record 213; food for Whakatōhea 218; food & shelter for pursuers 219; following in their footsteps 231, 233-38, 241-44

B
Baker, C.A. (surveyor) 136 f/n
Bay of Plenty and Paimārire 25; Crown invasion of Waikato 28; Volkner 30, 32; pursuit of Te Kooti 46; Waimana/Tauranga raid 86; reactions to Ōpape raid 91, 97; Ngāti Porou Urewera traverse 101, 111, 118; post Maraetahi events 152; events after return to Ōpōtiki 162, 165; myth of Ngāti Porou success 172, 175; outcomes for prisoners & Whakatōhea 187; fruits of war 203; growth of Ringatū religion 208, 210; effect of the Porter 'myth' on historical record 216
Binney, Dame Judith 115, 212
Blenheim 240
Booth, James (Resident Magistrate) 74
Bowen, Governor Sir George Ferguson 198, **199**, 208
Brills Bivvy 233, 234
British Government 23
British Imperial troops 23, 24, 29, 78, 216, 241
British subjects and rights 37
Brunt, Harvey 122 f/n, 128 f/n, 235, 244

C
Cameron, General 132
Campbell, J.H., Waiapu Resident Magistrate 101, 187, 188, 191
Catholic church, *see* Roman Catholic church.
Chapman, Thomas 78
Chatham Islands, *see* Wharekauri.
Clarke, Henry Tacey and Kōkōhīnau 56; Ōpape raid 59, 60, 64; Feb-early March 1870 events 83, 86, 89, 90, **91**, 93, 94, 96, 98; issue of Ngāti Porou prisoner numbers 116; Whanganui pursuit 124, 132; Ngāti Porou assault on Maraetahi pā 135; tactical comparison Maraetahi & Waipuna attacks 145; post Maraetahi events 152; events after return to Ōpōtiki 162, 163; myth of Ngāti Porou success 170-72, 174-77, 181; outcomes for prisoners & Whakatōhea 182, 183, 185, 187, 191, 193; fruits of war 202, 203, 203 f/n, 204; effect of the Porter 'myth' on historical record 213
Colenso, William 222
Cowan, James 116, 132, 141, 142, 212, 216 f/n
Crosby, Margy **52**, 240
Crosby, Ron **233, 238**
Crown aggression 22-27, 29, 35, 36

D
Daily Southern Cross 63, 176, 180
Department of Conservation 223 f/n, 224 f/n
Disturbed Districts Act 182
Dunedin 205

E
East Coast, *see* Te Tai Rāwhiti.
East Coast Land Titles Investigation Act 203, 203 f/n
Eclipse 31
Eclipse, HMS 32
Evening Post 90, 181

F
First World War 131
Fox, William (Premier) and post-Ōpape raid events 67; Whanganui Contingent 71-74, 77, 86; Waipuna pā 130, 131; Maraetahi attack 147; events after return to Ōpōtiki 162; fruits of war 202, **204**, 205, 206
Fraser, Lt Col 59, 60, 82
Fulloon, James Te Mautaranui 32, 33

G
Galatea, Fort (Waikaramuramu) 144
Gate Pā battle of, 28, 132
George Grey (Governor) and aggressive war 23, 24; Kingitanga invasion 28; relationship with Wi Marsh 65

INDEX 263

Gisborne, *see* Tūranga.
Governor Pipi 207
Gray, Chris **232**, 237–41

H
Hakara, *see* Māhika, Hakaraia.
Hakitara, Winiata 227, 228
Hakopa 132
Hangaroa River 104, 106
Hauhau aggressive approach of 25; Maraetahi 41; Ruatāhuna 51; Whanganui Contingent raid up the Waimana 57, 58; Ōpape raid 59–65; events after Ōpape raid 66, 67; Whanganui Contingent 76, 81, 85; news of Ōpape raid 87; Ngāti Porou Urewera traverse 109, 114, 118; Whanganui pursuit 122, 124; assault on Waipuna pā 131; Ngāti Porou assault on Maraetahi pā 138, 142, 147; post Maraetahi events 158; events after return to Ōpōtiki 161; myth of Ngāti Porou success 173, 180, 181; outcomes for prisoners & Whakatōhea 186, 191, 193; effect of Porter 'myth' on historical record 212
Haurere Point 186
Hawke, Tony 235
Hawke's Bay 46, 216
Hawkes Bay Herald 181
Heemi, Reeti **52**
Hewett, Captain 76, 76 f/n
Hicks Bay 32, 203
Hikurangi 105
Hīona church 27, 31
Hiwarau reserve 34, 183
Hocken Dr T.M. 23
Hopa 197
Hora Aruhe 79, 79 f/n
Horoeka pā 107, 109, 115, 116
Horomanga River 45, 50, 52, 221, 222
Hotene, Capt 101, 169
Houkamau, Iharaira 169, 203
Huhana, *see* Tamati, Huhana.
Hurakia 79, 79 f/n

J
Johnston, Justice **196**–99

K
Kaharoa 246 f/n
Kahunui River 225, 228
Kāhu NZ 234
Kaimai ranges 78, 216
Kaingaroa Plains 45, 50, 221
Kairakau 136, 136 f/n, 137
Kaiteriria 45, 175, 200

Kaituna River 78
Kaokaoroa 13, 28
Karanama 169, 174, 197
Kate 32–33
Kawakura, Hori (or Kerei) 86–88, 92, 161
Kāwanatanga and background 26; Crown invasion 29; after Tumunui 51, 52; post Ōpape raid events 67; Ngāti Porou assault on Maraetahi pā 137, 147; events after Maraetahi raid 149, 157
Kawepo, Renata 39
Kemp, Major, *see* Te Kepa
Keenan, Danny 213, 215
Kelly, Trooper 175
Kenana (location) 78
Kenana, Rua 103
Kepatu, Herepeta 227, 228
Kereopa (Te Rau) and role as emissary 25; denounces Volkner **30**–32; Ngāti Porou Urewera traverse 100; Waipuna pā 130–33; myth of Ngāti Porou success 169, 170, 172, 174, 176, 180; fruits of war 201, 206; effect of the Porter 'myth' on historical record 212
Kerikeri, Pene 109
King Country, *see* Kingitanga.
Kingi, Derek 136 f/n, 224
Kingi, Mete 73, 207
Kingitanga (King Country) 26; Te Kooti 38, 43, 69; Whanganui Contingent 72, 73, 75; Hakaraia 78; outcomes for prisoners & Whakatōhea 184; mid 1870–72 events 200; growth of Ringatū religion 208, 209
Kingites (includes King party) 72, 73, 88, 194, 201, 204
Kōhere, Mōkena 39, 169, 208
Kohi, Hapurona 51
Kohi a tau 206 f/n
Kohimarama 206, 206 f/n
Kōkōhinau 55–58, 231
Koranga River events in mid 1870–72 200; Feb–Mar 1870 routes for Te Kooti 225, 228–30; following in their footsteps 234
Koranga Forks 225, 236

L
Lambert, Thomas 118
Lamont, Luke 234
Law, Mark 234, 237, **238**, 239
Lloyd, Captain 76 f/n
Locke, S. (Resident Magistrate) 101
Lyall, A.C. 140, 212
Lyon, Lt Col 137, 174, 185

M
Mabbett, Barbara 213
Māhika, Hakaraia and Tapapa 44, 78, 80; Waipuna pā 130–32; events after Maraetahi 158; events after return to Ōpōtiki 163; myth of Ngāti Porou success 169, 171, 172, 176–78, 180, 181; fruits of war 201; following in their footsteps 235, 236
Maihi, Hātaraka (Heteraka) 62, 65
Mair, Capt Gilbert initial engagements with Te Kooti 44, **45**, 50; Hoani Te Paiaka 53; 80 f/n; Feb 1870 success 99; Maraetahi 144; events after Maraetahi 155, 156; events after return to Ōpōtiki 163; outcomes for prisoners & Whakatōhea 190, 193, 196; events in mid 1870–72 200; Feb–Mar 1870 routes for Te Kooti 221; following in their footsteps 243
Mair, Maj William Gilbert and initial engagements with Te Kooti 56; Ōpape raid 59, **60**, 64; Waimana/Tauranga raid 86–88; events after return to Ōpōtiki 166; outcomes for prisoners & Whakatōhea 191, 193–96
Makaretu 14, 39
Makeo **64**
Maketū 28, 92, 175
Mamaku ranges 44, 184
Manangaatiuhi Stream 222
Mangaaruhe River 49
Mangaoira Stream 136, 136 f/n
Mangatawhero Stream 223
Maniapoto, Rewi 44
Māori reaction to Crown aggression 22–27, 29, 35, 36
Maraekowhai 75 f/n
Maraemanuka Stream 79 f/n, 80 f/n
Maraenui 187
Maraetahi pā (includes Maraetai) (colour images **B5** lower, **B6**) and 1865 events 34; Ngātapa 39–41; Te Kooti returns 45, 50, 54; Whakatōhea support for Te Kooti 54; base for raids 55–57; Ōpape raid 58; events after Ōpape raid 66–68; Whanganui pursuit 124, 125, 131 f/n, 134; Ngāti Porou assault 135–39, 142–44; tactical comparison to Waipuna attack 145–47; post

264 TE KOOTI'S LAST FORAY

Maraetahi events 149-51, 153, 155-58; events after return to Ōpōtiki 163, 166, 167; myth of Ngāti Porou success 169-76, 181; outcomes for prisoners & Whakatōhea 184, 185, 188-90, 190 f/n, 191, 193, 199, mid 1870-72 events 200; effect of Porter 'myth' on historical record 211-15; food for Whakatōhea 218; 1870 routes for Te Kooti 221-30; following in their footsteps 231, 234, 236, 242, 245
Maraki, Te Whiu 206
Mataahu 119, 119 f/n, 203, 203 f/n
Mātaatua (iwi) 187
Matahanea 136
Matatā and Tai Rāwhiti taua 28; events of May 1869 42
Matawai 235
Matawhero 38, 39, 209
Matenga (Whānau a Apanui rangatira) 166
Maunga Kākaramea (Rainbow Mountain) 50
Maunganuioteao River 74
Maungapōhatu and Te Kooti's Feb 1870 traverse of Te Urewera 52, 53; Whanganui Contingent raid up the Waimana 56, 85-87, 89; Ngāti Porou Urewera traverse 102, **103**, 105-109, 109 f/n, 110, 111, 113, 115, 119; events after return to Ōpōtiki 163, 164; mid 1870-72 events 200; fruits of war 203, 203 f/n, 206 f/n; food for Whakatōhea 219; shelter for Whakatōhea 220; Feb-Mar 1870 routes for Te Kooti 222
Maungawhiorangi 136 f/n
Maxwell, Peter 214
McDonnell, Lt Col Thomas initial engagements with Te Kooti 43; McLean's decision 46; Volcanic Plateau events 69, 70, 71; Whanganui Contingent Dec 1869-Feb 1870 73, 77, 79-83; Feb-early March 1870 events 84, 90; report to Clarke 92-94
McLean, Donald and Feb 1870 decisions 46, 47; Whanganui Contingent raid up the Waimana 57; relationship with Whanganui Contingent, Te Kēpa & Topia Turoa 69-71, 73, 74, 83; Feb-early March 1870 events 84-87, 89, 91, 96; Ngāti Porou Urewera traverse 100-102, 113, 116, 117, 119; Whanganui pursuit 129,

131; Ngāti Porou assault on Maraetahi pā 137, 138; post Maraetahi events 152, 153, 156; events after return to Ōpōtiki 160-63, 165, 166; myth of Ngāti Porou success 173, 174, 177-81; outcomes for prisoners & Whakatōhea 183, 185-87, 191, 193, 195-99; fruits of war 201-205
Melanesia 25
Moanui Stream 234
Moerangi 43
Mohaka 39, 42
Mokena 203
mōkihi 103 f/n
Morton, Phil 235
Motu River 34, 83, 166, 167, 187, 216
Motu, Iharaira 110
Motumako Stream 223, 223 f/n
Motuohau 88
Motumako 52
Mount Cook Barracks 208
Murupara 31, 52
Musket Wars effects on Whakatōhea 26; Hakaraia 78; outcomes for prisoners & Whakatōhea 187

N

Napier 101, 178, 192, 205, 206
Napier-Taupō road 51 f/n
Neketuri 52, 53, 223
New Zealand Cross 44
New Zealand government (sometimes includes the Crown, Executive Council & government people) and Crown aggression against Māori 22-24, 26, 27; Volkner 33; 1865-70 events 34-36; confiscation policies 42; pursuit of Te Kooti on Volcanic Plateau 43; McLeans' decision 46, 47; Whanganui Contingent raid up the Waimana 56; Ōpape raid 63, 64; post Ōpape raid events 66; Whanganui Contingent 69, 72-74, 78, 83, 89-95; Ngāti Porou Urewera traverse 99, 102; Whanganui pursuit 132; post Maraetahi pursuits 149, 153-55, 157; events after return to Ōpōtiki 163-65, 167, 168; myth of Ngāti Porou success 176-78; outcomes for prisoners & Whakatōhea 183-86, 189-200; fruits of war 201, 203, 204, 206-208; growth of Ringatū religion 209, 210; effect of the Porter 'myth' on historical

record 214-17; Feb-Mar 1870 routes for Te Kooti 222, 225, 227-29; following in their footsteps 243
New Zealand Settlements Act 1863 31
New Zealand Wars 25, 132, 211-13, 215, 216, 216 f/n
Ngamu, Hoani 92
Ngā Rauru 72, 83
Ngāi Tai and background 26; Whanganui Contingent raid up the Waimana 57; raid on Ōpape 59, 64; Feb 1870 events 83, 85, 86, 88; Whanganui pursuit 120, 124, 129 f/n; events after return to Ōpōtiki 161, 162, 166, 167; outcomes for prisoners & Whakatōhea 183, 186, 188, 190; mid 1870-72 events 200; fruits of war 202; Anglican religion 210 f/n; effect of the Porter 'myth' on historical record 216
Ngāi Tamahaua 25, 183
Ngāi Tapuika 132
Ngāpuhi and Musket Wars 26, 78; Ngāti Porou Urewera traverse 110
Ngāruahoe 70
Ngātapa 39, **40**, 41, 42, 45, 54, 104, 105, 149, 168, 189, 198, 211
Ngātapa (location) 104 f/n
Ngāti Awa (includes Whakatāne people) and background 26, 32; Fulloon 33; 1865-70 events 34, 42, 51, 55; Feb-early March 1870 events 83, 85-87, 92; events after return to Ōpōtiki 161, 166, 167; outcomes for prisoners & Whakatōhea 190, 193; mid 1870-72 events 200; effect of the Porter 'Myth' on historical record 216
Ngāti Haka 49
Ngāti Ira and background 25; Tai Rāwhiti taua 28; Volkner 32, 33; post 1865 events 34; Ngātapa 41; support for Te Kooti 54; Kairakau 136 f/n; Maraetahi pā 140; post Maraetahi events 157; outcomes for prisoners & Whakatōhea 183, 184, 188-90, 193-96; effect of the Porter 'myth' on historical record 212, 214, 215; Feb-Mar 1870 routes for Te Kooti 224
Ngāti Kahungunu and Te Kooti's killings 39; Ngātapa 40; Mohaka 42; McLean's decision 46, 84; mid 1870-72 events 200
Ngāti Kahungunu Contingents relationship with Government

& McLean 69; fruits of war 206
Ngāti Kereru 86, 86 f/n
Ngāti Kōhatu 49, 105, 203
Ngāti Manawa 31, 52
Ngāti Maru 26
Ngāti Maniapoto 43, 44, 72
Ngāti Ngāhere 25, 32, 64, 183
Ngāti Patuheuheu 49, 163
Ngāti Patumoana 25, 183
Ngāti Pikiao 87
Ngāti Porou and background 26; Matawhero raid 39; Ngātapa 40, 41, Mohaka 42; McLean's decision 46, 47, 50; Urewera traverse 100-102, 113; events after return to Ōpōtiki 168; outcomes for prisoners & Whakatōhea 187, 191; fruits of war 203 f/n, 208; effect of the Porter 'myth' on historical record 214, 216
Ngāti Porou Contingent 54; and Whanganui Contingent raid up the Waimana 56; post Ōpape raid events 67 f/n, 68; relationship with government & McLean 69, 84, 94, 98; Maungapōhatu traverse 99, 101, 103, 105, 107, 108, 110-12, 114, 115; issue of Ngāti Porou prisoner numbers 119; Whanganui pursuit 124, 134; assault on Maraetahi pā 135-37, 139-44; tactical comparison Maraetahi & Waipuna attacks 145-47; post Maraetahi events 148, 151, 152, 155-58; events after return to Ōpōtiki 161, 163, 164, 167; myth of Ngāti Porou success 169-71, 173-76, 179; outcomes for prisoners & Whakatōhea 182, 190, 197; mid 1870-72 events 200; fruits of war 201, 202, 206, 206 f/n; effect of the Porter 'Myth' on historical record 212-15; food supplies & shelter for the pursuers 219, 220; Feb-Mar 1870 routes for Te Kooti 222, 227, 228; following in their footsteps 242, 245
Ngāti Pukeko 42, 83, 86, 87, 129 f/n, 161, 166, 167, 190
Ngāti Rangitihi 42, 65
Ngāti Rangiwewehi 65, 86 f/n
Ngāti Raukawa 78, 80
Ngāti Ruapani 49
Ngāti Rua (takenga) and background 25, 32; Ōpape raid 64
Ngāti Te Kōhera 80
Ngāti Tūwharetoa and initial response to Te Kooti 41, 42; Whanganui Contingent 72; Porter 97
Ngāti Whare 42, 49, 163
Ngutuoha 88, 88 f/n
Nihoniho, Tuta **102**, 141-43
Nikau Flat hut (colour image **B3 upper**) 235-37, 239
Nopenope, Eru 152, 153
North Island 56, 83
Nukuhou 55

O

Oamaru Times 181
Ōhaua o te Rangi marae 206, 222, 222 f/n
Ōhinemutu (Rotorua) 44, 45, 49
Ōhinemutu (Whanganui River) 72, 74, 205
Ōhiwa and 1865-70 events 34, 35, 39, 42, 55; Whanganui Contingent raid up the Waimana 56-58; Ōpape raid 59-61, 65; Whanganui Contingent Feb-early March 1870 events 82-85, 86, 87, 89, 95-98; Ngāti Porou Urewera traverse 101, 102, 110, 111, 113, 114, 116-19; Whanganui pursuit 120; events after return to Ōpōtiki 151 f/n, 162, 164, 165; outcomes for prisoners & Whakatōhea 183-85, 187; growth of Ringatū religion 208, 209; food supplies & shelter for the pursuers 220
Ōhope 82, 219
Ōhura River 74
Okama Stream 80 f/n
Ōkarika Stream 222, 222 f/n
Ōkaro, Lake 50, 221
Okiakia, Miriama 143
Old Testament 24, 25, 37
O'Malley, Vincent 213, 213 f/n, 215
Ōmarumutu pā and 1865-70 events 34, 35; Te Kooti's raid 57-59, 61-63; post Ōpape raid events 66, 67; Feb-early March 1870 events 83, 86, 87, 89, 90; outcomes for prisoners & Whakatōhea 184, 185, 188, 190; effect of the Porter 'myth' on historical record 211, 212, 215; following in their footsteps 231, 235, 238
Ōmaruteangi 50, 51, 52, 222
Ōmaukora Stream (colour images **A7 upper and lower**) and post Ōpape raid events 66; Whanganui pursuit 123, 126, 127, 133, 134; Whanganui ambush 147, 148; post Maraetahi events 158; myth of Ngāti Porou success 171, 175; Tahora pā 190 f/n; Feb-Mar 1870 routes for Te Kooti 229; following in their footsteps 231, 232, 234, 235, 237, 238, 243
Omdurman 131
Ōngarue River 76
Ōpape pā (colour images **A4 upper and lower**) and 1865-70 events 35, 56; Te Kooti's raid 57-60, 63; post Ōpape raid events 66, 67; Feb-early March 1870 events 83, 86, 87, 89-91, 94, 95; Whanganui pursuit 124, 127; events after return to Ōpōtiki 162; myth of Ngāti Porou success 170, 172, 176; outcomes for prisoners & Whakatōhea 182-86, 188, 190, 191, 193; effect of the Porter 'myth' on historical record 211, 212, 215, 217; following in their footsteps 231-35, 238, 239
Ōpape Native Reserve and post 1865 events 34
Ōpato Stream, see Tahora Stream.
Ōpeke 196
Open Bay, see Waipiro Bay.
Ōpepe 51 f/n
Ōponae Stream (colour image **B7 upper**) and 1865 events 34; Feb-Mar 1870 routes for Te Kooti 224-26, 245
Ōpōtiki and background 22, 23, 26, 27; Volkner 28, 30-33; 1865-70 events 34, 35, 39, 41, 47, 53, 55, 56; Whanganui Contingent raid up the Waimana 57; Ōpape raid 59, 61-64; post Ōpape raid events 67; early March 1870 events 87-98, 114, 116, 118, 119; Whanganui pursuit 120, 122, 122 f/n, 131; Ngāti Porou assault on Maraetahi pā 135, 137; post Maraetahi events 151, 152, 156, 157; events after return to Ōpōtiki 160, 162-64, 166, 167; myth of Ngāti Porou success 174-78, 180; outcomes for prisoners & Whakatōhea 182, 184, 185, 187-89, 191-93, 195; fruits of war 201-205; growth of Ringatū religion 208-210; effect of the Porter 'myth' on historical record 217; Feb-Mar 1870 routes for Te Kooti 224; following in their footsteps 236
Ōpōtiki River, *see* Ōtara River.
Ōpōtiki Volunteer Rangers (includes Rifles) 35, 61, 93
Orākau 80 f/n, 209

Oriwa or Otiwa 63
Ormond, J.D. 69, 70, 73, 74, 77, 101, 166, 191, **192**, 193
Otago Daily Times 161, 162
Otago Witness 95, 95 f/n, 181
Ōtamarakau 28
Ōtane Stream 155, 225, 227-29
Otanetea Hut 223, 223 f/n
Ōtapukawa Stream 224
Ōtara (location in Tauranga River valley) 87
Ōtara River (includes Ōpōtiki River) and background 26, 27; post Ōpape raid events 67, 97; Whanganui pursuit 122, 122 f/n, 124; following in their footsteps 235
Ōtetere (colour images **B8 upper and lower**) 224, 227

P

Paengaroa 82
Paerata, Hirini 80, 80 f/n
Paerau (Tūhoe rangatira) 155
Paimārire commencement 24, 25; Volkner 30, 31; Te Kooti 35, 38; upper Whanganui 43, 76 f/n; fruits of war 201, 208; effect of the Porter 'myth' on historical record 216
Paipai, Kawana 92
Panetaonga 81, 81 f/n, 82
Panewhero 112 f/n
Paora (Whanganui rangatira) 129
Pāpuni 38, 106, 106 f/n
Pararakau 136 f/n
Patara (Raukatauri) and emissary role 25; Volkner 30, 32
Patetere 80, 81
Patutahi 104 f/n
Pera 224
Pēwhairangi (Bay of Islands) 78
Pikowai Stream 28
Pinepine, Mere 65
Pinere 63
Pipiriki 74
Pōaka, Hoera 32
Pokaiwhenua River 81, 81 f/n
Pōkirikiri 55, 155, 224, 226-28, 245
Pollen, Dr 194, 194 f/n
Porter, Lt Col Thomas and McLean's decision 46; description of Maraetahi whare karakia 54; Ōpape raid 63, 67 f/n; arrival at Ōhiwa 96-98; Ngāti Porou Urewera traverse 101, **102**, 103-112; Ropata & Tamaikōwha meeting issue 113-15; issue of prisoner numbers 115, 116; issue of Ōhiwa meeting of Te Kepa & Ropata 117-19; Whanganui pursuit 134; Ngāti Porou assault on Maraetahi pā 135, 136, 136 f/n, 137-39, 141-44; tactical comparison Maraetahi & Waipuna attacks 145-47; post Maraetahi events 148, 149, 151, 152, 156, 156 f/n, 157, 158; events after return to Ōpōtiki 162, 167; myth of Ngāti Porou success 169, 170, 172-81; outcomes for prisoners & Whakatōhea 185, 191, 197; mid 1870-72 events 200; fruits of war 203 f/n, 206; growth of Ringatū religion 209; effect of the Porter 'myth' on historical record 211-15, 217; food for Whakatōhea 218; food supplies & shelter for the pursuers 219, 220; shelter for Whakatōhea 220; Feb-Mar 1870 routes for Te Kooti 222, 227; following in their footsteps 242, 245
Pouakani 80
Poutū 43, 70, 71, 72
Poverty Bay 101, 129, 133, 149, 199
Poverty Bay Herald 97, 113, 116, 118, 137, 139, 219
Preece, Capt George 81 f/n, 163, 200, 243
Pukareao Stream 222, 222 f/n
Puke nui a raho 136 f/n
Pukehinahina (Gate Pā) 78
Puketapu 38, 106, 106 f/n
Putiki 207

Q

Queen Victoria, *see* Victoria.

R

Raepawa, Ripawa & Raipawa, *see* Waipuna pā.
Raetakahia Stream (colour image **A6 top**) and Whanganui pursuit 123, 125; following in their footsteps 231-33, 237
Rakuraku 88, 177
Rānana 72-74, 205
Rangiora pā 229, 230, 234
Rangitaiki River 50, 51 f/n, 55, 156, 221, 222
Rangitaiki Plains 51, 52
Rangiwaha, Eru 146
Raukatauri, Patara, *see* Patara.
Raukokore 187
Raupō ridge (colour images **A6 middle and lower**) and post Ōpape raid events 66; Whanganui pursuit 125, 125 f/n, 126, 127; following in their footsteps 232, 233, 235, 237
Rawiri 64
Redpath, Bob 235, 241

Redpath, Dale 128 f/n, 235
Redpath, Geoff & Rebecca 238, 240
Redpath, Murray & Anne 128 f/n, 226, 235, 241, 244
Redpath, Stuart 241
Redpath Road 66 f/n, 226, 235
Rēkohu, *see* Wharekauri
Rere Falls 104
Retaruke River 75, 75 f/n
Rifleman 38
Ringatū (Te Hāhi Ringatū) and Te Kooti's escape 35; Hakaraia 78; fruits of war 201, growth of Ringatū religion 208-210; effect of the Porter 'myth' on historical record 214
Roman Catholic church 26, 27, 217
rongopai (includes treaty/peace agreement) and Tamaikōwha 94, 95, 97, 98; Ngāti Porou Urewera traverse 110, 111, 114, 118; events after return to Ōpōtiki 162-65
Rongowhakaata 40
Ropata, *see* Wahawaha, Ropata.
Rotoaira, Lake 43, 71
Rotoiti, Lake 28
Rotokākahi, Lake 200
Rotorua 40, 44, 45, 63, 78, 99, 208, 216, 221
Rua's Track 108
Ruakituri River and Te Kooti 38; Ngāti Porou Urewera traverse 103, 104, 106, 106 f/n, 107, 108; mid 1870-72 events 200
Ruamata 79, 79 f/n
Ruapehu, Mt 70
Ruatāhuna and Te Kooti accord 42, 45, 51-53, 55; Ngāti Porou Urewera traverse 99, 105, 111, 114, 115; post Maraetahi events 148, 155, 156; myth of Ngāti Porou success 173; fruits of war 206; Feb-Mar 1870 routes for Te Kooti 221-24, 227, 229; following in their footsteps 231, 245
Ruka 190
Runanga 51, 51f/n, 53, 222
Rushton, Ensign 93

S

St. John, Lt Col 112 f/n, 137, **164**, 165, 166, 174, 178, 185, 185 f/n, 187, 188, 190 f/n, 191- 93, 222, 227, 232
St Kilda 207
St Stephens Church 27
Selwyn, George Augustus (Bishop) 29
Shattky, Graye 241

INDEX 267

Southern Cross 94, 95 f/n
Spicer, Stuart **233**, 241, 243
Stallworthy, Dave 233, 241, 243
Stallworthy, Lynda 241, 243
Star of the South 178, 183, 205
Stormbird 207
Sturt 74, 84, 96, 100, 101, 202
Supreme Court 54, 57, 68, 143, 158, 196, 199, 215

T

Tahora (Stream & locality) and post Ōpape raid events 66–68; Whanganui pursuit 127–29, 132, 136 f/n, 140 f/n, 143; post Maraetahi events 156; events after return to Ōpōtiki 166, 190 f/n; food for Whakatōhea 218; Feb–Mar 1870 routes for Te Kooti 228–30, 234, 235, 243, 244. *See also* Opato Stream
Tahora pā 190 f/n
Tainui and Musket Wars 28; Whanganui Contingent 72
Takaputahi River and background 26; post 1865 events 34
Takurua Hut 223, 223 f/n
Tamaikōwha, Eruiti and 1865–70 events **35**, 41, 52; Whanganui Contingent raid up the Waimana 56, 57, 85–89, 93; rongopai 94, 95, 97, 98, 110; Ngāti Porou Urewera traverse 111, 112; issue of meeting with Ropata 112 f/n, 113–15; events after Whanganui return to Ōpōtiki 162–65; shelter for Whakatōhea 220; Feb–Mar 1870 routes for Te Kooti 223, 224
Tamapaoa, Mini 140 f/n
Tamatea 139, 140 f/n
Tamati, Huhana 68 and Ōpape raid 63; post Ōpape raid events 66; Maraetahi 144, 145; Porter claim that Te Kooti fired on, 146; post Maraetahi events 148, 153, **154**, 155; and mid 1870–72 events 200; Feb–Mar 1870 routes for Te Kooti 225–30, 230 f/n; following in their footsteps 231, 245
Taniora 166
Tapa (Whanganui rangatira) 129
Tapapa 44, 78, 80–82, 85, 90, 184, 205
Tapuaeharuru 73
Tarakeha Point 58, 16
Taranaki 22; and Paimārire 24; Crown invasion of, 27; land confiscations 31; south Taranaki & Titokowaru 70;

effect of the Porter 'myth' on historical record 216
Tarawera 51 f/n
Tataweka Stream 155, 225, 227–29
Tauaki pā 52, 53, 107, 109, 109 f/n, 111, 113, 114, 223
Tauaroa 45, 50
Taumarunui 76, 77, 78 f/n, 79
Taupō, Lake 43, 77, 80, 216
Taupō (area & town) 73, 77, 80, 91, 149, 184
Tauranga and background 22, 27; Tai Rāwhiti taua 28; Volkner 32; Whanganui shipping 47; Kōkōhinau raid 56; Whanganui Contingent raid up the Waimana 56; Ōpape raid 59, 61; Whanganui Contingent 77; Hakaraia 78; Volcanic Plateau & Mamaku engagements 80, 82; Feb–early March 1870 events 84, 90, 92, 96; Ngāti Porou Urewera traverse 99, 100, 119; Ngāti Porou assault on Maraetahi pā 135; myth of Ngāti Porou success 172, 175, 177; outcomes for prisoners & Whakatōhea 185, 193; fruits of war 202; effect of the Porter 'myth' on historical record 216
Tauranga-Taupō 41, 43
Taurawharona Hut 223, 223 f/n
Tauwharemanuka and Tūhoe & Te Kooti accord 42; Whanganui Contingent raid up the Waimana 57, 89, 95, 97; Ngāti Porou Urewera traverse **112**–15; events after return to Ōpōtiki 165; shelter for Whakatōhea 220; Feb–Mar 1870 routes for Te Kooti 224
Tawata 75 f/n
Tawhana pā and Tūhoe & Te Kooti accord 41, 42, 52, 53; Ōpape raid 64; Ngāti Porou Urewera traverse 110–13, 115; post Maraetahi events 155; Feb–Mar 1870 routes for Te Kooti 224, 225
Tawhana Stream 52, 223, 228
Tāwhiao, Matutaera Potatau and initial contacts with Te Kooti **43**, 44, 49; Whanganui Contingent 73, 75–77; Hakaraia 78; post Maraetahi events 149; mid 1870–72 events 200. *See also* Māori King.
Tawhiwhi Hut 223, 223 f/n
Te Aitanga a Māhaki 26
Te Ao Marama 72, 205, 206
Te Aowera 40, 136
Te Arawa and resistance to Te Tai

Rāwhiti taua 28; 1865–70 events 35; Ngātapa & Whakatāne 40, 42; Mamaku ranges & Tumunui 44, 45, 50; Kōkōhinau 56; Whanganui Contingent raid up the Waimana 57; Ōpape raid 59, 61–65, 67; relationship with NZ government & McLean 69; Hakaraia 78; Jan–early March 1870 events 79, 81 f/n, 83, 86 f/n, 87, 90, 92, 97–99, 113, 117, 118 f/n; Maraetahi 144; post Maraetahi events 155; events after return to Ōpōtiki 161, 165; outcomes for prisoners & Whakatōhea 184; mid 1870–72 events 200; effect of the Porter 'myth' on historical record 216; Feb–Mar 1870 routes for Te Kooti 221
Te Arei River 102
Te Atihaunui 53, 72, 74, 87, 92, 155, 157. *See also* Ngāti Haunui.
Te Aitanga a Hauiti mid 1870–72 events 200
Te Awaawa 62, 65
Te Awanui 64
Te Hapua 200
Te Haroto 51 f/n
Te Hata (Whānau a Apanui) 88, 166, 186, 187
Te Iharaira 203
Te Iki 193, 194
Te Kaha 26, 59, 60, 83, 187
Te Kaka, Timoti 40, 45
Te Kākari 107
Te Karetu 104
Te Karoro a Tamatea gorge (Hell's Gate) (colour images **B4, B5 upper**) and post Ōpape raid events 66, Maraetahi attack 134, 137–39, 140 f/n, 144; tactical comparison of Maraetahi & Waipuna attacks 145, 146; myth of Ngāti Porou success 172, 179; effect of the Porter 'myth' on historical record 214; Feb–Mar 1870 routes for Te Kooti 230
Te Kauau, Te Kerehama 227, 228
Te Kēpa, Te Rangihiwinui (Major Kemp) and initial engagements with Te Kooti 43, 44; McLean's decision 46; Whanganui Contingent raid up the Waimana 56–58; Ōpape raid 59, 61, 62; post Ōpape raid events 67, 67 f/n; Volcanic Plateau events 69–71; negotiations with Fox 72, **73**, 74, 76, 77; Volcanic Plateau & Mamaku events 78–82; Feb

1870 events 83, 84; Waimana/ Tauranga raid 85, 87–89; reaction to Ōpape raid 90, 92–98; Ngāti Porou Urewera traverse 100–102, 106, 109, 109 f/n, 110–14; meeting with Ropata at Ōhiwa 117–19; Whanganui pursuit 120, 123, 124, 129, 129 f/n, 130; assault on Waipuna pā & aftermath 131–33; Maraetahi pā 137, 138, 143; tactical comparison Maraetahi & Waipuna attacks 144, 145, 147; post Maraetahi events 149, 152; events after return to Ōpōtiki 161–64; myth of Ngāti Porou success 169–71, 174–79, 181; outcomes for prisoners & Whakatōhea 184–87, 189, 198, 199; fruits of war 202, 204, 205, 207, 208; effect of the Porter 'myth' on historical record 212, 213, 215

Te Kooti, Arikirangi Te Turuki and 1868 escape 35; relationship with Whakatōhea 36, **37**, 38; Matawhero raid 39; Ngātapa 40–42; accord with Tūhoe 43; Kīngitanga 44; at Rotorua 45; only Māori to pursue 46; arrival at Ruatāhuna & Maraetahi 49–54; raid on Kōkōhinau 55–57; Ōpape raid 58, 59, 61–64; post Ōpape raid events 66–68; earlier engagements against Whanganui 70, 72–77; Hakaraia Māhika 78; Mamaku events 80–82; Feb-early March 1870 events 83, 85–98; Ngāti Porou Urewera traverse 99, 100, 104–106, 110, 111, 114, 118, 119; Whanganui pursuit 120, 123, 124, 127–31, 131 f/n, 132–34; Ngāti Porou assault on Maraetahi pā 137–139, 41–44; tactical comparison of Maraetahi & Waipuna attacks 145–47; post Maraetahi events 148–57; events after pursuers' return to Ōpōtiki 162–64, 166–68; myth of Ngāti Porou success 169–81; outcomes for prisoners & Whakatōhea 182–99, mid 1870–72 events 200; fruits of war 201, 203–206; growth of Ringatū religion 208–210; effect of the Porter 'myth' on historical record 211, 214–17; food for Whakatōhea 218; food supplies & shelter for the pursuers 219; shelter for Whakatōhea 220; Feb–Mar 1870 routes for Te Kooti 221, 222, 224–30; 'Following in their footsteps' (Appendix 3) 231, 232, 234, 238, 242, 245

Te Kuiti 77
Te Maire Stream 119 f/n
Te Mamaku, Topine 74, **75**, 75 f/n, 76, 118
Te Meihana (Ngāti Pukeko rangatira) 129, 129 f/n, 161
Te Mokena 101
Te Paia, Wiremu Kingi and Ngātapa 40, 41; Rangitaiki to Maraetahi 50–53; Whakatōhea support 54; Te Kooti's raid on Kōkōhinau 57; raid on Ōpape 58; events post Ōpape raid 67, 67 f/n, 68; Waipuna 132; Maraetahi 144; myth of Ngāti Porou success 180; outcomes for prisoners & Whakatōhea 196, 197; Feb-Mar 1870 routes for Te Kooti 222–24, 230 f/n; following in their footsteps 231
Te Paiaka, Hoani and Ōhinemutu 44, 45; Feb 1870 Urewera traverse 53; Maraetahi 144; post Maraetahi events 155–58; outcomes for prisoners & Whakatōhea 190, 193; food for Whakatōhea 218; Feb-Mar 1870 routes for Te Kooti 229; following in their footsteps 231
Te Pahipoto 55
Te Pato Stream and post Ōpape raid events 68; post Maraetahi events 155, 156; food for Whakatōhea 218, 230; following in their footsteps 234–37, 240, 241
Te Ponanga 45
Te Popo, Hira and Tai Rāwhiti taua 28, **29**; 1865–70 events 33–35; Ngātapa 39–41; Te Kooti' return Feb 1870 50; Maraetahi pā 143, 144; post Maraetahi events 153, 157; events after pursuers' return to Ōpōtiki 167; outcomes for prisoners & Whakatōhea 183, 184, 188–91, 193–98; effect of the Porter 'myth' on historical record 215
Te Porere 44, 45, 49, 69, 71
Te Punga (Te Ponga) 112, 112 f/n, 117, 148, 173, 177, 227
Te Puke 82
Te Pukenui, Kereru 222
Te Ranapia and raid on Ōpape 58, 59, 62, 64; reaction against Whanganui 92, 94; Whanganui pursuit 120; events after return to Ōpōtiki 162; outcomes for prisoners & Whakatōhea 184–86, 187
Te Ranga 78
Te Rangikāheke, Wiremu (Wi) Maihi (includes Marsh) 65, 90, **117**, 118, 118 f/n
Te Rangikaitupuaki 51
Te Rangitukehu 56
Te Rau, Kereopa, see Kereopa.
Te Roau 206
Te Tahora pā 133, 188, 190, 193
Te Tai Rāwhiti (East Coast) and background & Paimārire 25, 26; taua to resist Crown invasion of Waikato 28, 31; raising of forces by Ropata & Uawa raid 47, 63, 84; Waimana/Tauranga raid 85, 87, 98; Ngāti Porou Urewera traverse 101, 114, 119; myth of Ngāti Porou success 178; outcomes for prisoners & Whakatōhea 187, 191, 196, mid 1870–72 events 200; fruits of war 202, 207; growth of Ringatū religion 208, 209; effect of the Porter 'myth' on historical record 215, 216
Te Tāpiri 31
Te Tarata 33, 131
Te Tatana Ngatawa (Whānau a Apanui) 186, 187
Te Teira 58, 64
Te Teko 55, 193, 200
Te Ua a te Rangi, Paora (Ngāti Ira rangatira) 188, 189, 194, 195, 197, 198
Te Ua Haumene and creation of Paimārire 24, 25; emissaries 30, 76 f/n
Te Ūpokorehe and background 25; 1865–70 events 34, 42; outcomes for prisoners & Whakatōhea 183
Te Urewera and Ngātapa 39, 41; accord with Te Kooti 42, 43; refuge for Te Kooti 44, 45; McLean's decision 46, 47; Te Kooti's Feb 1870 return 49–51, 53; Whanganui Contingent raid up the Waimana 56, 83, 85; events after Ōpape raid 90; Ngāti Porou traverse 99, 102–104, 108, 109, 111, 114, 117, 119; Waipuna assault 132; post Maraetahi events 153, 156; events after pursuers' return to Ōpōtiki 161, 163, 164, 167, 168; myth of Ngāti Porou success 174, 177, 178, 181; outcomes for prisoners & Whakatōhea 191; mid 1870–72 events 200;

fruits of war 202, 206, 206 f/n; growth of Ringatū religion 208, 210, 210 f/n; effect of the Porter 'myth' on historical record 211, 216; Feb–Mar 1870 routes for Te Kooti 221; Feb–Mar 1870 routes for Te Kooti 222, 223 f/n, 227; following in their footsteps 234, 240, 243
Te Urewera Education Lodge (Lion's Hut) 88 f/n
Te Uru Taumatua 223 f/n
Te Waimana 86, 87, 113
Te Wainui 209
Te Wera (and Te Weranga) 199, 229, 230, 234
Te Whaiti, *see* Ahikereru.
Te Wharau range 52
Temara, Tā Pou 105 f/n
three rivers junction, *see* Wairata
Tihoi Trading Post 79 f/n
Tieke 74
Timoti (a whakarau) 132
Tipene 165
Tirau 44
Titiokura 51 f/n
Titiraupenga 77, 77 f/n
Titokowaru 199, 216, 217
Tiwai, Te Piahana and raid on Ōpape 58, 59; post Ōpape raid events 68, 92, 94; Whanganui pursuit 120, **121**; Maraetahi 143; outcomes for prisoners & Whakatōhea 184, 185, 189, 191, 197
Toka a Kuku pā 187
Tokaanu 43, 77
Tokoroa 81
Tongariro 70
Toreatai pā 107, 109, 111, 113, 115
Tōrere and raid on Ōpape 58–60, 62, 64; Feb–early March 1870 events 83, 87; events after return to Ōpōtiki 167; outcomes for prisoners & Whakatōhea 186, 188; Anglican religion 210 f/n
torori 105
Treaty of Waitangi Article 2 rights 22, 23; post-Treaty period 25–27; 1865–70 events 35; Article 3 rights 36; Tiwai, Te Piahana and raid on Ōpape 58, 59; post Ōpape raid events 68, 92, 94; Whanganui pursuit 120, **121**; Maraetahi 143; outcomes for prisoners & Whakatōhea 189; growth of Ringatū religion 209, 210; effect of the Porter 'myth' on historical record 216
Tuhua 69, 205
Tūhoe (Ngāi) (includes Urewera people) and 1865-70 events 35; Ngātapa 39, 40; accord with Te Kooti 41–43; at & after Ōhinemutu 45, 49, 50; support for Te Kooti's people 51–53; Whanganui Contingent raid up the Waimana 56; Ōpape raid 59, 60; Waimana/Tauranga raid 85; early March, 1870 events 88, 89, 97; Ngāti Porou Urewera traverse 102, 103, 105, 108–111, 113–15, 118; Maraetahi 144; post Maraetahi events 148, 155, 157; events after pursuers' return to Ōpōtiki 162, 164, 165, 168; myth of Ngāti Porou success 173, 177; outcomes for prisoners & Whakatōhea 191, 192, 194, 197; mid 1870-72 events 200; fruits of war 206, 206 f/n; growth of Ringatū religion 208; effect of the Porter 'myth' on historical record 216; food for Whakatōhea 219; Feb–Mar 1870 routes for Te Kooti 222, 222 f/n, 223, 224 f/n, 225, 227
Tumunui 44
Tūranga(nui) (Gisborne) and Te Kooti's escape 36, 38; Matawhero raid 38, 39; Ngātapa 40; Ngāti Porou Urewera traverse 101, 102, 105, 116; Maraetahi 144; events after pursuers' return to Ōpōtiki 167; myth of Ngāti Porou success 174; growth of Ringatū religion 209; effect of the Porter 'myth' on historical record 211; Feb–Mar 1870 routes for Te Kooti 228; following in their footsteps 236
Turei, Mohi 47
Turoa, Te Pēhi 74, 76
Turoa, Topia Pehi and response to Te Kooti's killings 43, 44; McLean's decision 46; Whanganui Contingent raid up the Waimana 56, 57; Ōpape raid 60–62; post Ōpape raid events 67; negotiations with Fox 72, 73, 74, 76; Jan–early March 1870 events 77–81, 83, 84, 86–90, 92–96; Ngāti Porou Urewera traverse 101, 102, 118; Whanganui pursuit 120, 123, 132; Maraetahi 143, 144; tactical comparison Maraetahi & Waipuna attacks 147; post Maraetahi events 155; events after return to Ōpōtiki 161; myth of Ngāti Porou success 169, 170, 174–76, 178–80; outcomes for prisoners & Whakatōhea 183, 184, 189, 198; fruits of war 202, 204, 205, 207, 208; effect of the Porter 'myth' on historical record 213, 215
Tutaepukepuke pā 222
Tutaetoko River (colour image **A5**) and post Ōpape raid events 66, 67; Whanganui pursuit 122, 122 f/n 123; events after return to Ōpōtiki 166; following in their footsteps 231, 232, 235, 237
Tutahuarangi, Wiremu Kingi and raid on Ōpape 59, 62, 64; Waimana/Tauranga raid 85, 88; reaction to Ōpape raid 92; Whanganui pursuit 120, **121**, 124, 129, 129 f/n; events after return to Ōpōtiki 161, 162, 166; myth of Ngāti Porou success 170; outcomes for prisoners & Whakatōhea 183, 186, 188, 190 f/n, 193; mid 1870-72 events 200; following in their footsteps 232

U

Uawa (Tolaga Bay) 63, 153, mid 1870-72 events 200, 203
Uruteangina (Whanganui rangatira) 129
Urewera (iwi or people), *see* Tūhoe.
Urewera (country or ranges), *see* Te Urewera.

V

Victoria, Queen 76, 195, 196, 197, 199, 208
Volcanic Plateau 43, 69, 70, 72, 77, 79, 80, 94, 216
Volkner, Rev Carl Sylvius 30–32; and background **27–29**; Paimārire & killing 30–33; post-Maraetahi events 149; myth of Ngāti Porou success 178; outcomes for prisoners & Whakatōhea 191

W

Wahawaha, Maj Ropata and Matawhero raid 39, 40; McLean's decision 46, 47; Whanganui Contingent raid up the Waimana 56; Feb–early March 1870 events 84, 86, 89, 94, 96–98; Urewera traverse 99, 100–102, 104–107, 109–111; issue of meeting with Tamaikōwha 113–15; issue of Ngāti Porou prisoner

numbers 116; meeting with Te Kēpa at Ōhiwa 117–19, 119 f/n; Whanganui pursuit 120, 124, 132, 134; assault on Maraetahi pā 135, 137–39, 141, 143, 144; tactical comparison Maraetahi & Waipuna attacks 145, 147; post Maraetahi events 149, 150, 152, 152 f/n, 153, 156, 156 f/n, 157, 158; events after return to Ōpōtiki 161, 163, 164, 167–69; myth of Ngāti Porou success 170, 171, 175–81; outcomes for prisoners & Whakatōhea 183, 186–89, 191, 195, 196, 198; mid 1870–72 events 200; fruits of war 202, 203, 203 f/n, 206, 208; growth of Ringatū religion 209; effect of the Porter 'myth' on historical record 212, 214, 215; Feb–Mar 1870 routes for Te Kooti 227
Waiapu 101, 187, 191
Waiarua 51 f/n
Waiaua River and background 26, 27; gunpowder 54; raid on Ōpape 58, 61–64, 87; outcomes for prisoners & Whakatōhea 191, 193
Waihaha River 79
Waiiti Stream 112 f/n, 224, 224 f/n, 226, 227
Waikakariki Stream 104 f/n
Waikare River 52, 111, 191 f/n, 223, 223 f/n
Waikaremoana, Lake (also includes 'Waikare') 49, 51, 84, 99, 100, 156, 191, 191 f/n, 200, 203
Waikaretaheke River 49
Waikarewhenua clearing 223
Waikato River 22, and Crown invasion 27–29; Te Kooti 44; Whanganui Contingent 75; Hakaraia 78; Jan 1870 events 79, 80, 82; effect of the Porter 'myth' on historical record 216
Waikato/Tainui iwi 43, 77
Waikaramuramu (Fort Galatea) 144
Waimahana 80, 80 f/n
Waimana (Tauranga) River (colour image **B8 middle**) and 1865–70 events 35, 41, 52, 53, 55; Whanganui Contingent raid up the Waimana 56, 57, 61, 64, 83, 85, 86, 88, 93; rongopai 94, 95, 97; Ngāti Porou Urewera traverse 103, 110, 111, 112 f/n, 113, 116, 117; Whanganui pursuit 120; post Maraetahi events 148, 155; events after

pursuers' return to Ōpōtiki 163, 164, 167; myth of Ngāti Porou success 173, 177; Feb–Mar 1870 routes for Te Kooti 222, 223, 225–28; following in their footsteps 232, 245
Waioeka River (& country) (colour images **A8, B3 lower**) and background 26, 27; 1865–70 events 35; Ngātapa 39–41; Te Kooti returns 45, 53; Whakatōhea support for Te Kooti 54; base for Te Kooti's raids 55–57; raid on Ōpape 58, 59, 62, 63; post Ōpape raid events 66, 67 f/n; early March 1870 events 88, 94–98, 116–19; Whanganui pursuit 123–25, 125 f/n, 127, 128, 128 f/n, 129, 132, 134; Ngāti Porou assault on Maraetahi pā 135, 136 f/n, 137, 139, 142–44; tactical comparison of Maraetahi & Waipuna attacks 145; post Maraetahi events 150, 151, 153–55; events after pursuers' return to Ōpōtiki 162, 163, 166–68; myth of Ngāti Porou success 169, 171, 173–76, 178, 180, 181; outcomes for prisoners & Whakatōhea 182, 188, 190, 190 f/n, 192–94, 196–98, mid 1870–72 events 200; fruits of war 201–203, 208; growth of Ringatū religion 209; effect of the Porter 'myth' on historical record 212, 213, 215, 217; Feb-Mar 1870 routes for Te Kooti 221, 223, 225–30; following in their footsteps 231–40, 242–45
Waioeka gorge and 1865 events 33, 34; Te Kooti's return 50, 54; post Ōpape raid events 67; Feb-March 1870 events 83, 95; ambuscade 133, 134; Ngāti Porou assault on Maraetahi pā 136; post Maraetahi events 158; myth of Ngāti Porou success 176; outcomes for prisoners & Whakatōhea 187, 190–93, 196, 197; following in their footsteps 236
Waione Stream 79, 79 f/n
Waiotahe River 35, 209
Waipaoa River (Tūranga) 101, 102
Waipaoa River (Ruakituri) 200
Waipapa River 80 f/n
Waipari River 79, 79 f/n
Waipiro Bay (Open Bay) 119 f/n, 203, 203 f/n
Waipuna pā (includes Raepawa & Ripawa) (colour images

B1 lower, B2) 50, 54 and establishment 66, 66 f/n, 67, 68; Whanganui pursuit 120; Whanganui assault 130, 131, 131 f/n, 132, **133**, 134, 136 f/n, 137, 143; tactical comparison to Maraetahi attack 144, 145; post Maraetahi events 150, 154, 155, 157, 158; events after pursuers' return to Ōpōtiki 163, 166; myth of Ngāti Porou success 170–73, 175, 177, 178; outcomes for prisoners & Whakatōhea 182, 188–90, 190 f/n, 193, 196, 199, mid 1870–72 events 200; fruits of war 206; effect of the Porter 'myth' on historical record 211–13, 215; food for Whakatōhea 218; shelter for Whakatōhea 220; Feb–Mar 1870 routes for Te Kooti 226–28, 230; following in their footsteps 231, 232, 235, 236, 239–42, 244, 245
Waipunga River & falls 51 f/n
Wairata (includes 'three rivers junction') (colour images **A7 lower, B1 upper**) and 1865 events 34; post Ōpape raid events 66; Whanganui pursuit 127, 128 f/n, 130; post Maraetahi events 150; effect of the Porter 'myth' on historical record 212, 215; food for Whakatōhea 218; following in their footsteps 234–36, 238, 243, 244
Wairata Stream (colour image **B7 lower**) 66, 66 f/n, 154, 224, 226, 239, 241, 242
Wairenga a Hika 36, 183
Wairoa 46, 51
Waitaha 77
Waitangi Falls 107
Waitangi Tribunal 33, 72, 209, 210, 210 f/n, 224
Walker, Capt G.P. and Whanganui Contingent raid up the Waimana 57; Ōpape raid 59, **60**, 61, 63, 87; outcomes for prisoners & Whakatōhea 188, 191
Walker, Ranginui 212
Waotu 77, 77 f/n
Way, Lt Herbert 175
Wellington 143, 158, 168, 178, 196, 198, 205, 208, 215, 237
Wellington Independent 168, 177, 181, 189, 196, 197
Wesleyan church 217
Westrup, Maj 101
Whaanga, Ihaka and Matawhero raid 39

INDEX 271

Whakahoro pā 75, 75 f/n
Whakamaru 80 f/n
Whakapirau Stream 224, 227
Whakarae marae (modern location up Waimana/Tauranga River) 226, 227
Whakarae pā (old location at Ōhiwa) 95, 164, 165
Whakarau and Te Kooti's escape 35, 38; Matawhero raid 38; Rotorua 45; Feb 1870 Urewera traverse 53, 54; myth of Ngāti Porou success 170; effect of the Porter 'myth' on historical record 215. *See also* Chatham Islanders.
Whakatāne and background 28; Volkner 30, 32; 1865-70 events 34, 42, 51, 52, 56, 57; Waimana/Tauranga raid 85; events after Ōpape raid 95, 96; outcomes for prisoners & Whakatōhea 184, 188, 193; following in their footsteps 243
Whakatāne River 33, 51, 53, 55, 85, 87, 191 f/n, 103, 206, 222, 222 f/n, 223, 223 f/n
Whakatōhea and background 22, 23, 25-27; support for Kingitanga 28, 29; Volkner 30-32; 1865 events 33-35; relationship with Te Kooti 36, 39-42, 45, 53, 54; Whanganui Contingent raid up the Waimana 57; Ōpape raid 58-64; post Ōpape raid events 67, 67 f/n, 68; Feb-early March 1870 events 83, 85-89, 91-93; reaction to Ōpape raid 94, 95; Whanganui pursuit 120, 124, 130; assault on Waipuna pā 131, 134; Ngāti Porou assault on Maraetahi pā 137-40, 143, 144; tactical comparison Maraetahi & Waipuna attacks 146; post Maraetahi events 150, 152, 157; events after return to Ōpōtiki 161-63, 167; myth of Ngāti Porou success 170-72, 174-78, 180; outcomes for prisoners & Whakatōhea 182-91, 193-97; fruits of war 201; growth of Ringatū religion 208; effect of the Porter 'myth' on historical record 211, 212, 215, 216; food for Whakatōhea 219; Feb-Mar 1870 routes for Te Kooti 224, 229; following in their footsteps 231, 236, 238
Whānau a Apanui and background 26; Feb-early March 1870 events 83, 86, 88; events after return to Ōpōtiki 167; outcomes for prisoners & Whakatōhea 187; effect of the Porter 'myth' on historical record 216
Whangaipeke block 79 f/n
Whanganui Contingent and inital engagements with Te Kooti 43, 44; Waimana raid 56, 57; Ōpape raid 59-62; post Ōpape raid events 66, 68, 69; relationship with Government & McLean 69; earlier Dec 1869-Feb 1870 engagements against Te Kooti 70-77, 79, 80, 82-84; Waimana/Tauranga raid & news of Ōpape raid 86, 87, 89, 90; reaction to Ōpape 92-94, 96, 98; Ngāti Porou Urewera traverse 112, 119: pursuit 120, 122-24, 127, 128; Waipuna pā & aftermath 130, 132, 134; Maraetahi pā 135, 137, 143; tactical comparison Maraetahi & Waipuna attacks 145, 147; post Maraetahi events 148-152, 156, 158; events after return to Ōpōtiki 161-63, 168; myth of Ngāti Porou success 169-79; outcomes for prisoners & Whakatōhea 182-86, 190, 196; fruits of war 201-207; effect of the Porter 'myth' on historical record 212, 213, 215; food for Whakatōhea 218; food supplies & shelter for the pursuers 219; following in their footsteps 231, 232, 234, 238, 239, 241, 243, 244
Whanganui (iwi) and response to Te Kooti's killings 43; McLean's decision 46, 47; post Ōpape raid events 69, 74; Feb 1870 events 83, 86, 94; Maraetahi 144, 146; events after return to Ōpōtiki 163; myth of Ngāti Porou success 175; outcomes for prisoners & Whakatōhea 187, 190; fruits of war 203-205, 208; effect of the Porter 'myth' on historical record 216
Whanganui River 43, 70, 72, 74, 75 f/n, 79, 79 f/n, 80, 118, 205, 216
Whanganui (town & area) 24, 70-72, 74, 75, 77, 78, 199, 205, 207
Whanganui a Parua 156
Whangārei 233
Wharau range 223
Wharauroa marae 78 f/n
Wharekauri (Chatham Islands or Rēkohu) and Te Kooti 35-38; Waipuna 132-34; outcomes for prisoners & Whakatōhea 183; Feb-Mar 1870 routes for Te Kooti 228
Wharekopae River 40, 104
Wharepanga Bay 203 f/n
Whareongaonga Bay 38
Whareraupo, Ihaka 110
Whatawhata 78, 78 f/n
White, Bennett 113
Whitikau Stream and post 1865 events 34
Whitmore, Lt Col George 38, 92, 106, 168, 169, **179**
World War I 131

ABOUT THE AUTHOR

Brought up and educated in Auckland, Ron Crosby pursued his legal career in Blenheim, including 30 years as a court lawyer particularly in Treaty-related and Resource Management cases. He is a hearings commissioner under the Resource Management Act 1991 and was appointed to the Waitangi Tribunal in 2011.

Ron's first book, researched and written over a five-year period, was *The Musket Wars: A History of Inter-Iwi Conflict, 1806–1845* (1999), which was widely applauded as the first comprehensive account of this period. His subsequent books are *Gilbert Mair: Te Kooti's Nemesis* (2004), *Andris Apse: Odyssey and Images* (2006), *Albaneta: Lost Opportunity at Cassino* (2007), *NZSAS: The First Fifty Years* (2009), *A Desperate Dawn: The Battle for Turuturu Mokai* (2013), *Kūpapa: The Bitter Legacy of Māori Alliances with the Crown* (2015) and *The Forgotten Wars: Why the Musket Wars matter today* (2020). He retains a deep interest in New Zealand's back country and history.

His interest in te ao Māori is constantly reinforced by his whānau relationships, his wife Margy being of Te Rarawa and Te Aupōuri descent. They have three adult children and eight grandchildren, and live in Blenheim.

Ron is pictured above on the ridgeline linking the Waioeka and Waimana/Tauranga catchments in late October 2022.